Neutrality and Theory of Law

Law and Philosophy Library

VOLUME 106

For further volumes:
http://www.springer.com/series/6210

Jordi Ferrer Beltrán • José Juan Moreso
Diego M. Papayannis
Editors

Neutrality and Theory of Law

Springer

Editors
Jordi Ferrer Beltrán
Department of Law
University of Girona
Girona, Spain

José Juan Moreso
Department of Law
Pompeu Fabra University
Barcelona, Spain

Diego M. Papayannis
Department of Law
University of Girona
Girona, Spain

The Work was first published in 2012 by Madrid-Barcelona: Marcial Pons with the following title: Neutralidad y teoría del derecho.

ISSN 1572-4395
ISBN 978-94-007-6066-0   ISBN 978-94-007-6067-7 (eBook)
DOI 10.1007/978-94-007-6067-7
Springer Dordrecht Heidelberg New York London

Library of Congress Control Number: 2013933363

Printed on acid-free paper

Springer is part of Springer Science+Business Media (www.springer.com)

Preface

This volume is the result of a very special international conference in legal philosophy on the relationship between legal theory and evaluative judgments that took place in Girona in May 2010. "Can legal theory be neutral?" was our leading question. Within the narrow scope of a preface, we cannot dwell into the subject matter of the book. But we would like to account for the context in which both this volume and its preceding conference were conceived.

In 2004, the Spanish publishing house Marcial Pons issued the first books of the "Filosofía y Derecho" ("Philosophy and Law") series. The project was originally a relatively modest one. At the beginning of the twenty-first century, publishers find themselves in an impasse of sorts, between printed and digital editions, local and global scopes, commercial and cultural drives—the first element of each pair still the dominating one—and a series of philosophical books did not exactly look like a promising venture. Yet in 2008, only 4 years later, around 40 volumes of the collection could be found on the shelves of bookshops. With the invaluable support of Juan José Pons, Marcial's son, we began to kindle the idea of organizing an international conference to mark the 50th volume in our series—a conference bringing together Continental and Anglo-American analytic philosophers on some common jurisprudential subject. Because such a combination was already part of the identity of the book series, we decided to invite some of its authors as speakers. They all immediately agreed to participate.

During the 3 days of the conference, the University of Girona became an extraordinary meeting point for more than 300 scholars, judges, lawyers, and other specialists interested in the philosophy of law. Delegates came from all over the globe: Argentina, Australia, Brazil, Canada, Chile, Colombia, Denmark, Dominican Republic, Finland, France, Germany, Mexico, the Netherlands, Panama, Peru, Portugal, Romania, the United Kingdom, the United States of America, Uruguay, Venezuela, and other countries still. The oral presentations were delivered by Robert Alexy, Juan Carlos Bayón, Brian Bix, Eugenio Bulygin, Bruno Celano, Jules L. Coleman, Riccardo Guastini, Brian Leiter, Jorge L. Rodríguez, Frederick Schauer, Scott Shapiro, and Wilfrid Waluchow. The debates were lively and productive, and the authors took into account the various suggestions and criticisms, which had emerged during the public sessions, in preparing revised versions of their papers. All these papers are included in this volume; the only exception is Scott Shapiro's: His contribution corresponds, in substance, to the first chapter in his 2011 monograph *Legality*, soon to be published, in Spanish, in this very series.

Meanwhile, the "Filosofía y derecho" series kept growing; it now includes almost 70 volumes. This series showcases, we believe, the strength of the research group behind this project. The main areas of our research are legal, moral, and political philosophy, as is often the case in our field. However, there is a distinctive interest in methodological issues, and we constantly endeavor to highlight the congruous contributions made to our discipline's cultural heritage by Spanish, Anglo-American, and Italian scholarship. As for specific subjects, we seek to promote some research topics which are somewhat underdeveloped in the Continental tradition, including the philosophical foundations of procedural law, constitutional law, and private law. We aim to contribute, with our philosophical work, to the discussion of important problems in different branches of the law: we try, in other words, to synchronize the philosophers' and the lawyers' approaches to law and jurisprudence.

In choosing the general topic of our conference, and thus also of this book, we found that there were two compelling reasons in favor of the subject of value-neutrality. First, it is a methodological issue that cuts across our group's main lines of research. It may be true that sometimes one simply takes for granted either the possibility or the *im*possibility of theorizing about the law in a value-neutral manner. But neither view is obviously right, and in a fully worked-out theory of any area of law the topic is eventually unavoidable. Second, neutrality has been a central topic of jurisprudential discussion, in the twentieth and twenty-first centuries, in both the Continental and Anglo-American traditions. It was therefore, we realized, a topic particularly suited for an international intellectual exchange—which it was our goal to promote—between some of the most important authors currently working in the field.

All these factors play their part in making this volume a truly special collection of essays. We believe it will make a strong contribution to the field, and lastingly influence in jurisprudential debates to come.

Jordi Ferrer Beltrán
José Juan Moreso
Diego M. Papayannis

Contents

About the Authors

Dr. Robert Alexy, born in 1945, studied law and philosophy at the Georg-August-University in Göttingen. He wrote a dissertation entitled "A Theory of Legal Argumentation", published in 1978. In 1984, he qualified as university lecturer in the faculty of law at the University of Göttingen. His thesis, submitted as his *Habilitationsschrift*, was entitled "A Theory of Constitutional Rights". Since 1986, he is Professor of Public Law and Legal Philosophy at the Christian-Albrechts-University in Kiel. From 1994 to 1998, he was president of the German section of the IVR. Since 2002, he has been a member of the Academy of Sciences in Göttingen.

Dr. Juan Carlos Bayón Professor of Philosophy of Law at the Autonomous University of Madrid. Author of La normatividad del Derecho: Deber jurídico y razones para la acción (1991) and, together with Jorge Rodriguez, of Relevancia normativa en la justificación de las decisiones judiciales (2003), as well as a number of articles about the rationality of rule-following, the normative foundations of the economic analysis of law, legal positivism, the notion of defeasible norms and the defeasibility of legal reasoning, or the relationship between democracy and rights and the justification of constitutionalism.

Dr. Brian H. Bix is the Frederick W. Thomas Professor of Law and Philosophy at the University of Minnesota. He received his J.D. from Harvard University and his doctorate from Balliol College, Oxford University. He is the author, editor, or co-editor of 15 books, and has published over 100 articles; his works have been translated into seven languages. His publications include Contract Law: Rules, Theory, and Context (Cambridge University Press, 2012), The Oxford Introductions to U.S. Law: Family Law (Oxford University Press, forthcoming), and Jurisprudence: Theory and Context, 6th ed. (Sweet and Maxwell 2012). He is a Member of the American Law Institute.

Dr. Eugenio Bulygin (1931) is Doctor in Law and Social Sciences at the University of Buenos Aires (1963). Postgraduate studies at the universities of Cologne, Bonn (1963–1964) and Oxford/1968–1969). He teaches at the University of Buenos Aires

(UBA), and was visiting professor at many European and Latin American universities. He was awarded the Guggenheim (1975), the Konex (1986) and the Humboldt (1996) prizes. He also received honorary doctorates by the universities of Bahía Blanca (Argentina), Alicante (Spain) and Pompeu Fabra (Barcelona, Spain). He was Dean of the Faculty of Law at the UBA (1983–1986), Judge of the Federal Court of Appeals (1986–2002) and president of the International Association for Legal and Social Philosophy (IVR). 1999–2003. Now he is honorary professor of UBA and honorary president of IVR. His publications include 14 books, the most important being Normative Systems (1971) and Análisis Lógico y Derecho (1991)—both with Carlos E. Alchourrón—and more than 140 papers on topics of legal philosophy and deontic logic.

Dr. Bruno Celano, Ph.D. (University of Milan, Italy), is full professor of Legal philosophy at the University of Palermo (Italy). He is a member of the counselling committee of the journals Ragion pratica (Il Mulino, Bologna) and Diritti umani e diritto internazionale (Franco Angeli, Milan), and a member of the editorial board of the journals Diritto e questioni pubbliche (University of Palermo), Legal Theory (Cambridge University Press, Cambridge), Analisi e diritto (Marcial Pons, Madrid), Law, Ethics and Philosophy (Marcial Pons, Madrid), and revus—European Constitutionality Review (Slovenia). His publications include the books Dover essere e intenzionalità (Giappichelli, Turin 1990), Dialettica della giustificazione pratica. Saggio sulla Legge di Hume, (Giappichelli, Turin 1994), La teoria del diritto di Hans Kelsen. Una introduzione critica (Il Mulino, Bologna 1999), Dos estudios sobre la costumbre, (Fontamara, México 2000), Derecho, justicia, razones. Ensayos 2000–2007 (Centro de Estudios Políticos y Constitucionales, Madrid 2009), Fatti istituzionali, consuetudini, convenzioni (Aracne, Rome 2010), as well as several essays on various topics in practical philosophy and the philosophy of law.

Dr. Jules L. Coleman was Wesley Newcomb Hohfeld Professor of Theory of Law and Professor of Philosophy of Law at Yale Law School. He received his doctorate in philosophy at Brooklyn College of the Rockefeller University and an MSL at Yale Law School. He teaches philosophy of law, tort law, political philosophy and theory of rational choice. Among his works are Hart's Postscript, Risks and Wrongs (being translated in the collection Philosophy and Law, Marcial Pons), The Practice of Principle, and Oxford Handbook of Jurisprudence and the Philosophy of Law (co-authored with Scott Shapiro).

Dr. Riccardo Guastini is Director of the Ph.D. School of Law of the University of Genoa. Professor of Legal Philosophy and Constitutional Law. Co-founder and director of the journals "Ragion Pratica", "Analisi e diritto", and "Materiali per una storia della cultura giuridica". He has been visiting professor at the Centre de Théorie et analyse du droit, Université de Paris Ouest-Nanterre; Benjamin Cardozo School of Law, New York; Institut de Hautes Etudes Internationales, Université de Paris II, Panthéon-Assas; Universitat Pompeu Fabra, Barcelona; Université d'Aix-Marseille, Aix-en-Provence. He published several articles in international journals of legal philosophy and constitutional law. His most recent works are: Das fontes às normas (São Paulo, 2005); Lezioni di teoria del diritto e dello stato (Torino, 2006); Teoría e ideología de la interpretación constitucional (Madrid, 2008); Nuovi studi sull'interpretazione (2009); Interpretación, estado, y constitución (Lima, 2010); Le fonti del diritto. Fondamenti teorici (Milano, 2010); Leçons de théorie constitutionnelle (Paris, 2010); La sintassi del diritto (Torino, 2011); Interpretare e argomentare (Milano, 2011).

Dr. Brian Leiter is Karl N. Llewellyn Professor of Jurisprudence and Director of the Center for Law, Philosophy & Human Values at the University of Chicago. He is the author of Nietzsche on Morality (Routledge, 2002), Naturalizing Jurisprudence (Oxford, 2007; Spanish edition, Marcial Pons, 2012), and Why Tolerate Religion? (Princeton, 2013), as well as many articles.

Dr. Dan Priel is an Assistant professor at Osgoode Hall Law School in York University. He has published work in jurisprudence and on tort law and restitution. Right now he is particularly interested in the relationship between law and politics as a means for understanding contemporary jurisprudential debates, the history of legal theory, and the rule of law. He is also exploring whether closer ties between legal and political theory can be the basis for connecting general jurisprudence and the normative theories of particular areas of law.

Dr. Jorge L. Rodríguez is Professor and researcher at National University of Mar del Plata and University of Girona. Konex Award in Legal Theory and Philosophy of Law (2006). Young Scholar Award of the International Association for Philosophy of Law and Social Philosophy (1999). Has published several books—Lógica de los sistemas jurídicos (2002), and as co-author Relevancia normativa en la justificación de las decisiones judiciales (2003), Estudios sobre interpretación y dinámica de los sistemas constitucionales (2005), and Jerarquías normativas y dinámica de los sistemas jurídicos (2011)—as well as articles on legal theory, deontic logic and moral philosophy.

Dr. Frederick Schauer is David and Mary Harrison Distinguished Professor of Law at the University of Virginia. Previously (1990–2008) he was Frank Stanton Professor of the First Amendment at Harvard University, and (1983–1990) Professor of Law at the University of Michigan. He has held visiting faculty positions at Columbia University, the University of Chicago, Dartmouth College, the University of Toronto, and New York University, and in 2007–2008 was Eastman Professor and Fellow of Balliol College at Oxford University. A Fellow of the American Academy of Arts and Sciences and former holder of a Guggenheim Fellowship, Schauer is the author of The Law of Obscenity (1976), Free Speech: A Philosophical Enquiry (1982), Playing By the Rules: A Philosophical Examination of Rule-Based Decision-Making in Law and in Life (1991), Profiles, Probabilities, and Stereotypes (2003), and Thinking Like a Lawyer: A New Introduction to Legal Reasoning (2009); and edited Karl Llewellyn, The Theory of Rules (2011). He was a founding co-editor of Legal Theory, and chaired the Section on Constitutional Law of the Association of American Law Schools and the Committee on Philosophy and Law of the American Philosophical Association.

Dr. Kevin Walton is a Senior Lecturer and the Director of the Julius Stone Institute of Jurisprudence in Sydney Law School at the University of Sydney. He teaches and researches in legal philosophy. He is particularly interested in problems of political obligation—see his forthcoming paper "The Particularities of Legitimacy: John Simmons on Political Obligation"—as well as in questions of jurisprudential methodology. Before joining Sydney Law School in 2003, he was a Lecturer in the School of Law at the University of Aberdeen. He received his doctorate from the University of Edinburgh in 2007.

Dr. Wilfrid Waluchow is a Professor of Philosophy and the Senator William McMaster Chair in Constitutional Studies at McMaster University. He is also an Adjunct Member of the Graduate Faculty of Osgoode Hall Law School. Waluchow has a B.A. and M.A. in philosophy from the University of Western Ontario and a DPhil in the philosophy of law from Oxford University, where he studied under H.L.A. Hart. His research interests include the philosophy of constitutional law and general jurisprudence. Among his publications are: *Inclusive Legal Positivism (Oxford: Clarendon Press, 1994)*; *Free Expression: Essays in Law and Philosophy* (Oxford: Clarendon Press, 1994); *The Dimensions of Ethics* (Peterborough: Broadview Press, 2003); and *A Common Law Theory of Judicial Review: The Living Tree* (Cambridge: Cambridge University Press, 2007).

Chapter 1
The Province of Jurisprudence Underdetermined

Juan Carlos Bayón

To be sure, "jurisprudence" or "legal theory" can be, and is in fact, conceived of and carried on in a number of different ways, both with regard to the questions which are supposed to be its proper subject and as to the methods which are considered appropriate to deal with them. John Austin famously claimed that in order to pick out the proper subject of jurisprudence, that is, to "determine its province", what has to be ascertained is "the essence or nature which is common to all laws that are laws properly so called".[1] So, jurisprudence, as conceived of by Austin, is descriptive and general. It is descriptive, in that its task is to provide an account of what law *is* (which amounts to grasping its "essence or nature", something that according to him may be found out without asking what a legal order morally ought to be).[2] And it is general, in that it is an inquiry into the nature of any legal system "properly so called", unconcerned about the parochial (and therefore contingent or inessential) features of any particular practice that is to count as a legal order.

[1] Austin [1832/1863] 1954, 2. It is true that in "The Uses of the Study of Jurisprudence" [published in 1863] Austin says that he means "by General Jurisprudence, the science concerned with the exposition of the principles, notions and distinctions which *are common* to systems of law: understanding by systems of law, the ampler and maturer systems" (Austin [1832/1863] 1954, 367; emphasis added). Of course, to pick up the *common* features of a sample of systems of law ("the ampler and maturer"), or even the features which are common to any legal system, is not the same as elucidating which are the *necessary* or *essential* features that make those systems legal. But he immediately adds: "Of the principles, notions, and distinctions which are the subjects of general jurisprudence, some may be esteemed *necessary*. For we cannot imagine coherently a system of law (or a system of law as evolved in a refined community) without conceiving them as constituents parts of it" (*ibid.*; emphasis added). And a few pages later he resolutely asserts: "With us, Jurisprudence is the science of what is *essential* to law" (Austin [1832/1863] 1954, 372; emphasis added).

[2] See Austin [1832/1863] 1954, 184.

J.C. Bayón (✉)
Department of Public Law, Autonomous University of Madrid,
Kelsen, 1, Madrid, 28049, Spain
e-mail: juancarlos.bayon@uam.es

J. Ferrer Beltrán et al. (eds.), *Neutrality and Theory of Law*,
Law and Philosophy Library 106, DOI 10.1007/978-94-007-6067-7_1,

Measured from the vantage point of current philosophy, Austin's methodological stance was surely naïve and unrefined.[3] And besides that, after Hart it is conventional wisdom that his substantive views regarding what has to be deemed the "essence or nature" of law are seriously flawed anyway.[4] Still, what has proved to be rather lasting in mainstream analytical jurisprudence is the very idea that building a theory of law is a descriptive and general endeavor whose aim is to identify the nature of law, that is, the necessary (or "essential") properties that something has to have in order to count as law. The basic assumption that this is the proper way of understanding the aim and purpose of jurisprudence can be found among the most prominent contemporary theorists in the legal positivist tradition, even if it is now rooted in sophisticated philosophical frameworks (very far away from Austin's methodological simple-mindedness), and whatever they be the precise contours of the substantive theories of law which turn out to be sustained in each case. Thus, Hart famously claimed to have elucidated "two minimum conditions necessary and sufficient for the existence of a legal system",[5] and held that the union of primary and secondary rules "may be justly regarded as the 'essence' of law".[6] In quite the same vein, Raz contends that, unlike the sociology of law, a philosophical theory of law is concerned "with the necessary and universal", so that it "has to be content with those few features which all legal systems necessarily possess".[7] And also

[3]Raz points out that the failure of Austin's analysis ultimately derives from having mistakenly assumed that the legal philosopher's inquiry into the nature of law—which is an inquiry into the concept *law*—simply boils down to an inquiry into the meaning of the word "law": see Raz [1983] 1996, 196.

[4]But see Schauer (2010) and Bix (2010), arguing that the answer to the question whether the Austinian substantive account of law was or not a failure after all depends precisely on what the role and nature of a theory of law is supposed to be.

[5]To wit, officials' acceptance of the rule of recognition and general obedience by the population to the rules which are valid according to the criteria the rule of recognition specifies (Hart 1994, 116).

[6]Hart (1994), 155 (adding that "they may not always be found together wherever the world 'law' is correctly used", but that, in spite of this, the central place he assigns to their union is justified because of its "great explanatory power"). It has been sometimes said that, at least in certain moments, Hart's approach to the concept of law, far from being purely descriptive—something he was eager to underscore in the *Postscript*: see Hart (1994), 239–240—, was rather guided by moral-political considerations: see, for instance Dworkin (2006), 28, 30, or Murphy (2008), 1095–1096; for a contrary view, see Dickson (2004), 149–150 (although she seems less confident about the point in Dickson 2009, 164). In any case, as in this moment it is not exegetical work what interests me, I leave this question aside.

[7]Raz (1979), 104–105. See also, to the same effect, Raz [1996] 2009, 92 ("[t]he universality of the theses of the general theory of law is a result of the fact that they claim to be necessary truths, and there is nothing less that they can claim. [...] A claim to necessity is in the nature of the enterprise"). Yet, Raz's views are in fact more complex, as he adds that an explanation of the concept of law "sets out *some* of the necessary or essential features of the law" (Raz [1998] 2009, 55; emphasis added), given that there are necessary properties of law which are utterly uninteresting or unimportant and then unhelpful in order to get a proper understanding of our concept of law (see Raz [1985] 1996, 235, [2003] 2009, 169, [2004] 2009, 17).

Coleman has said that the "descriptive project of jurisprudence is to identify the essential or necessary features of *our* concept of law".[8]

However, it is well known that over the last two or three decades the idea of a general jurisprudence as a purely descriptive enterprise aiming at elucidating the nature of law through conceptual analysis has been challenged from different fronts. So different, in fact, that it is distracting to characterize the current discussions as opposing proponents of a "descriptive jurisprudence", on the one hand, against those that hold that jurisprudence has to be "normative", on the other. In the context of the discussion about the methodology of jurisprudence, both "descriptive jurisprudence" and "normative jurisprudence" turn out to be crude and potentially misleading labels which mistakenly suggest that there is a single divide between two clearly defined and internally homogeneous positions (which is not the case) that are at any rate antagonistic (which, depending on the way these labels are understood, need not be the case).[9]

1.1 Descriptive and Normative Jurisprudence: In What Sense?

Just to give a compressed and very simplified sketch of the different positions which are upheld in the current debates about the methodology of jurisprudence, let me notice to begin that at least four different senses should be distinguished in which the idea of a "descriptive jurisprudence" may be understood and vindicated. The simpler one—too simple and naïve, indeed[10]—has it that the nature of law, its defining features, can be grasped just by looking at the world "as it is", a task for which no value judgment of any kind would be needed. But this is a view that simply fails

[8]Coleman (2001a), 112 n. 24 (original emphasis). In Coleman (2001b), 173, he also says that the task of analytic jurisprudence is "uncovering necessary truths about our concept of law". However, Coleman's views are more nuanced. First, like Raz (see above n. 7), he also insists that the aim of conceptual analysis is to show us "something interesting, important, or essential about the nature of the thing the concept denotes" (Coleman 2001b, 179). But in Coleman and Simchen (2003), 40–41, the point is pressed even farther, going on to say that "it would be an unfortunate mistake to suppose that the only interesting jurisprudential questions are those that seek to identify properties that all and only systems of governance by law share", not only because some of these properties may be uninteresting, but also because "many properties that are central to our understanding of law need not be shared by all systems of governance by law" (i.e., need not be necessary properties), concluding that "[m]any of the features of legal practice that are most illuminating for what is to be law [...] are *neither necessary* nor sufficient conditions of legality" (emphasis added). As not every necessary property has to be interesting or important (whatever it be the criterion to determine what is or is not important), nor every interesting or important property has to be necessary, it makes a real difference to say that the project of descriptive jurisprudence is to disclose the necessary, the necessary and important, or the important (even if not necessary) properties of law.

[9]This point is emphasized in Coleman (2001b), 4 n. 3 and 176, (2002), 311–312 n. 2, (2007), 598–599, and (2009), 391–392.

[10]As it was forcefully pointed out by Finnis: see Finnis (1980), 4–6.

to realize the complexities involved in categorizing the data. For instance, were it wrongly assumed that an inquiry into what law is—which is an inquiry into the concept *law*—involves nothing more than seeing what is common to all the items to refer to which the word "law" is—or has been—used, jurisprudence would be unable to offer us but a "lowest common denominator" deprived of any explanatory value.[11]

A second and more refined view, which prevails today among positivist legal theorists, holds that to be explanatorily adequate a theory of law cannot be entirely value-free, in that it has to resort to value judgments to select what is significant about law and then pertains to its nature. But, according to this view, the fact that some kind of evaluation is required for jurisprudence to perform its task does not mean that it has to be *morally* evaluative, because the theorist does not have to take a moral or justificatory stance about the worth or value of law to understand its nature. Thus, even if it is admitted that jurisprudence is evaluative, it is conceived of in any case as a project that can be carried on without endorsing any substantive moral claim or purporting to justify anything.[12] Julie Dickson has coined the expression "indirectly evaluative" to convey the idea that jurisprudence has somehow to be evaluative without being morally evaluative, and we may follow her and adopt it as a helpful way of referring to this view.[13] And the main point here is that, insofar as indirectly evaluative jurisprudence is morally neutral, it would make sense to keep on considering it as basically descriptive[14] even if in a sense it is an evaluative or norm-governed enterprise.

A third view contends that legal theory has to be descriptive in an utterly different sense. According to this view,[15] legal theory should take seriously the lesson to be drawn from Quine's critique of the analytic-synthetic distinction, which would

[11] To recall a telling and often quoted remark by Finnis, "jurisprudence [...] aspires to be more than a conjunction of lexicography with local history, or even than a juxtaposition of all lexicographies conjoined with all local histories" (Finnis 1980, 4).

[12] Among those who have sustained that jurisprudence has to resort to some "theory-construction" values, but not to substantive moral values, see Raz [1983] 1996, 208–209, [1985] 1996, 235–237, [1998] 2009, 69, Waluchow (1994), 19, Dickson (2001), 65–67, Coleman (2001a), 108 n. 22, 112, (2001b), 3, 4 n. 3, 177–178, 196–197 and 200 n. 25, Marmor (2001), 153–159 and [2005] 2007, 143, 145. It has been a matter of contention whether or not this view can be ascribed to Hart: for an answer in the affirmative, see Dickson (2004), 118–123. Coleman's position, however, is not entirely clear to me (may be because of a misunderstanding on my part), given that he has occasionally gone on to say that conceptual analysis—of the pragmatist variety he defends—is "always responsive" to "practical considerations" (Coleman 2001b, 210), and, even more clearly, that he does not deny that an analysis of the concept of law "should in principle answer to practical-political considerations" (*ibid.*, n. 36).

[13] Dickson (2001), 10.

[14] Although Dickson herself does not share this view: to her, to call an indirectly evaluative legal theory "descriptive" is "misleading at best" (Dickson 2001, 67), "a misnomer" (Dickson 2004, 128). Leiter, instead, thinks that Dickson stance can be considered "descriptivist" (Leiter [2003] 2007, 175).

[15] Firmly defended by Brian Leiter: see Leiter (1998), [2001] 2007, [2003] 2007, and (2007), 183–199.

imply to put into question the fruitfulness of a priori conceptual analysis (and thus the very idea of law having a "nature" or any "essential properties", so that some propositions about it were "necessarily true", "true by definition"). Hence, we should proceed instead to a "naturalistic turn", so that jurisprudence should be absorbed into social science and the answer to the question of what law is should emerge from an empirical inquiry as the one with the greatest explanatory and predictive power.[16]

And finally, in a fourth and substantially different sense, it is still possible to ground the claim that jurisprudence is descriptive in some specific positions in metaphysics and the philosophy of language, whose applicability to the law is highly questionable and that most legal theorists today would be reluctant to accept. It is the case, for example, of Michael Moore's views about how the theory of law is to be constructed, which require to assume that law is a "functional kind" (in a sense akin to the notion of a "natural kind", so that ascertaining the nature of law would be something of an analog to scientists' discovery of the nature of the sort of things natural kind-terms refer to).[17]

The idea of a "normative jurisprudence", on the other hand, is likewise understood in different ways. The first one (that has been sometimes called "the Benthamite

---

[16]Several complaints have been raised against this program for a naturalized jurisprudence. Kenneth Himma, for instance, has even sustained that Quine's argument that "analyticity" and "syntheticity" cannot be defined in a non-circular way is not enough to ground the claim that traditional conceptual analysis should be abandoned (see Himma 2007). And John Oberdiek and Dennis Patterson have contended that there are in any case some forms of conceptual analysis that are not challenged by Quinean naturalism (see Oberdiek and Patterson 2007; but see also Leiter's rejoinder to them in Leiter 2007, 196, n. 49). Anyway, the most often repeated objections to Leiter's program are that it "changes the subject" of the jurisprudential debate, replacing it with a question that is just different; that conceptual analysis is logically prior to empirical research, and then that his project presupposes what seeks to replace; and that it is doubtful whether a naturalized jurisprudence could give us something really different from a mirroring of the morass of vague, partially different and partially confused self-understandings of the participants, without somehow embracing something akin to the very method it repudiates (see Leiter's replies in 2007, 183–199).

[17]Moore is adamant on the point: "ours is a quest in descriptive general jurisprudence" (Moore 2000, 309). But Moore's way to vindicate the project of a descriptive jurisprudence requires accepting some extremely controversial points. He begins by endorsing the Kripke-Putnam theory of causal reference, acknowledging that it has been defended with respect to natural kind terms—and proper names, but this is immaterial here—and that it is contested whether it could be properly applied to words designing artifacts (like "law"). But next he goes on to saying that law is a "functional kind" and that, as such, the items that "law" designates "have a nature that they share that is richer than [...] merely sharing a name in some language", albeit, unlike natural kinds, the nature they share "is a function and not a structure" (Moore 2000, 313). So, if jurisprudence studies the nature of law, this nature is to be found in law's function, and such function is—according to Moore, who also endorses moral realism—"a true moral value" that "can be served by law uniquely" (*ibid.*, 294), then jurisprudence could certainly be conceived of as a "descriptive" enterprise in as far as it would give us a proper account of what law "is" through a grasping of its "natural" function. But only provided all the above said metaphysical and semantic contentions are accepted (and, of course, there is the rub).

project",[18] or the "beneficial moral consequences" argument)[19] is in fact a prescriptive theory of the concept of law, in the sense that its aim is to recommend what our concept of law should be or should become in view of the moral consequences that would follow from embracing it. As such, this approach needs not to deny the possibility of a descriptive jurisprudence, that is, it needs not deny that we can get a successful explanation of our concept of law as it actually is without making any moral commitment. And, in particular, it needs not to sustain the fallacious argument that the beneficial moral consequences a certain concept of law would purportedly have support the conclusion that this actually is our concept of law.[20] The enterprise that the Benthamite project would be pursuing is simply different (and not necessarily antagonistic to the idea of a descriptive—i.e., morally neutral—theory of law).

We get at a second sense of the idea of a "normative jurisprudence" (seemingly related to the former one, but in fact different from it) when it is endorsed the claim that there simply may not be a single concept of law "we all share", that there rather are different concepts of law or, in other words, that "our" concept of law is to a significant extent indeterminate.[21] In this case there is leeway to decide to adopt one or other view of law—or to refine in a definite direction the partly indeterminate concept of law—on the basis of moral and political reasons, and this is precisely what jurisprudence would have to do. This is what has been called the "engineering or legislative project"[22] or the "practical-political argument".[23] Both this view and the former one—the "Benthamite project"—have been at times associated with what has come to be confusingly called "normative positivism", which, as it is usually presented, is by my lights more a cluster of logically independent theses than a single and well-defined theoretical position.[24] As far as I can see, normative positivism is primarily a substantive normative view about how legislation ought to be formulated and how it ought to be interpreted and applied by the judiciary. But under the rubric "normative positivism" one may sometimes also find specific jurisprudential claims about the content of the concept of law and the nature—descriptive or otherwise—of legal theory, claims that,

[18] Coleman (2001b), 209.

[19] Dickson (2001), 9, 83–93.

[20] This is clearly shown in Schauer (2005). See also Campbell (2005), 27–28.

[21] See Murphy (2001), 381, (2005), 7, (2007), 30, and (2008), 1093. Schauer (2005), 498–499 n. 21 and 501 n. 23 seems to leave open the possibility that Murphy be right on this point. And much the same can be said of Brian Bix (2003, 556: "we should at least be open to the possibility that our society contains multiple and conflicting concepts of law"; see also Bix 2005, 314–316, and 2007, 3).

[22] Coleman (2001b), 208.

[23] Dickson (2004), 145 ff.

[24] Moreover, a cluster variously denominated ("normative positivism", "ethical positivism", "prescriptive positivism"…), which also raises the question whether all those different names refer exactly to *the same* cluster of theses. On the reasons that have been adduced to choose (or to eschew) some of these names, see Campbell (1996), 79, Waldron (2001), 411–412 and Campbell (2004), 10. On the idea that the term "normative legal positivism" applies to at least five possible views, see Marmor [2005] 2007, 126–127.

as it turns out to be, most of the times are in the line either of "the Benthamite project" or of the "engineering" or "practical-political argument".[25] Thus, because of these ambiguities, I think that in the context of the present discussion it is better to avoid using the rubric "normative positivism" altogether.

And finally, there is a third, much stronger sense in which it has been said that jurisprudence is—and has to be indeed—normative. This is the sense embraced by any view according to which an analysis of the concept of law requires engaging in substantive moral or political argument, so that one has somehow to rely on moral judgments in order to give a proper account of what law is. Thus, unlike the "engineering" or "practical-political argument", what is contended now is, first, that there is indeed a definite concept of law and that the proper subject of jurisprudence is to get it right (not to propose a way of shaping the concept, attending to moral and political considerations). And second, that we simply cannot get it right without "understanding the point" of law, which would purportedly require endorsing substantive judgments of political morality about law's worth or purpose. In other words, a proper understanding of what law is should be grounded on an adequate understanding of law's morally valuable purpose or point, with the result of making conceptual analysis of law a part of moral or political philosophy.[26]

There is at present a growing literature about the methodology of jurisprudence, so that one can say that in recent years analytical legal theory is to a large extent turning its attention from substantive or first-order questions to methodological or second-order ones (or, as Alexy has helpfully put it, from debating the nature of law to debating the nature of arguments about the nature of law).[27] It is not my purpose here to offer a comprehensive overview of the current debates about the methodology of jurisprudence,[28] nor to engage in full discussion with each of the views I have briefly outlined. I will merely intend to pick out some salient points instead. First, I shall take issue with the idea—which seems to me to be mainstream among positivist legal theorists today—that jurisprudence is best conceived of as a general and basically descriptive enterprise whose aim is to adequately explain the nature of law through conceptual analysis and that, in order to accomplish this task, cannot be entirely value-free, but needs only be "indirectly evaluative". And then, I shall suggest that jurisprudence should be normative in the second of the three senses previously distinguished (that which have been called the "engineering" or "practical-political argument"), which of course would need to be more carefully elaborated. None of these arguments, as I shall put them forward, is entirely novel (nor do

---

[25] Therefore· I find rather uninformative and ultimately misleading to define "normative positivism" as Waldron did (in Waldron 2001, 412): "the view that positivism should be understood as a normative position". For example, this confusing definition leads Waldron to consider (albeit hesitatingly) that Raz might be a "normative positivist" (see Waldron 2001, 412 n. 7 and 432 n. 66).

[26] This skeletal structure may be shared by otherwise different conceptions of what we are trying to do in constructing a proper theory of law, as, for instance, those of Dworkin or Finnis.

[27] Alexy (2003), 4.

[28] For an extensive and helpful discussion of the literature on the subject see Coleman (2002) and Dickson (2004).

I claim they are). But I shall intend to show that some important points about them may be more sharply put and especially that some standard objections to the theses I shall endorse might be cleared up.

1.2 The Necessary Features of Our Concept of Law: A Dubious Idea

Thus, let me recall the mainstream view held by analytic jurisprudence in the legal positivist tradition, which Stephen Perry has helpfully called "the methodology of necessary features".[29] According to it,[30] the aim of jurisprudence is to give us an adequate explanation of the nature of law, and any claim about the nature of law is a claim about what law necessarily is. This entails that there is a set of features that law necessarily possesses, so that if a legal theory is successful insofar as it identifies this set—i.e., the features that something has to exhibit in order to be law—, the propositions that make up such a theory are necessarily true. However, it should be clear that—leaving aside the case of natural kinds—"the world as it is" does not come demarcated in kinds: our concepts set their boundaries. Hence, an explanation of the nature of law—of what law is—is an explanation of the concept of law.[31] Moreover, as the concept of law—any concept indeed—is a changing, historical product, what legal theory should identify are the necessary features of *our* concept of law.[32] In this way, it contributes to our self-understanding.[33] But in order to do that it has to highlight what is really significant for us, and then, among the necessary features of our concept of law, it has to select the subset of those which also are interesting or important.[34]

Then, this program has to face two significant problems. In the first place, it seems that in order to pick out the features that law "necessarily" possesses we should previously know what counts or does not count as law, but this depends in its turn on what features are deemed necessary to count as law. The second problem is that we should make clear how are we to determine which features are "important".

---

[29] Perry (2009), 316.

[30] See references in notes 5–8 above, and also the crisp presentation of this view in Dickson (2001), 17–18. Bix (1995, 2003, 2007) provide valuable background to clarify what is at stake in this discussion.

[31] See Coleman and Simchen (2003), 5 n. 9 (saying that the questions "what is law?", "what is the nature of law?" and "what is the concept of law?" can be treated as interchangeable).

[32] See Raz [1996] 2009, 96 and [2004] 2009, 32 ("Talk of *the* concept of law really means *our* concept of law"; original emphasis); and Coleman (2001a), 112 n. 24 (emphasizing that "there is a difference between the claim that a particular concept is necessary and the claim that there are necessary features of an admittedly contingent concept").

[33] Raz [1985] 1996, 237, [1996] 2009, 97 and [2004] 2009, 31 ("In large measure what we study when we study the nature of law is the nature of our own self-understanding").

[34] See notes 7 and 8 above.

Let me elaborate a bit on the first of these problems.[35] The difficulty lies in determining what belongs or does not belong to the set of things we are trying to explain, given that the theorist must be examining law and not anything else—and everything that counts as law, if his or her claim is to provide a *general* account of it—. It could be said that this is not a problem at all and that the mere fact of having thought otherwise reveals a deep misunderstanding of how conceptual analysis proceeds. Once we realize that what we are trying to identify are the necessary features of *our* concept of law, we would simply have to rely on *our* pre-theoretical shared understanding of the concept, and this would be all we need at the beginning to set a standard by which we could determine what counts as law[36] (before we articulate an explanation of its nature).

But now we have to ask—as Perry does—"who is this 'we'?",[37] who are those that have an agreed-upon, shared understanding of the concept of law? Among legal theorists, at least, it could hardly be said that there is agreement about which are the features that something has to exhibit in order to be law, the features that law "necessarily" possesses. It has been sustained both that every legal system is necessarily coercive[38] and also that resort to sanctions is not a necessary feature of our concept of law.[39] That it is implicit in our concept of law that every legal system claims to possess legitimate authority[40] and also that there is no convincing reason to suppose that.[41] That the gunman situation writ large—*pace* Hart—could in certain circumstances be considered law[42] and, to the contrary, that a purely arbitrary power which violates the principles of the rule of law altogether cannot be called a legal system.[43] That a claim to supremacy is essential to the law[44] and also that this does not have necessarily to be so.[45] And, of course, it remains contested whether extremely unjust law would still be law,[46] and it also remains contested whether it is conceptually possible to incorporate morality to law or not (the much discussed question that divides exclusive and inclusive legal positivists).

---

[35]Here I draw heavily on Priel (2007a, b). See also Perry (1996), 370–371.

[36]That is, as Hart said, "[t]he starting point for this clarificatory task is the widespread common knowledge of the salient features of a modern municipal legal system" that he attributes to "any educated man" (Hart 1994, 240).

[37]Perry (1996), 370–371.

[38]Just to pick up a couple of examples from the *non*-positivist camp, see Alexy (2003), 7 and Finnis (1980), 266.

[39]See Raz (1990), 158–159.

[40]Raz [1985] 1996, 215 and Alexy (2002), 32–34 (putting the idea as a "claim to correctness").

[41]Murphy (2001), 382 (disagreeing with Raz) and Bix (2006), 147–148 (disagreeing with Alexy).

[42]Kramer (1999), 96–98.

[43]Coleman (2001b), 192–193 ("in so far as a ruler exercises purely arbitrary power, he or she does not govern by law"); Waldron (2008), 79.

[44]Raz (1990), 151.

[45]Marmor (2001), 39–42.

[46]For an answer in the negative see Alexy (2002), 28–35, 40–68; or MacCormick (2007), 278 ("there is some moral minimum without which purported law becomes un-law").

But the real trouble is not disagreement among theorists. The real problem is that inasmuch as members of society also have partly different and in any case blurry pre-theoretical understandings of what counts as law, it seems that legal theorists will have nowhere to look to in order to resolve in a non circular or non question-begging way their disagreements about what features law "necessarily" possesses.[47] Every time it is claimed that something is a necessary feature of law and it is replied that we can conceive of systems of law where this feature is lacking, there are two possible reactions: either accepting that the claim was mistaken, or else retorting that the purported counter-example could not be properly called law. But if there is not a single concept of law we all share (the "ours"), but rather partly different concepts, there seems to be no principled way to decide which one of those reactions should be deemed appropriate in each case. Supporting one of these reactions or the other by giving an argument about what *is* the nature of law would simply be question-begging when different people consider different things to count as law, just because they have different concepts of law.

Two possible objections might be raised against this view. The first one would say, on the one hand, that it overstates the reach and depth of disagreement which actually exists about the concept of law, and, on the other hand, that, even if there is at the margins a certain extent of disagreement about its content, that is exactly what we can expect of any philosophically interesting concept.[48] But I think that the objection can be met. To be sure, it has to be conceded that if we have different concepts of law they overlap to a great extent[49]: otherwise, whenever we talk about law we would be talking past one another. But this overlap is not the same that there being a single concept of law, and it does not exclude that a number of interesting questions about the boundaries between law and non-law will remain for which we simply won't be able to find an answer in any shared understanding. Besides, if the aim of legal theory is to uncover what is necessary and important about law, a search for the features which all the different and overlapping concepts of law coincide in considering necessary would make us to lose sight of much of what is important from the point of view of each one of them.[50]

The second objection would go deeper. It would say that the contention that we have different concepts of law is the product of a dubious semantics. In fact, if would be the product of having endorsed "criterialism" in a dworkinian sense. As it is well known, Dworkin holds that the "sociological concept of law"—namely, our concept of law as a certain type of institutional social structure—is criterial, that is, the kind of concept we can say we share only on condition that we agree on a set of criteria for the correct application of the corresponding concept-word. Then, the sociological concept of law is simply imprecise, because there is no full agreement about these criteria. And therefore all we can do is to report this imprecision and to acknowledge

[47] See Priel (2007a, 150, b, 187–188).

[48] See on this point Coleman (2001b), 210.

[49] Murphy himself underlines this: see Murphy (2005, 18, 2008, 1108).

[50] Priel (2007b), 183.

that it is not the kind of concept whose analysis can yield philosophically interesting "essential or necessary features" (and eventually, for some purposes such as social science investigation, to stipulate a more precise definition).[51] But then, if criterialism (or Dworkin's account of it) is flawed as a theory of how the extension of a noun—or at least of a kind of nouns like "law"—is determined, and if the idea that there is not a single concept of law we all share, but rather partly different concepts, were a result of having assumed criterialism, then this idea would now be lacking any serious support.

This is not the place to engage in full discussion about criterialism, the right way of understanding criterialism, or the alternatives to it. Suffice it to say that to my mind the idea that there is not a single concept of law we all share does not depend on accepting that for individual speakers to share the meaning of a concept-word amounts to having propositional knowledge of a same extension-fixing set of criteria. We may think instead that these criteria need not be completely transparent for the people who share them and even that we can distinguish between ordinary and theoretical explanations (so that the theorist can somewhat redraw the boundaries of the concept as compared with what would superficially result from the data of actual usage by ordinary speakers).[52] Or we may think that for individuals to share the same concept all that is needed is agreement on paradigmatic cases or instances of the concept, and not on a set of criteria of application, because the ability to classify is practical, and then the beliefs required to fix the extension of a kind-term are basically *de re*, not *de dicto*.[53] Nothing of this, however, seems to me to be enough to rule out the possibility that there be partly different concepts and not a single concept of law we all share. One can grant that sharing the same concept does not imply sharing the same application criteria (and even less being able to formulate this set of criteria and doing it in the same way), but this could hardly assure that we do share a given concept (for instance, the concept of law).

1.3 What is Important About Law? The Inescapability of Substantive Valuations

If there is not a single concept of law we all share, but rather partly different concepts, the enterprise of picking out the necessary features of our concept of law cannot be carried on. Thus, the province of jurisprudence, the objective to be pursued in theorizing about the nature of law, seems to be left rather underdetermined, given the variety of available perspectives. But were this not enough, we still have the problem of how to establish which features of law are significant, interesting or important. What is at stake here is the very possibility of determining what is

[51] Dworkin (2006), 3, 9, 223–224, 228.

[52] Raz [1998] 2009, 67–76.

[53] See Coleman (2001b), 156–157 and Coleman and Simchen (2003), 30–38.

important in the way that the project of an "indirectly evaluative legal theory" purports it can be done. Then, we need to make clear by what standards could it be determined whether something is important or not and therefore how are we to choose among competing judgments of importance.

The minimal sense in which it is widely admitted that legal theory—any theory, indeed—cannot be entirely value-free has to do with the "banal truth"[54] that theorizing ought to fulfill some epistemic or metatheoretical requirements (such as simplicity, comprehensiveness, coherence, consilience, etc.). But it is doubtful whether these metatheoretical values alone can settle the question of what is important. On the contrary, it seems that we need to know in the first place what is important in order to test whether some of these requirements are satisfied or not (for instance, an explanation is not simple enough if it includes something unimportant, or it is not truly comprehensive if it fails to include something important).[55]

Thus, according to Dickson, legal theory has in fact to resort to something beyond epistemic or metatheoretical values in order to determine what is important or significant. She calls "indirectly evaluative propositions" those of the form "X is an important feature of the law", and she thinks that propositions of this type may find support in different kinds of considerations.[56] Some of them are in my view hardly useful, to wit, that "X is a feature which law invariably exhibits", or that something is important "on the basis of the prevalence of certain beliefs concerning that feature on the part of those subject to the law".[57] If there is not a single concept of law we all share, and therefore no correct account of "the" nature of law, then there is disagreement about which features the law "invariably" exhibits. Likewise, there will be disagreement among "those subject to the law" about what is important. If the legal theorist has to do something more than merely reporting those disagreements, it is not entirely clear upon which basis he or she is expected to do it. Especially when it is said that some self-understandings of the participants "will be confused" and some "will be more important and significant than others"[58] one cannot rely solely on the fact that the belief that something is important prevails among the participants to support the claim that it is in fact important.

The main support such a kind of claim can find in Dickson's account comes from a different source. According to her, an indirectly evaluative proposition of the form "X is important", even if it does not entail (directly evaluative) propositions stating that X is good or bad, may nevertheless be supported by the fact that it is a matter of practical concern to us whether a social institution that exhibits X is a good or a bad thing.[59] But as far as I can see, it is difficult to understand why the fact that something exhibits the feature X should be a matter of practical concern for me unless I think that X is or can be either a good or a bad thing, either something to

[54] See Dickson (2001), 33 and Leiter [2003] 2007, 167.

[55] This point is highlighted in Priel (2010), 657–658.

[56] Dickson (2001), 53, 57–65.

[57] *Ibid.*, 64, 59.

[58] Dickson (2004), 138.

[59] Dickson (2001), 53, 64.

hope for or something to fear. So, it is one thing to say that considering that X is important "is not in itself an ascription of goodness to that X",[60] and quite another to conclude that it is possible to identify what is important about law without making any substantive moral claim whatsoever (which of course does not entail purporting to justify what is qualified as important).[61]

1.4 Whither Jurisprudence? Shaping the Concept of Law on Normative Grounds

If it is accepted that there simply may not be a single concept of law "we all share", that there rather are different concepts of law, and that claims of importance have to be grounded on moral and political considerations, jurisprudence should be reconceived as a different enterprise, in the line, I think of what has been called the "engineering or legislative project" or the "practical-political argument". By now it should be clear, I think, that this does not amount to indulging in a form of wishful thinking, confusing a proposal about how it would be better (from a moral and political point of view) to shape the concept of law with the right account of the concept of law we have. Because what is denied, to begin, is that there be a single concept of law that we all share and that legal theory has to get right. If there is a hurdle to overcome before accepting the pertinence of this kind of project it probably lies elsewhere, and I would like, to conclude, to comment very briefly on this.

The problem is that the "engineering project" seems to presuppose that we can ascertain what social and political consequences will result from general convergence on a particular conception of what law is, and that these consequences will be different were we to converge on a different conception. And perhaps none of these assumptions can be granted. Perhaps it is uncertain what consequences will ensue, and maybe they will be the same whatever conception is adopted. If the kind of consequences we have in mind have mainly to do with people's critical or uncritical attitudes toward the law, as the classical instrumentalist approach would have it, then the doubts are probably founded.[62]

But things are different if the issue is considered from another point of view, the one that has to do with the relationship between the questions "what is law" and "what is *the* law (of a particular community at a given moment)".[63] It is a standard positivist criticism of Dworkin that he confuses these questions,[64] and in fact they are different. But their being different does not imply that the way we answer the first one has no bearing at all on how we are going to answer the last one. Coleman and

[60] *Ibid.*, 53.

[61] As Waldron says, "It is a mistake to think that all normative jurisprudence must extol or idealize law. Warnings and worries are part of normative jurisprudence when one's theories and concepts are organized so as to highlight them" (Waldron 2009, 696, n. 64).

[62] As Murphy himself acknowledges: see Murphy (2008), 1096–1102.

[63] *Ibid.* 1102.

[64] See, for instance, Coleman (2001b), 180 and Coleman and Simchen (2003), 7–8.

Simchen have pointed out that it is possible to disagree about the extension-fixing criteria for "law" without having to disagree about the claim that a certain proposition about the law of our community is true (or false),[65] and I think this is right. But this does not preclude the possibility of disagreeing about a claim of the last kind precisely because we disagree about the extension-fixing criteria for "law" in the first place.[66] We implicitly use a concept of law every time we state the content of the law.[67] And then, if "our" concept of law is partly indeterminate (or better, if we have different concepts of law), it makes sense to advocate for shaping the concept of law in a certain way in the light of the moral or political value one believes their consequences on legal practice would have.

References

Alexy, R. 2002. *The argument from injustice. A reply to legal positivism.* Trans. Litschewski Paulson, B., and S.L. Paulson. Oxford: Oxford University Press.

Alexy, R. 2003. The nature of arguments about the nature of law. In *Rights, culture, and the law. Themes from the legal and political philosophy of Joseph Raz*, ed. L.H. Meyer, S.L. Paulson, and T.W. Pogge, 3–16. Oxford: Oxford University Press.

Austin, J. [1832/1863] 1954. *The province of jurisprudence determined and the uses of the study of jurisprudence*, with and Introduction by H.L.A. Hart. London: Weidenfeld and Nicolson.

Bix, B. 1995. Conceptual questions and jurisprudence. *Legal Theory* 1: 465–479.

Bix, B. 2003. Raz on necessity. *Law and Philosophy* 22: 537–559.

Bix, B. 2005. Raz, authority, and conceptual analysis. *American Journal of Jurisprudence* 50: 311–316.

Bix, B. 2006. Robert Alexy, Radbruch's formula and the nature of legal theory. *Rechtstheorie* 37: 139–149.

Bix, B. 2007. Joseph Raz and conceptual analysis. *APA Newsletter* 6(2): 1–7.

Bix, B. 2010. John Austin and constructing theories of law. *University of Minnesota Law School: Legal studies research paper 10-07*. Available at: http://ssrn.com/abstract=1535386

Campbell, T. 1996. *The legal theory of ethical positivism.* Aldershot: Dartmouth.

Campbell, T. 2004. *Prescriptive legal positivism. Law, rights, and democracy.* London: UCL Press.

Campbell, T. 2005. Prescriptive conceptualism: Comments on Liam Murphy, 'Concepts of law'. *Australian Journal of Legal Philosophy* 30: 20–29.

Coleman, J.L. 2001a. Incorporationism, conventionality, and the practical difference thesis. In ed. Coleman 2001, 99–147.

Coleman, J.L. 2001b. *The practice of principle. In defence of a pragmatist approach to legal theory.* Oxford: Oxford University Press.

[65] Coleman and Simchen (2003), 8.

[66] As Brian Bix says "theory *can be* orthogonal to practice", in that "*frequently* [...] the results of legal disputes [...] can be explained or justified under most or all alternative theories" (Bix 2006, 144; emphasis added). But this leaves open the possibility that sometimes our theories—about what law is—do make a difference on the resolution of particular cases.

[67] And precisely because of that it is perplexing—as Schauer rightly stresses—that Dworkin suggest that the "sociological concept of law" (which is for him irredeemably imprecise) is immaterial to determining whether a proposition about the law is true: see Schauer (2009).

Coleman, J.L. 2002. Methodology. In *The Oxford handbook of jurisprudence and philosophy of law*, ed. J.L. Coleman, S. Shapiro, and K.E. Himma, 311–351. Oxford: Oxford University Press.
Coleman, J.L. 2007. Beyond the separability thesis: Moral semantics and the methodology of jurisprudence. *Oxford Journal of Legal Studies* 27: 581–608.
Coleman, J.L. 2009. Beyond inclusive legal positivism. *Ratio Juris* 22: 359–394.
Coleman, J.L., and O. Simchen. 2003. Law. *Legal Theory* 9: 1–41.
Dickson, J. 2001. *Evaluation and legal theory*. Oxford: Hart Publishing.
Dickson, J. 2004. Methodology in jurisprudence: A critical survey. *Legal Theory* 10: 117–156.
Dickson, J. 2009. Is bad law still law? Is bad law really law? In *Law as institutional normative order*, ed. M. Del Mar and Z. Bankowski, 161–183. Farnham: Ashgate.
Dworkin, R. 2006. *Justice in robes*. Cambridge: Harvard University Press.
Finnis, J. 1980. *Natural law and natural rights*. Oxford: Oxford University Press.
Hart, H.L.A. 1994. *The concept of law*, 2nd ed, ed. P.A. Bulloch and J. Raz. Oxford: Oxford University Press.
Himma, K.E. 2007. Reconsidering a Dogma: Conceptual analysis, the naturalistic turn, and legal philosophy. In *Law and philosophy*, Current legal issues, vol. 10, ed. M.D.A. Freeman and R. Harrison, 3–35. Oxford: Oxford University Press.
Kramer, M. 1999. *In defense of legal positivism. Law without trimmings*. Oxford: Oxford University Press.
Leiter, B. 1998. Naturalism and naturalized jurisprudence. In *Analyzing law. New essays in legal theory*, ed. B. Bix, 79–104. Oxford: Oxford University Press.
Leiter, B. 2007. *Naturalizing jurisprudence. Essays on American legal realism and naturalism in legal philosophy*. Oxford: Oxford University Press.
Leiter, B. [2001] 2007. Legal realism, hard positivism, and the limits of conceptual analysis. [2001], reprinted in Leiter 2007, 121–135.
Leiter, B. [2003] 2007. Beyond the Hart/Dworkin debate: The methodology problem in jurisprudence. [2003], reprinted in Leiter 2007, 153–181.
MacCormick, N. 2007. *Institutions of law. An essay in legal theory*. Oxford: Oxford University Press.
Marmor, A. 2001. *Positive law and objective values*. Oxford: Oxford University Press.
Marmor, A. [2005] 2007. Legal positivism: Still descriptive and morally neutral. [2005], reprinted in A. Marmor, *Law in the age of pluralism*, 125–151. Oxford: Oxford University Press.
Moore, M. 2000. *Educating oneself in public. Critical essays in jurisprudence*. Oxford: Oxford University Press.
Murphy, L. 2001. The political question of the concept of law. In *Hart's postscript: Essays on the postscript to "The concept of law"*, ed. J. Coleman, 371–409. Oxford: Oxford University Press.
Murphy, L. 2005. Concepts of law. *Australian Journal of Legal Philosophy* 30: 1–19.
Murphy, L. 2007. Razian concepts. *APA Newsletter* 6(2): 27–31.
Murphy, L. 2008. Better to see law this way. *New York University Law Review* 83: 1088–1108.
Oberdiek, J., and D. Patterson. 2007. Moral evaluation and conceptual analysis in jurisprudential methodology. In *Law and philosophy*, Current legal issues, vol. 10, ed. M.D.A. Freeman and R. Harrison, 60–75. Oxford: Oxford University Press.
Perry, S. 1996. The varieties of legal positivism. *Canadian Journal of Law and Jurisprudence* 9: 361–381.
Perry, S. 2009. Beyond the distinction between positivism and non-positivism. *Ratio Juris* 22: 311–325.
Priel, D. 2007a. Evaluating descriptive jurisprudence. *American Journal of Jurisprudence* 52: 139–158.
Priel, D. 2007b. Jurisprudence and necessity. *Canadian Journal of Law and Jurisprudence* 20: 173–200.
Priel, D. 2010. Description and evaluation in jurisprudence. *Law and Philosophy* 29: 633–667.
Raz, J. 1979. *The authority of law. Essays on law and morality*. Oxford: Oxford University Press.
Raz, J. 1990. *Practical reason and norms*, 2nd ed. Princeton: Princeton University Press.

Raz, J. 1996. *Ethics in the public domain. Essays in the morality of law and politics*, revised edition. Oxford: Oxford University Press.

Raz, J. [1983] 1996. The problem about the nature of law. [1983], reprinted in Raz 1996, 195–209.

Raz, J. [1985] 1996. Authority, law, and morality. [1985], reprinted in Raz 1996, 210–237.

Raz, J. 2009. *Between authority and interpretation. On the theory of law and practical reason.* Oxford: Oxford University Press.

Raz, J. [1996] 2009. On the nature of law. [1996], reprinted in Raz 2009, 91–125.

Raz, J. [1998] 2009. Two views of the nature of the theory of law: A partial comparison. [1998], reprinted in Raz 2009, 47–87.

Raz, J. [2003] 2009. About morality and the nature of law. [2003], reprinted in Raz 2009, 166–181.

Raz, J. [2004] 2009. Can there be a theory of law. [2004], reprinted in Raz 2009, 17–46.

Schauer, F. 2005. The social construction of the concept of law: A reply to Julie Dickson. *Oxford Journal of Legal Studies* 25: 493–501.

Schauer, F. 2009. Institutions and the concept of law: A reply to Ronald Dworkin (with some help from Neil MacCormick). In *Law as institutional normative order*, ed. M. Del Mar and Z. Bankowski, 35–44. Farnham: Aldershot.

Schauer, F. 2010. Was Austin right after all? On the role of sanctions in a theory of law. *Ratio Juris* 23: 1–21.

Waldron, J. 2001. Normative (or ethical) positivism. In *Hart's postscript. Essays on the postscript to "The Concept of Law"*, ed. J. Coleman, 410–433. Oxford: Oxford University Press.

Waldron, J. 2008. Hart on the principles of legality. In *The legacy of H.L.A. Hart. Legal, political, and moral philosophy*, ed. M. Kramer, C. Grant, B. Colburn, and A. Hatzistavrou, 67–83. Oxford: Oxford University Press.

Waldron, J. 2009. Can there be a democratic jurisprudence? *Emory Law Journal* 58: 675–712.

Waluchow, W.J. 1994. *Inclusive legal positivism.* Oxford: Oxford University Press.

Chapter 2
Necessity, Importance, and the Nature of Law

Frederick Schauer

It is a commonplace among scholars of general jurisprudence that a central goal—perhaps *the* central goal, or perhaps even the only goal—of general jurisprudence is to use the tools of philosophical analysis as a way of helping us to "understand" the "nature of law."[1] And although the question of what it is to "understand" some phenomenon is invariably a subjective and psychological determination, the object of that understanding—the "nature" of law—is not necessarily either subjective or psychological. Rather, the assumption in much contemporary writing on general jurisprudence is that the nature of the phenomenon of law has an observer-independent or theorist-independent existence, and that the task of the theorist is to discover and explain what that nature is.

There is much that is controversial embedded in the foregoing paragraph, and I will take note of some of these controversies presently. My principal goal in this

This paper was prepared for the conference on Neutrality and Theory of Law, University of Girona, Girona, Spain, May 20–22, 2010. The final version has benefited from audience questions in Girona, and from comments on the written draft by Brian Bix, Charles Barzun, Diana Constantinescu, and Brian Leiter.

[1]See Julie Dickson, *Evaluation and Legal Theory* (Oxford: Hart Publishing, 2001), p. 17; Leslie Green, "Positivism and the Inseparability of Law and Morals," *New York University Law Review*, vol. 83 (2008), pp. 1035–1058, at p. 1036; Kenneth M. Ehrenburg, "Defending the Possibility of a Neutral Functional Theory of Law," *Oxford Journal of Legal Studies*, vol. 29 (2009), pp. 91–113, at p. 91; Joseph Raz, "On the Nature of Law," *Archiv für Rechts—und Sozialphilosophie*, vol. 82 (1996), pp. 1–25; Joseph Raz, "Can There Be a Theory of Law,?" in Martin P. Golding & William A. Edmundson, eds., *The Blackwell Guide to the Philosophy of Law and Legal Theory* (Oxford: Blackwell, 2005), 324–342; Joseph Raz, "The Problem about the Nature of Law," in *Ethics in the Public Domain: Essays on the Morality of Law and Politics* (Oxford: Oxford University Press, 1994), pp. 195–213.

F. Schauer (✉)
School of Law, University of Virginia, 580 Massie Road, 22903 Charlottesville, VA, USA
e-mail: schauer@virginia.edu

J. Ferrer Beltrán et al. (eds.), *Neutrality and Theory of Law*,
Law and Philosophy Library 106, DOI 10.1007/978-94-007-6067-7_2,

paper, however, is to address the question of what it is for some phenomenon—law, in particular—to have a nature, and what it is for a theorist to try to ascertain it. More specifically, does the nature of something—or the concept of something, or the nature of the concept of something—consist of its necessary—or essential—properties?[2] Or does the nature of something consist, as some contemporary legal philosophers maintain, of the subset of the set of necessary or essential properties that are also in some way important, or that might be valuable to our understanding? Or does it, as I shall argue here, possibly consist of those properties that are important but not necessary? That is, might a full account of the nature of something include (or even consist in) those properties that are not exclusive to the phenomenon under analysis but which are, in an empirical and probabilistic way, concentrated in that phenomenon? If so, then might such a characterization be true of law, and might the nature of law thus best, or at least usefully, be explained, in important part if not necessarily entirely, by identifying those aspects of law that can be found elsewhere but which are contingently and empirically concentrated in law?[3] Such a conclusion might be philosophically unsatisfying, especially if we simply take an inquiry into the nature of something as necessarily being an inquiry into the concept of something, and then take an inquiry into the concept of something as necessarily being a search for necessary and sufficient conditions. But if the enterprise of jurisprudence is conceived to be about understanding law in its most theoretical way rather than necessarily and exclusively providing a useful application of certain traditional philosophical tools, then the philosophical itch created by probabilistic and empirical rather than logical conclusions perhaps ought still to be a concern, but perhaps not so much as to be fatal to the jurisprudential enterprise.

2.1 Some Preliminary Assumptions

Although this paper is an inquiry into one aspect of jurisprudential methodology, I will nevertheless bracket several other important and interesting methodological questions. Thus, I will not address the questions whether there are concepts at all, what the relationship is between concepts and what they are concepts of, whether conceptual analysis is possible, and, if it is, whether it is a task best (or necessarily) undertaken with non-empirical philosophical tools as opposed to, say, social scientific

[2] Throughout this paper I will treat "necessary" and "essential" as more or less synonymous. See Brian H. Bix, "Raz on Necessity," *Law and Philosophy*, vol. 22 (2003), pp. 537–559, at p. 537 n. 2.

[3] I make a similar claim about legal reasoning in Frederick Schauer, *Thinking Like a Lawyer: A New Introduction to Legal Reasoning* (Cambridge, Massachusetts: Harvard University Press, 2009), pp. 1–12.

ones.[4] There are rich debates in the literature on all of these questions, both outside of jurisprudence and within. And I do not deny that the resolution of these debates is highly pertinent to the specific question I address here. Nevertheless, I propose to focus more narrowly on the question of the relationship between conceptual necessity and jurisprudential inquiry, leaving issues about the implications of answers to that question for other occasions, and leaving it to the reader to evaluate the assumptions that may be implicit in my approach and my conclusions.

I will assume as well that law has a nature that it would be valuable to identify and understand. This too may not be so, and it is possible that law is such a diverse, loose, and shifting array of phenomena that there is no interesting nature of law itself, and no interesting concept of law.[5] Nevertheless I assume not only that there are concepts, and not only that they can be analyzed in terms of their necessary or essential properties, but also that there is a concept of law and that the concept of law is one of the concepts that can be so analyzed. This does not follow necessarily from the previous assumptions. It is possible that there are concepts susceptible to philosophical analysis but that the concept of law is not one of them. But I assume the contrary, and thus assume the possibility and even the value of conceptual analysis of the concept of law.

Finally, I assume that the analysis of the concept of law can be a descriptive one. There is, of course, an active debate about the possibility of a descriptive—in the

---

[4]Debates about some of these questions in the context of jurisprudence were launched, in part, by articles now reprinted in Brian Leiter, *Naturalizing Jurisprudence: Essays on American Legal Realism and Naturalism in Legal Philosophy* (Oxford: Oxford University Press, 2007), especially at pp. 121–199. Responses include, for example, Jules Coleman, *The Practice of Principle: In Defence of a Pragmatist Approach to Legal Theory* (Oxford: Oxford University Press, 2001), pp. 210–217; Scott Shapiro, *Legality* (Cambridge, Massachusetts: Harvard University Press, 2011), pp. 12–18; Julie Dickson, "Methodology in Jurisprudence: A Critical Survey," *Legal Theory*, vol. 10 (2004), pp. 117–156; Andrew Halpin, "Methodology and the Articulation of Insight: Some Lessons from MacCormick's *Institutions of* Law," in Maksymilian Del Mar & Zenon Bankowski, *Law as Institutional Normative Order* (Farnham, Surrey, England: Ashgate Publishing, 2009), pp. 145–159; Andrew Halpin, "The Methodology of Jurisprudence: Thirty Years Off the point," *Canadian Journal of Law and Jurisprudence*, vol, 19 (2006), pp. 67–105; Ian Farrell, "H.L.A. Hart and the Methodology of Jurisprudence," *Texas Law Review*, vol. 84 (2006), pp. 983–1011; John Oberdiek & Dennis Patterson, "Moral Evaluation and Conceptual Analysis in Jurisprudential Methodology," in Michael Freeman & Ross Harrison, eds., *Current Legal Issues*, vol. 10 (*Law and Philosophy*) (2007), pp. 60–76.

[5]I use the qualification "interesting" to make clear that there may be concepts in a strictly logical sense that have little non-logical interest. There may be a nature or concept of "shoppers at Wal-Mart on December 14, 2005, with last names beginning with the letter 'R' who had scrambled eggs for breakfast." But the analysis of that concept would surely be unilluminating. And the same might hold true of law, if law were only a sociological connection among various phenomena with scarcely more connection than exists with the elements of the "shoppers at Wal-Mart . . ." concept just noted. See Frederick Schauer, "Critical Notice," *Canadian Journal of Philosophy*, vol. 24 (1994), pp. 495–510. That may well be true, but, again, I will assume the contrary, and thus assume that there is a concept of law susceptible to non-trivial philosophical analysis.

sense of non-morally-normative but not necessarily in the sense of non-normative—analysis of the concept of law, with theorists including H.L.A. Hart,[6] Jules Coleman[7] and Andre Marmor[8] supporting such a possibility and others such as Ronald Dworkin,[9] John Finnis,[10] and Stephen Perry[11] denying it, with Joseph Raz[12] and Julie Dickson,[13] among others, offering interesting variations that include acknowledging that conceptual analysis necessitates identifying *important* features of the concept to be analyzed, but denying that the admittedly normative identification of importance must be morally-influenced or morally normative in any way. But for purposes of this paper I assume that descriptive analysis of the concept of law is possible,[14] although there is no need to take a position among the descriptivist methodologies of, for example, Coleman, Marmor, Raz, and Dickson.

2.2 On Concepts and Necessity

With these assumptions in hand, we can turn to the central issue: in engaging in the task of understanding the nature of law, is it mandatory that we understand "nature" in terms of conceptual analysis, and thus understand an inquiry into the nature of law as inquiry aimed at identifying properties or features that are *essential* or *necessary* to the concept of law? And, recognizing with Raz and others that some necessary properties may not be important, we can rephrase the question in terms of whether it is vital that we identify the properties that are both necessary and important?

---

[6]H.L.A. Hart, *The Concept of Law* (Oxford: Clarendon Press, Penelope A. Bulloch & Joseph Raz, eds., 2nd ed., 1994), pp. 239–244. Whether Hart's claim in the "Postscript" to always having been doing descriptive jurisprudence is consistent with some of his earlier statements, see below, note 9, and see also Dickson, *op. cit.* note 2, at p. 91 n. 14, is hardly clear.

[7]Jules Coleman, *The Practice of Principle*, *op. cit.* note 5, at pp. 175–179.

[8]Andre Marmor, "Legal Positivism: Still Descriptive and Morally Neutral," *Oxford Journal of Legal Studies*, vol. 26 (2006), pp. 683–704. See also Andre Marmor, *Positive Law and Objective Values* (Oxford: Clarendon Press, 2001), p. 153; Wil Waluchow, *Inclusive Legal Positivism* (Oxford: Clarendon Press, 1994), p. 19.

[9]Ronald Dworkin, *Law's Empire* (Cambridge, Massachusetts: Harvard University Press, 1986), pp. 50–59.

[10]John Finnis, *Natural Law and Natural Rights* (Oxford: Clarendon Press, 1980), pp. 14–17.

[11]Stephen R. Perry, "Hart's Methodological Positivism," in Jules Coleman, ed., *Hart's Postscript: Essays on the Postscript to the* Concept of Law (Oxford: Oxford University Press, 2001), pp. 311–354; Stephen R. Perry, "Interpretation and Methodology in Legal Theory," in Andre Marmor, ed., *Law and Interpretation* (Oxford: Oxford University Press, 1995), pp. 97–122.

[12]Raz, *op. cit.* note 2.

[13]Dickson, *op. cit.* note 2.

[14]For a recent and extensive argument to the contrary, see Dan Priel, "Description and Evaluation in Jurisprudence," *Law and Philosophy*, vol. 29 (forthcoming 2010).

In order to answer this question, we need to step back and look to the purpose or function of conceptual analysis of the concept of law. And when we do so, we see that for Raz and many others, it is to help us to understand (and to explain) the nature of law. Much then turns on what it is for some phenomenon to have a nature at all. The standard view is that no property can be part of the nature of some object of study unless that property is an essential feature of the object of study. To say that having feathers and a backbone is part of the nature of being a bird is to say that nothing can be a bird if it lacks feathers and lacks a backbone, and thus the properties of having feathers and a backbone are necessary conditions of both birds and the concept of bird, in a way that the property of the capacity for flight is not. Although most birds can fly, and although having feathers is apparently necessary for flight among vertebrates that are not bats,[15] there are some feathered vertebrates that cannot fly—penguins and ostriches, for example—and thus the standard view is that because flight is not necessary for birdness, the capacity for flight is not part of the nature of the concept of birds and not part of the nature of birds.

Birds are natural kinds, and it is more controversial whether the same analysis does or could apply to artifacts or to other social constructions. But it is at least plausible that it could. Perhaps usability for exchange is a necessary condition of the concept of money, for example, just as having pages may be (or may have been in the past) essential to the concept of book. And if that is so, then there is no reason to believe, contra Ronald Dworkin,[16] that the concept of law could not have necessary conditions. It is true that socially constructed concepts can change over time and vary across cultures, but that does not mean that there could not be a snapshot of some culture's concept of something socially constructed at some time. The concept of book might require pictures as well as pages (or may not require pages at all) in some cultures, just as the concept of money at some future time might not require usability for exchange, but *our* concept of book *now* (or at least in the recent past) requires pages and does not require pictures, and the possibility of that conclusion varying with time or place is not inconsistent with its soundness at this time in this place.[17] That the concept of law might be different in other cultures, that it might be different in this culture at other times, and that it

[15]So-called flying squirrels and flying fish, as well as flying frogs, flying snakes, and flying squid, are all gliders and not fliers. Bats are the only non-birds that can actually fly. (The foregoing obviously assumes a certain concept of flying, but analysis of *that* concept is obviously not my agenda here.)

[16]In Ronald Dworkin, *Justice in Robes*, (Cambridge, Massachusetts: Harvard University Press, 2006), Dworkin's argument for law being an interpretive concept hinges at numerous places on the claim that the concepts of human-created institutions such as law cannot have necessary and sufficient conditions in the way that natural kinds do.

[17]Compare Danny Priel, "Jurisprudence and Necessity," *Canadian Journal of Law and Jurisprudence*, vol. 20 (2007), pp. 173–200, which appears to adopt a less time—and culture—bound notion of (contingent) necessity than is actually present in the theorists that it questions.

might be better to have a concept of law other than the one we have[18] are all entirely consistent with there being a concept of law in this culture at this time which we can fruitfully describe.

2.3 The Varieties of Concepts

That there is a concept of law that we can describe, and perhaps describe without making morally normative commitments, does not necessarily mean that we can describe it by recourse to necessary and sufficient conditions. As H.L.A. Hart appeared to suggest in the opening pages of *The Concept of Law* (and then arguably retract later in the book[19]), law might well be a family resemblance concept, in Wittgenstein's sense, or a cluster concept, which is very similar but possibly not identical.[20] Against a more Fregean understanding of concepts, therefore, there may be no more of a set of necessary and sufficient conditions for the proper grasp and use of the concept of law than there are necessary and sufficient conditions for the proper grasp and use of the concept of game, to use Wittgenstein's example, or the concept of art, which is a common candidate for a family resemblance concept. That law is a family resemblance or cluster concept presupposes that there *are* family resemblance concepts, which remains contested. Moreover, it is possible that there are family resemblance concepts but that law is not among them, assuming that not *all* concepts are family resemblance concepts, which is also contested.

[18] On the possibility (and *not* the inevitability, and not necessarily the desirability) of normatively prescribing what concept of law we ought to have, see Frederick Schauer, "The Social Construction of the Concept of Law: A Reply to Julie Dickson," *Oxford Journal of Legal Studies*, vol. 25 (2005), pp. 493–501. Hart seems sympathetic to a normatively-selected concept of law in *The Concept of Law* (Oxford: Clarendon Press, 2nd ed., Penelope A. Bulloch & Joseph Raz eds., 1994), at 209–11, and in H.L.A. Hart, "Positivism and the Separation of Law and Morals," *Harvard Law Review*, vol. 71 (1958), pp. 593–629, as does, *inter alia*, Liam Murphy, "The Political Question of the Concept of Law," in Jules Coleman, ed., *Hart's Postscript: Essays on the Postscript to the* Concept of Law (Oxford: Oxford University Press, 2001), pp. 371–409. And see also Liam Murphy, "Better to See Law this Way," *New York University Law Review*, vol. 83 (2008), pp. 1088–1107; Frederick Schauer, "Positivism Before Hart" (paper presented at University College London, 16 December 2009); Jeremy Waldron, "Normative (or Ethical) Positivism," in Coleman, *ibid.*, pp. 411–433. This conclusion and this interpretation of Hart is questioned in Green, *op. cit.* note 3, at 1039, and perhaps by Hart himself in the "Postscript" to *The Concept of Law*, at 240, leading Julie Dickson to describe Hart's seemingly two-faced view of the issue as "awkward." Julie Dickson, "Is Bad Law Still Law? Is Bad Law Really Law,?" in Maksymilian Del Mar and Zenon Bankowski, eds., *Law as Institutional Normative Order* (Farnham, UK: Aldershot, 2009), pp. 161–183, at p. 164.

[19] "There are therefore two minimum conditions necessary and sufficient for the existence of a legal system." *The Concept of Law*, *op. cit.* note 5, at p. 116.

[20] See Max Black, *Problems of Analysis* (London: Routledge & Kegan Paul, 1954), Chap. 2; Max Black, "The Nature of Representation," in *Caveats and Critiques: Philosophical Essays in Language, Logic, and Art* (Ithaca, New York: Cornell University Press, 1975), pp. 139–179, and especially at pp. 177–179.

It could also be, as Ronald Dworkin has argued,[21] that law is an essentially contested concept, in W.B. Gallie's sense,[22] although it is again contested whether there are such concepts, whether all concepts are essentially contested, and whether Dworkin's understanding of the idea of an essentially contested concept is the correct one. For example, it may be that essentially contested concepts require an exemplar, and although whether that is so is again contested, to the extent that an exemplar is required it should be possible to identify the properties of the exemplar (or ideal-type, or paradigm case, or prototype case) which make it an exemplar in the first place, and without which is would not be an exemplar even though it might still lie within the domain of essential contestation. Moreover, Dworkin's application of the idea is even more challengeable, because it hardly follows from the fact of a concept being essentially contested that the contestation must be on moral or political grounds, as Dworkin maintains.

Although these are all valuable cautions to recognize before plunging headlong into the enterprise of searching for the necessary and sufficient conditions of the concept of law, they are no more than cautions. All of these cautions presuppose contested questions about the nature of concepts and about how we might go about recognizing and explaining them, and while it is important to recognize the contested nature of some of the assumptions, it is nevertheless far from unreasonable to engage in conceptual analysis of the concept of law on the assumption that there is a concept to be analyzed, and that the analysis will yield a set of necessary and sufficient conditions for application of the concept.

2.4 Necessity and Importance

That the concept of law may have necessary and sufficient conditions for its proper application does not entail the conclusion that philosophical analysis is the appropriate way of uncovering them. One or another variety of the challenge from naturalism[23] would suggest that even if there are concepts with necessary and sufficient conditions for their proper application, the way to discover those necessary and sufficient conditions is by empirical research and not by philosophical speculation.

Given that few legal theorists maintain that the necessary properties of the concept of law are necessary a priori or necessary by definition, however, it is not clear that the naturalist challenge is a fundamental rather than a methodological one. Most of the theorists who offer analyses of the concept of law acknowledge that they are describing empirical and contingent features of the world—in this case the

[21] Ronald Dworkin, *Taking Rights Seriously* (Cambridge, Massachusetts: Harvard University Press, 1978), p. 103.

[22] W.B. Gallie, "Essentially Contested Concepts," *Proceedings of the Aristotelian Society*, vol. 56 (1965), pp. 167–183.

[23] See Leiter, *op. cit.* note 5.

features that explain how people in some culture use the concept of law. Whether such description is better done by perceptive philosophers or instead by empirical social scientists is an interesting and important question, but there may be less disagreement than is commonly supposed between naturalists and non-naturalists except about the resources that should be used to learn about the concept of law that is used in this or that culture at this or that time.

There *is* disagreement, however, about whether such description can be divorced from morally-laden considerations about the value of law[24] and about the features of law that will best enable it to serve its essential functions. These debates are ongoing and important, but because they are peripheral to my main theme here I will put them to one side and assume that some description of the necessary features of the concept of law is possible, and that such description may not require making moral judgments.

That which is necessary or essential, however, may not be important.[25] And thus it should come as little surprise that numerous theorists, perhaps most notably on this issue Joseph Raz and Julie Dickson, have emphasized that of the set of necessary truths about the concept of law, the primary focus of general jurisprudence is and should be on the subset of those necessary truths consisting of the necessary truths that are in some way important, or whose identification and explanation will assist in our understanding. This conclusion—some would say concession, although I would not—has led some theorists to conclude that the enterprise of conceptual analysis of the concept of law is inevitably normative, but as long as we recognize, with Hart, that not all oughts are moral oughts, then we can acknowledge that selecting the important necessary truths from out of all the necessary truths requires choice and evaluation without committing to the view that moral choice or moral evaluation is necessarily part of so-called descriptive general jurisprudence.

2.5 On the Importance of the Contingent

But now we have reached the heart of the matter. If trying to "understand" the "nature of law" requires that we identify the necessary truths that are also important, then what about those important truths that are not necessary? And I do not refer here to those important truths that are simply contingent. There is nothing oxymoronic in the idea of a contingent necessary truth, for that which is necessary now and here could have been otherwise, and still may be otherwise. Rather, the question is whether there are things (ideas, or empirical observations, or philosophical explanations) of importance to the nature of law that are not—at this time and in this culture—necessary to the concept of law?

Of course if we understand and define the nature of something as being necessarily about the concept of that thing, and understand the concept of something as necessarily being about necessary or essential properties, then there is no question to be asked.

---

[24] See above, notes 6–13 and accompanying text.

[25] As Leslie Green says, with examples, "not all necessary truths are important truths." Green, *op. cit.* note 2, at 1043.

But might there instead be another understanding of the nature of something that could also (and *not* instead) be useful? And to entertain this possibility, it will be useful to return to birds. More particularly, we should ask whether there is not something about *flying* that will help us to "understand" the "nature" (in the non-technical sense) of birds. It is true that penguins and emus are birds and do not fly, and that bats fly but are not birds, so flying is neither a necessary nor a sufficient condition for birdness. But it is surely of great interest that almost all birds fly and almost all non-bird vertebrates do not fly, and thus if we think about why, how, and when birds fly we are likely to learn something of great interest about birds. Moreover, what we learn may increase knowledge for its own sake, but may also have practical importance for understanding birds and understanding the physics of flight.

Flying is thus a property highly concentrated in birds but neither exclusive nor necessary for birds, yet still of great importance. Much the same might be said about the Maasai and the Mandinka of Africa, tribes whose women average close to 2 m in height and the men well over that. There are, of course, short Massai and Mandinka, and very tall people of other ethnicities, but to fail to note or consider the height of these peoples is to miss something of importance and interest. And so too with the whiteness of swans or the promptness of German trains, properties that are again not exclusive to these objects or institutions, but whose probabilistic concentration makes them of substantial importance to *us*—and it is *our* understanding that is at issue, just as it is *our* concept of law that we are considering when we look for the necessary properties of that concept.

If I am right about the foregoing examples, then it is plausible to suppose that much the same might apply to law. If there are properties that are highly concentrated in law, that probabilistically are far more likely to be concentrated in law than in other institutions even if their presence is neither necessary nor sufficient for law, would it not be a mistake to ignore their importance?[26]

2.6 Coercion and the Nature of Law

With respect to law, it may well be that coercion is the most important of these non-necessary but probabilistically concentrated properties. It is true, as numerous theorists, including Hart but also before[27] and after[28] him, have observed, that coercion

[26] A stronger but compatible claim is hinted at in Ehrenburg, *op. cit.* note 2, at p. 193, suggesting that law may consist in a "particular combination[] of non-unique elements."

[27] "[I]t is because a rule is regarded as obligatory that a measure of coercion may be attached to it; it is not obligatory because there is coercion." Arthur L. Goodhart, *English Law and Moral Law* (London: Stevens & Sons, 1953), p. 17.

[28] For example, John Gardner, "How Law Claims, What Law Claims" (paper presented at Symposium on "Rights, Law, and Morality: Themes from the Legal Philosophy of Robert Alexy," New College, Oxford University, September 10–11, 2008); Leslie Green, "Law and Obligations," in Jules Coleman & Scott Shapiro, eds., *Oxford Encyclopedia of Jurisprudence and Philosophy of Law* (Oxford: Oxford University Press, 2008), pp. 514–547; Joseph Raz, "Authority, Law, and Morality," *The Monist*, vol. 68 (1985), pp. 295–324.

is not (or at least may not be) a necessary condition for law. If we had a group of officials who non-coercively accepted the ultimate rule of recognition, if we had a population that similarly accepted the same ultimate rule of recognition, and if pursuant to that ultimate rule of recognition we had a system of primary and secondary rules, we would have law and a legal system even with no coercion whatsoever.

As Hart and countless others have recognized, however, it is likely that no such legal system exists now, and none may have existed even in the past. All or at least almost all actual legal systems have their coercive elements, and thus it is a salient feature of real legal systems that they coerce at least some subjects into compliance with the system's laws.[29] Indeed, even though Hart is undoubtedly correct in identifying the figure of the puzzled man who wishes simply to know what the law is so he can comply, and then in claiming that at least some such subjects exist in most real legal systems, it is an open question as to just how many such people there are in any legal system. Yet although we are uncertain, it is plausible to suppose that puzzled men are far outnumbered by bad (in Holmes's and Hart's sense) men, which explains why coercion is an omnipresent even if contingent and even if non-necessary feature of all or virtually all actual legal systems.

Thus, if we take "nature" to refer to salient and important characteristics rather than strictly essential or necessary ones, or if we substitute a word like "character" for "nature," it is highly plausible that coercion is as much part of the actual character of law as flying is of birds. To say this is to remain agnostic on questions relating to concepts or conceptual analysis, but only to conclude that there may be highly important and probabilistically concentrated features of some phenomenon that are not strictly necessary to the phenomenon, that may not be part of the concept of the phenomenon, but which may nonetheless be important to understanding the phenomenon as it exists in the world, and whose importance may well be illuminated by the use of broad theoretical, including philosophical, tools.

It is important to emphasize that I am using coercion here only as an example. Although I do believe that coercion is, post-Hart, an unfortunately neglected feature of law,[30] supporting that claim is not my agenda here. Attention to the importance of pervasive and concentrated but non-essential features of law may well support an increased focus on the role of sanctions and coercion, but even if it does not, there may be other such pervasive and concentrated but non-essential features whose importance should be noticed and analyzed with philosophical tools. Thus, although coercion may well be a good example of the consequences of my methodological

[29] Increased attention to the coercive dimensions of law is urged in Leslie Green, "The Concept of Law Revisited," *Michigan Law Review*, vol. 94 (1996), pp. 1687–1717. See also Danny Priel, "Sanction and Obligation in Hart's Theory of Law," *Ratio Juris*, vol. 21 (2008), pp. 404–411.

[30] Frederick Schauer, "Was Austin Right All Along?: On the Role of Sanctions in a Theory of Law", *Ratio Juris*, vol. 26 (2010), pp. 1–21.

claim, nothing in that claim depends on the ultimate soundness of coercion as an example.

That said, it is possible, as a claim about the history of ideas, that Austin's insistence on the central role of sanctions and coercion[31] has played a causal role in generating some of the contemporary methodological stances. Once Hart was taken to have demonstrated that sanctions could not be essential to legality and legal obligation, there remained the question of how something so obviously important to how law is actually lived, experienced, and structured in the legal systems we know could not be part of the theoretical explanation for the nature of law. One answer to this question, therefore, could be that the theoretical explanation of the nature of law was—and this is an answer plainly suggested by the title of Hart's book and by the philosophical methodological controversies of the day—an inquiry into the essential or necessary features of the concept of law and not an inquiry into what is important about law as it is actually experienced. Moreover, if part of the increasingly dominant positivist project was (and is) to distinguish law from other normative rule systems—etiquette, for example—then it was seen to be necessary to search for the features of law without which it would not be law at all, and which in addition were not present in seemingly similar non-law institutions and phenomena.[32] Hence (although my causal claim is a highly tentative one) there arose the focus on the necessary and sufficient conditions for the concept of law, as opposed to the jurisprudential examination on the important features of actual legal systems, and thus a decreased focus on coercion.

My reconstruction of the history of the modern methodology of jurisprudence may well be mistaken, and in addition omits the important methodological roles played by Joseph Raz, by the opening portions of John Finnis's *Natural Law and Natural Rights*, by the increasing philosophication of jurisprudence,[33] and by responses to Ronald Dworkin's proud refusal to give either a definition of "law" or to abjure doing what others have denigrated as particular as opposed to general jurisprudence. Nevertheless, for whatever reason, the enterprise of jurisprudence has increasingly avoided attention to that which is important but not necessary, and it is by no means clear that this development has been entirely or even substantially for the good.

---

[31] John Austin, *The Province of Jurisprudence Determined* (Cambridge: Cambridge University Press, W.E. Rumble, ed., 1995) (1st ed. 1832).

[32] See Joseph Raz, "Incorporation by Law," *Legal Theory*, vol. 10 (2004), pp. 1–26; Joseph Raz, "Legal Principles and the Limits of Law," *Yale Law Journal*, vol. 81 (1972), pp. 823–48, at p. 842. See also Ruth Gavison, "Comment," in Ruth Gavison, ed., *Issues in Contemporary Legal Philosophy: The Influence of H.L.A. Hart* (Oxford: Oxford University Press, 1987), pp. 21–28, at p. 25. For the view that distinguishing law from institutions that are similar in some but not all important aspects is unlikely to be fruitful, see Brian Z. Tamanaha, *A General Jurisprudence of Law and Society* (Oxford: Oxford University Press, 2001).

[33] See Frederick Schauer, "(Re)Taking Hart," *Harvard Law Review*, vol. 119 (2006), pp. 852–883.

2.7 The Boundaries of Jurisprudence

I cannot emphasize strongly enough what I am not claiming here. Although a number of prominent legal theorists have questioned the value of some are all of the debates in contemporary jurisprudence,[34] I do not join them. Thus it is not my goal here to challenge the usefulness of conceptual analysis of the concept of law as a worthy jurisprudential exercise. What I do challenge is the view that conceptual analysis of the concept of law—and a conceptual analysis seeking to explain with philosophical tools the necessary or essential features of law—is the *only* worthy jurisprudential enterprise. And thus I offer a challenge to any definition of jurisprudence that would exclude from the field anything other than a search for those necessary features. I question not conceptual analysis's importance, but only its hegemony.

My target is hardly made of straw. Joseph Raz has described the analysis of features present in anything less than all possible legal systems as (mere) sociology of law, as opposed to philosophy of law,[35] as if it were impossible to employ philosophical methods to illuminate our understanding of features present in some or all actual legal systems even if not a defining feature of legality itself. Julie Dickson follows suit, producing a definition of jurisprudence which understands Dworkin, for example, as not simply being mistaken in his jurisprudential claims, but as not doing jurisprudence, or at least not analytical jurisprudence, at all.[36] Under Jules Coleman's definition of jurisprudence, it is a field which excludes attention to sanctions and other methods of enforcement,[37] thereby excluding Austin and Bentham, among others, from jurisprudence entirely. If the field or discipline of jurisprudence is defined so as to assume the conclusion of jurisprudential inquiry, and also to exclude from the field not only Dworkin and Austin, but also a host of others who

[34] Thus, Brian Bix thinks it appropriate to ask whether the objectives and achievements of conceptual analysis of the concept of law are "substantial." Brian Bix, "Joseph Raz and Conceptual Analysis," *APA Newsletter on Philosophy and Law*, vol. 6(2) (2007), pp. 1–6, at p. 5. Kent Greenawalt suggests that the question about what is true of all and all possible legal systems "does not seem very important for understanding the legal systems under which we live." Kent Greenawalt, "Too Thin and Too Rich: Distinguishing Features of Legal Positivism," in Robert P. George, ed., *The Autonomy of Law: Essays on Legal Positivism* (Oxford: Clarendon Press, 1996), pp. 1–30, at p. 14. To much the same (skeptical) effect is Danny Priel, "The Boundaries of Law and the Scope of Legal Philosophy," *Law and Philosophy*, vol. 27 (2008), pp. 643–695.

[35] "Sociology of law provides a wealth of detailed information and analysis of the functions of law in some particular societies. Legal philosophy has to be content with those few features which all legal systems necessarily possess." Joseph Raz, *The Authority of Law: Essays on Law and Morality* (Oxford: Clarendon Press, 1979), pp. 104–105.

[36] Dickson, *op. cit.* note 2, at pp. 17–25.

[37] Coleman, *op. cit.* note 5, at p. 72 n. 12.

have sought to look philosophically at features present in some or most legal systems,[38] then something seems gravely wrong at the level of field definition.[39]

Thus, I do not deny that understanding the conceptual aspect of law is important, nor that seeking to understand legality just for sake of understanding is an important application of the philosophical enterprise. Kenneth Himma worries that challenges to conceptual analysis in jurisprudence have an odor of anti-intellectualism,[40] but Himma's charge is well-placed only if aimed at those who question the value in seeking knowledge for its own sake, or who question the philosophical enterprise more generally. But to question a too-narrow definition of jurisprudence or the philosophy of law is to object neither to conceptual analysis nor to non-practically-useful philosophical pursuit.[41] On the contrary, it is to object to a definition of the philosophy of law that excludes so much from the field as to narrow rather than broaden the domains in which we may seek knowledge simply for its own sake.[42]

2.8 Necessity and Logical Priority

One argument for the primacy, even if not the exclusivity, of conceptual analysis is the argument from logical priority. How could we think about or research law at all unless we knew what we were talking about and what we were researching?

---

[38] Ironically, Raz's definition of the philosophy of law may exclude some of his own work, such as his valuable analysis of precedent (Joseph Raz, *The Authority of Law: Essays on Law and Morality* (Oxford: Clarendon Press, 1979), pp. 180–193), a form of legal decision-making neither definitional of law nor present in even all actual legal systems.

[39] Thus, Brian Leiter appears to question the attitude under which "proximity to High Street in Oxford [is] a necessary condition for entry into the halls of serious legal philosophy." Brian Leiter, "Why Legal Positivism,?" paper presented at the annual meeting of the Association of American Law Schools, January 9, 2010 (draft of December 10, 2009, at pp. 2–3). And Andrew Halpin quotes in the context of a discussion of jurisprudential methodology Simon Blackburn's observation that that many methodological disputes are "political bids for ascendancy within a discipline." Andrew Halpin, "Methodology," in Dennis Patterson, ed., *Blackwell Companion to Philosophy of Law and Legal Theory* (Oxford: Blackwell, 2nd ed., forthcoming).

[40] Kenneth Einar Himma, "Substance and Method in Conceptual Jurisprudence and Legal Theory," *Virginia Law Review*, vol. 88 (2002), pp. 1119–1228, at pp. 1218–1227. See also Brian Bix, "Patrolling the Boundaries: Inclusive Legal Positivism and the Nature of Jurisprudential Debate," *Canadian Journal of Law and Jurisprudence*, vol. 12 (1999), pp. 17–33, at p. 24, arguing for the value of analytical jurisprudence as producing knowledge for its own sake.

[41] It is important, however, to avoid defining the scope of jurisprudence in such a way as to treat it exclusively as a philosopher's subject. To treat non-philosophers such as Lon Fuller and Arthur Goodhart as not doing jurisprudence at all seems a knowledge-limiting and insight-limiting mistake. See Schauer, *op. cit.* note 28.

[42] Thus, Ronald Dworkin has observed that "[t]he philosophy of law studies philosophical problems raised by the existence and practice of law," R.M. Dworkin, "Introduction," in *The Philosophy of Law* (Oxford: Oxford University Press, 1977), pp. 1–16, at p. 1. That definition seems correct, and it is one significantly and unfortunately narrowed by limiting it to *only* the philosophical problems raised in trying to identify the essential features of the concept of law itself.

Conceptual analysis of the concept of law is the necessary prologue to any attempt to understand actual legal systems by any method, so the argument goes, and is thus entitled to a special or even exclusive place in the jurisprudential pantheon.

Two responses to such a claim are possible. First, as Roger Shiner[43] and, more recently, Brian Leiter have argued,[44] the concept of law we need to ground further empirical or even philosophical work need not be a fully worked-out one, and can rely simply on common linguistic usage or on the institutions that are ordinarily designated as legal ones. On further analysis, we may discover that some of the things commonly thought of as legal may best be understood as otherwise, and vice versa, but there is no reason to believe that a complete analysis of the concept of law is necessary in order to examine the institutions that people commonly and pre-theoretically think and talk about as "law."

In addition, it is often the case that that which is presupposed or logically prior is not necessarily that which is most or exclusively important, or at least most or exclusively important in some context or domain. Even if conceptual analysis is logically prior to evaluation,[45] that which is logically subsequent may sometimes be more important or more conducive to understanding. Consider the theory of natural selection. In order for the theory of natural selection to be sound, there must exist a mind-independent physical reality, which some people deny. Thus, there is a form of epistemic objectivism, controversial in some circles (but not mine), which is a necessary condition for the soundness of the evolutionary theory of natural selection. Still, to take the claim about a mind-independent physical reality is being in some way more important or more central than the claim about natural selection misses the point of natural selection entirely. Even though the theory of natural selection, like any other scientific theory, is a descriptive one, a descriptive theory—or account—has a point, and we lose the point of a descriptive theory if we treat it as necessarily subservient to the sometimes contested facts and theories that are preconditions of its plausibility. Even if, the previous paragraph notwithstanding, conceptual analysis is logically prior to fruitful empirical or philosophical observation about law, it does not follow from this that the latter is of lesser importance or less entitled to be a significant part of jurisprudence.

---

[43]Roger Shiner, *Norm and Nature: The Movements of Legal Thought* (Oxford: Clarendon Press, 1992), pp. 4–9. Shiner refers to certain "preanalytic" and "philosophically aseptic" facts about the world (and about our commonsense understanding of law) as sufficient to get the analytic and philosophical enterprises started.

[44]Brian Leiter, "Naturalism in Legal Philosophy," *Stanford Encyclopedia of Philosophy*, http://plato.stanford.edu/entries/lawphil-naturalism/ (last revised February 20, 2007).

[45]See David Lyons, "Founders and Foundations of Legal Positivism," *Michigan Law Review*, vol. 82 (1984), pp. 722–739.

2.9 Conclusion

Thus, the goal of this paper is not, to repeat, to challenge the agenda of conceptual analysis of the concept of law, but only to challenge its jurisprudential hegemony. That which is contingent, non-essential, and even particular may be vitally important, and in need of empirical and philosophical illumination. If the non-essential is excluded from the "province of jurisprudence," we may hinder rather than help the effort to understand the nature of law, and thus frustrate the very goal that conceptual analysis is designed to serve. "What law is" is an important area of inquiry, but so too is "What law is like." The two are not the same, and there is no reason why the two cannot co-exist within the province of jurisprudence.

Chapter 3
Ideals, Practices, and Concepts in Legal Theory

Brian H. Bix

One persistent mystery of jurisprudence is the wide range of theories about the nature of law (even if one only includes theories that have been put forward by well-regarded theorists and have at least to some extent survived the test of time). If we are all theorizing about the same subject, law—and this subject is one that is well known and mundane, not esoteric—why do the theories vary so much?

One basic disagreement seems to come at a foundational level, regarding what it is that theories of (the nature of) law are describing, analyzing, or explaining. Does the theory explain the practice of law, and, if so, is it the practices only of our legal system or a select number of similar legal systems, or does it apply to all (and all possible) legal systems? Alternatively, is the theory explaining an idea or ideal of law that transcends current or past practices: perhaps a Platonic Form or some moral or political ideal?

This paper will offer an overview of the different approaches to theorizing about the nature of law, focusing on the justification and value of theories grounded in ideals or objectives. Part I discusses how many mainstream theorists have transformed theorizing about the practice of law into theories about the concept of law; Part II offers a quick overview of a number of theorists who offer theories fairly characterized as based on an ideal or teleology of law; and Part III revisits some basic methodological issues relating to the evaluation of the differing approaches to legal theory, before concluding.

This paper was presented at the Conference, "Neutrality and the Theory of Law," Girona, Spain, May 2010. I am grateful for the comments and suggestions of the Conference participants, and William Edmundson and Andrew Halpin.

B.H. Bix (✉)
School of Law, University of Minnesota, 229 19th Ave. S,
55455-0400 Minneapolis, MN, USA
e-mail: bix@umn.edu

J. Ferrer Beltrán et al. (eds.), *Neutrality and Theory of Law*,
Law and Philosophy Library 106, DOI 10.1007/978-94-007-6067-7_3,

3.1 Practices and Concepts

Jurisprudence articles, books, and courses often focus on, or at least begin with, what are described as "theories of law." However, it is only on rare occasions when it is made clear what is being explained by the theory. Is it the particular institutions and practices that go under the label "law" or "legal system"? That would seem the obvious response, but it immediately raises problems. If the theory extends beyond the theorist's own legal system (after all, it is usually labeled "a theory of law," not "a theory of American [or English or German or Russian, etc.] law"[1]), how do we know which normative systems are included and which are not?

In other words, if the theory extends beyond a single identified normative system, to a group or category of systems, then there needs to be some way to identify the category, to determine its boundary lines. One cannot go simply by the term—here, (the English word) "law"—first, because this term, like most (if not all) labels has uncertain and imprecise boundaries, and, second, because communities where English is not spoken may not have a word which corresponds sufficiently to "law" (the term in the local language may be broader, or narrower, or overlap only in part).

One alternative is that perhaps something entirely independent of us can ground the category "law." In other areas of philosophy, this external grounding might be a Platonic "Form" or "Idea": that there is a category "Law" in some other realm, which all past and current legal systems have only been imperfect realizations (just as all present, past, and future existing "leaves" are just imperfect realizations of the Platonic Idea of "Leaf").

Another alternative, advocated (to varying degrees of explicitness) by H. L. A. Hart, Jules Coleman, Joseph Raz, and others, is that the proper focus of a theory of law is the concept of law. Thus is Hart's famous book on legal theory called *The Concept of Law*.[2] However, it is Joseph Raz who has given the most attention to articulating the nature and justification of conceptual analysis as a methodology.

Raz has argued that theories of (the nature of) law are theories explaining *our* concept, law.[3] There are no significant metaphysical assumptions to such a claim: a concept is just a thought-category that helps us order our world. For conceptual analysis of this sort, we do not need to assume (with the Platonists) that there is some object in another realm of existence that the concept tracks, nor need we

[1]At times, Ronald Dworkin appears to be an exception, as he offers his theory as an interpretation of *particular* legal systems, the legal systems of the U.S. or the U.K. (and, at times, implies that any theory about *all* legal systems would have to make claims so general or so vague as to be of no interest). At the same time, his interpretive approach is itself meant to be true universally, applicable to all present, past, and possible legal systems. *See*, e.g., Ronald Dworkin, *Law's Empire* (Harvard, 1986), pp. 176–275; Ronald Dworkin, *Justice in Robes* (Harvard, 2006), pp. 168–178.

[2]H. L. A. Hart, *The Concept of Law* (rev. ed., Oxford, 1994).

[3]*See*, e.g., Joseph Raz, *Between Authority and Interpretation* (Oxford, 2009), pp. 17–125.

assume (with the natural kinds theorists) that the world somehow sets the boundary for the category the concept names.

At first glance, then, conceptual analysis is primarily a matter of identification and boundary lines: how do we determine what is inside this category ("law") and what is outside?[4] Through conceptual analysis, we ascertain what the essential properties are (in this case, the essential or necessary properties of law), keeping in mind that "essential" and "necessary" properties here refer to nothing more ambitious than the criteria our concept sets for the category in question. Additionally, Raz argues, our concept of law is part of our collective self-understanding. Theorists are not free to choose just any concept of law (e.g., according to its usefulness in social scientific research). As *our* concept of law, the concept is, in one sense, parochial[5] (other communities, past and present, have had different concepts); however, as a concept that we can (and do) apply to all other communities (present, historical, or hypothetical), the concept is, in a different sense, universal.[6]

The connections between the concept and the objects or practices referred to by the concept are not easy to delineate clearly. Nigel Simmonds once asked whether our concept of law was "true to the nature of law," [7] but this assumes that we can speak of "the nature of law" separate from our concept(s), and that may not be possible. Of course, one can criticize a theorist for mis-identifying or mis-describing what our concepts are, but the concepts (understood this way[8]) themselves seem to be, in a sense, beyond criticism. However, if one focuses on the way concepts interrelate (e.g., according Raz, that our concept of "law" is connected in basic ways with our concepts of "authority" and "reasons for action"[9]), there does seem to be

[4] At the Girona Conference, Frederick Schauer argued for a different kind of theory: one that would emphasize characteristics that are "important" to law, even if not defining that category (i.e., not necessary or universal). Frederick Schauer, "Necessity, Importance, and the Nature of Law," available at http://papers.ssrn.com/sol3/papers.cfm?abstract_id=1594930.

[5] Alexy attributes to Raz the view that all concepts are parochial. Robert Alexy, "On Two Juxtapositions: Concept and Nature, Law and Philosophy. Some Comments on Joseph Raz's 'Can There Be a Theory of Law?,'" *Ratio Juris*, vol. 20 (2007), pp. 162–169, at 163–164, and while Alexy disagrees with that conclusion, id., he does not deny that a concept of law would or could be parochial. In a reply, Raz agrees that some concepts are not historical but may be "necessary for the very possibility of thought." Joseph Raz, "Theories and Concepts: Responding to Alexy and Bulygin," in *Una Discusion Sobre la Teoria del Derecho* (Marcial Pons, 2007) (in Spanish); in English, available at http://sites.google.com/site/josephnraz/theory%26concepts. (The reference is to p. 4 of the English text.)

[6] Raz, *Between Authority and Interpretation*, *supra* note 4, at pp. 31–41.

[7] N. E. Simmonds, "Law as a Moral Idea," *University of Toronto Law Journal*, vol. 55 (2005), pp. 61–92, at pp. 70–71.

[8] If one disagreed with Raz's approach, and viewed concepts as matters subject to short-term choice (short-term manipulation), then the concepts themselves still might not be the sort of things that were "true" or "false," but they could be judged as more or less useful for the purpose for which they were created or modified.

[9] And as other concepts change, the relationship of the concept of law and those other concepts may change as well. See Raz, "Theories and Concepts," *supra* note 6.

potential grounds for criticism—e.g., that *the network of concepts* does not fit well with our practices.[10]

Additionally, a focus on concepts for a practice is unlikely to pick out the consequences in the world of that practice—at least, the concepts will likely not pick out *all* such consequences. One response is that this merely reflects a difference in disciplines or a difference in projects: that in our conceptual analysis we are doing *philosophy of law*, not sociology of law.

In a series of papers,[11] Brian Leiter has challenged the use of conceptual analysis in legal philosophy (and, indeed, all philosophy) in general, and in theories of the nature of law in particular. He argues, following W.V.O. Quine, that there are no a priori truths, and that conceptual analysis, insofar as it purports to discover such truths, is just armchair philosophy based on the philosopher's intuitions, where there is no reason to assume that these intuitions are shared by others. This is not the time to consider that critique at length.[12] Suffice it to say that Leiter's critique appears to allow, indeed to assume, a concept of "law"—if only at a rough, "folk" level—which seems to leave the door open to the possibility and possible value of analyzing that concept.[13]

3.2 Theories Grounded on Ideals, Paradigms or Teleology

It is a central assumption of modern theories of social practices and institutions (at least for hermeneutic/*Verstehen* approaches, as contrasted with behavioralist approaches) that since these practices are established to serve some human purpose, a reference to and focus upon that purpose is valuable, and perhaps necessary, for a proper understanding or explanation of the practice. And it is a commonplace that for many purposive activities, having the purpose in mind is necessary and central to understanding them. For example, one can imagine two people throwing a ball back and forth, where, alternatively, (a) they might be doing this just for the joy of throwing and catching a ball; (b) it could be a competitive game, where one wins by making the other person miss; or (c) it could be a cooperative game, where the objective is to see how many times the ball can be thrown back and forth without either person missing. There is an obvious sense in which one cannot be said to understand, either fully or adequately, the activity one is watching if one does not know which of those three characterizations of the activity was correct.

---

[10] I take this to be roughly what Robert Alexy is gesturing at in Alexy, "On Two Juxtapositions," *supra* note 5, at p. 164.

[11] Many of them collected in Brian Leiter, *Naturalizing Jurisprudence* (Oxford, 2007).

[12] I have a bit more to say on the subject in Brian Bix, "Joseph Raz and Conceptual Analysis," *APA Newsletter on Philosophy and Law*, vol. 06(2) (Spring 2007), available at http://papers.ssrn.com/sol3/papers.cfm?abstract_id=948766.

[13] In a paper presented at the Girona Conference, Prof. Leiter argued against all efforts to demarcate "law" from "non-law" (or "law" from "philosophy"). Brian Leiter, "The Demarcation Problem in Jurisprudence: A New Case for Skepticism," available at http://papers.ssrn.com/sol3/papers.cfm?abstract_id=1599620.

Perhaps, then, it is a natural step to believe that even complex social practices like law are best understood by focusing on the objective(s) they seek or the ideal(s) at which they aim. There are a number of prominent legal theorists who have built their legal theories on some variation of an ideal, paradigm, or objective. A brief overview follows of six prominent legal theories that seem to partake of this approach, to a greater or lesser extent: Nigel Simmonds, Mark Greenberg, Robert Alexy, Lon Fuller and Ronald Dworkin, and John Finnis.

3.2.1 Nigel Simmonds

Nigel Simmonds advocates an "archetype" approach to legal theory.[14] His arguments for this approach include the claim that such an approach allows theorists to account for the different and seemingly contrary uses of the term "law." In particular, the theory can account both for a value-neutral sense of law, in which legal rules can be used for both morally good and morally bad actions, and a value-laden sense, such that significantly immoral rules do not warrant the label "law." Additionally, Simmonds argues, the theory is able to include "laws of nature" with "positive laws" within a broader theory of law.

Simmonds refers to "the idea of law."[15] By this, he means the "archetype" against which systems are determined to be (however imperfectly) "legal" and against which all systems are evaluated. For Simmonds, this is necessarily a moral idea,[16] for the practice of law pervasively involves its use in the justification of state coercion, and so the proper question is: "'what must law be, that it can justify the use of force?'"[17] Simmonds' position might be seen as a bridge between conceptual and ideal-based approaches: a theory that can focus on the concept of law, and also see the way that concept works *within* our practices; and how our beliefs about law structure our practices.[18]

---

[14]See Nigel Simmonds, *Law as a Moral Idea* (Oxford, 2007); N. E. Simmonds, "Law as a Moral Idea," *University of Toronto Law Journal*, vol. 55 (2005), pp. 61–92; N. E. Simmonds, "Jurisprudence as a Moral and Historical Inquiry," *Canadian Journal of Law and Jurisprudence*, vol. 18 (2005), pp. 249–276.

[15]As in the title of his book, *Law as a Moral Idea* (*supra* note 14). As John Finnis has pointed out, Simmonds tends to use "idea" and "ideal" interchangeably. John Finnis, "Comment on Simmonds, *Law as a Moral Idea*" (unpublished manuscript on file with author; paper presented on December 3, 2009, Oxford University).

[16]To be clear, Simmonds expressly states that not all archetypes are moral, but that the archetype of law is.

[17]Simmonds, *Law as a Moral Idea*, *supra* note 14, at p. 172.

[18]In the course of commenting on Simmonds' works, John Finnis offered an interestingly different reading: not so much "law as idea" as "law*s* as ideas." Legal rules begin as ideas, objectives, reasons, and only if this origin is understood can *laws*, and also *law*, be understood. Finnis, "Comment on Simmonds, *Law as a Moral Idea*," *supra* note 15.

3.2.2 Mark Greenberg

Mark Greenberg, in a series of recent papers,[19] has challenged conventional assumptions underlying most analytical legal theories, in particular challenging the assumption that social facts and practices can determine the content of law without the addition of value facts. Along with this important critique, Mark Greenberg has also presented a positive view of law, in which it is in the nature of law that legal systems are "supposed to operate by arranging matters so that for every legal obligation, there is a moral obligation with the same content."[20] Here there is a seemingly clear connection between the theory of the nature of law and the aspiration all legal systems (are said to) have.

Again, under this approach, law is to be understood in terms of what it does when it is operating at its best—an event which may be rare, to the point of never occurring, but it is still the objective towards which legal systems allegedly strive, and which the morally very best legal systems sometimes approximate.

3.2.3 Robert Alexy

Robert Alexy asserts that, to be legal, an individual norm or a system of norms, must "claim correctness," and that a legal system (or legal norm) that did not *succeed* at being correct/authoritative would be, for that reason, "defective."[21] This claim of correctness carries obvious parallels to Joseph Raz's well-known claim that, by its nature, law necessarily claims authoritative status.[22] However, while Raz takes this point as consistent with his ("exclusive") legal positivist theory (separating determinations of legal validity and the content of legal norms from moral evaluation), Alexy believes that his version of the same claim requires an anti-legal positivist conclusion (denying that separation).

I have argued elsewhere that Alexy's analysis confuses a general point about language and advocacy for something peculiar to, or essential to, law. If one is trying to sell, persuade, or encourage, one uses positive language. To not in *some* sense claim correctness, in *any* context that calls for support or persuasion is, at least initially, paradoxical ("you should buy this product, but it is not very good"; "vote for me—I am the least qualified of the candidates"; or "I order you to do X, but you

[19] E.g., Mark Greenberg, "How Facts Make Law," *Legal Theory*, vol. 10 (2004), pp. 157–198; Mark Greenberg, "On Practices and the Law," *Legal Theory*, vol. 12 (2006), pp. 113–136; Mark Greenberg, "The Standard Picture and Its Discontents" (2008), available at http://papers.ssrn.com/sol3/papers.cfm?abstract_id=1103569.

[20] Greenberg, "The Standard Picture and Its Discontents," *supra* note 19, SSRN manuscript at p. 50.

[21] Robert Alexy, *The Argument From Injustice: A Reply to Legal Positivism* (Stanley L. Paulson & Bonnie Litschewski Paulson, trans., Oxford, 2002), pp. 35, 36.

[22] Joseph Raz, *Ethics in the Public Domain* (Oxford, 1994), p. 199.

probably should not do X").[23] This is a point about language and rhetoric, not about law and morality.

Alexy might respond that even if his correctness thesis is not *distinctive* to law, it is nonetheless *essential* to law. However, I am not sure that even this is supportable. What if a country were to say (in its constitution, or in some other official forum) the following: "We have no time for so-called 'justice': that is the talk of weak countries; our nation is all about commercial efficiency and doing the best we can for the citizens of our great nation." Would a country's public dismissal of justice mean that its rule system would not warrant the label "law"? I am not convinced.

Alexy might respond: surely, a government or rule system that does not purport to being doing *something*, to be following some theory or purpose, cannot be characterized as "legal."[24] However, this brings us back to the comparison with Raz's idea of law's claim to legitimate authority, and the observation that such a claim need not entail either any (objectively grounded) claim that the legal system in question has succeeded at *being* a legitimate authority, or any conclusion that the system is "legally" or "conceptually" defective (as opposed to being morally defective—that is, subject to moral criticism) if it fails under some objective test of correctness.

3.2.4 Lon Fuller

Lon Fuller is an American theorist who wrote in the middle decades of the twentieth century. He was best known among legal theorists for his procedural natural law theory, built around what he called the "internal morality of law."[25] Fuller's "internal morality of law" consisted of eight "principles of legality"—a list that is a mixture of what others call "the rule of law" or "procedural justice," and basic advice for

---

[23] Alexy does consider and reject the view that his correctness thesis is merely a convention of constitution writing. Alexy, *The Argument from Injustice*, *supra* note 21, at p. 37. However, that response misses the generality of the criticism: that it is a convention, or a general shared expectation, of *all* promotional speech. Much closer is Alexy's concession that the paradox of the unjust constitution is like asserting that "the cat is on the mat but I do not believe it is." *Id*, at p. 38 n. 66.

[24] What is the basis of—the grounds for—Alexy's conceptual judgments (and for his analytical claims)? The basic analysis seems to be an inquiry on when and whether an ascription of legal status or legal character would seem absurd or contradictory: an inquiry on which reasonable commentators could (and likely would) differ. E.g., Robert Alexy, "A Defence of Radbruch's Formula," in David Dyzenhaus (ed.), *Recrafting the Rule of Law* (Hart, 1999), pp. 15–39, at 25–26; Alexy, *The Argument from Injustice*, *supra* note 21, at pp. 23–31.

[25] Lon L. Fuller, "Positivism and Fidelity to Law—A Reply to Professor Hart," 71 *Harvard Law Review* 630 (1958); Lon L. Fuller, *The Morality of Law* (rev. ed., Yale, 1969). In the United States, Fuller is also well known for his work on alternative dispute resolution, his writings on contract law and remedies, his critique of the American legal realists, and his influence on an American approach to law known as the "legal process school."

effective law-making. Sometimes, Fuller described the eight principles as minimal criteria a system must meet to be a "legal" system. At other times, he wrote of different systems being "legal" to different degrees (and he noted that some of his eight principles, like the one regarding avoiding retroactivity, as more an ideal to be sought than a standard that is likely to be fully met). At one point, he wrote of how law should be understood in terms of the tension between "order" and "good order."[26] Fuller's theory partakes of an ideal theory in the way he ties the existence of law to meeting, or at least aspiring to meet, requirements of procedural justice (even if, as Fuller himself concedes, this can be consistent with significant substantive injustice).

3.2.5 Ronald Dworkin

Within Ronald Dworkin's Interpretivist approach, the relationship between the theory of law and the ideal or objective of law is unique. First, while most analytical legal theorists would insist on a sharp division between a theory of the nature of law and a theory of how to resolve particular disputes within the legal system, for Dworkin there is no such division, and the ultimate purpose of law plays a role in resolving particular legal questions.[27] Second, the objective of law plays a central role (in Dworkin's theory) in determining *what the law is*.

Dworkin's theory occupies an important intermediate role for the purposes of this article. According to Dworkin, the proper approach to understanding law (and other social practices, and artistic creations as well), constructive interpretation, involves making of the object of interpretation the best it can be of its genre.[28] The connection with ideal-focused theories of law is indirect. One objection sometimes raised against Dworkin's approach is that it sees law through "rose-colored glasses," rather than seeing law "as it really is."[29] His response was basically that there is no law "as it really is" separate from interpretation—the "pre-interpretive data" are merely isolated actions and decisions of officials, that require form to be imposed upon them to have any useful (legal) sense—and that this interpretation must be responsive to the point of the practice. Lawyers and judges know that claims about "what the law is" inevitably involve some amount of interpretation from the "data points" of statutes, judicial decisions, and the like. It is rare to have a legal dispute whose facts fit perfectly with the language of some statute or recent court decision, and even when one has an authoritative legal text that appears to be

---

[26] Fuller, "Positivism and Fidelity to Law," *supra* note 25, at p. 644.

[27] Ronald Dworkin, "Legal Theory and the Problem of Sense," in Ruth Gavison (ed.), *Issues in Contemporary Legal Philosophy* (Oxford, 1987), pp. 9–20, at pp. 14–15.

[28] Dworkin, *Law's Empire*, *supra* note 1, at pp. 46–68, 87–101.

[29] Dworkin himself notes the criticism, and responds to it. Dworkin, *Law's Empire*, *supra* note 1, at p. 54.

"directly on point," one must still consider the possibility that there are other legal norms that might require the prior case or the statute to be read differently from its apparent clear meaning.

Under Dworkin's analysis, all claims about what the law requires are thus interpretations of past actions by state officials, "constructive interpretations" sensitive to the purpose of the practice. And since the purpose of the legal practice is (as Dworkin sees it) the justification of state coercion, then the interpretation of the past official actions must be as morally-politically good as possible. Under Dworkin's approach, it is not so much the theory, but the act of legal interpretation prescribed by the theory, that aims at an ideal.

3.2.6 John Finnis

John Finnis is the foremost theorist of our time applying the natural law approach to law and legal theory. In an early chapter of his book, *Natural Law and Natural Rights*, Finnis cites with approval an Aristotelian approach to definition and explanation, in which social practices like "friendship" are given a "focal meaning" which describes the "central case" of the practice. Arguing that this is also the best approach to theorizing about law, Finnis contrasts the approach of Hans Kelsen, which Finnis characterizes as seeking "the lowest common denominator" of all instances of law, seeking those characteristics that are present in all instances of law.[30] For Finnis, the "central case" is a richer or fuller instance of a practice, with connotations of being or approaching an ideal version of the practice.

There is a second sense in which Finnis's view is relevant to a discussion of legal theories focused on ideals, teleologies, or paradigms. Finnis, in a number of his works, discusses the way that reasons should be understood of terms of "good reason," and views of practical reasoning should be based on the perspective of one who is (most) practically reasonable. Finnis writes:

> Where the subject-matter of the projected descriptive *general* account is some practice or institution devised by (more or less adequate exercises of) reason, and addressed to the rational deliberations of individuals and groups, there will normally be no good reason not to prioritise those forms of the practice or institution which are more rational, more reasonable, more responsive to reasons, than other forms of the "same" or analogous practices and institutions. The standard for assessing reasonableness for this theoretical purpose is, in the last analysis, the set of criteria of reasonableness that the descriptive theorist would use in dealing with similar practical issues in his or her own life.[31]

[30] John Finnis, *Natural Law and Natural Rights* (Oxford, 1980), pp. 5–6. Finnis observes that while Simmonds (see above) views his "archetypes" as somehow different from "central cases," Finnis does not see a difference. Finnis, "Comment on Simmonds, *Law as a Moral Idea*," *supra* note 15.

[31] John Finnis, "Natural Law Theories," in *Stanford Encyclopedia of Philosophy*, http://plato.stanford.edu/entries/natural-law-theories/ (2007).

For Finnis, the central case of law is a system which makes more determinate general moral obligations, solves coordination problems, helps citizens to achieve moral goods and the common good, and in these and other ways adds to our moral reasons for action.[32] He has argued that the theory of law must be true to the objectives of the practices—the good being sought through the practice, and the evil the participants hope to avoid through it.[33]

3.3 Revisiting the Nature and Objective of Theories of Law

3.3.1 Two Aspects of Law

Law has multiple aspects, which are sufficiently distinct that this may explain the difficulty—perhaps impossibility—of any single theory capturing law adequately; the corollary is that a number of quite distinct approaches manage each simultaneously to give insight into a part of law, even if not the whole (and each, thus, in a sense, "talks past" the others, so that no real engagement in debate occurs among competing theories). John Finnis has written of law's "double life"[34]: that law is both the history of past political actions (statutes, judicial decisions, constitutional provisions, etc.), and the use of those past political actions, *supplemented by other considerations* (moral and otherwise), in resolving disputes.[35] Law in the first of those two senses is primarily descriptive or historical; law in the second sense is primarily prescriptive.

In other writings, John Finnis described his approach as asking not "*what* is law?," but rather "*why* is law?" I think this captures a similar contrast of aspects (while also highlighting the teleological aspects of Finnis's own theory). "What is law" is the descriptive side, focusing on a particular sort of process or institutional structure. "Why is law," for Finnis, shows the way in which creating a legal system,

---

[32] H. L. A. Hart also wrote about why we should focus on sophisticated legal systems rather than marginal examples of the category, Hart, *The Concept of Law*, *supra* note 2, at pp. 3–4, and Joseph Raz endorses in his work a focus on central cases of law. Joseph Raz, "About Morality and the Nature of Law," *American Journal of Jurisprudence*, vol. 48. pp. 1–16 (2003), at p. 5.

[33] John Finnis, "On Hart's Ways: Law as Reason and as Fact," in Matthew H. Kramer, Claire Grant, Ben Colburn & Antony Hatzistavrou (eds.), *The Legacy of H.L.A. Hart* (Oxford, 2008), pp. 3–27, at 6.

[34] E.g., John Finnis, "The Fairy Tale's Moral," *Law Quarterly Review*, vol. 115 (1999), pp. 170–175, at pp. 174–175; John Finnis, "On the Incoherence of Legal Positivism," *Notre Dame Law Review*, vol. 75, pp. 1597–1611 (2000), at pp. 1602–1603.

[35] This "double life" is broadly analogous to, but in the end importantly different from, Hans Kelsen's argument that some people see law as "a fact, a definitive behavior of men" while others (properly, in his view) see law as a norm (or collection of norms). Hans Kelsen, "What is the Pure Theory of Law," *Tulane Law Review*, vol. 34 (1960), pp. 269–276, at p. 269.

and a certain kind of legal system, responds not just to a moral ideal, but, in certain instances, to moral requirements or prudential needs.[36]

A third, overlapping way of seeing the same sort of contrast is the difference between seeing law is essentially a kind of social institution, and seeing law as primarily a form of practical reasoning. That law can be shown in to have both aspects—a sort of "wave" and "particle" duality—may go a long way to explaining why theories as different as legal positivism and natural law theory can both appear to capture basic truths about law.

3.3.2 *Ideals and Teleologies*

What are the arguments for—and against—seeing an institution like law in terms of its ideal or its objectives? One ground for such an approach goes to a basic point at the heart of modern hermeneutic-style social theories: the argument that theories about the social practices and institutions need to be different from theories (e.g.) in the physical sciences, for the reason that social practices are established and maintained for some (human) purpose. It is then seemingly a short and easy step to say that theories of a purposive enterprise should focus on that purpose, including, or especially, when the purpose is an ideal towards which the practice is striving.

On the other hand, the viewing of objects in terms of some ultimate goal or perfect formation seems to invoke a classical Platonism, with its Forms or Ideas, or the teleological analysis found in Aristotle's work and some medieval thinkers, all of which were long ago rejected by mainstream (secular) philosophy, at least for understanding human beings and their social practices.[37] Additionally, even a more modest purposive analysis would need to consider the objection that law serves many purposes, none of which could be said to define law.[38]

3.3.3 *A Science of Law?*

In the classical and medieval works in the Western tradition—from Plato to Aristotle to Aquinas and beyond—it is most common to see law considered as a sub-topic of a more general discussion of political theory, moral theory, or theology, a tradition

---

[36] John Finnis, "Law and What I Should Truly Decide," *American Journal of Jurisprudence*, vol. 48 (2003), pp. 107–129.

[37] For a modern consideration of teleological explanation, see Andrew Woodfield, *Teleology* (Cambridge, 1976).

[38] Michael Moore, though sympathetic to a natural law approach to law, perhaps grounded in viewing law as a "functional kind," concludes that it may be difficult to locate a distinctive function/objective of law. Michael S. Moore, "Law as a Functional Kind," in Robert S. George, *Natural Law Theory: Contemporary Essays* (Oxford, 1992), pp. 188–242.

that continues through most of the great European Enlightenment thinkers as well. Arguably, it is only with John Austin in the nineteenth century that there is a strong push to refer to a study (a "science") of law, consciously separated from political and moral prescription.

There is a sense in which approaches to law like those of Nigel Simmonds and, to a less clear extent, John Finnis,[39] seek to return theories of law to being segments of larger theories of politics or morality. Simmonds is explicit on this point: "This book [*Law as a Moral Idea*] is … an effort to push jurisprudence back towards those more unified models of inquiry that preceded the so-called 'analytical' jurisprudence as a distinct enterprise…."[40] With Finnis, it is more the questioning of theoretical objectives other than the determination of how law fits within practical reasoning and our moral reasons for action; at one point, Finnis declared that legal positivism's claims are all either trivial or matters competent lawyers have always known.[41]

3.3.4 Responses and Criticisms

What arguments can be brought against the construction of theories of law around ideals, objectives or teleologies? One standard objection is that while references to objectives and ideals are worthy of investigation, they are extraneous to determining the nature of the object or practice. As John Austin put it almost 200 years ago, "law as it is" needs to be separated from "law as it ought to be."[42] However, this sort of response, without more, simply begs the question. If the true nature of law *is* best understood relative to an ideal or an objective, then one *cannot* separate "law as it is" from "law as it ought to be."

There is also an intuitive sense that an object, entity, practice or process can and should be understood separately from the standard by which it is evaluated. The definition of "human being" is rarely thought to take in all of morality (or even all of particularly apt types of moral thinking, like virtue ethics, built around a view of ultimate human flourishing (*eudaimonia*) or the types of natural law theory grounded on a view of human beings' place in a divine plan). This does not deny the importance of evaluation, or the connection between the standards of evaluation and the nature of the object, practice or process to be evaluated. Therefore, folding into one's descriptive theory the basis of evaluation or the ideal to be sought seems to be a mistake. On the other hand, one must take seriously an argument like Finnis's, that one can only understand "argument" if one understands what a "good argument" is.

---

[39] Here one might also mention the works of Sean Coyle. E.g., Sean Coyle, *From Positivism to Idealism* (Ashgate, 2007).

[40] Simmonds, *Law as a Moral Idea*, *supra* note 14, at p. 3.

[41] Finnis, "On the Incoherence of Legal Positivism," *supra* note 34, at p. 1611.

[42] John Austin, *The Province of Jurisprudence Determined* (W. Rumble, ed., Cambridge, 1995) (original edition, 1832), at Lecture V, p. 157.

There are objects and concepts which seem explicable primarily through their highest or most perfect instantiation (even if such perfection is unlikely ever to be seen in the actual world).

A different objection is grounded in what may be the dominant current approach to theories of law: conceptual analysis. If what we are investigating *is*, as a growing number of theorists claim, "*our concept of law*," a category within our society's inter-connected collection of concepts that sets the dividing line between "law" and "not law," what reason is there to suppose that the concept will pick out the best or most developed version of a legal system? To the contrary, it would seem that the criteria of "our concept" would be much more likely to do exactly what John Finnis (criticizing Hans Kelsen)[43] denied: it would pick out the "lowest common denominator," that which is true of all legal systems (by definition, as it were).

Finnis's response is that a concept of a practice like law would apply "focally" to the fullest instance of the practice, and "non-focally" to secondary (marginal or defective) instantiations.[44] Part of the question is how broad of a (sub-)category is the "central [focal] case," and how narrow is the exceptional or residual category of marginal/defective cases. For Finnis, the focal case of law is a form that approaches an ideal: legal systems which practically reasonable people (would) judge, in a practically reasonable way, to be creating new moral obligations through the promulgation of (positive) law.[45]

In response: one might agree that concepts do, and theories should, refer to "central cases," but by that mean the large range of the average and the near-average, excluding only the rare instances of extremes of different kinds. In the case of law, the "central cases" would arguably be the large range in the statistical middle of instances, likely including many forms of legal systems that frequently fall far short of what the moral (practically reasonable) citizens would want from their legal system.[46]

H. L. A. Hart reminds us that there is a need and a value to theories whose purpose is the description and analysis of a particular kind of social practice.[47] Additionally, there is also the reasonable fear (expressed by a wide range of theorists)[48] that theories too tied to ideals will lead to the legitimation of unjust practices.

---

[43] Finnis, *Natural Law and Natural Rights*, *supra* note 30, at pp. 5–6.

[44] Finnis, *Natural Law and Natural Rights*, *supra* note 30, at pp. 9–18; Finnis, "Comment on Simmonds, *Law as a Moral Idea*," *supra* note 15.

[45] *See* id.

[46] A separate point, of course, is that the range and operation of our concepts is, in principle, both contingent and a matter open to investigation. In the text, I made my own (armchair) speculation regarding our concept of law, but a more careful investigation should in principle be possible.

[47] See Hart, *The Concept of Law*, *supra* note 2, at pp. 239–241.

[48] See, e.g., Frederick Schauer, "Positivism Through Thick and Thin," in Brian Bix (ed.), *Analyzing Law* (Oxford, 1998), pp. 65–78; at pp. 75–78; H. L. A. Hart, "Positivism and the Separation of Law and Morality," *Harvard Law Review*, vol. 71 (1958), pp. 593–629, at pp. 594–600; Peter Gabel, Book Review (reviewing Ronald Dworkin, *Taking Rights Seriously*), *Harvard Law Review*, vol. 91 (1977), pp. 302–315.

3.4 Conclusion

At the most basic levels of legal philosophy, there is pervasive disagreement: is there some truth about the nature of law, or can we choose the theory of law which best suits our purposes or which has the best consequences? And are our theories about law, at their most basic, about concepts, practices, or reasons? Are they most essentially descriptions of criteria of an existing concept, construction of the most useful concept, or discovery of an ideal or paradigm? While this paper does not attempt finally to resolve these questions, it attempts to canvass the factors that must be considered in selecting among the alternatives.

There are various purposes that theories about (the nature of) law can and do serve. Conceptual analysis identifies the necessary terms of our concept of "law," setting its boundary lines. To the extent that the concept is, as Raz argues, part of our collective self-understanding, theories of the nature of law may also allow us to understand law better by seeing the internal connections among (our) concepts.

Even a fairly broad and general concept will set up a distinction between conventional cases and marginal/extreme/degenerate cases. One could also present a narrower concept that picks out the highest or (morally) best version of some practice. This narrower (best, paradigm) concept certainly would be central to a prescriptive theory. However, the case for paradigm case theories entirely supplanting analytical/descriptive theories has arguably not yet been made out.

While theories that disclose necessary and sufficient conditions, and the connections among (our) concepts, go some distance towards "explaining" the object or practice that the concept names, one might argue there is "explanation" left to do, and a role for different sorts of theory. Some of these "supplementary" theories will come from other disciplines, like sociology, anthropology, and history. Others may come from within philosophy, including its sub-branches of moral and political theory.

Some of the ideal theories can indeed be seen as bringing legal theory back to its roots as subordinate to a broader political, moral, or even theological system, as contrasted with theories that focus on law alone (whether one characterizes such a theory as "scientific," "social science," "jurisprudential," or the like). Even if an ideal makes sense of a practice in a way that one might otherwise miss,[49] one might still argue that a theory that focuses analytically or descriptively, without recourse to ideals, has independent value and significance. Perhaps the difference between "central cases" and ideal cases of "friendship," on one hand, and one's concept or theory of law, on the other hand, is that in the case of law, highly imperfect and significantly non-ideal instances numerically predominate; some might argue that fully just legal systems are in fact never seen.

One need not deny that law aspires to an ideal. It is perhaps sufficient to note that law aspires to many ideals, and this can be seen in the theories of law themselves.

---

[49] Simmonds, *Law as a Moral Idea*, *supra* note 14, at p. 14.

Thus, while Ronald Dworkin argues (or assumes) that law is primarily about the justifying state coercion,[50] other theorists argue that it is primarily about guiding behavior; and while many theorists believe that law "aims" at justice, the law and economics theorists assert that it "aims" at "efficiency."[51] There is a multiplicity of both purposes and aspects within law: law as reason and as social theory, as historical record of official actions and as guide for decision-making. This multiplicity may explain why quite different theories each seem to capture basic truths about law, and why we might never find the one right or best theory.

[50] Dworkin, *Law's Empire*, *supra* note 1, at p. 96.

[51] Richard A. Posner, *The Economic Analysis of Law* (7th ed., Aspen, 2007); Richard A. Posner, *The Economics of Justice* (Harvard, 1981).

Chapter 4
Alexy Between Positivism and Non-positivism

Eugenio Bulygin

4.1 Law and Morality: Legal Positivism Versus Non-positivism

In his book originally published in German[1] and later translated into English under the title **The Argument from Injustice. A Reply to Legal Positivism**,[2] Robert Alexy, a well known adversary of legal positivism, is concerned with the problem of the definition of law, in which the dispute about the relation of law and morality occupies a central position. In his opinion, there are two main conflicting trends regarding this question: the positivism and the non-positivism. All positivistic theories defend the *separation thesis*, according to which there is no conceptually necessary connection between law and morality. Accordingly, the positivistic concept of law does not include any reference to morality and is defined by means of two characteristics: issuance in accordance with the system, and social efficacy. So for all positivistic theories what law is depends on what has been issued and/or is efficacious (4).

The non-positivistic theories defend the *connection thesis*, according to which the concept of law includes moral elements. Therefore it is defined by means of three characteristics: the two that are shared with positivism, plus the correctness of the contents of legal norms. Alexy insists that in contradistinction to some natural law theories, a non-positivist regards both issuance and efficacy as defining characteristics of law,[3] together with a reference to morality.

[1] **Begriff und Geltung des Rechts**, Karl Alber Verlag, Freiburg-München 1994.

[2] Clarendon Press, Oxford 2002, translation by Stanley L. Paulson and Bonnie Litschewski Paulson. The quotations and the numbers of pages in the text refer to the English edition.

[3] "No serious non-positivist is thereby excluding from the concept of law either the element of authoritative issuance or the element of social efficacy. Rather, what distinguishes the non-positivist from the positivist is the view that the concept of law is to be defined such that, alongside these fact-oriented properties, moral elements are also included." (4).

E. Bulygin (✉)
University of Buenos Aires, Arroyo 963, 1007 Buenos Aires, Argentina
e-mail: ebulygin@gmail.com

J. Ferrer Beltrán et al. (eds.), *Neutrality and Theory of Law*,
Law and Philosophy Library 106, DOI 10.1007/978-94-007-6067-7_4,

4.2 Analytic and Normative Arguments

According to Alexy there are two kinds of arguments that can support either the separation or the connection thesis: analytical and normative. The analytical argument refers to the conceptual connection between law and morality, which is denied by legal positivism and affirmed by non-positivism. But the situation of the two is not symmetrical: the positivist is bound to deny this connection, for if he admits it, he can no longer maintain that moral elements are excluded from the definition of law, whereas a non-positivist, even if he does not prove the conceptual connection, can still argue that the connection thesis is normatively necessary.

The idea of a normative necessity seems to me extremely doubtful. Alexy admits that this kind of necessity cannot be distinguished from being commanded:

> Normative necessity is strictly to be distinguished from conceptual necessity. That something is normatively necessary means nothing other than that it is commanded. One can, without contradicting oneself, challenge the validity of a command, but not the existence of a conceptual necessity. It is clear that only in a broader sense, then, is normative necessity a necessity. (21).

If something is commanded, then one says normally that it is obligatory or that one is bound to do it, but not that it is necessary. I see no advantage to use the term "necessary" instead of "obligatory" or "binding", for it can only lead to linguistic confusions. If normative necessity means that the connection between law and morality is commanded, then one should ask who is it that can command the connection thesis. Is it an agent empowered by the positive law, or is it a non-positive authority? Alexy gives no answer to these questions.

Moreover, he admits that "The conceptual argument will prove to be limited both in range and in force; and beyond that range, as well as to strengthen the conceptual argument, normative arguments are necessary. The thesis runs, first, there is a conceptually necessary connection between law and morality, and, second, there are normative arguments for including moral elements in the concept of law, arguments that in part strengthen and in part go beyond the conceptually necessary connection. In short, there are conceptually necessary as well as normatively necessary connections between law and morality" (22–23).

All this sounds extremely strange. If there are conceptual connections between law and morality, then there is no need to resort to normative arguments. Either the element of morality is included in the concept of law, or it is not. If it is included, then normative arguments are superfluous; if it is not included, they are useless. In this question there is no room for grading. So we can concentrate on analytical arguments. These are essentially two: the famous Radbruch formula (extremely unjust norms are not law) and, secondly, the thesis of the claim to correctness. Both arguments are closely linked with the distinction between the perspective of an observer and that of a participant. Let us examine them separately.

4.3 The Observer's Perspective

The observer's perspective is the standpoint of those persons that pretend to describe the law without being committed to obey or to follow its norms. A typical case is that of a jurist or legal scientist. The task of legal science is to determine or to identify which norms belong to the legal system and what they prescribe, i.e. which actions are obligatory, prohibited or permitted by law. So it is primarily a problem of cognition of law and the identification of its norms. But the dichotomy between observers and participants is not so sharp as Alexy seems to believe. Most observers are at the same time participants and all participants are also observers.[4]

Alexy is concerned with the question whether particular legal norms or whole legal systems loose, according to the Radbruch formula, their legal status by surpassing a determinate ("intolerable") degree of injustice. Now, regarding particular norms, Alexy's answer is clear: he rejects the Radbruch formula and declares to agree with positivism:

> From the perspective of an observer, Radbruch's connection thesis cannot be supported by appeal to a conceptually necessary connection between law and morality-" (30)."Thus, analytical as well as normative considerations lead to the conclusion that, from the standpoint of an observer, who looks at individual norms and enquires into a classifying connection, **the positivistic separation thesis is correct**. Radbruch's argument from injustice is not acceptable from this standpoint." (31). (Emphasis mine). Regarding whole legal system the situation, according to Alexy, is different: "What applies to an individual norm need not apply to a legal system as a whole. (31).

This assertion is not exceedingly clear. A legal system is normally defined as a set of legal norms and so it is rather doubtful why a set of norms, all of which are legal norms, should not be regarded as a legal system. Moreover, Alexy gives no reasons for the application of the Radbruch formula for legal systems. He only mentions three examples of social orders, the first of which, called senseless or desperado order contains no norms at all and so is clearly no normative order, and therefore not a legal order. The two other examples, predatory or bandit's order and governor system are normative orders, but only the second is, in Alexy's view, a legal order, in spite of the fact that it is "unjust in the extreme" (34).

The crucial question is now: What distinguishes the governor system from the bandit system? Alexy's answer to this question is:

> The difference is not that here general rules of some kind prevail, for that is already the case in the bandit system. And the difference is not that the governor system is equally advantageous for all, even if only at the minimum level of protecting life, liberty, and property; for in this system, too, killing and robbing the governed remains possible at any time. Rather, the decisive point is that a *claim to* correctness is anchored in the practice of the governor system, a claim that is made to every one. The claim to correctness is a necessary element of the concept of law." (34)

---

[4]Cf. the excellent paper by Liborio Hierro, "¿Por qué ser positivista?", *Doxa* 25 (2002), 263–302 and E. Bulygin, "Sobre observadores y participantes", *Doxa* 21, vol. I (1998), 41–48.

It follows from this quotation that the Radbruch formula is never applicable in the perspective of an observer, neither to particular norms, nor to legal systems: Both can be extremely unjust without loosing their status of law.

But in spite of admitting that the Radbruch formula is never applicable in the observer's perspective, neither to particular norms, nor to systems as a whole, Alexy insists that the claim to correctness restricts the positivistic separation thesis a good bit even in the observer's perspective "albeit only in extreme and indeed improbable cases" (35). Here "the separation thesis … reaches a limit defined by the claim to correctness".

There is a clear contradiction between the thesis that the non-positivistic concept of law necessarily includes moral elements (4) and Alexy's assertion that even an extremely unjust system as the governor order[5] is nevertheless a legal system. What moral elements does this order contain?

The difference between the bandit's order and the governor system lies, according to Alexy, in the claim to correctness. The governor system raises this claim and though it does not satisfy it; the mere fact that this purely rhetorical claim is raised is enough for changing the predatory order into a legal system. From a moral point of view, an order that claims to be correct, but is unjust in the extreme, is considerably worse than an openly predatory order. When somebody uses the pretext of moral correctness to commit immoral actions, it is usually called hypocrisy. The transformations of a bandit's order into a legal system and a gang of bandits into legal authorities seem to be grounded on mere hypocrisy. This sounds more than strange and is certainly incompatible with the assertion that the concept of law necessarily includes moral elements.

The only plausible explanation of this inconsistency is that Alexy, while describing the observer's perspective tacitly adopts the positivistic concept of law that does not include any reference to morality. But in this case the predatory order, as well as the governor system, would be both legal systems, for both are socially efficacious and from the moral point of view they are equally unjust and moreover, if there is a difference it favors the predatory order, because it is less hypocrite.

4.4 The Participant's Perspective

Alexy maintains that in the perspective of a participant, e.g. a judge, the situation regarding the relation between law and justice is different. Whereas from the observer's perspective the positivistic separation thesis is essentially correct, from

[5] Alexy's description of the governor system is rather eloquent: "In the long run, the predatory order proves not to be expedient, so the bandits strive to acquire legitimacy. They develop into governors and thereby transform the predatory order into a *governor system*. They continue to exploit their subjects… *The killing and robbing of governed individuals, acts that in point of fact serve only the exploitative interests of the governors, remain possible at any time*." (33–34). The stress is mine.

the participant's perspective, the separation thesis is inadequate, and the connection thesis is correct (35). A norm or a system of norms must contain a minimal of justice in order to be legal, or, expressed in negative terms, they must not surpass a given threshold of injustice without loosing their character of law.

Alexy speaks of "participant's perspective" and of the "standpoint of a judge", as if these two expressions were synonymous. But if fact, their meaning is different.

Participants in the "legal game" are those persons that are interested not in a mere description of the law, but in the solution of a legal problem, for example, judges, barristers, legal councils and private persons. While the observer's perspective is based on the *description of the law*, the participant's perspective is connected to the *application of the law* for solving practical problems. In this sense judges are indeed its most important actors. But in the activity of a judge two different phases must be distinguished. When a judge has to solve a legal problem, he must adopt in the first place the perspective of an observer in order to determine what prescribes the existing law. Here there are only two possibilities: either the existing legal rules determine a univocal and clear solution of the case, or they do it not. In the first case the judge has the obligation to apply this solution. In such situation only the observer's perspective is relevant also for the judge.

But it can happen, that the existing law contains no univocal solution for a legal problem, that the solution is undetermined. Such a situation can arise, pace Dworkin, for different reasons. In the first place, certain logical flaws may occur in the legal system, like *normative gaps* (when the law contains no solution for a given case) or *normative contradictions* (when there are several incompatible solutions). Another source are what has been called *penumbra cases* or *gaps of recognition.*[6] In all these cases the judge has to *decide* which solution is to be applied. This means that in the case of a normative gap he must "create" a new norm, in the case of a contradiction he must derogate (completely or partially) at least one of conflicting norms and in a penumbra case he must change the meaning of the relevant expressions. In all these cases the judge changes the existing law.

There is another especially interesting possibility, namely, when the law contains a univocal solution for the case, but the judge regards this solution as extremely unjust, either because the legislator did not take into account a relevant property (*axiological gap*[7]), or because the judge does not approve the value criteria of the legislator. In such cases it is possible that the judge decides not to apply the existing norm and to resort to another norm (eventually created by himself) that does not belong to the system at the time of his decision.

The application of norms not belonging to the system of the judge is nothing new. It occurs so often that there is a special branch of legal science, dealing with such cases, namely, the private international law. But in our case there is a considerable difference: What the judge applies is not foreign law, but a norm that has

[6]Cf. H.L.A. Hart, "Positivism and the Separation of Law and Morals", *Harvard Law Review* 71 (1958), 593–629, C.R. Carrió, **Notas sobre Derecho y Lenguaje**, Buenos Aires 1965, and C.E. Alchourrón—E. Bulygin, **Normative Systems**, Springer Verlag, Wien—NewYork, 1971.

[7]**Normative Systems,** 106–116.

been modified by him, i.e. a norm created by the judge. This means that judges participate—even if only in exceptional cases—in the creation of the law. This is what Hart called *judicial discretion*. But it does by no means imply arbitrariness. The judge applies his own value criteria for creating, changing or derogating legal norms. It must be stressed that all these problems are typical for *application*, not for *identification* of law.

In which way can these facts influence the concept of law? Does it mean that the judge uses another concept of law than the external observer that wants to describe it? I don't think so. When the judge does not apply a valid norm because in his opinion its application would lead to a great injustice and instead applies another norm, eventually created by him, this cannot be described as modification of the concept of law. What is modified in such cases are the norms or rules of a legal system, not the concept of law.

4.5 Judicial Decisions and Opinions of the Judge

How far can the argument from injustice, i.e. the Radbruch formula or the claim to correctness, influence the controversy between legal positivism, and the non-positivism, i.e. the relation between law and morality? We have already seen that for Alexy the Radbruch formula is not applicable, neither to particular norms, nor to legal systems. That the claim to correctness can perform this task is also doubtful. In any case, Alexy gives no argument in this sense. But he seems to be of the opinion that what judges say in their verdicts is relevant for the question which concept of law is more adequate.

In his book he mentions two practical cases. The first is destined to show that judges adduce the extreme injustice (Radbruch's formula) in order to stress that very unjust norms are not legal norms. The second example tries to show that the positivistic concept of law is not adequate from the standpoint of a judge. I am afraid that none of these examples is able to fulfill its purpose.

The first case concerns the so-called "statutory injustice". In 1941 a legal disposition (Ordinance 11) stripped emigrant Jews of German citizenship on ground of race. The Federal Constitutional Court decided in 1954 (long after the fall of Nazism) that Ordinance 11 was null and void, i.e. invalid from the outset, because "its conflict with justice reached an intolerable degree". Does this decision mean that this Ordinance was not a legal norm, in spite of the fact that it was regarded as valid and peacefully applied by German judges and administrative organs during several years? I don't think so. It was a valid norm of the German law during the Nazism and later was annulled *ex tunc*, i.e. retroactively, by the democratic court. The sole fact that the Constitutional Court took the trouble to invalidate this ordinance shows clearly that it was a valid legal norm. If it were not a legal norm, but e.g. a mere manifestation of a Nazi personality like Goebbels or Streicher, no court would take the trouble to declare it void.

The second case concerns the permissibility of judicial development of the law by judges, when it is contrary to a statute, i.e. *contra legem*. According to German Civil Code, monetary compensation for non-material harm is precluded except in cases provided by statute. In the case of Princess Soraya, the ex-wife of the last Shah of Iran the competent court awarded a compensation that clearly did not fall into one of the exceptions. The Constitutional Court, which declared that the law is not identical with the totality of written statutes, confirmed this decision and also declared that the judiciary is bound not only by statute (Gesetz), but by "statute and law" (Gesetz und Recht). So a judicial decision *contra* legem is not necessarily unconstitutional.

The only thing that shows this decision is that the Constitutional Court rejects the narrow statutory positivism, i.e. the idea that law is identical with written statutes. The trouble is that no serious positivist maintains nowadays this obsolete form of positivism. Consequently, this decision cannot be adduced as a reason for considering that the non-positivistic concept of law is more adequate than the positivistic one.

What these examples clearly show is the convenience of distinguishing between what judges say that they do and what they are doing really. Judges rather frequently give rhetoric arguments destined to conceal what they are really doing. This happens, e.g., because sometimes the demands of the positive law are logically impossible to satisfy.

The following requirements that a judge must satisfy when he has to decide a legal case are a good example:

1. The judge has the duty to give a verdict (he is forbidden to decline to decide).
2. His decision must be justified.
3. It must be grounded on valid legal norms.

Each of these requirements is fully justified, but in certain situations it is impossible to fulfill all of them. In cases of normative gaps or inconsistencies judges cannot justify their decision by means of existing law and so instead of applying an existent norm they change the law, applying a new norm, created by themselves.[8] This means that judges participate in the creation of the law. But as according to the dominant ideology, that stems from the doctrine of the division of powers, judges have the duty to apply the existent law and they are prohibited to modify it, most judges try to conceal by means of different rhetorical devices that they really changing the law in such situations. In this sense the formula used by the Suisse Civil Code is considerably more realistic: "A défaut d'une disposition légal applicable, le juge prononce selon droit coutumier, et á défaut d'une coutume, selon les règles qui'il établirait s'il avait á faire un acte de législateur."

Instead of presupposing that all cases can be decided according to existent law, judges are empowered by this rule to create new norms in critical cases.

---

[8]Cf. C.E. Alchourrón—E. Bulygin, **Normative Systems**, 256–268 and 287–291.

4.6 The Claim to Correctness

This topic gave rise to a long discussion with my friend Robert Alexy,[9] and I do not wish to repeat my arguments against this thesis, nor his replies. But two additional remarks should be in order.

4.6.1 *The Necessity of the Claim*

Alexy maintains that every law-creating act is conceptually connected with the claim to correctness. Normative systems that do not raise this claim are not legal systems, and if this claim is raised but not fulfilled, then they are legally faulty systems. A particular norm that does not raise this claim is still a legal norm, but it is legally faulty. The same happens if it raises the claim without fulfilling it.

Alexy introduces the notion of legal faultiness as a proof of the necessity of the claim. On the other hand, this faultiness is a very peculiar property of the law, which is basically different from other properties. Indeed, Alexy's position on this problem is ambiguous. On the one hand he says that the sentences (10): "Legally faulty systems are faulty" is an ordinary tautology like the sentence (11): "Continental legal systems are continental" and both are trivial.[10] On the other hand, he maintains that

> Nevertheless, there is a difference concerning the relation of the predicates "faulty" and "continental" to the concept of legal system (Alexy 2000, 146).

But then the sentence (10) is not as trivial as (11) and consequently it is not an ordinary tautology. This sounds very rare; I would say that both sentences are analytically true and in this sense both are trivial. Alexy's contention that the peculiarity of (10) consists in the fact that legal systems necessarily raise the claim to correctness, while they do not claim to be continental[11] is not only not convincing, but it

---

[9]Cf. R. Alexy, "On Necessary Relations between Law and Morality", *Ratio Juris*, vol.2, No.2, 1989, 167; E. Bulygin "Alexy und das Richtigkeitsargument" in Aulis Aarnio et al. (eds.), **Rechtsnorm und Rechtswirklichkeit. Festschrift für Werner Krawietz zum 60. Geburtstag**, Duncker & Humblot, Berlin 1993, 19–24; R. Alexy, "Bulygins Kritik des Richtigkeitsarguments" in E. Garzón Valdés et al. (eds.), **Normative Systems in Legal and Moral Theory. Festschrift for Carlos E. Alchourrón and Eugenio Bulygin**, Duncker & Humblot, Berlin 1997, 235–250; E. Bulygin, "Alexy's Thesis of the Necessary Connection between Law and Morality", and R. Alexy, "On the Thesis of a Necessary Connection between Law and Morality: Bulygin's Critique", both in *Ratio Juris*, vol.13, No.2, 2000, 133–137 and 138–147. All these papers have been reproduced in Spanish in P. Gaido (ed.), **La pretension de la corrección del derecho. La polémica sobre relación entre derecho y moral,** Universidad Externado de Colombia, 2001.

[10]Alexy 2000, 146: "The sentence (10) 'Faulty legal systems are faulty' is indeed trivial. Its triviality is of the same kind as the triviality of the sentence (11) 'Continental legal systems are continental'".

[11]"It is the necessity of the claim to correctness which gives faultiness a special character. This special character consists in that faultiness contradicts correctness, which is necessarily claimed by law." Alexy 2000, p. 146.

makes his argumentation circular: The claim to correctness is necessary because normative systems that raise it without fulfilling it are faulty. And this faultiness has a special character because it is based on the necessity of the claim. So the necessity of the claim is at the same time a reason and a consequence of this claim.

4.6.2 *Necessary Inclusion of Moral Elements into the Concept of Law*

As the claim to correctness, according to Alexy, is necessary and it implies moral correctness, it follows that the law necessarily includes moral elements. But this sentence is ambiguous: it can mean, first, that every legal system includes always some, but not necessarily the same, morality or, secondly, that there is one special morality that is included in every law. The difference appears quite clear if one uses predicate logic notation. If we symbolize law by L, morality by M and the relation of inclusion by I, then the first version says:

$$(x)Lx \rightarrow (Ey)\ (My\&xIy),$$

whereas the second version says:

$$(Ey)My\ \&\ (x)(Lx \rightarrow xIy)$$

The first version, that Alexy calls the weak connection thesis, is completely innocuous. No positivist would deny that every law includes some moral principles. The second version (the strong connection thesis) asserts something quite different, namely, that there is a necessary connection between every legal system and a certain morality, or as Alexy puts it, the idea of a correct or justified morality.[12]

There are at least two objections that can be raised against this idea: In the first place it is by no means clear that there is something like **the** correct or true morality and secondly, one must distinguish between the correct morality and the **idea** of a correct morality.[13] Even if there were one correct morality, there certainly are many different ideas of it.

In order to prove that the strong connection thesis is true one should be able to show that all persons have the same idea of a correct morality. This is extremely

---

[12]"...one must distinguish between two versions of the thesis of a necessary connection between law and morality: a weak version and a strong version. In the weak version, the thesis says that a necessary connection exists between law and *some* morality. The strong version has it that a necessary connection exists between law and the *right* or *correct* morality." 75.

[13]"The qualifying or soft connection that emerges when he system is considered as a system of procedures, too, from the perspective of a participant leads not to a necessary connection between law and a particular morality, to be labelled as correct in terms of content, but, rather, *to a necessary connection between law and the idea of correct morality as a justified morality*." 80 (The stress is mine).

improbable. Is it the same what such people as Kant, Hitler, Stalin, Gandhi or Bush have understood by a correct morality?

4.7 Coincidences and Differences Between the Positivism and the Non-positivism

The recognition that "the positivistic separation thesis is from the observer's perspective essentially correct" puts an end to the debate between positivism and non-positivism, at least concerning the concept of law, because positivism is interested not in the application of law, but in its identification. The positivistic separation thesis means that the contents of a legal system can be determined without any reference to morality. On this point agree all serious positivists from Bentham, Kelsen and Hart to Raz and Hoerster, and Alexy agrees too, something that might surprise some of his followers. On the other hand, no positivist denies that judges often use moral arguments.

If one compares the ideas of a positivist like Kelsen or Hart with those of a non positivist like Alexy one arrives to strange results.

1. Both parties agree that authoritative issuance and social efficacy are defining characteristics of law. Alexy adds to them the connection with morality, but it is not clear what this means, taking into account that he regards extremely unjust and hence immoral normative orders as legal orders.
2. Both parties agree (1) that in the observer's perspective, e.g. in the perspective of a jurist, the concept of law does not include any moral element and (2) that legal systems, as well as particular norms, can be immoral without loosing their legal character. The Radbruch formula is not applicable in this perspective. Not even an extreme injustice can deprive a norm issued by a competent legal authority and the corresponding legal system of their legal character.
3. From Alexy's book it follows clearly that for an external observer, who only wants to describe the law it is possible to identify all legal norms without resorting to moral values. And this is exactly what all serious positivists, from Bentham to Raz, maintain. And Alexy agrees with them, at least concerning the observer's perspective. This means that the legal science is, or rather can be, purely descriptive. Though legal norms express valuations, there is nothing that would make impossible a purely descriptive legal science. As Hart states in his famous *Postscript*: "My account is *descriptive* in that it is morally neutral and has no justificatory aims: it does not seek to justify or commend on moral or other grounds the forms and structures which appear in my general account of law.... A description is still a description even if what is described are values".[14]

[14] H.L.A. Hart, **The Concept of Law**, second edition, Clarendon Press, Oxford, 1994, 244 and 240.

And though Alexy is not very explicit on this point, there is nothing in his writings that would be incompatible with the ideal of a purely descriptive science of law except his metaphorical invocation of the ideal dimension of the law.[15]

4. Regarding the participant's perspective both parties agree that judges sometimes do not apply those norms, which they regard as very unjust. For a positivist they do it for moral reasons, for Alexy for legal reasons. But both agree that they do it. So where lies here the big difference?

One could think that Alexy concedes more importance to the participant's perspective than the positivists. This might be true regarding Kelsen, but not regarding Hart.[16]

I have the impression that the discrepancy looks very like a verbal one. Alexy is not very enthusiastic about the recognition that an unjust normative order can be regarded as law, though he does not deny it, while a positivist asserts that the positive law, like any other product of human activity can be good or bad, just or unjust. By denying calling "law" an unjust normative order, we do not remove the injustice. Unjust normative orders certainly deserve to be sharply criticized, but there is no reason not to call them "legal orders".

[15]"Thus, the claim to correctness leads to an ideal dimension that is necessarily linked with the law." 81.

[16]"… there is nothing in the project of a descriptive jurisprudence as exemplifies in my book to preclude a non-participant external observer from describing the way in which participants view the law from such an internal point of view." **The Concept of Law**, 242.

Chapter 5
The Architecture of Jurisprudence

Jules L. Coleman

5.1 Introduction

Two marks of a mature field of inquiry are that its central problems are well-formulated and that its conventional wisdom is sound. Even in the most mature fields, however, the conventional wisdom can sometimes be misleading and the central problems poorly cast. Unfortunately, this is the state of affairs in analytic jurisprudence. Progress can be made only if much of the conventional wisdom is displaced and its central questions are reframed.

This Article does just that. It characterizes two central tenets of the conventional wisdom in jurisprudence and argues that both must be discarded if progress in jurisprudence is to be made. Having discarded both tenets of conventional wisdom, the Article then demonstrates the progress that can be made and indicates the direction in which prospects for further progress have been enhanced.[1] We begin by loosening the grip of conventional wisdom.

Originally published at *Yale Law Journal*, 121 (1): 2–80. The editors are greatful to Yale Law Journal for their permission to reprint this paper.

[1]As a Torts teacher, I feel compelled to issue a warning; whether it is adequate to relieve me of responsibility is another matter. I pride myself on writing clearly and especially in having the ability to communicate difficult and technically demanding material in an accessible manner. I try to do the same here and for the most part, I believe, successfully. That said, the discussion in Part VI is very demanding, and I could find no way of getting the points across that makes for pleasurable reading. I believe, however, that anyone who is prepared to work through the argument can understand it (whether they agree with the conclusions or not). I have avoided the use of logical notation and technical jargon wherever doing so is at all possible. To be honest, it is not as if, but for Part VI, the Article reads like a summer novel, but it should provide no special barriers to comprehension beyond the need to read carefully and stay awake while doing so.

J.L. Coleman (✉)
Office of the Provost, New York University, 70 Washington Square South, 10012-1091 New York, NY, USA
e-mail: jules.coleman@nyu.edu

J. Ferrer Beltrán et al. (eds.), *Neutrality and Theory of Law*, Law and Philosophy Library 106, DOI 10.1007/978-94-007-6067-7_5,

5.2 The Conventional Wisdom and the Separability Thesis

5.2.1 Its Place in the Conventional Wisdom

Though most academic lawyers are unschooled in the finer points of contemporary jurisprudence, nearly all are confident of their ability to distinguish legal positivism from natural law theory. They tell us that natural lawyers assert and positivists deny the existence of necessary connections between law and morality; that positivists endorse and natural lawyers reject what I have termed 'the separability thesis'.[2] Academic lawyers may even tell us that legal positivism is defined by its commitment to the separability thesis and natural law by its rejection of it. Finally, they may say that, among positivists, there has been no more ardent proponent of the separability thesis than H.L.A. Hart.

There is a difference between the claim that the separability thesis is *compatible* with legal positivism and the claim that it is *essential* to it. Claims are compatible if they all *can* be true at the same time, and they are incompatible otherwise. In contrast, were the separability thesis essential to legal positivism, then it *would have to be true were positivism true*.

The separability thesis would suffice to distinguish legal positivism from natural law theory were it compatible with one of them—positivism—but not the other—natural law theory. Thus, the separability thesis need not be essential to legal positivism in order for it to distinguish positivism from natural law theory.

At the same time, the separability thesis could be essential to legal positivism yet fail to distinguish positivism from natural law theory. Depending on how all these views are to be formulated precisely, the separability thesis might turn out to be compatible with natural law theory despite being essential to positivism. In that case, its being essential to legal positivism would not be enough to distinguish legal positivism from natural law theory.[3]

Taken together, these considerations demonstrate that the conventional wisdom regarding the separability thesis actually consists in the conjunction of three related but nevertheless quite distinct claims. The first is that the separability thesis is essential to legal positivism. The second is that the separability thesis distinguishes

[2] *See* Jules L. Coleman, *Negative and Positive Positivism*, 11 J. Legal Stud. 139, 140–141 (1982).

[3] In a private correspondence, Ori Simchen has suggested that the *necessity* of the separability thesis in fact distinguishes legal positivism from natural law theory insofar as legal positivism is compatible with the necessity of the separability thesis, whereas natural law theory is not. That is, the separability thesis may be compatible with natural law theory, but its necessity is not. I do not disagree, but my claim is that the *separability thesis* (not the necessity of the separability thesis) is inadequate to distinguish legal positivism from natural law. Beyond that, as I demonstrate below, nothing in legal positivism requires the separability thesis, so it hardly can be essential to it. In fact, the most compelling arguments for certain forms of legal positivism rely on rejecting the separability thesis, not endorsing it—let alone its necessity!

legal positivism from natural law theory. The third is that the separability thesis distinguishes legal positivism from natural law theory *because* it is both essential to legal positivism and incompatible with natural law theory. Together, these claims comprise the conventional wisdom regarding the place of the separability thesis in jurisprudence. This much is conventional. Whether it is wisdom is an entirely different matter.

5.2.2 *Its Claims*

5.2.2.1 The Coherence of Immoral Law

In order to assess the conventional wisdom, we need first to settle on an interpretation of the separability thesis. Unfortunately, this is easier said than done—a striking fact given how influential the separability thesis has been. Part—though not all—of the problem is that whereas the separability thesis is often taken to be a claim about the conditions of *legal validity*—that is, the conditions that must be satisfied in order for a *norm* to count as among a community's laws—it has also been taken to be a claim about the *existence conditions of legal systems*—that is, the conditions that must be satisfied in order for a *system of rules* (or norms) regulating affairs to count as a *legal* system.[4] The greater part of the problem is that in both cases, the claim that the thesis makes is open to several different and by no means equally plausible interpretations, few of which have been explicitly articulated and fewer still adequately defended.

The truth is that positivists have no one to blame but themselves for much of the confusion that has grown up around the separability thesis. In many ways, the main culprit may well be H.L.A. Hart, no doubt the most prominent positivist of the modern era who, as Leslie Green has correctly observed, endorsed a particularly broad int.rpretation of it.[5]

Though Green is right both to attribute to Hart a promiscuous interpretation of the separability thesis and to criticize him for it, there is no question that Hart emphasized a much narrower formulation of the separability thesis owed originally to Austin. As Austin put it, "The existence of law is one thing; its merit or demerit

[4] *Compare* Fernando Atria, *Legal Reasoning and Legal Theory Revisited*, 18 Law & Phil. 537, 547 n.6 (1999) (describing the separability thesis as the proposition that "from the fact that a legal solution is morally objectionable it does not follow that it is legally mistaken"), *with* Kenneth Einar Himma, *Inclusive Legal Positivism*, *in* The Oxford Handbook of Jurisprudence and Philosophy of Law 125, 136 (Jules Coleman & Scott Shapiro eds., 2002) ("[T]he Separability Thesis asserts that there exists at least one conceptually possible legal system in which the criteria of validity are exclusively source- or pedigree-based.").

[5] Leslie Green, *Positivism and the Inseparability of Law and Morals*, 83 N.Y.U. L. Rev. 1035, 1040 (2008).

another. Whether it be or be not is one enquiry; whether it be or be not conformable to an assumed standard, is a different enquiry."[6]

The claim that the 'law is one thing, its merit or demerit another' calls attention to the fact that valid laws can be either morally estimable or reprehensible: their moral character neither settles their legal status nor is settled by it. Neither natural lawyers nor legal positivists dispute the latter claim, so the focus of the dispute has been on whether the morality of a norm settles, in whole or in part, the legal validity of a norm. The view typically associated with natural law theory is that even if the morality of a norm is not sufficient to establish its legal validity, a norm cannot count as law unless it meets an appropriate moral test—unless, that is, it satisfies (or at least is not incompatible with) relevant moral demands. The standard way to put this is to say that, for the natural lawyer, morality is a necessary condition of legal validity. Positivists reject this claim, and in so doing, they endorse the separability thesis—the claim that morality is not a necessary condition of legal validity.

All this should be familiar enough, but even so, some slight but important modifications of the standard formulation of the separability thesis are required. The phrase 'conditions of legal validity' is so common and so much a part of jurisprudential discourse that it is easy to miss that the concept of legal validity is itself probably an artifact of jurisprudential theories and not a feature of law that such theories must explain or accommodate.[7] The concept of legal validity does not figure prominently, if at all, in many jurisprudential theories—Ronald Dworkin's most notable among them.[8]

It is an important but overlooked point that it is sometimes difficult to distinguish concepts that are essential to legal practice—and thus which call for explanation—from those concepts that are theoretical constructs employed to help us explain legal practice. Fortunately, we do not have to settle the general matter here, nor even must we determine the category to which the concept of 'legal validity' belongs.

---

[6]John Austin, The Province of Jurisprudence Determined (1832), *reprinted in* The Province of Jurisprudence Determined and the Uses of the Study of Jurisprudence, xxiii, 184 (Hackett Publishing Co. 1998).

[7]The pervasiveness of the concept of legal validity attests again to the influence of Hart's *The Concept of Law*, in which there is a rule of recognition and other rules subsidiary to it. The authority of these rules as law depends on their validity under a rule of recognition that is itself neither valid nor invalid, but merely exists or not. *See* H.L.A. Hart, The Concept of Law 94–95 (Penelope A. Bulloch & Joseph Raz eds., Oxford Univ. Press 2d ed. 1997) (1961). Following Hart, legal philosophers have invoked a way of thinking according to which a norm is a law only if it is *valid* and valid only if it satisfies appropriate criteria of validity. *See, e.g.*, Stephen Munzer, *Validity and Legal Conflicts*, 82 Yale L.J. 1140, 1148–1150 (1973).

[8]On my reading, Dworkin also resists the corollary idea that a legal system is a code of any sort—let alone a code of rules that must satisfy membership or validity conditions. Indeed, both Dworkin and Mark Greenberg have developed jurisprudential outlooks that do not rely on the idea of 'a law'—at least insofar as particular laws are to be identified with statutes, regulations, or particular authoritative acts of any sort. Ronald Dworkin, Justice in Robes (2006); Ronald Dworkin, Law's Empire 410–413 (1986); Mark Greenberg, *How Facts Make Law*, 10 Legal Theory 157 (2004) [hereinafter Greenberg, *How Facts Make Law*]; Mark Greenberg, *The Standard Picture and Its Discontents*, *in* 1 Oxford Studies in Philosophy of Law 39 (Leslie Green & Brian Leiter eds., 2011) [hereinafter Greenberg, *Standard Picture*].

It is enough for our purposes that we are able to reformulate the separability thesis in a way that does not invoke the concept of legal validity (so as not to beg any questions against views that do not avail themselves of it) while capturing the gist of the disagreement about its truth.

Instead of formulating the separability thesis as a claim about the conditions of legal validity, we might express it in either of the following ways:

(a) The concept of immoral law *is* coherent; or
(b) Sentences asserting that a particular legal requirement or directive is immoral do not—*for that reason alone*—constitute contradictions.

Again, the conventional wisdom is that natural law rejects the separability thesis, which means that it rejects (a) and (b). Thus, natural law must endorse either (most likely both) of the following:

(c) The concept of immoral law is *incoherent*; or
(d) Sentences asserting the existence of particular immoral legal directives or requirements—for that reason alone—constitute contradictions.

Thus, *as a claim about laws*, the separability thesis is best represented as either (a) or (b), and if the conventional wisdom is sound, that means that positivism endorses either (most likely both) (a) or (b), whereas natural law endorses either (and most likely both) (c) or (d).[9]

5.2.2.2 The Existence Conditions of Law

As I noted, the separability thesis is often associated with a claim about the existence conditions for legal systems, and not exclusively with a claim about the conditions of legal validity. On this way of understanding it, the separability thesis is the claim that, whatever other constraints legal systems must satisfy, moral constraints are not among those conditions. There are, in other words, no necessary moral constraints on the existence of a legal system or on the possibility of governance by law.

The idea that there are or could be moral constraints on the existence of legal systems can be understood in a variety of ways. For example, one idea would be that no scheme of governance could count as a legal system unless it had or pursued a moral aim. Another might be that no scheme of governance could count as law unless it had 'minimal' moral content, constituted a legitimate authority, or claimed to constitute such an authority. Shifting gears, another set of ideas might express the

[9] In putting the point in terms of the conceptual coherence of immoral law, I do not mean to be committing jurisprudence to conceptual analysis. The point I am making, in a way that is explicitly neutral about conceptual analysis, would go as follows. The natural lawyer could just as easily suppose (and a legal positivist deny) that the concept of immoral law is necessarily empty but not semantically incoherent (much like the concept of a water molecule applying to nothing as a matter of logical necessity), and a natural lawyer could just as easily suppose (and a legal positivist deny) that a sentence asserting a particular legal requirement to be immoral is necessarily false rather than contradictory (much like the sentence 'water is an element'). Again, I am grateful to Ori Simchen for this more precise formulation.

demand that no system of regulating human affairs could count as law unless its demands generally met the requirements of morality, its characteristic modes of lawmaking comported with moral demands, or its distinctive mode of governance embodied or expressed certain moral virtues or values. All of these formulations express moral constraints on the existence of legal systems.

While not denying that any or all of these constraints would render governance by law desirable, (the conventional wisdom has it that) positivism holds that no such constraints must be satisfied in order for a system of regulating human affairs to constitute a legal system. At the same time it attributes to the natural lawyer not just the view that legal systems that satisfy these constraints are desirable for their doing so, but that their doing so is necessary to their counting as legal systems. Because satisfying some or other such constraint is distinctive of law as a form of governance, the natural lawyer must reject the separability thesis that the positivist is committed to endorsing—or so conventional wisdom has it.[10]

We have now distinguished between the separability thesis as a claim about laws and as a claim about the existence conditions of legal systems (or the possibility conditions of governance by law). As a claim about laws, the separability thesis holds that the concept of immoral law is coherent; as a claim about the existence conditions of legal systems, it holds that there are no moral constraints that a scheme of governance must satisfy in order to count as a legal system. We turn now to assessing whether, conceived in any of these ways, the separability thesis is up to the task that conventional wisdom has set for it. We begin with the separability thesis as a claim about laws and thus with the assertion that the concept of immoral law is coherent.

5.3 Assessing the Conventional Wisdom: The Separability Thesis

5.3.1 Is the Separability Thesis Adequate to Distinguish Positivism from Natural Law? The Possibility of Immoral Law

As I noted at the outset, the separability thesis would suffice to distinguish legal positivism from natural law were it compatible with the former and incompatible with the latter (or vice versa). We therefore set aside for the moment the question of

[10] *See,* e.g., Kenneth Einar Himma, *Final Authority To Bind with Moral Mistakes: On the Explanatory Potential of Inclusive Legal Positivism*, 24 Law & Phil. 1, 7 (2005) ("Classical natural law theorists . . . argue that there are necessary moral constraints on the content of the law. . . . In contrast, positivists hold it is the conventional practices of officials that determine the second-order legal norms which constrain judicial decision-making.").

whether the separability thesis is *essential* to legal positivism and ask first whether it is *compatible* with legal positivism but not with natural law theory. Thus, we have to answer two questions: (1) Is the separability thesis compatible with legal positivism? (2) Is the separability thesis incompatible with natural law theory?

The separability thesis (as a claim about laws and not about legal systems) asserts that the concept of immoral laws is coherent (or that sentences expressing the existence of immoral laws are not contradictory). If the morality of a norm neither settles its legal status nor is settled by it, then it is possible for there to be legal norms that are not moral, just as there could be moral norms that are not law. In that case, immoral laws are possible, and if they are, the concept of immoral laws is coherent. This suggests that the conventional view is at least partially right in that positivism is compatible with the separability thesis.

This leaves us with the matter of whether the separability thesis is incompatible with natural law theory. At first blush the separability thesis appears to be clearly incompatible with natural law theory. After all, both classical and modern natural lawyers echo Augustine's famous assertion, reaffirmed by Aquinas, that "an unjust law is no law at all."[11] Taken literally, this amounts to the view that it is conceptually impossible for something to be both law and bad (i.e., immoral), and that entails the view that the concept of immoral law—a norm that is both law and morally bad—is incoherent.

If history is to be a guide, one cannot help but be struck by the fact that morally bad law is not merely conceptually possible but all too frequently realized. If natural law holds that the concept of immoral law is incoherent, then it is not simply false but foolish. No doubt, for many of its critics, these considerations provide ample grounds for dismissing natural law theory out of hand.

Worthwhile arguments are rarely that easily won. What we need to do, then, is to see if we can interpret the claim that 'an unjust law is no law at all' in a way that renders it plausible and potentially illuminating, rather than obviously false and uninteresting. In what follows, I provide several plausible ways of interpreting the claim (or the motivation behind it) that renders it compatible with the possibility of immoral laws and thus with the separability thesis.[12]

[11] Augustine, On Free Choice of the Will bk. I, § 5, at 8 (Thomas Williams trans., Hackett Publ'g Co. 1993) (c. 400 AD); *see also* 2 Thomas Aquinas, Summa Theologica, question 96, art. 4, at 70 (Fathers of the English Dominican Province trans., 1915) (c. 1274) ("[A] law that is not just, seems to be no law at all.").

[12] To be sure, one need not identify natural law theory with the claim that 'an unjust law is no law at all', and some important contemporary natural lawyers do not. In the case of some of these scholars, there is no question that natural law theory is compatible with the possibility of immoral laws, and so, I spend no time in what follows focusing on their work. *See,* e.g., John Finnis, Natural Law and Natural Rights 360–363 (1980); Mark C. Murphy, Natural Law in Jurisprudence and Politics (2006). Instead, I focus on those versions of natural law theory that initially seem inconsistent with the possibility of immoral laws and take my task to be showing that, even in those cases, initial appearances are misleading.

5.3.1.1 Making Sense

The phrase 'immoral law' makes sense insofar as we understand what a speaker using it intends to convey by it. Someone asserting the existence of immoral laws is claiming that there are norms that satisfy the criteria of legality that are nonetheless morally objectionable. True or false, there is no problem understanding what one who makes this assertion has in mind. Expressions can make sense, however, even if the objects to which they purport to refer do not exist—indeed even if the objects to which they purportedly refer could not possibly exist.

Because there is no problem understanding what someone who asserts the existence of immoral laws intends to convey, we should not interpret the claim that 'an unjust law is no law at all' as asserting that the phrase 'immoral law' makes no sense. Of course it does. The better interpretation is that the set of immoral laws is necessarily empty—that nothing can be both law and immoral at the same time. On this reading, someone asserting the existence of immoral laws would be in the same boat as someone asserting the existence of square circles and the largest prime number. When we understand his claim in this way, it should not surprise us that the natural lawyer is steadfastly unmoved by our protests that the concept of immoral law makes sense. For he does not deny that the expression has application conditions, only that those conditions could possibly be satisfied.

Alas, this suggestion does not seem capable of rendering the claim that 'an unjust law is no law at all' either plausible or interesting. Far from being necessarily empty, the set of immoral laws suffers an embarrassment of riches. Strange that something unrealizable could be such a familiar part of our lives—and the source of so much misery and injustice.

The problem is that we are treating the natural lawyer's claim as if he were invoking the ordinary concept of law—when in fact he is not. In the ordinary sense of the term, there clearly are immoral laws, and it would be odd to treat the natural lawyer as somehow not noticing this obvious fact. The more charitable view is that the natural lawyer's claim invokes a distinctive concept of law that departs from the ordinary one. Until we specify more concretely the concept of law that the natural lawyer has in mind, however, we remain only part of the way to finding a charitable interpretation of the phrase 'an unjust law is no law at all' that renders it compatible with the separability thesis. We turn now to that task.

5.3.1.2 A Revisionist Concept

In the classical natural law tradition it is common to identify law with the category of norms that *necessarily bind the conscience*. The phrase 'a law that binds the conscience' is ambiguous. On the one hand, rules that bind the conscience might be ones that *necessarily motivate* compliance with them. On the other hand, rules that bind the conscience might be ones that *necessarily provide reasons for action*. A norm can create reasons to act that are inadequate to motivate compliance with the reasons it provides, as in the case of *akrasia* (weakness of the will). Or a rule that fails to provide reasons for acting, in virtue of its other features, can motivate compliance with it. Therefore, we need to disambiguate the expression 'law that binds the conscience'.

In doing so, we should be mindful of the emphasis that the natural law tradition places on the relationship between law and reason. Unless there are other considerations that warrant a different interpretation, the sensible place to begin is by assuming that, in restricting law to those norms that bind the conscience, the natural lawyer intends to limit law to norms that are necessarily reason-giving. Certainly, a well-motivated person will comply with laws that create compelling reasons for acting. Thus, we can assume that the natural lawyer holds that in the ideal or successful case, law that binds the conscience provides reasons and, as a result, motivates compliance.

However we disambiguate the expression, restricting law to norms that bind the conscience involves departing from the ordinary concept of law. That concept is much more closely associated with a norm's distinctive human or institutional source or, to use Dworkin's term, its 'pedigree',[13] as well as with particular institutions like courts and legislatures and familiar relationships of authority between 'command-giver' and 'recipient'. Given the ordinary concept, it is an open question whether what the law directs us to do is something we ought to do and whether, if it is, we ought to do what the law demands *because* the law demands it. In other words, binding the conscience in any sense of the expression is no part of our ordinary concept of law; it is neither essential to the concept nor is it entailed by anything that is.

Someone proposing an alternative concept of law may allow that the ordinary concept is well-suited to both normal practical engagement with the law and to many theoretical projects in the social sciences—economics, political science, sociology, and anthropology. Research in those fields can proceed nicely with a thin concept of law that emphasizes law's institutional structure, social source, and coerciveness. Someone proposing a revised concept merely resists the view that the ordinary concept is suitable for jurisprudence.

Normally, revision of a concept is justified when the ordinary concept is misleading and confusing or when it does not serve theoretical or practical purposes well. The revised concept is offered as otherwise providing insight or being particularly well-suited to certain explanatory or justificatory projects. Given that the ordinary concept is adequate for both practical engagement and the theoretical purposes of the social sciences, it is natural to ask what is special about the projects of jurisprudence that calls for revision in the concept of law.

Among the aims of jurisprudence is to explain the distinctive forms of life that governance by law makes available. Jurisprudence engages law in its 'aspirational mode'. To understand law is to know what forms of achievement are distinctive of it. Without law, these forms of life would not be attainable, or if attainable, only incompletely so. It is an open question what those forms of life are and the aim of

[13]Ronald Dworkin, Taking Rights Seriously 17 (1978).

jurisprudence is to identify, characterize, and explain the way in which law helps create and sustain them.

One way of expressing the idea that jurisprudence must focus on law in its aspirational mode is to say the concept of law suitable to jurisprudence is a 'success concept'—that the term we use to refer to that concept, i.e. 'law', is itself a 'success term'. To say that 'law' is a success term is to say that the conditions of law's success are among the application conditions of the term 'law'. Because law's aspirations are part of the application conditions of the concept of law, no norm that fails to meet the standards of law's success is law in the full sense of the term. If we associate law's success with its binding the conscience, then a norm's failure fully to bind the conscience renders it 'defective' as law—as less law than it would be were it to bind fully the conscience of those to whom it is directed. In the same way as one cannot *know* something untrue or *deceive* someone without getting her to believe a falsehood, a norm cannot be law in the full sense without succeeding in binding the conscience: primarily by obligating those to whom it is directed, and secondarily by motivating their compliance with the obligations thereby incurred. This is the concept of law suitable for jurisprudence.

There are several ideas here that are very easy to confuse with one another. One is that law is essentially aspirational; the second is that the best way to capture this idea is to characterize 'law' as a success term. The third is that the standard of success appropriate to law in its aspirational mode is binding the conscience of those to whom the law is addressed. Fourth, to bind the conscience is necessarily to provide those to whom the law is directed with moral reasons for acting (which, if those to whom the law is addressed are rational or well-motivated, are sufficient, if not necessary, to motivate their compliance with it).

We have already explained the concept of binding the conscience. Part of the point of claiming that law is an aspirational concept is to emphasize that there is an essentially normative aspect of law. When we characterize a norm as law or a set of rules as a legal system, we are not merely describing it but expressing some form of positive evaluation. Its being law is a desirable, attractive, or valuable feature of a norm or of a system of norms—or so the argument goes. The claim that 'law is an aspirational concept', then, is part of a more general view about the essentially normative character of the concept of law. We take up this more general claim in a bit and so postpone discussing its merits at this time. Instead, we assume for the sake of the current discussion that the concept of law suitable for jurisprudence reflects an aspirational component and turn our attention to the suggestion that the way to express this aspirational dimension of law is to treat the term 'law' as a success term.

To say that 'law' is a success term implies that a norm's failure to satisfy its success conditions—whatever they are—entails that it falls short of being law. It is either not law, defective as law, or not law in the full sense.

We need to distinguish the claim that 'law' is a success term from the more familiar idea that there are standards appropriate to evaluating law and that law can be either successful or not depending on whether it meets those standards. Law that falls short of meeting its standards for success is law in every relevant sense.

Because it is unsuccessful law, it is less valuable or desirable than it would otherwise be; but it is fully and completely law, nonetheless.[14]

The difference we are emphasizing—between standards of success applicable to various things and treating the terms that refer to them as 'success' terms—is quite general and broadly applicable. We can assess the success of our team's performance without 'team' being a success term. I have aspirations for my essays—including this one—without the term 'essay' being a success term. So too law. One can quite appropriately inquire into the success of laws and legal systems—in particular or in general—without 'law' being a success term. Whatever the criteria for 'law' may be, it will always make sense to evaluate it as good or bad, desirable or not, fair or unfair, just or unjust, and so on. This does not make 'law' a success term, even though both laws and legal systems are apt for evaluation as successful or not.

Still, even if we grant that 'law' is a success term or that law embodies certain aspirations, it hardly follows that the natural lawyer's substantive revision must be accepted—namely, that law can be said to succeed *only if* it binds the conscience, and that fully to be law is to bind the conscience. After all, there are other ways of taking 'law' to be a success term or of characterizing law's aspirations. For instance, law might be thought to succeed to the extent that it coordinates large-scale human interaction or provides the framework within which individuals can make rational investments in their projects and pursue them with minimal interference from others.

While this way of understanding the natural lawyer's claim that 'an unjust law is no law at all' raises more questions than it answers, it is plain that natural law is compatible with the separability thesis. For in claiming that 'an unjust law is no law at all', we simply must take the natural lawyer to be holding that, in the ordinary sense of the term 'law', immoral law is possible, but in the sense appropriate to jurisprudence, it is not. Roughly, he insists that if in referring to norms as law our aim is merely to call attention to various formal or institutional features, then of course there can be and are immoral laws; but if our aim is to grasp law's aspirations, to inspire and not merely to report, then, in the sense of law suitable for those projects, immoral law is impossible.

5.3.1.3 A Methodological Suggestion

Instead of treating the natural lawyer's claim as involving a proposed revision in the concept of law suitable for jurisprudence, we might reach what is essentially the same interpretation of the claim that 'an unjust law is no law at all' by understanding the natural lawyer as offering a *methodological* suggestion as to how jurisprudence

[14] This latter idea is suggested by the fact that law is a social construct, designed by persons to pursue certain aims and goals and measurable or evaluable in terms of whether it achieves them. In this sense the failure to succeed does not rob a norm or a system of governance of the status of law; it is merely a way of evaluating the law—as successful or not.

should proceed. There is a wide range of cases of law and of legal systems. On which instances or cases of law ought jurisprudence to focus? The thought is that the central case of law is the successful one,[15] and the successful law is the one that imposes obligations on those to whom it is directed. Understood in this way, the natural lawyer is not suggesting that we abandon the ordinary concept of law in favor of a revised one suitable for the purposes of jurisprudence. Instead, his claim is that in order to understand even the ordinary concept of law we have to focus on the core or paradigmatic instantiations of it. The core instance of law is not law that fails, but law that succeeds—as measured by the standards of success, which, for this type of natural lawyer, is law that binds the conscience.[16]

By way of analogy, in order to understand what it is to be a heart, one would not look to all hearts to uncover what, if anything, they share. Rather, one would look to the successful heart to discover what is essential to its success. The successful heart pumps blood efficiently. Thus, we identify hearts as the organ that pumps blood with some minimal degree of effectiveness. Successful hearts perform this function well, unsuccessful ones less so, or not at all.

Like hearts, one might think that laws, too, have functions. When they perform their functions well, they do what they are designed to do. Among laws' functions is to bind the conscience of those to whom they apply. If so, then the core case of law—the appropriate object of study in jurisprudence—is law that binds the conscience. Understood in this way, the natural lawyer's claim that 'an unjust law is no law at all' is best understood as a claim about the core case of law—the proper object of jurisprudential inquiry.

One might agree that jurisprudence should study the core case of law and that the core case of law is the one in which law succeeds at doing what it is meant or designed to do. It achieves its aim—whether the aim is instrumental or intrinsic to it. On the other hand, one might object that there is nothing special about binding the conscience that makes law's doing so—when it does—the core or paradigmatic case of law.

But the natural lawyer has the makings of a good response and one that has the ironic feature of enlisting the aid of the leading positivist of our time, Joseph Raz. Raz famously holds that law necessarily claims to be a legitimate authority.[17] To claim legitimate authority is to claim that one's directives provide reasons for acting that apply to those over whom one claims authority. If that claim is essential to law, then one could argue that the successful case of law is the one in which the claim

[15]It is important to note that 'success' here is being used in its evaluative sense, not as a criterion for applying the concept. The assumption is that whatever the criteria for 'law' may be, jurisprudence should proceed by studying the cases in which laws do what they are designed to do—cases in which they succeed. Here, then, binding the conscience is a substantive claim about what constitutes success for law.

[16]I take John Finnis to be a natural lawyer who adopts the general methodology of focusing on the central case and as someone who identifies the central case with the successful one. *See* Finnis, *supra* note 12, at 9–16.

[17]Joseph Raz, The Authority of Law 28–33 (1979).

law necessarily makes is vindicated. The proper object of jurisprudence is the case in which law's claim is true, not the many cases in which it is false.

If we understand the natural lawyer as offering a methodological suggestion about how jurisprudence should proceed, we need not read him as insisting on the impossibility of immoral laws. Nor should we read him as claiming that there is a distinctive notion of law that is suitable for theoretical inquiry into the forms of life and organization made possible through governance by law. Rather, he is suggesting that in the same way we will fail to grasp what hearts are if we focus on what all hearts have in common rather than on what makes for a successful heart, we will miss what is essential to law unless we focus on the cases of law in which its directives bind the conscience. None of this entails that immoral laws are impossible, however, and so there is no reason to think that a natural lawyer must resist the separability thesis.

5.3.1.4 Legality as a Normative Notion

We noted earlier that some might argue that law is an essentially aspirational concept. We indicated, as well, that such a view takes law to be a normative concept: that is, in addition to having a descriptive component, the *concept of legality has a normative component (or is an essentially normative predicate).* To say that a norm is law is not merely to mark it as belonging to or being a part of a legal system, but also to *evaluate* it (presumably, positively) or to *endorse* it. Evaluation and endorsement are two different ways of making out the claim that legality is a normative notion. One can evaluate the law without endorsing it; to do so is to judge or assess the value or desirability of the law without accepting its moral presuppositions, taking on its characteristic point of view, or promoting or encouraging its fundamental aims.

Thus, we have two distinct versions of the claim that legality is normative: either that marking a norm as law constitutes a form of evaluation or that it constitutes a form of endorsement.

In saying that legality constitutes a form of evaluation, it is important that we distinguish between different possible objects of assessment: particular laws on the one hand and legal institutions or legal systems on the other. On the one hand, to identify a norm as law (on the view under consideration) is to assess it as valuable or desirable. A norm's having the property of legality—of being law—would imply something about its worth, desirability, or value. In this view, then, the moral worth of a norm would be settled at least in part by its having the property of legality. Someone pressing this view of the normativity of legality would have difficulty squaring it with a narrow formulation of the separability thesis, according to which the legality of a norm and the worth of a norm represent two distinct inquiries. So if we understand legality as a normative notion in *this* sense, the natural lawyer's position may not be compatible with the separability thesis.

Alternatively, in claiming that legality is a normative concept of assessment, one can be understood as calling attention to the idea that a system of law or a legal institution embodies or expresses a particular kind of political virtue. This, I take it, is an important feature of Ronald Dworkin's jurisprudence. For Dworkin, the distinctive virtue of law is not justice, but what he calls "integrity."[18] Indeed Dworkin can sometimes be read as claiming that a theory of law is a theory of legality, by which he has in mind an account of the kind of value or political virtue displayed by 'the legal'. Possessing the virtues distinctive of law, like possessing most ordinary virtues, is a matter of degree. Thus, legal systems can display integrity, for example, even if some of its laws are immoral. Integrity is the virtue that law strives to achieve but, as with the rest of us, often falls short of doing. Thus, understood in this way, the claim that legality is a normative concept is perfectly compatible with the possibility of immoral laws and thus with the narrow formulation of the separability thesis.

Let us turn now to the view that legality constitutes or expresses a kind of endorsement. The rough idea is that because laws are generally enforceable by the use of coercion, to mark a norm as law is to identify it as a suitable object of justified coercion. Thus, to mark a norm as law is unavoidably (at least provisionally) to endorse coercively enforcing it (if necessary).

With this conception of the endorsement feature of ascriptions of legality in hand, we can then understand the claim that 'an unjust law is no law at all' in either of two ways: (1) unjust laws are not entitled to the endorsement that being law normally warrants; or (2) because unjust 'laws' are not fit for the endorsement that predicating legality of a norm warrants, they fall short of being law in the full sense—they are somehow defective as laws. Either view is compatible with the coherence of immoral laws and thus with the narrow formulation of the separability thesis.

To sum up the discussion of the relationship between the separability thesis and the claim that 'an unjust law is no law at all': I have offered several ways of interpreting the claim that 'an unjust law is no law at all' that are consistent with the possibility of immoral law. I considered first the idea that the most charitable interpretation of the claim that 'an unjust law is no law at all' takes the natural lawyer as offering a revision in the concept of law suitable for the purposes of jurisprudence.

According to the revised concept of law, the term 'law' is reserved for norms that bind the conscience in the sense of providing reasons for action for those to whom they are directed. The claim that 'an unjust law is no law at all' is just the claim that nothing can be both bad (immoral) and bind the conscience at the same time. The positivist interprets this claim in the light of the ordinary concept of law, but the natural lawyer does so employing the revised concept. Thus, rather than being engaged in a dispute in which, at most, one of them can be right, the fact is that they are talking past one another. Given the particular concept each employs, they can both be right at the same time, and that means that the separability thesis is inadequate to distinguish between them.

[18]Dworkin, Law's Empire, *supra* note 8, at 400–413.

I next considered whether jurisprudence is better served by interpreting the natural lawyer's substantive claim as a methodological directive: a view about how jurisprudence should proceed. In order to uncover the nature of law, one should study law that succeeds, and law succeeds if it binds the conscience. Understood in this way, there is nothing in the natural lawyer's position that precludes the possibility of immoral laws. His point is simply that such laws are defective in an important sense and that by focusing on them, the legal philosopher misses more than he uncovers about the nature of law.

Finally, I considered the possibility that, in claiming that 'an unjust law is no law at all', the natural lawyer is looking to exploit the very different idea that legality is a normative notion: that certain kinds of legal statements are evaluations or endorsements. Whereas there are problems in rendering the claim that legal judgments are positive assessments consistent with the claim that the concept of immoral law is coherent, both the claim that a particular kind of political virtue is associated with law and the claim that legal judgments convey an endorsement are compatible with any narrow formulation of the separability thesis. Understood in either of these ways, the claim that 'an unjust law is no law at all' is compatible with the separability thesis.

Thus, there is no reason to suppose that, charitably understood, the natural lawyer must reject the separability thesis understood as a claim about the coherence of immoral law. Both legal positivists traditionally understood and natural lawyers *charitably* understood can endorse the separability thesis understood as a claim about the coherence of immoral law. The next question is whether both can endorse the separability thesis as a claim about the existence conditions of legal systems. Before we take on that question directly, let's pursue some of the interesting ideas raised in this section concerning the relationship between law and endorsement.

5.3.2 The Internal Point of View and the Law's Point of View

Arguably, the natural lawyer claims that *no system* of norms can count as a legal system unless it satisfies certain moral standards or displays certain moral ideals or virtues. This is an importantly different claim from the one expressed by Hart, for example, that a legal system can exist only if the bulk of legal officials adopt a distinctive kind of *attitude* toward those norms.[19] He refers to this attitude as the "internal point of view."[20] In the previous discussion, we introduced the idea that there might be a connection between law and the concept of endorsement. We have two interesting ideas before us. The first is that the possibility of law depends on substantive moral constraints; the second is that it depends on a distinctive kind

[19]Hart, *supra* note 7, at 55–57 (discussing the "internal aspect").

[20]Id. at 89–91.

of attitude. The first question is how we should understand that attitude: as moralized or not. On Hart's view, it is enough that officials are disposed to treat legal norms in a characteristic way in their actions and in their practical reasoning. They need not regard the norms as morally legitimate. Alternatively, one can hold the view that the relevant practical attitude is moralized in that those who adopt the law's most fundamental norms regard them as morally legitimate. They endorse the law as legitimate, and their doing so is a necessary condition of legal governance. Let's begin our discussion by first characterizing this view.

As is often true, it is helpful to begin with Raz's familiar idea that law necessarily claims to be a legitimate authority. One way to understand the claim to legitimate authority is this: the law is, among other things, a 'point of view' about what is morally required and permitted. You and I can have different or similar points of view about what reason or morality requires. Oddly perhaps, the law is no different. It, too, takes up or is a point of view about its directives, which is to say that it adopts something like an attitude towards them. It regards them as stating moral requirements and permissions. So as a first approximation, the claim to legitimate authority should be interpreted as the law asserting that—*from its point of view*—its directives always have the appropriate moral force; that is, they express true moral authorizations, permissions, and requirements.

Before pursuing this line of thought further, we need to dispense with a natural but misguided objection. Some might argue that the law is not a person and only persons can have a point of view and so the law has no point of view because it is incapable of having one.[21] Law is not a person, but that does not imply that it is not a point of view, nor does it imply that law cannot take up or express a point of view. Talk of 'the law's point of view' is a way of expressing an idea about law: namely, that there is an underlying moral theory that is implicit in the existence of law, according to which the law's directives not only turn out to be systematically connected to one another, and thus satisfy the demands of rationality and coherence, but also turn out to be morally legitimate. The requirement of systematicity is necessary in order that one can legitimately reason using the law—that is, draw inferences—and the requirement of moral legitimacy is responsive to the fact that law is to play a certain kind of role in practical reason: namely, as a ground for action for officials and those governed by law.

The law does not 'adopt' the law's point of view. It just *is* the law's point of view, or better, expresses a point of view—a way of regarding its norms—which others can adopt or decline to adopt. And if they do, then they accept the idea that there is such a moral theory according to which the law's directives are rationally connected to one another and express morally legitimate authorizations, permissions, and prescriptions. When Dworkin claims that jurisprudence is the silent partner in adjudication, we can understand him as saying that adjudication presupposes the existence of such a theory and judges are each charged with the responsibility of

[21] *See,* e.g., Kenneth Einar Himma, *Positivism and Interpreting Legal Content: Does Law Call for a Moral Semantics?*, 22 Ratio Juris 24, 26–27 (2009).

characterizing as best they can the theory that makes law systematic (or rational—his term is 'fit'[22]) and defensible.[23]

It would be linguistically awkward to characterize the law as *endorsing* its directives, but in a sense that is what law implicitly does. It takes its directives, authorizations, and permissions as invariably justifiable and as appropriately enforceable through coercive means. It holds, as well, that those to whom the law is directed have good reason so to regard it, and it prescribes that they do so or at least that they act as if they had done so.

5.3.2.1 Adopting the Law's Point of View

With this interpretation of the law's relationship to its directives in hand, we can introduce the idea of 'adopting the law's point of view'. To adopt the law's point of view is to adopt the attitude the law takes toward its directives, which is to endorse them as legitimate: to regard them as legitimate and to dispose oneself to reflect that regard in one's actions and practical reasoning.

Our question now is whether the existence of law depends in any way on individuals adopting the law's point of view. The obvious subsidiary questions concern who, if anyone, must adopt the law's point of view. Though it may be desirable that ordinary citizens adopt the law's point of view—thus contributing to what some call the conditions of 'democratic legitimacy'—it is not obvious that ordinary citizens must regard the law as morally legitimate in order for the rules they follow to count as part of a legal system. Hart, for one, was sensitive to the importance of the distinction between citizen and official, for he argued that, in order for law to exist, it is necessary that the bulk of those to whom the law is addressed must comply with its demands, whereas the bulk of officials must adopt a distinctive attitude toward the law—what he famously called "the internal point of view." He also referred to the requirement that there be widespread compliance as an "efficacy condition" of law as opposed to a conceptual constraint on the possibility of law, thereby signaling the kind of significance given to compliance within his conception of law.[24]

If the existence of law depends upon some individuals adopting the law's point of view, those bound to do so are those charged with creating, enforcing, and adjudicating law—officials. It is not necessary that all officials adopt the law's point of

---

[22] *See*, e.g., Dworkin, Law's Empire, *supra* note 8, at 247–266 (discussing the role of "fit").

[23] Among the best discussions of the law's point of view are Raz, *supra* note 23, at 140–143; and Scott J. Shapiro, Legality 184–188 (2011).

[24] Hart, *supra* note 7, at 103–104. My view is that democratic legitimacy does not require that citizens adopt the law's point of view but requires instead an element of fidelity to law. Fidelity is expressed in terms of actions and attitudes displaying 'support' for political institutions: doing one's share to sustain them and to encourage them to act for the common good in accord with the demands of justice. All this is quite different from regarding the law's demands as stating moral requirements or permissions; that is a much stronger constraint.

view—only that most do. Alienation is not an idle possibility, but a common and sometimes welcome and appropriate attitude to take to law—even for legal officials—and any theory of law must have the capacity to explain its possibility and perhaps help us to identify the conditions that are likely to foster it.

Still, law is not possible if *all* (or even if *most*) officials are alienated from it. The very possibility of law thus requires that the bulk of those authorized to exercise the power to constrain the freedom of others adopt the law's point of view. There can be no law if the majority of those situated by law to judge the conduct of others and to determine whether coercion is called for do not adopt the law's point of view—if, for example, they do little more than 'go through the motions' or act in bad faith. The possibility of law allows for alienation and bad faith, but legal governance cannot rest on a foundation of either. There is an important difference between action under the law and acting as if there were law—or so one might plausibly argue.

Particular legal judgments—statements of what the law is, what it requires, permits, or authorizes—may or may not convey an endorsement of its legitimacy. One can report what the law is without endorsing it and without adopting the law's point of view towards it. When such statements are made by someone adopting the law's point of view, however, they express an endorsement of the law's legitimacy and all that legitimacy in the circumstances implies. On the other hand, though adopting the law's point of view entails that those who do so are disposed to endorse its directives, it is not necessary that one adopt the law's point of view in order to endorse the law's directives. One can endorse particular directives—or indeed all of the law's directives individually—without having adopted a disposition to do so.

5.3.2.2 The Internal Point of View and the Law's Point of View

The suggestion to this point is that law presupposes that officials by and large adopt what I am calling the law's point of view, which is to say that they dispose themselves to regard the law's demands as morally legitimate. It is a good question to ask what the relationship is between the law's point of view, so understood, and Hart's notion of the internal point of view.

In Hart's account, law exists only if there is a rule of recognition that is adopted from the internal point of view by those whose conduct is regulated by it—namely, officials.[25] What is the relationship, if any, between this idea and the law's point of view? The internal point of view is a *practical attitude* in two senses of the term 'practical'. First, it is practical in the sense that to adopt the internal point of view towards a rule is *to employ the rule in one's practical reasoning in a distinctive way.* One who adopts the internal point of view towards the rule of recognition disposes

[25] Hart, *supra* note 7, at 116–117; *see also* Shapiro, *supra* note 23, at 93 (describing Hart's account of the internal point of view); Scott J. Shapiro, *What Is the Internal Point of View?*, 75 Fordham L. Rev. 1157, 1164 (2006) (same).

oneself to treating the rule as a standard or norm for determining which rules count as legal standards, which act as authoritative, and so on. Secondly, the internal point of view is practical in that one who adopts it characteristically *acts* in a certain way. To adopt the internal point of view is to dispose oneself to engage in practices of reason giving—displayed in contexts of offering explanations and justifications. As a result, one who adopts the internal point of view towards the rule of recognition offers the rule as a reason for one's judgments of legality and as a basis of one's criticisms of others, and so on. Thus, to adopt the internal point of view is to dispose oneself to reason and to act in certain characteristic ways.

It looks as if there is no real difference between what I am calling "the law's point of view" and what Hart calls "the internal point of view." But this is a mistake as there is an enormous difference between the two. Once we see what the difference is, we can ask which, if either, is necessary for the existence of law.

To see the difference, recall first that in Hart's account one may adopt the internal point of view for a wide array of quite disparate reasons—from the basest of instrumental reasons to the loftiest of moral ones. Law depends on the existence of a collective practice of 'norm adoption' among officials. Hart's account is explicitly inattentive to possible constraints on the reasons officials might have for adopting the rule of recognition as their fundamental guiding norm.

The same cannot be said for adopting the law's point of view towards a rule in general or towards a rule of recognition in particular. To adopt the law's point of view is to be disposed to regard the rule as *morally legitimate* and to act accordingly. One cannot dispose oneself to regard norms as morally legitimate for any old reason. We have to distinguish between reasons (or considerations) of the right kind and reasons of the wrong kind for the adoption of attitudes.

Like belief, resentment, and indignation, both the 'internal point of view' and the 'law's point of view' are attitudes. Attitudes have standards of correctness. These standards identify the grounds for appropriately holding, having, or maintaining the attitude in question. The norms of correctness partially determine what it is to be the attitude in question. They enable us to distinguish between reasons of the right kind and wrong kind for having the attitude in question. Let's see how this works.

The objects of beliefs are propositions. The prevailing—if not universal—view is that the standard of correctness for belief is truth. The only good reasons for believing a proposition are those that bear on its truth. Similar considerations apply to resentment: that is, only considerations tending to show that the person resented has wronged another are reasons of the right sort for resenting him.

Now consider the attitude of 'adopting the law's point of view'. In adopting the law's point of view, one is disposed to regard the law's demands as legitimate. In that case, only considerations that bear on the legitimacy of the law's directives are reasons of the right kind for adopting the attitude. Thus, it is plain that one cannot appropriately adopt the law's point of view for financial or self-interested reasons.

Not so the 'internal point of view'. While Hart tells us nothing about what the standard of correctness for the internal point of view is, he makes very clear that he takes all sorts of considerations for adopting it to be appropriate that would *not* be appropriate for adopting 'the law's point of view'.

If this is right, then the internal point of view is a very different kind of attitude than is the law's point of view. The question is, which, if either, is a necessary condition for the existence of law.

Hart and I differ on this. His view is that the possibility of legal governance presupposes that a sufficient number of officials adopt the internal point of view, whereas I am advancing the view that law is possible only if a sufficient number of relevant officials adopt the law's point of view. It is not enough, in my view, that relevant officials employ the rule of recognition or the other fundamental norms of the legal system in a distinctive way in their practical reasoning and display their adoption of it in characteristic behavior. Their doing so must be part of a practice in which they also regard the norms they are applying as legitimate.

What explains the difference between Hart's view and mine? One reason is that, like Raz and other positivists, I hold that the normative concepts that figure prominently in law—obligation, right, duty, and so on—are employed in their moral sense. Raz and I, for example, hold that legal directives are best understood as claims about what those to whom they are directed are morally required, authorized, or permitted to do.[26]

In contrast, Hart does not believe that the law's normative concepts are employed in their moral sense. He does not deny that law can make a moral difference nor does he deny that law, in fact, often makes a moral difference. He simply resists the idea that law's making a moral difference or its purporting to do so is an essential feature of it. So while those who are empowered by law to create, interpret, and enforce it must, by and large, adopt and be committed to the law's fundamental norms (including the rule of recognition)—a commitment displayed in characteristic behavior—there is no reason why this commitment must be moralized since the law makes no essential moral claims. Thus, Hart's account requires the internal point of view but there is no need to 'moralize' it by connecting it to what I am calling the 'law's point of view'.

Is there a positivist reason for adopting one formulation of the attitude towards law's fundamental norms over the other? A natural thought is that the requirement that officials adopt the law's point of view is inconsistent with positivism and thus unavailable to a positivist. After all, to adopt the law's point of view is to dispose oneself to treating the law's requirements as morally legitimate. How can a positivist insist that the existence of law depends on judges treating legal directives as morally legitimate? If that is right, then Hart's view—that officials must adopt the internal point of view—is best understood as a consequence of his being a positivist. This suggests that I am in the awkward position of being a positivist and yet insisting on the claim that legal governance requires that officials adopt the law's point of view.

Natural though it may be, this thought is seriously mistaken. Remember that to adopt the law's point of view is to adopt an attitude toward the law's directives.

[26] *See,* e.g., Raz, *supra* note 17, at 19 (discussing authority).

It is to regard those laws as morally legitimate and to act accordingly. This does not mean that the laws are legitimate or that their being law depends on their being morally legitimate. Requiring that individuals believe that propositions are true does not render them true. Requiring that individuals regard norms as legitimate does not render them so. Even if legal positivism were incompatible with requiring that norms be morally legitimate to count as law, it is hardly incompatible with positivism to require that officials regard or believe the fundamental legal norms to be morally legitimate.

The requirement that officials regard the law as having that legitimacy—even the requirement that officials regard laws as having that legitimacy entirely in virtue of their being law—is likewise compatible with positivism. The view I am suggesting is not simply that such a requirement is compatible with positivism. Rather, it is that if law is to play the role in our practical and moral lives that it does, then the bulk of those who are charged with making, interpreting, and enforcing law must endorse law as morally legitimate. There is simply no reason that positivism must resist the view that the social practice at the foundation of law is an essentially moralized one. If I am right, it is.

The argument of this Section is twofold: first, that law is possible only if, as a whole, those who are empowered by law and charged by law with its creation, modification, interpretation, and application adopt a moralized attitude toward law—that is, regard the bulk of its directives as morally legitimate; and second, that the existence of such a constraint on legality is perfectly compatible with positivism. If there is a reason for choosing, as Hart does, the internal point of view over what I am calling (following others) 'the law's point of view', the reason cannot be because positivism requires it.

We turn now to two similar but importantly different concerns: First, does the existence of law presuppose substantive moral constraints on governance? Second, if it does, is its doing so compatible with positivism?

5.3.3 Is the Separability Thesis Adequate to Distinguish Positivism from Natural Law? The Existence Conditions of a Legal System

Does a scheme of governance count as a legal system only if it complies with certain moral requirements, embodies certain moral principles, secures or promotes certain moral ends, or some such thing? Are there substantive or procedural moral constraints on the possibility of governance by law? The separability thesis claims that there are no moral constraints on the possibility of governance by law.

Understood as a claim about the existence conditions of legal systems, the separability thesis was an important bone of contention among legal theorists in debates that arose after World War II surrounding the issue of whether Nazi Germany or Vichy France had legal systems. Historically, natural lawyers have insisted that neither had a legal system,[27] whereas positivists have been more inclined to the view that both were governed by law—evil law, but law nonetheless.[28]

Perhaps some self-identified legal positivists hold that there are *no* necessary moral constraints on the existence of legal systems. But without more, their doing so reveals more about them than it does about positivism. No doubt we can imagine some moral constraints on the existence of legal systems that would be at odds with positivism—for example, the constraint that nothing could be a legal system unless the legality of a norm was fully determined by its moral worth. But it hardly follows from the fact that positivism recoils at some moral constraints on legality that it must take a similar attitude to all such constraints. At the same time, we can be sure that natural lawyers endorse some moral constraints on legality—for example, Fuller's so-called 'internal morality of law'. But it hardly follows that natural law endorses any or all possible moral constraints on legality.

If we are going to identify a dispute worth having—or even one worth exploring—we are going to have to identify a class of moral constraints on legal governance that natural lawyers are particularly concerned to endorse that, at least on first blush, one might think legal positivists are especially concerned to resist.

Without pinning the natural lawyer down too narrowly and thereby excluding without argument perfectly plausible formulations of his position, we can identify at least two kinds of relationships between morality and the possibility of law that natural lawyers have been anxious to press. The first is that there are moral principles or ideals that are constitutive of law or distinctive of governance by law. The second is that there are moral ends or aims that governance by law necessarily achieves or necessarily seeks to achieve.

Many legal positivists are quite sympathetic to the second kind of concern. Hart claims that law must have a 'minimal moral content'. Raz claims that law necessarily claims to be a legitimate authority. And Shapiro claims that law has a necessary moral aim. The real bone of contention, then, must be that natural lawyers believe that there are moral principles or ideals that are distinctive of governance by law whereas positivists demur.

Lon Fuller is the paradigmatic example of a natural lawyer who advances the view that there is a morality that is distinctive of legal governance: that is partially constitutive of it. He refers to this as the "internal morality of law": the morality that makes law possible.[29] It is defined by eight canons that include the requirements that the rules must be expressed in general terms, publicly promulgated, prospective in effect, understandable, consistent, capable of being complied with, and so on.[30] In Fuller's view, these canons express moral requirements and satisfying each of

---

[27] *See,* e.g., Lon L. Fuller, *Positivism and Fidelity to Law—A Reply to Professor Hart,* 71 Harv. L. Rev. 630, 633 (1958).

[28] *See,* e.g., H.L.A. Hart, Book Review, 78 Harv. L. Rev. 1281, 1289–1290 (1965) (reviewing Lon L. Fuller, The Morality of Law (1964)).

[29] Lon L. Fuller, The Morality of Law 33–94 (1964).

[30] Id. at 39.

them (to some degree) is necessary to make law. The more fully the canons are satisfied, the better the substance of the law is likely to be. For Fuller, these canons represent a morality that is distinctive of legal governance and constitutive of the very idea of legality.

Fuller's view has been roundly criticized by positivists and anti-positivists alike. Critics have resisted Fuller's claims that the eight canons represent a moral ideal. Hart, for one, argues that the eight canons state norms of efficiency—that is, they are tools one should follow to make laws that are likely to work—not morality.[31] Effective laws can serve immoral—as well as moral— ends.

Fuller's critics are perhaps too quick to dismiss his claim that the eight canons constitute a morality of lawmaking. The fact that the canons express norms of efficiency does not mean that they do not also state requirements of fairness. Arguably, fairness, too, dictates that the coercive authority of the state can only be imposed on individuals for their failure to comply with norms that are, among other things, clearly expressed, capable of being complied with, and articulated in advance.

Even if Fuller is mistaken in thinking that the eight canons he identifies constitute the morality intrinsic to governance by law, the deeper question is whether his critics should be hostile to the idea that there is a morality or a normativity that is distinctive of governance by law. Fuller may or may not have been right in identifying the particular set of principles that are distinctive of legal governance, but he may well have been right in thinking that part of what is distinctive of law is a set of moral ideals, values, or norms partially constitutive of it.

Arguably, one of the ways in which law differs from other ways of regulating or impacting behavior—for example, pricing and sanctioning schemes—is that it reflects or embodies a range of moral ideals and principles. This is my view, for example.

I am inclined to think that part of what makes law the distinctive form of governance that it is—and therefore part of what distinguishes law from other schemes of regulating human affairs, including sanctioning and pricing systems—is that its normative structure reflects a distinctive form of address: a way in which those who make law address those governed by law and the way in which those who are governed by law regard one another. Following Stephen Darwall, I treat law as a system of accountability.[32]

Systems of accountability are characterized by a distinctive interrelated set of concepts—obligation, wrong, guilt, resentment, indignation, authority, and demand—and by modes of regarding one another as equals entitled to respect and concern. Being obligated to another confers on those to whom one is obligated a form of authority. In the first instance, it is an authority to demand compliance.

---

[31] Hart, *supra* note 28, at 1285–1287. Others may argue that those who, in making law, try but fail to comply with these canons need not be morally at fault for their failures; and if this is so, then the canons cannot express moral requirements.

[32] Cf. Stephen Darwall, *Authority and Reasons: Exclusionary and Second-Personal*, 120 Ethics 257, 257–261 (2010) (discussing accountability).

In the event that compliance is not forthcoming, it is an authority to demand an accounting, explanation, and, in many cases, redress or repair. The failure to measure up to one's obligations warrants in others indignation, and where appropriate, resentment. These are simply not features of pricing systems. One responds to a price and acts accordingly in a pricing system. One does not owe others an explanation for what one has done; nor is there a place for notions of redress, recourse, and restitution. Further, failures to respond to prices are not the source of appropriate reactive attitudes of indignation and resentment.

It is not unreasonable to suppose that part of what is distinctive of governance by law is that it embodies or expresses certain moral ideals, and that this is at bottom what distinguishes it from pricing and sanctioning systems. Whether such an argument can be successfully made is not our current concern, though it is clear that I am inclined to think that there is some such argument in the offing.

The existence of unjust laws and evil legal systems is perfectly compatible with law as a form of address that recognizes a person's capacity to respond to reasons and to act upon and for reasons, to respond to demands of compliance, and to redress in the light of the failure adequately to do so. I see no reason why positivism must hold otherwise, and if it must, then I see no reason to be a positivist.

There is an interesting symmetry in our discussion of the separability thesis understood as a claim about the coherence of immoral laws and as a claim about the existence conditions of legal systems. In the first case, our efforts were aimed at demonstrating that, contrary to conventional wisdom, there is no reason to suppose that natural law cannot allow for the coherence of immoral laws, and therefore no reason to suppose that it is incompatible with the narrow formulation of the separability thesis. In the latter case, we find ourselves in the opposite position, arguing that there is nothing in positivism that requires that it resist the possibility of moral constraints on the very possibility of governance by law.

The separability thesis is inadequate to distinguish legal positivism from natural law theory, either as a claim about laws or legal systems. The question that remains is whether it is nevertheless essential to legal positivism.

5.3.4 Is the Separability Thesis Essential to Legal Positivism?

Recall that the conventional wisdom consists of three claims. The first is that the separability thesis is essential to legal positivism. The second is that the separability thesis distinguishes legal positivism from natural law theory. The third is that the separability thesis distinguishes legal positivism from natural law theory *because* it is both essential to legal positivism and incompatible with natural law theory.

The argument to this point shows that neither of the latter two claims is sustainable. Even if the separability thesis is inadequate to distinguish positivism from natural law theory, it may nevertheless be essential to legal positivism. Were it, the significance of its being so would be greatly reduced since part of the interest in its being essential to positivism is based on the importance that fact about it plays in distinguishing natural law from positivism. On the other hand, many take the separability thesis to be the defining characteristic of positivism, so this aspect of the conventional wisdom needs to be addressed as well.

Again, the conventional wisdom comes up short—at least insofar as it purports to represent wisdom. In the first place, I have just argued that legal positivism need not endorse the separability thesis as a claim about constraints on the possibility conditions of law. I argued that law involves a distinctive form of governance marked in part by its commitment to forms of 'address'. These forms of address are constitutive of modes of accountability, which, in turn, reflect certain ideals of equality and concern. To be sure, these ideals are more often than not imperfectly realized (at best) in actual legal systems, but they are constitutive nonetheless of the very idea of governance by law. They are, moreover, part of what distinguishes law from other modes of regulating human affairs, including, notably, pricing and sanctioning systems. If distinctive modes of moral address are a prerequisite of governance by law, then the separability thesis as a claim about the existence conditions of law or the possibility conditions of governance by law is mistaken—and there is no reason why a positivist should insist otherwise. If positivism about legal systems is compatible with rejecting the separability thesis, how can the separability thesis be essential to positivism? That is a rhetorical question.

But there is a much more powerful argument against associating legal positivim with the separability thesis that—at least to my knowledge—has gone unnoticed in the literature. Early on, we demonstrated that legal positivism is compatible with the separability thesis understood as drawing attention to the possibility of immoral laws. It is time to take notice that the arguments that demonstrate the compatibility of legal positivism and the separability thesis, in fact, leave open the possibility that legal positivism is also compatible with rejecting the separability thesis. If positivism could be both compatible and incompatible with the separability thesis, then the obvious conclusion is that legal positivism and the separability thesis have very little, if anything, to do with one another. And that would be a rather shocking conclusion.

In fact, legal positivism is perfectly as compatible with the falsity of the separability thesis as it is with its truth. How can that be?

Note first that legal positivism has been characterized in terms of either of two claims: (1) that an inquiry into the legality of a norm is one thing and that an inquiry into the moral worth of a norm is another; or (2) that the morality of a norm neither settles a norm's legality nor is it settled by it. Legal positivism may well endorse both of these claims (as may other jurisprudential outlooks), yet neither claim is adequate to guarantee immoral laws.

Suppose that there is a necessary constraint on legality, *C*, such that nothing could be law unless it satisfied *C*. *C* is *not* the constraint that 'nothing can be law unless it satisfies the demands of morality', but *C* is such that only moral norms satisfy or can satisfy it. In other words, any norm that satisfies *C* also has the property of being compatible or consistent with the relevant standards of morality.[33]

[33] We set aside the question of whether it is a necessary or contingent truth that any norm that satisfies *C* also satisfies the demands of morality.

In that case: (1) the inquiry into a norm's morality and into its legality would remain two distinct activities; yet, (2) no norm could count as law unless it satisfied the relevant requirements of morality. This means that, understood in the usual way, legal positivism is compatible with either endorsing or rejecting the separability thesis, and this is surely something of a surprise.

If legal positivism is compatible both with the separability thesis and its rejection, the separability thesis can hardly be an essential feature of positivism or otherwise definitional of it.

I have, thus, made good on all the claims with which the discussion began. For we have shown that the separability thesis is inadequate to distinguish legal positivism from natural law theory and that it is not essential to legal positivism. Much remains to be done, however. First, we must take up the second nugget of the conventional wisdom: namely, the view that substantive and methodological views in jurisprudence travel together. Second, we can ask, if the separability thesis fails to distinguish legal positivism from natural law theory, then what, if anything, does. Third, we can ask, once we have discarded the conventional wisdom, with what are we to replace it. The answer is a new architecture of jurisprudence.

5.4 The Methodology of Jurisprudence

A substantive jurisprudence provides a (hopefully) unified set of solutions to fundamental problems that arise regarding law and legal practice. Though it is controversial which issues a jurisprudence must address, most commentators would agree the most basic issues concern the essential nature of law or our concept of it, the role law plays in our practical lives, and the relationship between the two. In contrast, a methodological jurisprudence is a view about the way in which these substantive issues should be approached—the methods apt for the inquiry at hand and the tools appropriate to those methods.

The conventional view is that substantive and methodological views in jurisprudence 'travel together'. Legal positivists about the nature of law are positivists (or descriptivists) about the methods and philosophical tools suitable to jurisprudence, and natural lawyers about law are 'normativists' about the methods appropriate to jurisprudential inquiry. Before we can assess the conventional wisdom we need to be much more precise about the differences between normative and descriptive or analytic methodologies in jurisprudence.

For expository purposes, let's suppose, along with Hart, that the main project of a substantive jurisprudence is to analyze or provide an account of the concept of law, and that to provide an account of the concept of law is to characterize what it is about law that makes it the thing that it is. Once we understand what it is that makes law the thing that it is, we would then be in a position to explain the ways in which it is both similar to—and different from—other mechanisms for regulating human affairs. And hopefully, we will have the resources to explain how it is that law plays the role it does in our practical lives. If this is not the entirety of jurisprudence or its main focus, it has been a large and important part of it, and thus provides a useful vehicle for distinguishing among different methodological approaches.

5.4.1 In What Sense Is Normative Jurisprudence Normative?

Unsurprisingly, there are a number of quite distinct ways in which a methodology can be said to be normative and so a good deal of clarification is in order.

Norms and criteria. In one sense, every philosophical theory of a concept,[34] whether otherwise normative or descriptive, has a normative dimension or ambition. After all, a philosophical account of a concept sets out criteria for its proper use. This is true of a theory of the concepts of liberty, justice, and law, but it is also true of the concepts of mind, truth, and knowledge. All theories of all concepts are thus necessarily normative in this limited sense, and if this is all one means by calling a theory of law normative, then all theories of law are normative. In that case, there is nothing of interest or importance in the distinction between normative and analytic or descriptive theories for the simple reason that all theories of concepts—including descriptive ones—are normative. There is no distinction worth making: no 'fight' worth having.

Norms and theory assessment. How do we choose among different theories of the nature of law or, for that matter, the nature of anything—liberty, law, justice, truth, knowledge, or mind? What are the criteria of theory assessment?

Criteria are norms and so there is a sense in which all theory assessment is normative. But criteria for assessing theories can be either theoretical or normative in a further sense. What is that further sense, and how does theory assessment that is normative differ from descriptive or analytic norms of theory assessment? We can illustrate the distinctions I have in mind if we focus for a moment on the concept of liberty.

On one conception of it, liberty is understood in terms of a capacity to impose a distinctive form of constraint, namely, self-regulation; on another, it is associated with the absence of constraint altogether; while on a third it is associated with the absence of a particular kind of constraint, namely, political coercion; yet, on still another, it is associated with the special place of agency in our lives; and so on. How would we choose among these (and other possible conceptions) as the correct or best account of the nature of liberty?

Descriptive or analytic criteria focus on theoretical grounds for assessing theories. These include a theory's predictive and explanatory prowess; its consilience, elegance,

[34] My emphasis is on philosophical theories of concepts, for we can imagine a certain kind of sociological theory of a concept whose ambition is merely to describe existing use, or differences among existing usages in different cultures. My claim that all theories are normative in this sense is confined to philosophical theories.

and simplicity; and especially its intuitive plausibility or relative invulnerability to hypothetical counterexamples—what Wayne Sumner calls "descriptive adequacy."[35]

Arguably, the way we think about certain fundamental ideas has an impact on how our lives go—individually and collectively. Ideas matter in the sense of having practical consequences. To say that theories can be assessed normatively might be to say that they should be chosen by their political or practical consequences. The best theory of liberty is the one that has the best practical consequences: that is, the one that makes or is likely to make the biggest improvement in individuals' lives.

Concepts need not have practical consequences in order for the criteria of correctness for them to be normative. Instead, theories of concepts can be assessed by their fit within sound political arguments or theories. In this sense, the best theory of liberty falls out of the best political theory of the place of liberty in political, social, and economic life.

Norms and theory construction. We can distinguish the view that theory assessment must be normative from a related but nevertheless distinct view that *theory construction* must be normative. There is a familiar view in philosophy that an analysis of a concept should not be any normative questions.[36] So, for example, an account of the nature of 'valuable', 'desirable', or 'blameworthy' should not exclude or beg the question against any plausible substantive view about what is valuable, desirable, or blameworthy. In the case of liberty, an account of the nature of liberty should leave open questions about whether liberty is valuable and, if so, why.

Others worry that to characterize liberty in a way that is removed from its place in the normative landscape cannot help but render our understanding of the nature of liberty fundamentally flawed or incomplete. Surely liberty is something of value and in order to determine the nature of liberty we must begin with a working hypothesis of why having liberty is valuable to those who have it and why those who lack political and personal liberty are disadvantaged or wronged as a result.

If one accepts that the value of liberty partly makes liberty the thing that it is, then, in order to analyze what liberty is, one needs to identify the value that it has. It is one thing to say that liberty is valuable and another to identify what its value is. One kind of theorist might ascribe the Kantian values of self-regulation to liberty and then provide an account of what liberty is that picks out or privileges certain features of liberty in the light of the significance of liberty for self-regulation. A utilitarian might ascribe to liberty various values associated with maximizing human welfare and then illuminate the nature of liberty by picking out or emphasizing

---

[35]L.W. Sumner, Welfare, Happiness, and Ethics 10–20 (1996).

[36]It is common in philosophy to refer to the project of providing an analysis of a normative concept as metaethics. So to give an account of the nature of a normative predicate like 'good' or 'desirable' is not to determine which things are good or desirable. Thus, the view on which to say that something is 'desirable' or 'valuable' is to say no more than that 'there are reasons to desire or to value it' is a view that offers at least a partial account of those predicates. It is not to determine which things in the world are desirable or valuable. A theory whose aim is to provide criteria for determining which things, if any, are desirable or valuable is a normative, not a metaethical, theory.

those features of it that are especially significant for liberty to contribute to maximizing human well-being.

Only with this value in place can we proceed to identify what is central to liberty or of what it consists. The account of liberty explains why it has the value that the theory assigns to it and, thus, cannot proceed other than by ascribing a substantive yet contestable value to it. The differences between conflicting theories of the nature of liberty can thus often be traced to the fact that theorists ascribe different values to having liberty or weigh the same or similar values differently.[37]

We can distinguish between narrower and broader forms of normativism about theory construction. Narrower versions restrict themselves to the claim that one must ascribe a value only to normative predicates or concepts in order to understand their nature or to uncover the content of the concepts that refer to them. Broader versions hold that the set of interpretive concepts extends beyond the set of normative predicates and that in principle most, if not all, philosophically interesting concepts call for normative theory construction.

Given this formulation of normativism in theory construction, how would we best characterize analytic or descriptivist alternatives? One form of descriptivism is simply unmoved by this alleged normativist insight and insists that normative concepts like liberty and law are no different from other philosophically interesting concepts such as belief, knowledge, mind, and truth. One does not have to ascribe a value to belief, knowledge, mind, and truth to analyze them, and the same is true of normative predicates.

To support his claim, the descriptivist may call attention to familiar debates in the metaethics of normative predicates that have little, if anything, to do with fundamental normative matters, and whose resolution does not depend in any obvious way on matters of first-order morality—that is, on matters of value, goodness, rightness, or the like. Here is an example of what he has in mind.

There is a familiar and important dispute among metaethicists whether something's being valuable or desirable is a fact about it that can be a ground or reason for valuing or desiring it. Some hold that it can be.[38] Others disagree. They hold what is nowadays called a 'buck-passer' view according to which to say that something is valuable or desirable is just to say that there are grounds for valuing or desiring it; it is to assert the existence of grounds or reasons, not to provide one.[39]

---

[37]Dworkin refers to concepts in which the ascription of value is essential to their analysis as "interpretive concepts." *See,* e.g., Dworkin, Law's Empire, *supra* note 8, at 49.

[38]*See,* e.g., T.M. Scanlon, What We Owe to Each Other 97 (1998) (attributing this view to G.E. Moore); Pekka Väyrynen, *Resisting the Buck-Passing Account of Value*, *in* 1 Oxford Studies in Metaethics 295–324 (Russ Shafer-Landa ed., 2006), *available at* http://www.personal.leeds.ac.uk/~phlpv/papers/buck.pdf; Wlodek Rabinowicz & Toni Rønnow-Rasmussen, *The Strike of the Demon: On Fitting Pro-Attitudes and Value*, 114 Ethics 391 (2004).

[39]*See,* e.g., Franz Brentano, The Origin of Our Knowledge of Right and Wrong 18–19 (Roderick M. Chisholm ed., Roderick M. Chisholm & Elizabeth H. Schneewind trans., Routledge & Kegan Paul 1969) (1889); Scanlon, *supra* note 38, at 97; Richard Brandt, *Moral Valuation*, 56 Ethics 106, 113 (1946).

Something is desirable if and only if there are good reasons for desiring it; something is valuable if and only if there are good grounds for valuing it; and so on.[40]

There is little reason to suppose that in order to resolve this dispute (or many others) in the metaethics of normative predicates one needs first to determine which things in the world are valuable and why. There is no pressure to ascribe a value to the valuable or to the desirable in order to work out accounts of these concepts. Surely, metaethics is possible. There is no reason to suppose that analytic or descriptive accounts of normative predicates in general are impossible and no reason to suppose therefore that they are unavailable for 'law' and 'liberty'.

In a way, this descriptivist is entirely unmoved by the difference between normative and other predicates. He sees no reason to abandon traditional metaethics in favor of the view that 'it is all normative or first-order ethics' all the way down. I do not mean to dispute this formulation of descriptivism, but it is not the only one that is available. It is possible to give the normativist more credit than this descriptivist does. For the normativist is surely right that liberty, for example, is something of value and to miss this fact about it is to distort the nature of liberty. The question is how to capture this feature of liberty—its value—in constructing an account of what liberty is.

We begin by assuming that any theory of the concept of liberty must be responsive to liberty being something of value: those who have it possess something valuable and desirable; and those who have less, little, or none of it are missing something valuable or desirable. The normative methodologist believes that the way to represent this fact about liberty is to ascribe a contestable conception of its value as the first step in constructing an account of it.

This is not the only way to accommodate in theory construction the fact that liberty is valuable. As a descriptivist, I think there is a better way of responding to this fact about liberty. The better approach is to accommodate the fact that liberty is valuable by imposing an *adequacy condition* on a theory of the nature of liberty to the effect that in order to be adequate or persuasive, an account of the nature of liberty must have the resources to explain what is valuable about liberty. Just as consilience, predictive efficiency, explanatory power, and resistance to counterexamples are criteria for assessing accounts of liberty, so, too, is explaining its value. One might even argue that this desideratum of a theory of liberty is simply a consequence of the others—especially, perhaps, consilience and immunity to counterexamples.

To get a better idea of how this line of argument goes, recall Hart's powerful objection to Austin's theory of law.[41] Austin characterized law as the command of a sovereign properly so called backed by a threat of sanction.[42] Thus, the conceptual resources available in Austin's account include commands, threats, habits of obedience, and sovereigns, some of which—like the concept of the sovereign—are

[40] *See* Scanlon, *supra* note 38, at 96–98 (1998).

[41] Hart, *supra* note 7, at 18–25.

[42] Austin, *supra* note 6, at 13–33.

defined in terms of the others. Hart objected on the grounds that the concept of obligation is central to law and that the resources available in Austin's jurisprudence provide inadequate resources to draw the distinction law makes between being *obliged* to comply with a directive and being *obligated* to do so. At gunpoint, one can be *obliged* to do all manner of things one is under no obligation to do; indeed, one may be obliged to do things one is obligated *not* to do. This is the upshot of Hart's notorious 'gunman example'.[43]

In effect, I am making the same kind of argument about liberty that Hart makes about law. Among the phenomena that a theory of law must explain is the difference between being obligated (by law) and being obliged. The resources available in Austin's account are not up to that task and thus his theory of law is unpersuasive. Among the phenomena that a theory of liberty must explain is its value or significance. A theory does not have to proceed as the normativist would have by assuming a particular contestable conception of its value. Quite the contrary, in fact, the theorist must confront the fact that whatever theory he offers, it must have the resources adequate to explain why liberty is valuable. Arguably, it is a comparative advantage of this form of descriptivism that the better accounts of liberty will be those that can explain why having liberty is valuable within a wide range of quite distinct political or moral theories, from liberalism to libertarianism to utilitarianism—all of which value liberty but do so for different reasons. In contrast, those who adopt the normative approach to theorizing about liberty begin by ascribing a *particular* contestable value to liberty, and then provide an account of liberty that is fit to *that* value—and not to the many different ways in which liberty is valuable according to different political theories.

We have now distinguished among three ways in which a normative jurisprudence could be normative: criteria of usage, assessment, and construction. The next step is to determine which notion of normative methodology is being presupposed by the conventional wisdom. All theories are normative in the first sense—as setting out criteria—and so this is not the sense of normative that can be at stake in the conventional wisdom. This leaves us with two options: the normativity that may or may not be suitable to theory assessment or the normativity that may or may not be involved in theory construction. The claim that theories should be assessed by normative criteria holds that the test of correctness for theories of the concept of law is 'normative', and that by normative, one could mean either 'best political consequences' or 'best political argument'.

In either case, the conventional wisdom that substantive and methodological theories 'travel together' would be ill-fated and could not withstand even cursory analysis. That is because many contemporary legal positivists defend positivism as the correct theory of law on straightforwardly *normative* grounds. And many defending versions of substantive natural law do so employing the traditional methods of analytic philosophy. Tom Campbell, Jeremy Waldron, and Gerald Postema

---

[43]*See* Hart, *supra* note 7, at 6–7 (arguing that treating laws as commands backed by threats collapses the distinction between being obligated and being obliged).

fall into the first category[44]; Michael Moore, Nicos Stavropoulos, and Mark Greenberg fall into the second.[45]

If there is a viable claim to be recovered from this piece of the conventional wisdom, it is that those defending substantive positivism adopt a descriptive or analytic methodology of theory *construction*, whereas those who defend a natural law substantive jurisprudence adopt the view that an account of law must proceed through substantive political theory. This is the only plausible claim that those who endorse the conventional wisdom could have in mind.

Is it accurate?

5.4.2 Do Substantive and Methodological Jurisprudential Views 'Travel Together'?

When it comes to substantive jurisprudence, Hart famously held the narrow formulation of the separability thesis and insisted on the distinction between inquiry into the validity of a norm and the norm's moral worth. And when it came to methodological matters, in the preface to *The Concept of Law*, Hart famously referred to his method as "descriptive sociology."[46] For Hart, to determine the nature of law one must inquire into its usage—the linguistic practices in which it figures. The analysis of the concept of law proceeds independently of and prior to the normative project of determining the distinctive value (if any) of governance by law. Thus, Hart is both a substantive positivist and a methodological descriptivist.

For Ronald Dworkin, the project of substantive jurisprudence is to settle on the grounds of law, the facts that are the truth makers for propositions of law. These necessarily include normative facts: facts about the distinctive value of law that purport to justify the use of coercion. When it comes to methodology, Dworkin holds that law is an interpretive concept and that one can understand its nature only in the light of the value one assigns to it. Thus, Dworkin is both a substantive and a methodological normativist. As for the conventional wisdom, then, so far so good. Unfortunately, the good news ends here.

There are many important issues that political theory addresses, few if any more pressing than the justification of coercion—the use of collective force in the name of all against some. A natural view is that political coercion is justified if and only

---

[44] *See* Tom Campbell, Prescriptive Legal Positivism: Law, Rights and Democracy (2004); Gerald J. Postema, Bentham and the Common Law Tradition 302–336 (1986); Jeremy Waldron, Law and Disagreement (1999).

[45] Nicos Stavropoulos, Objectivity in Law (1996); Greenberg, *How Facts Make Law*, *supra* note 8; Michael S. Moore, *Legal Reality: A Naturalist Approach to Legal Ontology*, 21 Law & Phil. 619 (2002); Stephen R. Perry, *Hart's Methodological Positivism*, *in* Hart's Postscript 311 (Jules Coleman ed., 2001).

[46] Hart, *supra* note 7, at vi.

if justice requires it. Though initially plausible, this answer simply will not do, for there are many valid claims of personal or private justice that are not the business of the state, while the state's power may be legitimately deployed for reasons other than justice.

Dworkin's view is that a necessary feature of law is that it purports to answer the question what, if anything, justifies political coercion. From the law's point of view, the collective use of force is justified 'when the law calls for it'. This is both a way of expressing and of exploiting a view about law's possible connection to political coercion.

If law is connected to political morality in the sense of purporting to express the conditions under which political coercion is justified, law must be the sort of thing that in principle could justify coercion. This means that there must be some value associated with governance by law that could serve (in principle) to justify coercion. An analysis of the nature of law then proceeds first by ascribing a value to law presumably adequate or at least of the right sort to justify coercion. With that value in place, various features of law and their relationship to one another are explained by reference to it. The value helps to identify the features that are central to law, while weeding out less important ones. These features, once woven together, help explain the fact that law has the value that it does. The value ascribed to law is itself presumably adequate to justify the collective use of force. Different jurisprudential outlooks ascribe different, even conflicting values to law and thus identify somewhat different features of law as central to it.

The reader familiar with Dworkin's methodology will recognize that this is the core of his interpretive method.[47] While it should surprise no one that Dworkin adopts a normative methodology of jurisprudence, it surely will surprise many to learn that the leading contemporary legal positivist Joseph Raz also adopts a normative methodology of jurisprudence. Whereas for Dworkin the key legal relationship is coercion, for Raz, it is *authority*. According to Raz, law necessarily claims to be a legitimate authority.[48] Raz does not require that law's claim to authority be true, let alone that it be necessarily true. In fact, Raz believes that the state lacks authority over some subjects.[49] Raz's point is that even if the claim is often false, it cannot be necessarily false—that is, it must be the sort of claim that could be true.[50]

---

[47] *See* Dworkin, Law's Empire, *supra* note 8. It is worth noting that the standard understanding of that method in which 'fit' and 'value' are taken to be not only distinct standards an interpretation must satisfy, but independent standards as well, is mistaken. For the features of law that must fit together are, in fact, partially determined by the value ascribed to law, and so, fit and value are not wholly independent. And it is certainly not true that first one applies the criterion of fit and then the criterion of value. Quite the opposite is the case. In any event, given our current purposes, the important point is that an inquiry into the nature of law proceeds through substantive political theory in the form of an account of the conditions that justify political coercion.

[48] Raz, *supra* note 17, at 28–33.

[49] Joseph Raz, The Morality of Freedom 76–80 (1986).

[50] Joseph Raz, *Authority, Law and Morality*, 68 Monist 295, 301 (1985).

If the claim to legitimate authority could be true of law—whether or not it actually is in a given case—then law must be the sort of thing of which the claim to legitimate authority could be true. Thus, the nature of law is constrained by the account of the conditions of legitimate authority; for whatever law is, it must be the sort of thing that could be a legitimate authority, whatever consists in being a legitimate authority. For Raz, the nature of law must be approached through first-order political philosophy—the theory of legitimate authority.

For both Dworkin and Raz, one must approach the nature of law by addressing a problem in first-order political philosophy: the justification of coercion in Dworkin's case, the conditions of legitimate authority in Raz's.[51] For our purposes, the important point is that Dworkin, the natural lawyer, and Raz, the substantive positivist, are both normativists when it comes to the methodology suitable for jurisprudence. Both hold that one can determine the nature of law only by first addressing a fundamental problem in first-order political philosophy. The nature or essence of law is accessible only by understanding law's relationship to fundamental issues of substantive political morality. Consequently, Raz, the substantive positivist, is a methodological normativist.

Thus, the nugget of conventional wisdom that substantive and methodological positivism travel with one another cannot be sustained. If the separability thesis does little more than distract us from the core issues of jurisprudence, shifting focus to the methodological dispute between descriptivists and normativists does even less to illuminate the important differences among jurisprudential views, and less still the fundamental problems of jurisprudence.

If I am right, then both nuggets of the conventional wisdom must be set aside. Freed from the grasp of the conventional wisdom, I want first to get clear the truth about the relationship between legal positivism and the separability thesis. The conventional wisdom is not only mistaken, but to an extent it actually has the relationship backwards. The most familiar and persuasive forms of positivism actually presuppose that law and morality are necessarily connected. That's right: they are based on rejecting the separability thesis, not on endorsing it. If discarding the conventional wisdom means that progress is to be made, let's start by making some.

5.5 The Truth About Positivism and the Separability Thesis

Let's start with a simple idea. Assume for a moment that legal statements are assertions—rather than, say, commands, orders, or expressions of attitudes. Assertions are distinguishable from commands since they can be either true or false. If I order you to

[51] Coercion can be justified in the absence of authority. And authority (in my view) is essential to law in a way in which coercion (for all its importance) is not. These are points that to his credit Raz has long emphasized and exploited.

close the door, the sentence, 'I ordered you to close the door' asserts something that can either be true or false (true if I did so order, false if I did not), whereas the sentence 'Close the door!' is not capable of being true or false. It is a command, not an assertion. For the purposes of the following discussion, we assume that legal sentences are assertions: they assert that one is prohibited from doing *X*; is authorized to do *Y*; or has the power to do *Z*; and so on.

Because legal sentences are assertions, they can be either true or false. They assert the existence of facts that, if they obtain, would make the assertions true. Legal sentences are true if true to the facts and false otherwise. But which facts make legal sentences true? The answer is the obvious one: the relevant legal facts. Legal facts are the truth makers of legal sentences. In some sense, this answer is surprisingly illuminating. If it is a fact in a particular jurisdiction, *J*, that individuals under the law possess the power to *Z*, then the sentence 'In *J* individuals are free under the law to *Z*' is true.

Legal facts are not basic facts, which is to say that they are facts that obtain in virtue of other facts obtaining. The idea is simple enough. Let's suppose that it is a fact in our imaginary jurisdiction, *J*, that individuals have the power and discretion to *Z*. They are neither required to *Z* nor does the law prohibit them from doing so. We might ask, what makes it a fact that in *J* people have the power to *Z* if they want to? Is it because it would be good for people to have that power? Is it because most people believe they have that power? Is it because a legislature gave them that power? Is it because people want to have that power? Is it because a court said they have that power? And so on. It is some or all of these other facts that create the relevant legal facts.

In philosophy, we typically express this idea in terms of the notion of supervenience.[52] Legal facts supervene on other facts. The facts on which legal facts supervene make legal facts the facts that they are. The most fundamental question in the metaphysics of law is: What kinds of facts can contribute to legal content—to the law having the content that it does? What are the facts on which legal facts supervene? A related question is: How do these facts come together to give law the content that it has? In this Article, our focus will be limited to the first of these questions.

Let's begin by distinguishing between two different views about the kinds of facts that can contribute to legal content—to the law having the content that it has. Let's use the examples already at our disposal. We are imagining that in jurisdiction *J*, it is a crime to *X* and also that everyone is free to *Z*. Now we ask ourselves: How are those the facts about the law in *J*? Is it the case that it is a crime to *X* because *X*-ing is a particularly bad thing to do? Or is it the case that it is a crime to *X* in *J* because the legislature acted in a particular way, i.e., passed a rule prohibiting *X*-ing

[52] There are many definitions of supervenience. Supervenience is a 'dependence relationship'. *A* supervenes upon *B* implies that *A* depends on *B*. Supervenience is a distinctive kind of dependence relationship that for our purposes we will characterize as: *A* supervenes upon *B* if and only if there can be no change in *A* without a corresponding change in *B*.

or making it a crime to *X*? Similar remarks are in order regarding the power to *Z*. Is it the case in *J* that individuals have the power to *Z* in virtue of it being desirable, efficient, or wonderful that individuals be allowed to *Z*, or is it the case that persons are free to *Z* in *J* because a court recognized such a privilege or liberty or because a legislature conferred it?

On one view, the content of the law—what it requires, permits, or authorizes those to whom it is addressed to do—is fixed by facts about behavior and attitude: what individuals say and do and the attitudes (including intentions and beliefs) they and others have or take in response to or as part of those sayings and doings. This is the view that if it is a crime to *X* in *J* or if individuals have the power to *Z* in *J* it is because certain individuals (e.g., legislatures and courts) acted in a particular way. To be sure, a judge or legislator may have been moved to act in the requisite way—cast one's vote for the enactment of a statute for example—having been moved by the fact that *X*-ing is bad or that it would be good for individuals to have a power to *Z*. Still, it is the action that makes it the law, not the morality of *X*-ing and *Z*-ing. *X* may be a bad thing to do and *Z* a good option for persons to have, but unless and until legislatures or courts act, it is neither against the law to *X* nor a power under the law to *Z*. This is what it means to say that, on one view, legal facts supervene on social facts: facts about behavior, attitudes and beliefs. It is controversial whose behavior and attitudes count, but there is no reason for us to reach that question at this stage of the argument.

On another view, what the law requires of those to whom it is directed depends on what is *right*, *good*, *just*, *fair*, or *valuable* in addition to what individuals feel, say, and do.[53] We can distinguish between two versions of this view. According to the first, the law supervenes on normative facts alone. So in this view, if we wanted to know whether or not it is the law in *J* that it is a crime to *X*, we need only determine whether *X*-ing is wrong or otherwise undesirable or unsavory. The more familiar and promising version of the view at hand is that normative facts as well as social facts contribute to the law having the content that it does. On this view, it is not enough that *X*-ing is bad or *Z*-ing desirable to make the former criminal and the latter legally optional. In addition, the legislature or the courts must act. On the other hand, their acting is not enough to make it law either. The moral worth of the directives they issue bear on what the legal facts of the matter are.

We can say that on the first view, only social facts—facts about behavior and attitude—contribute to legal content; whereas in the second view, normative

[53] Thus the view that what the U.S. Constitution requires or permits is determined not only by what the Framers said and did and what judges and Justices since the Founding have said and done, but also by how it is received within the community as a whole—what Robert Post calls the "constitutional culture"—falls into the first category. *See* Robert C. Post, *The Supreme Court, 2002 Term—Foreword: Fashioning the Legal Constitution: Culture, Courts, and Law*, 117 Harv. L. Rev. 4, 8 (2003). A view that holds that what the law requires depends on what individuals *believe* is just or fair to demand of one another is also a view of the first sort. The view that the content of the law depends on what is in fact just or fair, right or wrong, etc., represents a view of the second sort.

facts—including especially, moral facts—contribute to law having the content that it does.

We may put these distinctions more precisely:

(1) Only social facts can determine the content of law. Law has the content that it does *in virtue of facts about individual (or group) behavior and attitudes: that is, in virtue of social facts.*

If only social facts can contribute to determining what the law requires of those to whom it is directed or what it authorizes or permits them to do, then moral or evaluative facts—facts about what ought to be done, what would be good to do or valuable (and the like)—cannot. This feature of (1) makes for a natural contrast with:

(2) Only normative (evaluative or moral) facts contribute to the content of law. Legal facts are the facts that they are—i.e., have the content that they do—in virtue only of certain moral or evaluative facts obtaining. What the law is—what it requires, permits, or authorizes—depends entirely on what is good, desirable, valuable, or ought morally to be done.

(1) and (2) do not exhaust the possibilities. Thus:

(3) Both normative and social facts contribute to legal content. According to this view, what the law is—how it is that it has the content that it does—can depend on either or both social as well as normative facts.

In *Negative and Positive Positivism*,[54] I defended (3) as consistent with the core ideals of legal positivism. I argued there that positivism is compatible with incorporating moral facts into law provided those facts are incorporated in a way that is consistent with positivism. The question is: What does 'incorporation consistent with positivism' mean? In that paper, I exploited Hart's idea of a rule of recognition. The rule of recognition is a social rule. A social rule is the conjunction of shared behavior and a shared attitude towards that behavior. The latter is Hart's notion of the internal point of view. So a social rule is constituted by social facts: facts about behavior and attitudes towards that behavior. Thus, I argued if the rule of recognition incorporates morality, its doing so is compatible with legal positivism because it is compatible with the idea that the foundation of all law is social facts or social practices. Law ultimately depends on what people do and say and the attitudes they have, and not on what is just, fair, good, right, or wrong.

So for now if we treat (1) as characterizing exclusive legal positivism, (2) as natural law theory, and (3) as inclusive legal positivism, we can uncover the truth about the relationship between positivism and the separability thesis.[55] And a surprising truth it is.

---

[54] Coleman, *supra* note 2.

[55] We will have occasion below to reconsider these characterizations and to make significant changes. The argument below is not impacted by whatever modifications in characterizing these notions we ultimately come to.

5.5.1 *Judges Are People Too*

Joseph Raz recently has offered an objection to the view that the law can incorporate morality and, thus, to the view that normative or moral facts can contribute to legal content. This objection is based on the obvious and uncontroversial fact that judges are people too.[56] In a nutshell, the argument goes something like this:

Judges are people, and people generally have the capacity for agency. To have the capacity for agency is to be responsive to reasons. Rational agency requires that one respond to the reasons that apply to him. The issue each agent faces is what to do—what action to undertake. The answer depends on the balance of reasons that apply to the agent at that time. This is true whether one is a judge or an ordinary citizen. It is the nature of morality that its reasons always apply to agents. That is, it is always the case that what one ought to do depends in part (or in whole, depending on one's view of normativity) on what morality calls for. Moral considerations may be silent in a particular case or leave one free to pursue an option of one's own choosing, but they always bear on the question of what is to be done.

If morality always applies to agents, then it is a confusion to think—as inclusive legal positivism does—that it is within law's power to make moral reasons apply to officials. In other words, if inclusive legal positivism were correct, then, short of the law incorporating morality, moral considerations would not bear on what a judge ought to do. But this cannot be right since moral considerations always bear on what one ought to do, whether one is a judge or an ordinary citizen to whom the law is directed. The problem with inclusive legal positivism is that it attributes to law a power that law simply could not possess. Morality's role in determining what a judge ought to do cannot depend on what the law has to say about it.[57]

---

[56] Joseph Raz, *Incorporation by Law*, 10 Legal Theory 1, 2 (2004).

[57] In conversation, Alex Sarch has suggested a possible response to the Razian argument that I will not pursue in this paper, but that needs to be addressed more fully at some point. His argument is this:

Against inclusive legal positivism (ILP), Raz in effect argues that: (1) If ILP is true, then in the absence of a practice among officials of 'incorporating' morality into law, moral considerations would not apply to them (i.e., would not constrain judges' legal decisions). (2) But moral considerations *do* apply to judges (since "judges are people too"). (3) Therefore, ILP is not true.

Sarch suggests that a proponent of ILP might respond to this argument by rejecting premise (1). Perhaps he could say that even if there were no practice of incorporation, morality would still apply to judges, except that the (moral) reasons he would have to decide this way or that would be different, i.e., different from they would be had a practice of incorporation existed. Regardless of whether there is a practice of incorporation or not, morality would still direct judges to *do their duty*, i.e., to vigilantly and indifferently apply the law as given. The only difference is that without a practice of incorporation, the law to be applied would not contain moral tests, while *with* such a practice, the law to be applied would contain such tests. Thus, whether or not there is a practice of incorporation, morality would still "apply" to judges; i.e., it would direct them to do their duty and apply the law as given. It is just that the content of the law to be applied would be different depending on whether a practice of incorporation exists.

5.5.2 *Morality and Law's Place*

Because morality applies regardless of the content of the law, it cannot be up to law to determine the nature and scope of morality's application to actions governed by law. If anything, rather than law incorporating morality, as the inclusive legal positivist would have it, morality 'incorporates' law. Whereas law lacks the power to incorporate morality, morality and only morality has the power to 'incorporate' law.

What does it mean to say that morality and only morality has the power to incorporate law? We can suppose that there are any number of different considerations that can bear on what one has reason to do—what one ought to do all things considered. Law, etiquette, self-interest, autonomy, and more can bear on what we have reason to do. So, too, can prices: if I have reason to feed my family as best as possible within my budget, then if the price of a luxury item increases, I have reason to buy less of it, other things being equal. A change in prices impacts what I have reason to do.

The question is whether and in what way law and other considerations bear on what we have moral reason to do. If we must always do what morality requires us to do, then the only time we would be permitted to act on the basis of considerations that appear to be 'non-moral' is when morality itself counsels us to do so. It follows that one should act on the basis of *the law's reasons* only when morality counsels that one do so.

Of course, this immediately raises the question of when morality so counsels. The answer is that acting on the basis of law's directives is required by morality only when doing so 'serves' morality—that is, makes it more likely that one will conform to the requirements of morality than one otherwise would. Law serves morality insofar as it creates new moral reasons for acting, identifies the action called for by the balance of reasons, or makes concrete, in a given set of circumstances, what morality requires. To the extent that law serves morality, morality provides a place for law. Morality defines the place of law within rational agency and for action based on law's demands. This is the sense in which morality incorporates law, and not, as inclusive legal positivism would have it, the other way around.

5.5.3 *From Law to Positivism About Law*

Working from the simple premise that judges are people too, we have been able to put in place two important and related ideas: the first is that it is not up to law to incorporate morality; the second is that the place of law is determined by morality. To this pool of resources we should add a proper formulation of Raz's claim about authority. In *Authority and Justification*, Raz provides a familiar formulation of the 'normal justification thesis'. He writes:

> [T]he normal and primary way to establish that a person should be acknowledged to have authority over another person involves showing that the alleged subject is likely better to

> comply with reasons which apply to him (other than the alleged authoritative directives) if he accepts the directives of the alleged authority as authoritatively binding and tries to follow them, rather than by trying to follow the reasons which apply to him directly.[58]

With these elements in place, we can derive exclusive legal positivism as a conclusion of a valid argument employing the idea that law serves morality, the claim that law is a legitimate authority, and Raz's particular theory of authority.

(1) One should always act on the balance of reasons, which is to say that one ought to do what morality calls for (or permits).
(2) If one should always act as morality directs or permits, could one ever be justified in acting on something other than one's own assessment of the reasons that apply to oneself?
(3) Yes, one would be justified in doing so provided that morality counsels it.
(4) When would morality so counsel?
(5) Morality counsels one to act on the law's directives instead of acting on one's own assessment of the moral reasons that apply to oneself when doing so would actually make it more likely that one will fully comply with morality's demands.
(6) From the law's point of view, legal reasons always satisfy the requirement set out in (5). In other words, law claims that (in the areas where law applies) one will more fully comply with the balance of reasons by acting on law's directives than one will do by acting on one's own assessment of the balance of reasons.
(7) (6) expresses law's claim to being a legitimate authority.
(8) Law *necessarily* claims to be a legitimate authority.
(9) The claim to being a legitimate authority may be false, but it *canno*t be necessarily false.
(10) If the claim to being a legitimate authority cannot be necessarily false, then it could be true (even if it is not—indeed even if it never is).
(11) Therefore law must be the sort of thing of which the claim to being a legitimate authority could be true.
(12) What would make the law's claim to being a legitimate authority true?
(13) The claim would be true if and only if one were in fact likely to do better complying with the balance of reasons by acting on law's directives than one would do by acting on one's own assessment of what the balance of reasons calls for.
(14) Whether the law can satisfy the condition in (13) depends on whether it is capable of functioning in the way authorities in general do.
(15) The essential feature of an authority is that it substitutes its judgment about what one ought to do for the assessment of those over whom it purports to exercise or claim authority.

[58] Joseph Raz, *Authority and Justification*, 14 Phil. & Pub. Aff. 3, 18–19 (1985) (emphasis omitted).

(16) If one must appeal directly to the reasons that apply to oneself in order to determine what the law's directives are or what they call upon oneself to do, then in doing so one vitiates law's claim to authority.
(17) Why? Because if one must appeal directly to the reasons that apply to oneself in order to determine the nature or content of an authoritative directive or judgment, then determining its content would require one to engage in precisely the assessment of the balance of reasons that one must be turning over to the authority.
(18) Thus, the identity and content of law cannot be determined by appeal to reasons (that is, moral facts) and must instead be determined by social facts alone. This is the 'sources thesis', which is the core claim of exclusive legal positivism.

Neither the validity nor the soundness of the argument is our immediate concern.[59] For what is important for our current purposes is the nature and structure of the argument for exclusive legal positivism, including especially the key premises from which it is thought to follow.

The first thing to note is that exclusive legal positivism is not a premise offered as part of an interpretation of legal practice. Instead, it is the conclusion of an argument whose central premises include a claim about the nature of law: namely, that law claims to be a legitimate authority.

The second (and for our purposes, even more important) thing to note about the argument is that exclusive legal positivism is the conclusion of an argument that relies on the premise that *law and morality are necessarily connected* in a distinctive way. Here, the idea is that the place of law is in general determined by morality, and that specifically its place is to serve morality. *Necessarily, law is an instrument in the service of morality.*

The third thing to note is that law serves morality through the mechanism of authoritative directives. Essential to law is its claim to being a legitimate authority—that is, its claim in fact to serve morality.

The fourth thing to note is that the argument requires that the claim to authority must be capable of being true even if, in fact, it turns out to be false.

The final thing I want to draw the reader's attention to is the fact that the substantive theory of authority—that is, the account of the conditions under which the claim to authority is true—ties the elements of the argument together and drives the inference to the sources thesis as the conclusion of the argument. Equally important, the conception of authority is itself normative and is defended on normative grounds.[60]

---

[59] For doubts about both its validity and soundness, see, for example, Jules Coleman, The Practice of Principle: In Defence of a Pragmatist Approach to Legal Theory (2001). For doubts about its soundness, see, for example, Darwall, *supra* note 32; Scott Hershovitz, *The Role of Authority*, Philosopher's Imprint, Mar. 2011, at 1; and Scott Hershovitz, *The Authority of Law*, *in* Routledge Companion to Philosophy of Law (Andrei Marmor ed., forthcoming 2011).

[60] We take up below the question of whether this renders Raz a normativist and not a positivist.

Taken together, these considerations reveal that the argument from authority is itself nested in a much deeper set of considerations that bear on law's place, and in particular, on the relationship between morality and law's place. For at the heart of the argument is the claim that law necessarily serves morality. And this means that the core premise in the defense of legal positivism is the idea that law and morality are necessarily connected.

Ironically, commentators (quite correctly) associate exclusive legal positivism with the view that moral considerations cannot bear on determining the identity or content of law: that, as regards these issues, morality and law must be separated. Yet the conventional understanding is that exclusive legal positivism is the natural and correct way of giving expression to the separability thesis. This is a natural mistake but a deep one. The Razian version of exclusive legal positivism is not a way of giving expression to the separability thesis for it derives from rejecting the separability thesis. It is only because at the most fundamental levels law and morality are necessarily connected that, at the level of determining the identity and content of law, they necessarily must be kept apart. If there is a more surprising conclusion in jurisprudence in the offing, I, for one, am unaware of it.[61]

5.5.4 Extending the Argument

This line of argument is not peculiar to Raz's version of positivism. Recently, Scott Shapiro has developed a very similar argument to roughly the same effect.[62] Shapiro argues that laws are plans and that legal activity is planning activity. The distinctiveness of law as planning activity is that it has a 'moral aim'; it aims to respond to or solve a certain category of moral problems. Law's legitimacy depends on its capacity to solve the problems it aims to solve. Thus, like Raz, Shapiro is committed to a necessary connection between law and morality and also to a service conception of that relationship. Shapiro then argues that plans cannot serve their function if those whom the plans are supposed to guide must appeal to moral considerations in order to determine what the plans require of them. In effect, Shapiro argues for positivism about plans, which is a version of the sources thesis about plans. Since laws are plans, Shapiro defends a version of exclusive legal positivism about law.[63]

Freed from the grip of the conventional wisdom, our first conclusion is that instead of the separability thesis being essential to legal positivism and its defining feature, the most familiar form of positivism is grounded in rejecting the separability thesis.

---

[61] One does not reach positivism by adopting the separability thesis. If anything, one is drawn to exclusive legal positivism only by rejecting the broadest forms of the separability thesis. It is no wonder that so many have missed this deep and important point caught in the grasp of the conventional wisdom, which would have us believe instead that nothing is more central to legal positivism than the separability thesis.

[62] Shapiro, *supra* note 23.

[63] *See* id.; Scott J. Shapiro, *Was Inclusive Legal Positivism Founded on a Mistake?*, 22 Ratio Juris 326 (2009).

Exclusive legal positivism does not deny that law and morality are necessarily connected. If anything, its plausibility turns on insisting that law and morality are necessarily connected.

5.6 What About Inclusive Legal Positivism?

To be precise, I have not established that every form of exclusive legal positivism derives from rejecting the separability thesis. I have established, however, that the two most well developed versions of exclusive legal positivism—Raz's and Shapiro's—do. It is interesting that in the conventional wisdom the distinguishing feature of all forms of positivism is adherence to the separability thesis. In effect, the argument to this point goes some considerable way to turning the conventional wisdom upside down. All that is left would be to show that inclusive legal positivism also rejects the separability thesis. If it did, then we would not merely have discarded the conventional wisdom, but turned it on its head.

Ironically, one reason why some commentators have been suspicious of inclusive legal positivism's bona fides as a form of positivism is precisely that it allows normative as well as social facts to contribute to law's content. This encourages the thought that inclusive legal positivism is inconsistent with the separability thesis. Were that true, both inclusive and exclusive legal positivism would reject the separability thesis and that indeed would turn conventional wisdom on its head.

To be sure, inclusive legal positivism rejects the idea that normative or moral facts cannot contribute to the law's content, but it does not endorse thereby the claim that law and morality are necessarily connected. It holds that they can be connected: that there is nothing in positivism that precludes law and morality being connected. The deep point about exclusive legal positivism is that it holds that moral facts necessarily cannot contribute to legal content precisely because (among other reasons), at a more fundamental level, law and morality are necessarily connected. That is by no means a claim one can make on behalf of inclusive legal positivism.

If neither endorsing nor rejecting the separability thesis grounds or anchors inclusive legal positivism, what does? If natural law theory at some level insists that law and morality are necessarily connected (but not in a way that precludes the possibility of immoral law), then isn't exclusive legal positivism, which also insists that law and morality are necessarily connected more like natural law theory than it is like inclusive legal positivism? And how can that be? One can be forgiven for thinking that, having discarded the conventional wisdom, jurisprudence has lost its bearings entirely. Whatever its failings may have been, at least the conventional wisdom provided a good deal of structure and stability to jurisprudential inquiry. For all its failings, we are apparently in worse shape without the conventional wisdom to rely upon. Not only are we unable to identify any core claims that the various forms of legal positivism share with one another; it also seems that the main adversaries in the conventional story—exclusive legal positivism and natural law theory—have turned out to be bosom buddies if not kissing cousins. Talk about sleeping with the enemy.

Fear not. The next sections create order from the apparent chaos of living without a conventional wisdom. We do so by addressing each of these three concerns beginning with the last: If both natural law and exclusive legal positivism insist on the existence of necessary connections between law and morality, how are we to distinguish between them?

5.6.1 Exclusive Positivism and Natural Law: Redux

If asked to distinguish (exclusive) legal positivism from natural law, most commentators who had not read this Article would likely say, "That's easy; the latter asserts what the former denies, namely the existence of a necessary connection between law and morality." We have shown that such an answer would be mistaken, for as it happens, both natural lawyers and exclusive legal positivists insist that law and morality are necessarily connected.

Whereas both are committed to necessary connections between law and morality, they have very different accounts of the nature of that relationship. The exclusive positivist is committed to the view that the relationship is instrumental: law necessarily serves morality. The natural lawyer holds that the relationship is at least in part intrinsic; morality is intrinsic to the nature of law.

This difference has important implications. The exclusive positivist holds that in order for law to service morality there must be something of a firewall between law and morality. One is not free to consult the moral principles that justify the law when determining what the law requires. To do so, as we have seen, would vitiate the law's claim to authority. This is the reason why, for the exclusive positivist, the necessary connection between law and morality entails the sources thesis.

The fact that law and morality are intrinsically or constitutively connected implies for the natural lawyer that, in order to determine what the law requires, those to whom it is directed must be able to 'see through' the law to the principles that justify it. Rather than positing a firewall between law and morality, the natural lawyer takes the law to be translucent—if not transparent—regarding the principles that would justify it.

We turn now to consider the relationship between inclusive and exclusive legal positivism.

5.6.2 Exclusive and Inclusive Legal Positivism: Redux

Exclusive legal positivism is part of (or flows from) a comprehensive picture of the law and of its place in the normative landscape. Not so inclusive legal positivism. From the outset inclusive legal positivism or incorporationism has always been much more a view about the nature of *legal positivism* than about the nature of law. I first introduced it as a way of meeting Dworkin's objection to Hart that positivism lacks the resources adequate to explain how moral principles could be binding legal standards.

There may be much to be said on its behalf as an account of positivism, but the more pressing question is whether there is much, or indeed, anything to be said for inclusive positivism as a theory of law—or as a way of understanding law's place in the normative landscape. Without a defense of it as flowing from essential features of law or of law's place in the normative landscape, inclusive legal positivism will always remain—in my view at least—'unanchored' as a jurisprudence. How might one defend inclusive legal positivism as a theory of law and not just as an alternative conception of legal positivism?

5.6.2.1 The Argument for Inclusive Positivism

The prevailing defense of inclusive legal positivism proceeds in two stages. First, one defends positivism as a general theory of law, and then inclusive legal positivism as the better formulation of positivism.[64] If we suppose that one could defend positivism as a general matter first then the argument on behalf of inclusive legal positivism must be that there are features of legal practice that can only be explained by it or which can better be explained by it than by the exclusive positivist alternative. What might those features be?

The standard view is that inclusive legal positivism provides a more natural interpretation than does exclusive legal positivism of the fact that many legal texts refer directly to moral principles and to moral considerations more broadly. So, for example, the Fourteenth Amendment to the United States Constitution has the famous Equal Protection Clause and the natural reading of it suggests that the Clause represents a moral constraint on legality: nothing that is unequal in the relevant sense can constitute valid law under the Constitution. Thus, the Fourteenth Amendment explicitly conjures a moral test on legality such that what the law is must be based on moral or normative facts about the nature of equality. This is no problem for the inclusive legal positivist who allows that substantive morality can be incorporated into law. The Fourteenth Amendment merely proves the point. In contrast, the exclusive legal positivist rejects the possibility of morality being incorporated into law and so must read all such putative moral constraints on legality as directives to officials to appeal to considerations that are not themselves part of the law in order to assess whether or not a norm counts as law. Morality has the same standing as the law of France would

[64] Alternatively, one might defend the view that moral facts are among the determinants of the content of the law. This rejects exclusive legal positivism, but then defends inclusive legal positivism as a better account of the way that normative facts figure in legal judgments. I am grateful to Scott Hershovitz for this suggestion, which he takes to be a more promising way of defending inclusive legal positivism. As we shall see below, I find none of these approaches ultimately persuasive because, on my reading, inclusive legal positivism is not an alternative or competitor to either natural law or to exclusive legal positivism. It has a different logical object. It answers a different set of questions. It purports to play a different philosophical role. In short, the view I defend here is that virtually everyone (including me) has mischaracterized the relationship between inclusive legal positivism and other theories—understood as accounts of the metaphysics of legal content.

have in a conflicts case between French and German companies litigated in the United States (since both do business there). Suppose the relevant law in the jurisdiction holds that French law governs. In effect, the law directs the judge to appeal to French law in order to resolve the dispute. This does not make French law part of American law. It merely makes French law *binding* on officials in these cases. After all, our officials have no authority to alter French law, which is a power they do have over our law. The Equal Protection Clause is to be interpreted in the same way. It is a directive to officials to appeal to morality to resolve the dispute without it being the case that morality is part of our law.

Inclusive legal positivism allows us to credit the surface syntax of legal discourse whereas exclusive legal positivism requires that we treat the surface syntax as misleading with regard to its underlying semantics. Thus, the way to defend inclusive legal positivism is first to defend positivism and then to argue that inclusive legal positivism is the better version of the two because it provides the more satisfying explanation of the syntax of legal discourse.

The problem is that, if the argument for exclusive legal positivism is sound, this strategy for defending inclusive legal positivism is simply unavailable. The point of that argument is that the correct jurisprudential view is, as it were, thrust upon us by certain essential features of law or of our concept of it. As long as law necessarily claims to be a legitimate authority, where the legitimacy of that authority is expressed by the service conception, there is no room for normative facts to contribute to the law's content. Only exclusive legal positivism is compatible with law's claim to authority and so there is no choice among jurisprudential views to be had—positivist or otherwise.

In a sense, then, it is misleading to characterize the argument for the sources thesis as a defense of exclusive legal positivism. Rather, its point is that the essential nature of law entails the sources thesis. And if sound, this means that any plausible jurisprudential theory must begin not only with a laundry list of features of legal practice that it seeks to explain but also with the constraint that (whatever explanation is in the offing) it must be consistent with the fact that the content and identity of law is a matter of facts about behavior and attitude: social facts. Thus, if one offers up an account of the nature of law that explains how law can be a source of moral obligations by arguing that part of what makes a norm law is its moral worth, then this account must fail because it violates the sources thesis. It offers an account of an important feature of law that is inconsistent with a necessary truth about law: namely, that its content is fixed by social facts alone.

The better understanding of what we normally think of as the argument for exclusive legal positivism is that it is not so much a proof of the truth of exclusive legal positivism, but the demonstration of a necessary constraint on any jurisprudential view. If one insists on referring to the argument as a defense of exclusive legal positivism, then the most accurate way of characterizing the argument's conclusion is that all plausible jurisprudential theories are forms of exclusive legal positivism.

I cannot emphasize enough the significance of the argument in Part IV. If we think of the argument as a defense of exclusive legal positivism, then it demonstrates vividly that this particular form of positivism gets its traction by rejecting the separability thesis, not by endorsing it. Exclusive legal positivism is not a way of giving content to or expressing the separability thesis. It is an implication (in conjunction with other premises) of rejecting the separability thesis.

If we simply remove the labels and focus instead on what the argument (if sound) establishes as an implication of our concept of law (along with other premises), a metaphysical view about the sources of law's content results. In philosophy we draw a distinction between essential and other kinds of necessary features. The essential features of something are those features that make it the thing that it is. The essence of water is H_2O. Everything that is water is H_2O, and nothing that lacks that property can be water. There are other properties that are or can be necessary without being essential; they include the logical implications of essential properties, but need not be limited to those properties. So I tell the following "joke" to illustrate the point. I have never met a Canadian who is not a nice person. Of course, being nice is not what makes one a Canadian. There are presumably some formal criteria that determine whether one is Canadian; nevertheless, it is a necessary feature of anyone who is Canadian that he is nice.

Applying this distinction to the argument in Part IV, the essential feature of law that we are drawing on is its claim to being a legitimate authority. The necessary implication of it is the claim that the content of law must be fixed by social facts alone. So just as a theory of law is constrained by its essential features, it is likewise constrained by necessary implications of those features. The argument does not defend exclusive legal positivism so much as it purports to demonstrate that any jurisprudential theory must work with the constraint that legal content is necessarily a matter of social facts alone. If it is a burden of a jurisprudence to show how law creates reasons for acting, then it falls to jurisprudence to explain how social facts can give rise to reasons. If it is a burden of a jurisprudence to explain the moral semantics of legal discourse, then it falls to all jurisprudential theories to show how a moral semantics of law can be compatible with a social facts metaphysics. The argument in Part IV (if sound) establishes necessary constraints on all jurisprudential outlooks. It does not merely establish the plausibility of one such outlook.

5.6.2.2 The Argument Against Exclusive Positivism

With so much at stake then, it is not surprising that inclusive legal positivists are moved to question the argument's soundness.[65] The argument relies on three basic claims.

[65] And not just the inclusive legal positivist either. It is not enough for the natural lawyer to agree with the exclusive legal positivist that law and morality are necessarily connected and then to distinguish between different ways in which they are. If the argument in Part IV is sound, the natural lawyer's claim that the law must be transparent or translucent to the principles that justify it cannot be sustained. This does not mean that natural law theory is unavailable. If the argument in Part IV is sound, the forms of natural law theory that are available must accept the sources thesis.

These are: (1) law necessarily claims to be a legitimate authority; (2) the claim to being a legitimate authority cannot be necessarily false, and thus, necessarily it must be capable of being true; and (3) the particular substantive theory of authority is the service conception.

In fact, all three premises are problematic.[66] Consider the second and third. We can agree that law's claim to being a legitimate authority is not incoherent or contradictory and thus that it is not necessarily false. Well, not quite: we can agree that the claim to legitimate authority cannot be necessarily false in virtue of incoherence or inconsistency—for it is neither. That does not mean that it cannot be necessarily false for other reasons—as it would be, for example, were anarchism true.

Anarchism is the view that no practical or political authority could be legitimate. Necessarily all authorities are illegitimate; thus, any claim to legitimacy is necessarily false. Surely one cannot argue that anarchism must be false because law's claim to being a legitimate authority must be capable of being true. That simply begs the question. Even if anarchism is not true, it could be true, and were it true, the claim to being a legitimate authority would be necessarily false. In that case, the premise that the claim to legitimate authority cannot be necessarily false would be incorrect.

In addition, the argument for the Razian version of exclusive legal positivism relies on the so-called 'service conception' of authority, which is to say that law's authority depends on its relative ability to service the demands of reason or morality. It is the service conception of authority that draws the necessary connection between law and morality. According to the service conception, a practical authority is legitimate when its claim to superior service is true. In claiming to have legitimate authority over *B* (in some domain of activity), *A* implies that *B* will do better in complying with the demands of reason that apply to him by following *A*'s directives than by following *B*'s own assessment of the balance of reason. In the service conception, the authority relationship is between agents and reasons.[67]

It is by no means clear, however, that the service conception provides the best or most illuminating way to think about the authority relationship, or that the argument for the sources thesis would go through with some other theory of authority in its place. At the very least, the service conception does not capture our ordinary notion of authority, which is a relationship between persons.[68] The service conception of

[66] I have also argued, notably in *The Practice of Principle*, that some versions of the argument are not valid—namely, that its conclusion does not follow even granting its premises. Roughly, the idea is this: even if appealing to the moral principles that would justify a directive would vitiate the claim to authority, it does not follow that appealing to other moral principles or facts would; and so it does not follow that all appeals to moral principles or facts to determine law's content or identity are inconsistent with law's claim to authority. *See* Coleman, *supra* note 59, at 103–119.

[67] Raz, *supra* note 49, at 55–56.

[68] My interpretation is that the Razian account is a revisionist account of authority. As I see it, his deep point is that when it comes to reason, no one has a status authority over anyone else. There are just reasons that apply to persons and the only 'status' anyone has with respect to anyone else is a matter of competence—capacities for judging or executing what reason requires. There is no place for a status- as opposed to a competence-based notion of authority.

authority makes authority a matter of 'competence'. The ordinary notion of authority is one of 'standing'.

If the argument for the sources thesis is unsound, then one does not have to treat the claim that legal content must be fixed by social facts alone as a constraint on all jurisprudential theories. At the same time, both inclusive legal positivism and natural law theory in their traditional forms remain options. But this leaves us with more work to do. After all, the conventional wisdom was framed in terms of conceptual claims about the relationship of law to morality, none of which could be sustained. Absent such claims, however, we are hard-pressed to identify what the core claim of any particular jurisprudential view is or must be. It is clear that the core claim of exclusive legal positivism is a claim about the metaphysics of legal content, and not a claim about the relationship of law to morality—certainly not the claim about the relationship of law to morality that the conventional wisdom assigns to it.

We will go nowhere fast if we insist on characterizing a taxonomical project in jurisprudence in terms of any kind of conceptual claims relating law to morality. The simple truth is that there are necessary conceptual connections of some sort or other between law and morality, and there are some alleged conceptual truths about the relationship between law and morality that do not obtain. Further, it is impossible to distinguish among jurisprudential views in the light of their commitment to some of these and not to others. Every plausible jurisprudential view has no reason not to accept the true ones and even less reason not to reject the false ones.

If we want to make progress, then we should at least begin by shifting focus from conceptual claims about the relationship of law to morality to some other feature of law and legal practice. We might take note of the fact that the core claim of exclusive legal positivism is the sources thesis and that the sources thesis is a claim about the metaphysics of legal content: the facts that give law the content that it has. Perhaps then we should see if we can recast traditional jurisprudential views in terms of core claims each makes about the sources of legal content.

5.7 It Is About the Metaphysics: Maybe

As we have already noted, legal facts are not basic facts. They supervene on other facts. These other facts, the law's supervenience base, give law the content that it has. Arguably the most basic question in jurisprudence is a metaphysical one: What are the sources of legal content? Once we have an answer to that question, we can pursue a range of other related concerns. If, for example, only facts about behavior and attitude contribute to the content of law, then we may ask whose behavior, which of their behaviors, whose attitudes, which of their attitudes, and so on. If normative facts can contribute to law, then which normative facts? If both normative and social facts contribute to the law having the content that it does, then how do normative and social facts operate with or on one another to give law the content that it has? More generally, how do the facts on which the law supervenes come together to give law the content that it has?[69]

What kind of stuff is 'legal stuff', or better, what is the stuff law is made of? What, in other words, is law's metaphysical foundation?[70]

5.7.1 *Meet the New Boss, Same as the Old Boss!*

We have already identified three distinct claims about the possible contributors to legal content.

(1) Only social facts determine the content of law. Law has the content that it does *in virtue of facts about individual (or group) behavior and attitudes: that is, in virtue of social facts.*
(2) Only normative (evaluative or moral) facts contribute to the content of law. Legal facts are the facts that they are—i.e., have the content that they do—in virtue only of certain moral or evaluative facts obtaining. What the law is—what it requires, permits, or authorizes—depends entirely on what is good, desirable, valuable, or ought morally to be done.
(3) Both normative and social facts contribute to legal content. According to this view, what the law is—how it is that it has the content that it does—depends on either or both social and normative facts.[71]

We have formulated (1), (2), and (3) as *contingent* claims. This is not the only alternative. Claims about legal content may express the idea that law's content *must* have a particular supervenience basis. In that case we get:

(4) Necessarily only social facts contribute to legal content;
(5) Necessarily only normative facts contribute to legal content; and
(6) Necessarily both normative and social facts contribute to legal content.

Thus, (4) claims that it is a necessary truth about law that its content must be determined by social facts alone, and (5) claims that it is a necessary truth about

---

[69] For an excellent discussion of precisely this issue, see Greenberg, *How Facts Make Law*, *supra* note 8.

[70] The discussion that follows is more demanding and requires more careful attention than any of the arguments to this point. I wish I could make it easier and more enjoyable to read, but it is more important that it be precise than that it be fun to read.

[71] Still, however precise and technical the discussion in this and subsequent sections is, it necessarily remains partial and incomplete. In addition to setting aside the two biggest questions—whether the right metaphysical relationship is supervenience and how it is that facts come to make *legal* facts—we do not take up a wide range of other equally interesting and important issues: for example, whether social facts can also be normative; whether normative or moral facts are basic or whether instead they supervene on other facts—in particular, social facts; whether normative facts are reducible to social facts; and so on. Even setting these matters aside for now, there remains much work to do.

law that its content must be determined by normative facts alone. And, of course (6) claims that it is a necessary truth about law that its content must be determined by the conjunction of social and normative facts.

Propositions (1)–(6) represent alternative hypotheses about the supervenience base of law. Each offers a general claim about the facts that somehow come together to make law: to give law the content that it has. One important difference among them is that (4)–(6) assert that wherever there is law (whether in the actual or in any possible world), law is the kind of thing that must have a particular supervenience base. Propositions (1)–(3) make no such claim. While each gives a specific source of legal content, propositions (1)–(3) allow for the possibility that it could have been otherwise. It is actually true, but not necessarily true.

So (1) says, in effect, that law is what it is because judges, legislators, and perhaps ordinary folk have said, intended, or believed certain things. On the other hand, (1) is also consistent with the view that things could have been different from how they are; law would have the content that it does—not just because courts and legislatures acted in particular ways (and believed or intended certain things)—but also because the source of legal content is good, right, just, fair, desirable, and so on. In other words, (1) claims that the sources thesis happens to be true of law and thus that (2) and (3), for example, are false; but it holds as well that (2) or (3) could have been true of law, and may well be true of law in some possible world. Proposition (1), however, is true of law in our world. In effect, (4) shares with (1) the claim that the sources thesis is true of law in our world, but differs in that it claims, unlike (1), that the sources thesis must be true of law in all possible worlds. Thus, according to (4), it is not just that alternative accounts of the sources of law are mistaken about the nature of law in our world; they are wrong for all possible worlds.[72]

Having introduced these distinctions in the potential supervenience bases of law, the natural question to ask what the ultimate point is of doing so. What projects does this inquiry further? A natural and immediate thought is that we have introduced the metaphysics of legal content in order to recharacterize various forms of positivism and natural law theory. The old architecture is characterized by the separability thesis; the new architecture is defined by views about the nature of legal content. If our aim is to recharacterize positivism and natural law theories in terms of claims about the metaphysics of law, the natural thought would be that the distinguishing feature of legal positivism is that it endorses either (1), (3), (4), or (6) whereas natural law endorses (2) or (5). Then we would distinguish inclusive legal positivists from exclusive positivists insofar as the latter endorse (1) or (4) whereas the former endorse (3) or (6).

---

[72]The view that only social facts contribute to legal content is the sources thesis. The question is whether the sources thesis is best represented as (1) or as (4), or better, whether those who endorse the sources thesis endorse (1) or (4). The argument for the sources thesis in Part IV purports to demonstrate that it is a necessary implication of the premises and so it is reasonable to suppose that those who endorse the sources thesis endorse (4), not (1). Similar questions arise regarding (2) and (5), and (3) and (6).

Were this our main objective, succeeding in it would be an achievement, but a modest one. One could wonder what all the fuss has been about. Worse, a skeptic might wonder whether it is an achievement at all. Notice that while explicitly framed in terms of the sources of legal content, the distinctions among the various theories are all formulated in terms of the relationship of legal facts to moral and social facts. And if this is all the 'new architecture of jurisprudence' amounts to, couldn't one argue that the new architecture merely recharacterizes the separability thesis as a claim about legal content instead of as a claim about the concepts of law and morality, the conditions of legal validity, or the possibility conditions of law? In that case, we have not abandoned or discarded the separability thesis, my protestations notwithstanding; we have instead simply identified its proper domain. Meet the new boss—same as the old boss.

5.7.2 *There Is Something Happening Here!*

The concern is understandable but ultimately unwarranted. While it may be correct to identify exclusive legal positivism with (1) or (4), it is a mistake to identify inclusive legal positivism with either (3) or (6). It is also a mistake to characterize natural law theory in terms of (2) or (5).

By identifying natural law with either (2) or (5), one attributes to it the view that what judges and legislatures say and do cannot contribute to what the law is. This would leave the natural law tradition bereft of resources to explain the institutional nature of law. It may be one thing to attribute to the natural lawyer the view that others too easily dismiss or misrepresent law's normative dimensions; it is quite another to attribute to the natural lawyer a total disregard of law's social or institutional nature. In truth, the natural lawyer holds that normative facts in addition to—and not to the exclusion of —social facts contribute to legal content. If anything, it is more plausible to identify natural law with either (3) or (6) than with (2) or (5). But then if natural law theory is understood in terms of (3) or (6), how are we to characterize inclusive legal positivism? After all, didn't we characterize it as (3) or (6)? But if natural law is (3) or (6), inclusive legal positivism cannot be—unless it is indistinguishable from natural law theory!

Interesting. We begin by associating natural law with (2) or (5) and inclusive legal positivism with (3) or (6). But no sooner do we press on these formulations that we come to see that, if anything, natural law holds (3) or (6) and not (2) or (5).[73]

[73]Depending on how one thinks of natural law, a natural lawyer could adopt (1) or (4) as regards legal content. That is, one could in principle hold that the law depends only on what people say and do and yet claim that there are some necessary connections between law and morality. So, in fact, it is just not helpful at all to think that what we are doing is merely recharacterizing the conventional disputes between positivists and natural lawyers in terms of differences about the sources of legal content. We are doing something else altogether, as the remainder of this discussion makes very clear.

Of course, inclusive legal positivism also holds that social and normative facts contribute to legal content. So this suggests that inclusive legal positivism and natural law theory hold the same views of legal content. If that is so, what distinguishes them from one another?

The answer is that inclusive legal positivism is consistent with (3) and (6), but is not defined or characterized by either. If there is a plausible formulation of the core of inclusive legal positivism it is:

(7) Only *social facts* determine which facts contribute to the law having the content that it does; or
(8) *Necessarily,* only social facts can determine which facts contribute to the law having the content that it does.

Inclusive legal positivism is compatible with (3) or (6), one might think, because of its commitment to (7). Social and normative facts contribute to legal content if and only if social facts allow that to be the case. Isn't this the point I made in *Negative and Positive Positivism,*[74] which has been the calling card of inclusive legal positivism ever since? It is natural to identify inclusive legal positivism with (3) or (6) just because the point of inclusive legal positivism is that law *can incorporate* morality and, if it does, either (3) or (6) will obtain. And once one sees that, one realizes that it is really (7) (or (8)) and not (3) or (6) that represents inclusive legal positivism. But (7) and (8) are altogether different animals from (1) to (6). Let's see just how different.

5.7.3 A Brand New Day

Taking the surface syntax of (7) seriously invites the thought that (7) merely specifies the conditions under which (1)–(6) obtain.[75] That is, the content of the law is a matter of social facts only, (1), or necessarily a matter of social facts only, (4), when there are social facts (e.g., a rule of recognition) to the effect that in the relevant jurisdiction only facts about what legal officials and others say, do, believe, and intend contribute to the law having the content that it does. Or, the content of the law is a matter of normative facts, (2), or necessarily a matter of normative facts only, (5), when there are social facts (e.g., a rule of recognition) to the effect that in the relevant jurisdiction only facts about what is good, right, valuable, just, and fair determine what the law calls for. Similar considerations would apply to the relationship between (7) and (3) and (6). (7) is a 'meta' claim in the sense that it is a claim about (1)–(6); in particular, it is a claim about when (1)–(6) obtain.

---

[74] Coleman, *supra* note 2.

[75] Much of the argument that follows was stimulated by a discussion with David Plunkett. I have no idea if he would agree with the claims I make in this section, but our discussion stimulated me to stake out the theses that are presented here.

One consequence of interpreting (7) (and (8)) in this way is that there is no real conflict between inclusive and exclusive legal positivism. In either of its formulations, inclusive legal positivism would be the more fundamental claim. As a positivist, one would always be committed to the claim that social facts ground legal content, but one would interpret that claim along the lines of (7) or (8). Exclusive legal positivism would be the derivative and not strictly speaking alternative claim.

But can this be right? Can it really be the case that inclusive and exclusive legal positivism are not competing theories of law or of legal content? Can it really be correct that inclusive legal positivism is the core claim of positivism, and exclusive legal positivism subsidiary to it? If this is right, just about everything positivists and their critics have believed up until this point must be mistaken.

In fact, my view is that most of what positivists and their critics have believed about positivism and its alternatives is mistaken or, if not mistaken, terribly misleading. I include myself among the confused and misguided. Indeed, I include myself among those responsible for much of the confusion that has passed as insight. But this is the conclusion of the arguments that follow, and a *mea culpa* at this point is jumping ahead a bit.

Before we abandon the view that inclusive and exclusive legal positivism are not in fact competitors, we need first to capture why interpreting (7) and (8) as claims about when (1)–(6) obtain might be problematic. In order to do so, it will be helpful if we begin by simplifying the discussion a bit for ease of exposition. Instead of asking what the relationship is between (7) or (8) on the one hand and (1)–(6) on the other, let's restrict the discussion to the relationship between (7) on the one hand and (4)–(6) on the other. Why choose (7) rather than (8)? Why choose (4)–(6) rather than (1)–(3)?

The reason for choosing (7) rather than (8) is that, with the exception of Hart, I know of no inclusive legal positivist who holds that it is a necessary truth that the determinants of legal content are fixed by social facts. No inclusive positivist to my knowledge explicitly has argued that it is a necessary truth that social facts determine which facts contribute to legal content. All to my knowledge—and certainly me in particular—introduce inclusive legal positivism as a way of characterizing positivism, not as a necessary truth about law. Again, Hart may be the exception. This is just another way of making the point I made before that inclusive legal positivism is unanchored.

There are several reasons for choosing (4)–(6) rather than (1)–(3). The first is that I know of no exclusive legal positivist who believes that it is a mere contingent fact that legal content is fixed by social facts. For example, the arguments that we attribute to Shapiro or a Razian, for example, demonstrate, if sound, that legal content is necessarily a matter of social facts. And the normativist who can be represented as holding either (3) or (6) does not merely claim that normative facts contribute to legal content, but that given the nature of law and its connection to morality, necessarily they do.

Even more important, given our current purposes, is that by focusing on the relationship of (7) to (4)–(6) we really heighten the burden on the inclusive legal positivist who claims that inclusive legal positivism is a claim about the determinants of the contributors to legal content. And that is because (7) and (4)–(6) differ in their modalities in important ways: (7) is a contingent claim whereas (4)–(6) express necessity claims. Thus, someone who holds that inclusive legal positivism is the ground of different claims about legal content is faced with the burden of showing how necessities can be derived from contingencies.

With these preliminaries out of the way, we can now express some of the reasons for thinking that the interpretation of the relationship between (7) and (4)–(6) as being about different things is likely to strike many as problematic. We can begin with the worry that the interpretation on the table does not do justice to the claims (4)–(6) make. Take (4) first. It is not claiming that the content of law is necessarily fixed by social facts *if and when social facts of a certain kind so determine it*! It claims that the content of law is fixed by social facts—full stop. The same holds for (5), which (rightly or wrongly) does not claim that the content of law is necessarily fixed by normative facts only *if and when social facts of a certain kind determine that to be the case.* Proposition (5) claims that necessarily legal content is fixed by normative facts alone—full stop. The same for (6).

Someone pressing the case may go further and argue that if any of (4)–(6) is true, then (7) must be false. To see this, suppose that (4) is true. If (4) is true, then necessarily legal content is determined by social facts alone. And if legal content is necessarily determined by social facts alone, then (5) and (6) must be false. And so it is not, as it were, optional for (7) to make them true. They cannot be true if (4) is. By the same token, if (5) is true, then (4) and (6) must be false, and if they are false, (7) does not have the power as it were to make them true. Same for (6): if it is true, then (4) and (5) are false, and (7) simply has nothing to say about it. Proposition (7) cannot be the master claim that makes (4)–(6) true, when they are true. If one of them is true, the others are false, and there is nothing, as it were, that (7) can do about it.

If any of (4)–(6) is true, then (7) is false; and if (7) is true, (4), (5), and (6) are false. These considerations require that we abandon the view that (7) is a claim about when (4)–(6) obtain. If anything, they suggest that (7) is in the same boat as (4)–(6). If any one of them is true, the others must be false. That is what makes them competitive theories of the nature of legal content. If (7) is in the same boat as (1)–(6), then it is a substantive theory of legal content and a genuine competitor to exclusive legal positivism. These considerations suggest that (7)—one version of inclusive legal positivism—is incompatible with (4)—exclusive legal positivism—and that the standard view of their relationship—as competitors—must be correct. Despite its syntax, (7) is not about (4)–(6). It is just another claim about legal content on par with them: false, if any of the others are true.

But this is a mistake, one that virtually everyone has been guilty of—including me—and the time has come to correct it. Once we do we will be on our way to putting in place a solid foundation on which a new architecture of jurisprudence can be erected.

5.7.3.1 Semantics and Meta-Semantics

In the philosophy of language, there is an important distinction between the inquiry into the meaning of a term and the inquiry into how the term gets the meaning it has. It is the difference between the question, for example, of what 'gold', 'water', or 'law' refers to and the question of how it is that 'gold', 'water', or 'law' come to refer to the things to which they refer.[76] This is the difference between semantics and meta-semantics.

I want to suggest as a first approximation (that we will modify in due course) that the difference between exclusive and inclusive legal positivism is analogous to the difference between semantics and meta-semantics. Exclusive legal positivism or the sources thesis is a claim about the metaphysics of legal content; it is a claim about the determinants of legal content. Inclusive legal positivism is not a claim about the determinants of legal content. It is a claim about the grounds on which the determinants of legal content are determined. Inclusive legal positivism is, to coin a particularly ungainly phrase, a claim in meta-metaphysics.

Contrary to the prevailing wisdom, inclusive and exclusive legal positivism are not alternative jurisprudential views—either about legal content or the nature of law more generally. The problem is to spell out precisely what their relationship to one another is. In doing so, the first order of business is to meet the challenge posed in the previous section that (7) cannot be a claim about when (4)–(6) obtain. That worry has been in expressed in a variety of different ways, but they all boil down to one fundamental concern: How can (7) be a ground or an explanation of (4) when it obtains, (5) when it obtains, or (6) when it obtains? Proposition (7), after all, is a contingent claim. (4)–(6) express necessary claims. Even if we suppose that (7) were to make (4) true, to acknowledge that (7) is a contingent claim is to recognize that (7) could have grounded (5) or (6) instead of (4). This makes it seem that the fact that (4) obtains is a contingent truth about legal content—whose truth depends on what the social facts happen to be. But (4) asserts a necessity claim: How can a necessity claim's obtaining depend on contingent (social) facts? More generally, the worry, to put it starkly, is that necessity cannot depend on contingency.

The fact is that there is no problem in a contingent claim grounding a necessary truth. Let's make the idea concrete with an illustration. Let's take (7) to be instantiated by a Hartian rule of recognition. That rule, we can suppose, establishes criteria of legality such that only social facts contribute to legal content. In saying that (7) is contingent, we are committed to saying that the rule could have been otherwise; it could have incorporated normative facts as well as social facts. It is a matter of fact, not a necessary truth, that it makes law a matter of social fact alone.

So far so good. Presumably there is no problem were we to understand the claim that only social facts contribute to legal content to itself be a contingent claim,

---

[76] I have explored this issue in great detail as regards 'law' in another paper, and I will not rehearse the arguments of that paper here. *See* Jules L. Coleman & Ori Simchen, *"Law,"* 9 Legal Theory 1 (2003).

i.e., (1). After all, (7) is a contingent claim, and there is no special issue in seeing how it could ground another contingent claim. The rule of recognition makes it the case that only social facts contribute to legal content, but the rule could have been different, and so the contributors to legal content could have been different. The contributors to legal content are only social facts, but that is not a necessary truth; it could have been otherwise. Again, no problem.

The problem emerges if someone claims that (7) is a potential ground of (4)–(6), and one must make that claim in order to sustain the view that (7) purports to determine the sources of legal content and is not itself a claim about what those sources are. Proposition (7) must therefore be capable of determining (or explaining) (4), (5), or (6) when they obtain. Again, referring back to our illustration, this means that the rule of recognition would have to be able to make it the case not only that social facts alone contribute to legal content, but that necessarily only social facts contribute to legal content. Necessity claims cannot follow from 'contingency' or 'could have been otherwise' claims—or can they?

They can, for the contingency of determinants of the determinants of *X* need not entail the contingency of the determinants of *X*. The determinants of my existence are contingent—those gametes could have failed to fuse—and yet my existence determines my self-identity as a matter of necessity rather than contingency. The determinants of the game of chess in its current state are contingent, and yet the game of chess in its current state determines the way the rook moves as a matter of necessity rather than contingency. Such examples are not hard to come by. 'Musts' regularly follow from 'could have been otherwise', and there is no reason why they could not in the case of legal content.[77]

There is no problem then in understanding (7) as a meta-metaphysical claim about the determinants of legal content. It is a putative hypothesis about how it is that some facts and not others contribute to legal content. The explanation it provides is that these facts and not those contribute to legal content in virtue of some set of social facts (7)—like Hart's rule of recognition, or Shapiro's collective planning practices. This explanation is perfectly compatible with the claim that these facts—and not others—contribute to legal content being a necessary and not merely a contingent truth.

This is a deep and important point. It removes the main obstacle to my claim that inclusive and exclusive legal positivism are not competitive theories of legal content. Propositions (1)–(6) are competitors with one another. In doing so, it raises the

[77] For this point, I am grateful to Ori Simchen, who provides a way of making the same point when it comes to the case of legal content directly. Suppose (7) is true. It so happens as a matter of mere contingency that social facts alone fix which facts are to contribute to legal content: say that it is social facts belonging to some clearly demarcated class *C* of facts and that nothing more is thus determined—as a matter of mere contingency again—to be whatever is to determine legal content. It seems not so implausible to me to suppose that this contingent determination of *C* as whatever determines legal content also thereby fixes the nature or essence of legal content. If so, then it will not be merely contingent that *C* is whatever determines legal content—it will be necessary given the nature of legal content.

question: What are possible competitors to (7) other than (8)? In other words, what are some competing claims about how the determinants of legal content are themselves determined?

One obvious alternative to (7) would be:

(9) Normative facts determine the determinants of legal content. (Let's call this normativism.)

Another alternative would be:

(10) Necessarily normative facts determine the determinants of legal content. (This is just a modally more stringent form of normativism.) Proposition (10) stands to (9) as (8) does to (7).

Yet another particularly interesting alternative to (7) would be:

(11) The determinants of legal content derive from truths about the essential nature of law. (For convenience, let's call this conceptualism.)

And so on.

We really do have two different kinds of questions here. The first is:

(A) What determines legal content?
The second is:

(B) What determines the determinants of legal content? In virtue of what set of considerations does it happen that these facts and not others constitute the contributors to legal content? What are the grounds of the determinants of legal content? Or even better perhaps, what explains why these facts and not others determine the content of law?[78]

Inclusive legal positivism, normativism, and conceptualism are all competing accounts at the metalevel: putative accounts of how it is that these facts (and not others) contribute to legal content. They are not competitors to (1)–(6). With respect to (1)–(6), whichever turns out to be the right account of the contributors to legal

[78] The distinction I am emphasizing between the determinants of legal content and the determinants of the determinants of legal content invites two possible objections. The first is that the determination relationship is transitive and so the determinants of the determinants of legal content are themselves determinants of legal content. So the distinction collapses. The second objection takes the opposite tack. If the determinants of legal content have determinants, then so, too, do those determinants, ad inf.nitum. The second objection is in a form that does not lead to a serious objection. Whenever one claims that *A* is a ground of *B*, it is possible to ask what is a ground of *A*? So what?

In principle, the first objection is more interesting—at least at first blush. If being a shade of red determines something's being red, and its being red determines that it is a color, then it is true that its being a shade of red determines that something has a color. But this is a different kind of relationship, which is transitive; it is the relationship of greater specificity (being a shade of red) to lesser specificity (being red) to even lesser specificity (being a color). That is not the relationship we are after. The relationship between the first- and second-order determinants of legal content is a metaphysical notion of being a ground (or being the explanation) and this relationship is not transitive. Again, I am grateful to Ori Simchen for clarification of the relevant distinctions.

content, (7)–(11) are competitive accounts of how it is that that is the right account. If, for example, it turns out that necessarily both social and normative facts contribute to legal content, i.e., (6), then (7)–(11) offer conflicting accounts of why that is so. Proposition (7), for example, says that necessarily social and normative facts contribute to legal content in virtue of some other set of social facts, for example, the rule of recognition. Proposition (9) says, for example, that necessarily social and normative facts contribute to legal content as a result of some other set of normative facts, for example, that law is a moral good. Finally, (11), for example, would hold that necessarily social and normative facts contribute to legal content in virtue of some truth about the nature of law, for example, that law is necessarily a source of institutional moral reasons for acting.[79]

If all this is right, and I obviously believe that it is, inclusive and exclusive legal positivism are not strictly speaking alternative theories of legal content. And if that is right, they are not strictly speaking alternative formulations of positivism. Indeed, as we shall see momentarily, there may be no interesting unifying core idea that ties theories that have been labeled 'positivistic' together.

5.7.3.2 It Is Always About Everything: All the Way Down

There is no question that when it comes to matters of legal content there is an important distinction between problems at the object level and others at the metalevel. On the other hand, it is also true that whatever the differences, both questions concern the metaphysics of legal content. A full accounting of the metaphysics of legal content will answer both questions; it will provide an account of the contributors to legal content and how it is that these facts (and not others) determine why law has the content that it does. One consequence of this realization is that theories of law that appear identical or at least very similar because they provide the same or similar answers at the 'object level' can also provide very different answers at the metalevel. I want to illustrate this point by focusing on Joseph Raz's and Scott Shapiro's versions of exclusive legal positivism.

Both Raz and Shapiro adopt the sources thesis. Thus they are exclusive legal positivists and endorse either (1) or (4), and most likely (4). That is their first-order or object-level views. For Raz, the sources thesis follows from the conjunction of several premises, notably the assertion that law necessarily claims to be a legitimate authority, as well as his substantive view of the nature of authority.[80] For Shapiro, the sources thesis follows from the view that law necessarily aims to solve a distinctive class of moral problems and that it seeks to do so through a characteristic activity—a form of complex social planning.[81] The sources thesis follows from Shapiro's view of the nature of plans and how they work in practical reasoning.

---

[79] The reader should note that I am not defending any of these arguments. I am merely identifying the kinds of arguments that would bear on answering these kinds of questions.

[80] *See* Raz, *supra* note 17, at 28–33, and accompanying text.

[81] *See* Shapiro, *supra* note 23; *see also supra* text accompanying note 62.

Thus, both Raz and Shapiro adopt some version of (11): the determinants of legal content themselves derive from claims about the nature or essence of law or of our concept of it. For Raz, the essential nature of law includes the claim to authority and a distinctive account of the nature of authority. For Shapiro, the essential nature of law includes its having a 'moral aim' and its pursuing that aim through a distinctive kind of social activity: planning. The key concept is that of a plan. Together these ideas determine that necessarily only social facts contribute to legal content. Thus, they agree not only at the object level but also at the metalevel: at least this far up the meta-chain.

Because both agree on the first and second-order metaphysical claims, they reject the second-order claim that I am associating with inclusive legal positivism: namely, that social facts determine the determinants of legal content. Now, we have to be careful here. The standard view is that Raz, Shapiro, and those moved by their arguments actually reject inclusive legal positivism because, on their views of the nature of law, they are committed to the sources thesis. I am arguing that the standard view is mistaken (or very misleading). Their arguments against inclusive legal positivism are much more complex and interesting than that. They believe that the determinants of legal content derive from essential or necessary truths about law; they begin by adopting (11). Interestingly, Hart, the inclusive legal positivist, also adopts the view that contributors to legal content follow from necessary truths about law. This distinguishes him from almost all other inclusive legal positivists, who, like me, fail to anchor the theory in any fundamental claims about the nature of law. The differences between Raz and Shapiro, on the one hand, and Hart, on the other, have to do with what each identifies as necessary truths about law. For Raz, it is the claim to authority. For Shapiro, it is the conjunction of law's moral aim and the idea of plans. For Hart, it is the rule of recognition. The rule of recognition is a social rule, and thus, for Hart, (11) turns out to yield (7). The features of law that Raz and Shapiro pick out are incompatible with (7)—or so I have demonstrated. And that is why they reject inclusive legal positivism. It is not their commitment to the sources thesis (4) that explains their rejection of (7), but is instead the way they each spell out their commitment to (11). In fact, as I have also demonstrated, (7) is perfectly compatible with (4)! It turns out not to be on the views of exclusive legal positivists like Raz and Shapiro—but only because they accept (11) and understand law's necessary or essential features in ways that they believe preclude the truth of (7). But as I have also demonstrated, Hart, like Raz and Shapiro, accepts (11). The key, then, is what one's views are about law's essential features and what, if anything, follows from them!

There is even more to see if we now focus on the ways in which Raz and Shapiro go about defending and characterizing what each takes to be law's essential features. For they not only identify different features of law as essential to it, but they defend their claims in very different ways. In Raz's overall argument, the key idea is that of the service conception of authority, but it is well known that Raz's argument for that conception is explicitly normative. The Razian argument for the sources thesis, then, is really a mixture of conceptual claims and normative ones. The 'positivistic' claim about legal content ultimately rests on alleged truths about the nature of law and the nature of authority; importantly, whereas the claim about the nature of law is itself a conceptual claim, the claim about authority is a normative claim and it is defended as such. So we have a positivistic first-order metaphysical claim supported by a conceptual claim (about the nature of law) and a normative defense of another claim (about the nature of authority).

Not so for Shapiro. For Shapiro, laws are plans. But Shapiro's argument for laws as plans is not normative in the same way that Raz's argument for authority is. Nor is Shapiro's account of what plans are normative. Thus, in his case, we have the same 'positivistic' claim about legal content derived from conceptual claims about the nature of law and about the nature of plans. There is no normative argument in sight. No normative or moral considerations are doing any heavy lifting. In this regard, Shapiro is more like Hart than like Raz. Yet, unlike Hart who, like me, rejects the sources thesis, Shapiro, like Raz, endorses it.

What are we to make of this? One thing we could say is that Raz actually is committed to (9) and not to (11). To be sure, Raz holds that the determinants of legal content derive from claims about the essential nature of law, but at least some of those claims are, in his account, defended on normative grounds—as (9) would have it. And that means that in an obvious sense Raz seems committed to the view that the determinants of legal content are ultimately fixed by normative facts! If that is right, there is something to be said for the claim that Raz adopts (9), not (11). And what is the proper conclusion to draw from this? Is it that Raz is not really a positivist? And since Hart adopts (6), not (4), does that imply that he is not a positivist even though he argues for (6) first through (7) and ultimately through (11)?[82]

Are we to say that at the end of the day Raz is not a positivist, and that to be a positivist is to start with the sources thesis and work backwards to its foundation without once ever invoking moral or normative considerations? Thus, Hart would only pass part of this test and the same at best would hold for me. Shapiro would be a positivist, but who else? Why care?

What is to be gained, what insights gleaned, by the labels: positivism, normativism, natural law, inclusive positivism, and so on? For my money, there is no one claim any theory makes or no one answer we can point to and say, "That is what makes this a positivist theory," or "That is what makes it a normativist theory or natural law theory." If the relevant question is, "What facts can contribute to legal content?" then Raz is a positivist as is Shapiro, whereas maybe Hart and I are not. The lesson is that there is no place in theory construction where we can draw a line to distinguish a positivistic jurisprudence from a natural law or normativist one. There will no doubt be pure forms of each kind, but they are likely to be rare and of no special significance.

They are of no interest because they are merely taxonomical concerns that do not point us in the direction of the right questions, let alone the right answers. What we have are questions in jurisprudence and theories that seek to answer them and to do so in a systematic way. The goal of jurisprudence is to identify the problems and

[82] Remember, on my reading, which Hart himself accepts in the postscript to the second edition of the *Concept of Law*, (3) holds because of the rule of recognition, which is an instance of (7); further, the rule of recognition is a feature of the concept of law—an essential feature of law—which means that (3) ultimately derives from (11). Cf. Hart, *supra* note 7, at 265 and n.59.

questions of jurisprudence and to make progress in responding to and answering them. There is little reason to suppose that labeling any particular kind of answer will contribute much to our success at either. We need an architecture within which the right questions are asked and the prospects for progress on their resolution are enhanced. We have taken one big step—discarding the conventional wisdom—and a few smaller ones—including identifying the importance of the metaphysics of legal content and the difference among different kinds of metaphysical questions about content we can ask—in this essay. Our aim is to construct an architecture with a sturdy foundation. That foundation is the metaphysics of legal content. The question is: Where do we go from here? What lies ahead?

5.8 A New Beginning

I want to close this Article by taking a look ahead to the next two essays in this series. The aim of both is to continue to pursue the projects of jurisprudence once freed of the conventional wisdom. As I understand it, the aim of jurisprudence is to identify its core concerns and problems and to make progress on their resolution. In my view, the core problems of philosophical, as opposed to say sociological, jurisprudence are very much the same kinds of problems that arise elsewhere in philosophy—as much in the philosophy of language and metaphysics, the philosophy of action, mind, social, and natural science as in ethics and political philosophy. The character of the problems is affected, no doubt, by the fact the subject matter is a distinctive kind of social institution, law. But the tradition in legal philosophy has been to isolate jurisprudence—to treat its problems as only marginally connected to the core concerns of philosophy more generally. This has been bad for jurisprudence because it has isolated those who work in the field from both lawyers and legal theorists of all stripes on the one hand and from philosophers more generally on the other. It has been even worse for jurisprudence because it has robbed the subject of the tools of philosophy more generally and the talents of philosophers in other areas of philosophy. Progress has stalled for all the wrong reasons: not because the problems are too hard or too deep, but because too much effort has been devoted to the wrong issues. One deepens and confirms the importance of jurisprudence not by displaying its 'uniqueness' but by showing the ways in which its problems are the problems of philosophy more generally. The question is: What are those problems?

5.8.1 Legal Content and Legal Semantics

One important problem concerns the relationship between legal content and legal semantics. A theory of legal semantics is a theory of the meaning of legal sentences. In the first instance it is an account of how to understand statements of the form: 'It is the law in jurisdiction *J* that *p*'. Some hold that such statements are not reports but actually *predictions* about what judges will do. This is certainly the view widely attributed to Holmes. Others hold that such statements are not reports but *authorizations* directing officials to impose sanctions on those who fail to *p* (at least where *p* is a prohibition or duty-imposing rule). Arguably this is Kelsen's account of the semantics of legal discourse. Still others hold the view that the law does not merely report the existence of a moral duty or an important moral reason to act; it should be understood as imposing such a duty. We can call this the 'moral semantics view of legal discourse', some or other version of which is held by Raz, myself, and others.

The view that legal statements call for a moral semantics of this sort is thought to raise a particularly serious worry for those who adopt a broadly speaking 'positivistic' account of legal content. The problem is this: If legal facts are or can be only social facts, how can legal claims be moral assertions? Or to put it the other way around: If moral facts need not (my view) or cannot (Raz's view) contribute to the content of law, how can legal statements be claims about what one has (sometimes conclusive) moral reason to do? How can such a 'thin' metaphysics of law support a 'rich' moral semantics of legal discourse?

The problem may be particularly pressing for a positivist, but it is actually a quite general problem in jurisprudence: Namely, what metaphysics of law is adequate to support a given semantics of legal discourse? Indeed, this is a general problem in philosophy and not just in jurisprudence.

5.8.2 *Hume's Problem*

The second issue, often confused with the first, concerns the relationship between *propositional contents*. Again, let's begin with metaphysics of law. On the view that only social facts can contribute to legal content, sentences that express the facts in virtue of which the law is what it is are sentences describing behavior and attitudes: the judge did this or intended that or believed this and that, the legislature did that, and so on. Legal statements, however, express claims about what ought to be done or what one is at liberty to do: citizens must do this or are free to do that, and so on.[83]

Sentences asserting or characterizing what officials say and do (and the attitudes they have towards the sayings and doings) are descriptive; they are 'is' statements. In contrast, legal statements (on all but the 'predictive' interpretation of them) are normative; they are 'oughts' of one sort or another. The problem is: How can 'is' premises lead to 'ought' conclusions? How can one derive 'ought' from 'is'? This is Hume's problem, of course.[84] It is a problem about the relationship between descriptive and normative claims or the propositional contents of descriptive and

[83]One need not understand these statements as expressing *moral* oughts or obligations in order for the problem to arise. It is enough that they are normative in any sense.

[84]*See* David Hume, A Treatise of Human Nature, bk. III, pt. 1, § 1, at 456–470 (L.A. Selby-Bigge ed., Oxford Univ. Press 1978) (1740).

normative sentences. It thus differs from the first problem, which expresses a concern about the relationship between the metaphysics of legal content and the semantics of legal discourse.

5.8.3 Directives and Reasons

The third issue is different from the first two but is all too often confused with either or both of them. Law claims to create reasons for acting. Some think that it claims to create a distinct class of reasons for acting—legal reasons. Arguably, Hart held the view that legal obligation constituted a distinctive kind of obligation which was not just a species of moral obligations. Others, again including positivists like Raz and me, believe that the law claims to have an impact on what we have moral reason to do. Sometimes law makes concrete what we already have moral reason to do and yet other times it creates moral reasons for acting that in the absence of law we might not otherwise have. For my part, I think it best to put the point as broadly and generally as possible. Law impacts what we have reason to do: reason, moreover, that is appropriately enforced by coercion. After all, a number of activities can impact what we have moral reason to do without those reasons being suitable objects of coercion. Promising is a good example. Arguably, my promising to meet you for lunch impacts what I have moral reason to do, but not in a way that normally calls for its coercive enforcement.

From the law's point of view, each of its directives has an impact on what we have moral reason to do. The law could well be wrong about this, but it would be odd for law to hold that it is justified in enforcing its directives through coercive means yet remain agnostic as to whether its directives bear on what we have moral reason to do. (The reader will recall that it is considerations of this sort that lead me to the view that, in order for law to exist, an appropriate group of officials must adopt the law's point of view and not merely the internal point of view.)

The question, therefore, is: How can acts of asserting and commanding—among the paradigmatic cases of legal activity—impact what those to whom they are addressed have moral reason to do? How can legal activity, the issuance of authoritative directives, and judicial opinions create moral reasons for acting or otherwise impact what we have moral reason to do?[85] Moreover, distinctive of law (but not unique to it) is that the law claims to give rise to content-independent reasons: that is, the law purports to make a difference in normative space—in terms of what we have reason to do—quite apart from what the content of a particular legal directive or command is.

---

[85] In fact, the issue can be generalized and extended. The same problem arises for those who satisfy themselves thinking that law only creates 'legal' reasons and not moral reasons. After all, the issue is how commanding, asserting, and directing creates any sort of reason for acting, moral or otherwise.

5.8.4 *Law's Place*

The third essay in this trilogy turns to a problem whose solution, for all I know, may forever elude us. For as long as I can recall, commentators have characterized law as a normative social practice—and that seems right. What these commentators have had in mind, more often than not, is what I address in the second essay. They claim that, due to legal positivism's impoverished resources (social facts), positivism cannot account for the normative semantics of law, law's capacity to create reasons for action, and the gap between 'legal is' statements and 'legal ought' statements. The second essay makes clear that I do not believe that any of these charges stick. A thin metaphysics can support a thick semantics. There is no special Humean problem in law. And legal activity can create moral reasons or impact more generally what we have moral reason to do.

On the other hand, there is something of a dual nature to law—its sociality and its normativity—that is a problem of much wider scope, one that cuts across the natural law/positivism divide. I am inclined (for now anyway) to frame the problem in the following way.

Law is indeed a normative social practice. An adequate theory of law will explain its sociality and its normativity. It turns out, however, that there is a major divide in jurisprudence between those who think that the primary project of jurisprudence is to explain the normative dimensions of law and those who think the project is to display the sociality of law, which they take to be the requirement of showing the ways in which law is continuous with other aspects of our social life.[86] For some, like Shapiro, this amounts to showing the continuity between individual intentional and planning activity to group action to group organization to complex organizations to law.[87] The normativity of law is then the normativity suitable to social organizations; this turns out to be largely the normativity of instrumental rationality. The worry that all such accounts invite is that the normativity of law is not the normativity of instrumental rationality. Is there more that can be said about ways in which law's normativity can be connected to instrumental rationality if not strictly speaking reducible to it?

But, of course, law is not just any old social organization, just more complex. The plans, rules, and directives of the law purport to—and sometimes, if not always, do—make a difference in what those to whom it is directed have moral reason to do. Other theorists, including natural lawyers, but not only natural lawyers—Raz, for example—think of law in terms of its continuity with morality. For them, to understand or to grasp law is to appreciate the ways in which law makes a moral difference. For them, the most fundamental feature of law is its continuity with morality and moral life more generally.

---

[86] Hart, Shapiro, and I are among those who emphasize the sociality of law—Hart in emphasizing social rules, Shapiro in emphasizing plans, and I in emphasizing law's conventionality.

[87] Shapiro, *supra* note 23, at 118–233.

It should turn out to be no surprise that those who have focused on the difference law makes in moral space have said little about the social dimensions of law, whereas those who have emphasized law's continuity with social orderings more generally have been largely unconvincing in their accounts of the normativity of law.

The duality of law is the problem of law's place. An adequate jurisprudence is ultimately an account of law's place. The project of the third essay is to find law's place. Failing that, its aim is to provide us with a roadmap adequate to insure that we look for law's place in the right neighborhood.

Chapter 6
Norms, Truth, and Legal Statements

Jorge L. Rodríguez

6.1 Introduction

In a widely discussed decision in August 2009, Argentina's Supreme Court declared unconstitutional the second paragraph of article 14 of the Drug Control Act (number 23.737), which sanctions the possession of drugs for personal use as a criminal offence.[1] The arguments of the Court centered on the scope of the principle of privacy contemplated in article 19 of the Federal Constitution and several international protocols ranked with constitutional hierarchy. The controversial character of the issue was recognized by the Court itself when it acknowledged that its own jurisprudence on the topic had been unstable over the years: in 1978, in 'Colavini',[2] the Court legitimized a criminal penalty for such conduct; in 1986, both 'Bazterrica'[3] and 'Capalbo' rulings reversed 'Colavini', declaring the paragraph in question unconstitutional; in 1990, in 'Montalvo',[4] the Court returned to the first interpretation and, finally—at least by now—the 2009 new ruling represented a return to the view held in 'Bazterrica'.

Among the different interesting questions this set of cases offers for analysis, I want to focus for the purpose of my paper only on one: the difficulties involved in the truth conditions of legal statements. The statement 'In Argentina it is a criminal offence to possess drugs for personal use' seems to have been successively asserted and denied in these different decisions of the High Court.

---

[1] CSJN, 'Recurso de hecho en Arriola, Sebastián y otros s/causa no 9080', A. 891, XLIV, 25/08/09.

[2] *Fallos* 300:254.

[3] *Fallos* 308:1392.

[4] *Fallos* 313:1333.

J.L. Rodríguez (✉)
School of Law, National University of Mar del Plata and University of Girona,
Rawson 318, 7600 Mar del Plata, Argentina
e-mail: jorgerodriguez64@yahoo.com

J. Ferrer Beltrán et al. (eds.), *Neutrality and Theory of Law*,
Law and Philosophy Library 106, DOI 10.1007/978-94-007-6067-7_6,

The problem the Court faced in these cases is with no doubt very complex, a *hard case* in which the key difficulty was interpretative in character. In fact, on the one hand, it is a controversial issue whether in hard cases like this one the law is truly determined, and therefore whether there is something that allows assessing the truth or falsehood of statements about what the law requires. On the other hand, the Court *decided* in each of the cases mentioned whether a criminal provision sanctioning drugs possession for personal use could be justified on constitutional grounds; accordingly, the words of the Court cannot be taken as theoretical statements about the law. However, let us consider a simpler example: a law professor or just a common citizen making the following statement: 'In Argentina murder is a crime'. What is the nature of such a statement? Is it susceptible of truth or falsehood? And if the answer is affirmative, what does its truth or falsehood depend upon?

I think the most intuitive answers to these questions are that it is possible to make true or false assertions about the law, and that their truth values depend mainly on the content of legal rules. But on a closer look, the justification of these or whatever other answers requires to assume a certain position regarding the most important problems of legal theory. Just to mention some of the most fundamental of them: the identification of the law and the relations between law and morality, the interpretation and validity of legal rules and the theory of adjudication.

In this paper I will present some preliminary remarks on this problem of the truth-values of legal statements. More specifically, I will try to defend the following theses:

1. It is possible to distinguish legal rules from true or false statements about what these rules require.
2. Not all kinds of legal statements are purely descriptive in character and susceptible of truth values. Moreover, some of them seem to share the normative character of von Wright's *technical norms* or Schauer's *instructions*.
3. The possibility of maintaining the distinction between legal rules and true or false statements about the law depends on the acceptance of a certain conception of legal rules.
4. The conception of legal rules that allows a defense of such a distinction turns problematic the acceptance of logical relations among legal rules.
5. However, the determination of the truth or falsehood of many legal statements requires taking into account the logical consequences of legal rules.

6.2 Norms and Normative Propositions

As a starting point for the analysis of the problem, it seems of the utmost importance to remember von Wright's distinction between norms and normative propositions.[5] Norms are expressed by means of norm-formulations, they are the meaning of

[5]See Georg Henrik von Wright, *Norm and Action. A Logical Inquiry*, London, Routledge & Kegan Paul, 1963, p. 106.

sentences used to prescribe, i.e., to command, forbid or permit certain actions, and they are neither true nor false.[6] On the other hand, normative propositions are propositions about the existence of norms, and they are true or false depending on the existence or non-existence of the norm referred to. One of the reasons why these two notions have not always been appropriately discriminated is because the very same words (e.g., 'Parking is not allowed here') may be used, depending on the context, either to formulate a norm or to express a normative proposition.

Transposing this distinction to the legal domain, we might say at first sight that legal statements are statements referring to the existence of legal norms, and therefore they express true or false normative propositions about the content of law. Consequently, a statement like 'In Argentina murder is a crime' expressed, not by a legal authority but by a legal theorist, would not express a norm but a normative proposition relative to the existence in Argentina of a legal rule to the effect that murder is a crime.

The relevance of the distinction for legal analysis is apparent and may be shown through the consideration of the problem of legal gaps. In spite of the insistence of Hartian legal positivists on the rejection of the existence of one right answer for any legal problem, Dworkin has claimed that the Social Sources Thesis, a defining tenet of Legal Positivism, implies the counterintuitive consequence that legal systems are necessarily complete. Dworkin's argument can be formalized as follows:

(1)	$p \leftrightarrow Sp$	Sources thesis
(2)	$\sim p \leftrightarrow \sim Sp$	By transposition in (1)
(3)	$\sim p \leftrightarrow S\sim p$	By substitution of *p* by ~*p* in (1)
(4)	$\sim Sp \leftrightarrow S\sim p$	By transitivity of biconditional in (2) and (3).[7]

Let us rephrase the point in clearer terms: if from a positivistic point of view the truth of a legal proposition like 'Murder is forbidden' is—at least—materially equivalent to the existence of a social source for such a proposition, this would logically imply that the falsehood of the proposition 'Murder is forbidden' is materially equivalent to the absence of a social source for such a proposition, but also that the falsehood of the same proposition is materially equivalent to the existence of a social source for the proposition 'Murder is not forbidden' ('Murder is permitted'). By transitivity, this allows to conclude that the absence of a social source for the proposition 'Murder is forbidden' would be materially equivalent to the existence of a social source for the proposition 'Murder is permitted'. In a few words, what is not legally prohibited is legally permitted.

At first sight, the rejection of this consequence seems to force legal positivists to abandon the principle of bivalence regarding legal propositions. Let me introduce

[6]Actually, von Wright claims that it would be misleading to conceive of the relation between norms and their expressions in language only by following the pattern of the semantic dimensions of sense and reference (see von Wright, supra note 5, p. 94).

[7]See Ronald Dworkin, 'Is There Really No Right Answer in Hard Cases?', in Ronald Dworkin, *A Matter of Principle*, Cambridge-London, Harvard University Press, 1985, p. 133.

the following slight variation on the reconstruction of the preceding argument. Instead of representing the truth of a legal proposition simply as *p*, I will use the expression ‘T*p*’, where ‘T’ stands for the predicate ‘true’.[8]

(1′)	$Tp \leftrightarrow Sp$	Social sources thesis
(2′)	$\sim Tp \leftrightarrow \sim Sp$	By transposition in (1′)
(3′)	$T\sim p \leftrightarrow S\sim p$	By substitution of *p* by ~*p* in (1′)

Classical logic not only assumes the principle of excluded middle, i.e., that a certain proposition is either true or not true ($Tp \vee T\sim p$), but also the principle of bivalence, i.e., that either a certain proposition is true, or its negation is true ($Tp \vee T\sim p$). So, under the assumption of these two principles, the claim that a certain proposition is not true and the claim that its negation is true—i.e., that the proposition is false—are equivalent ($\sim Tp \leftrightarrow T\sim p$). Of course, if the principle of bivalence is rejected this equivalence does not hold any more. From the rejection of the principle of bivalence it follows that a certain proposition may be (1) true; (2) false, or (3) neither true nor false ($Tp \vee T\sim p \vee (\sim Tp \wedge \sim T\sim p)$), and so ‘not true’ ($\sim Tp$) cannot be taken now as equivalent to false ($T\sim p$), as the former formula now comprises not only cases (2) but cases (3) as well.[9] Therefore, if we reject the principle of bivalence regarding legal propositions, the analogous to step (4) in the former reconstruction of the argument would not be admissible and Dworkin’s conclusion could be avoided because the first terms of the biconditionals in (2′) and (3′) would not be equivalent.

This seems to be the path followed by different scholars, under the idea that a realist thesis regarding legal statements, implying that every legal statement is true or false according to a certain objective reality whose existence and constitution is independent of our knowledge, is incompatible with the basic thesis of Legal Positivism.[10] From this perspective, the truth of legal propositions under a positivistic

[8] Here I follow Georg Henrik von Wright, ‘Truth Logic’, in Georg Henrik von Wright, *Truth, Knowledge and Modality. Philosophical Papers Volume III*, Oxford, Basil Blackwell, 1984, pp. 26–41. See also José Juan Moreso, Pablo Navarro and Cristina Redondo, ‘Sobre la lógica de las lagunas en el derecho’, in *Critica. Revista Hispanoamericana de Filosofía*, vol. 33, No 99, 2001, pp. 47–73.

[9] See von Wright, *supra* note 8.

[10] See, for instance, Andrei Marmor, *Interpretation and Legal Theory*, Oxford, Clarendon Press, 1992, p. 90. However, in *Positive Law and Objective Values*, Marmor claims that the possibility of legal gaps is compatible with the view that maintains the applicability of the logical principles of bivalence and of excluded middle to the legal domain. The justification Marmor offers is that statements about the law purport to describe authoritative resolutions, and so if the authority’s prescription is for some reason indeterminate due to vagueness or any other reason, then there would be no authoritative resolution on the matter, which would mean that it is false that the law requires whatever it is that it might prescribe in the circumstances. In an example, suppose that the law prescribes that all subjects of type *P* have a legal duty to do *X*, that the category *P* consists of a vague concept, and that *p* is a borderline case of *P*. Here the appropriate conclusion would be that *p* is not legally obliged to do *X* (see Andrei Marmor, *Positive Law and Objective Values*, Oxford, Clarendon Press, 2001, pp. 142–143). I agree with Marmor on this point, but it should be added that if we now ask whether in such case it is legally permitted for *p* not to do *X*, the answer should be that *p* has only a negative permission no to do *X*, as will be explained in the text.

approach could not be conceived independently of the conditions for the recognition of such truth.[11] If the Social Sources Thesis claims that a proposition like 'In Argentina murder is forbidden' is true if there exists a social convention supporting that proposition, then Legal Positivism would be committed to the rejection of the principle of bivalence regarding the truth conditions of legal propositions. This is so because it seems plain that either there is a convention in Argentina that murder is forbidden, or there is a convention in Argentina that murder is not forbidden, or there is not a convention on neither of those things.[12]

But there is an alternative way of avoiding the undesirable conclusion of the argument, that has the advantage of being more deferential to Quine's *minimal mutilation maxim.*[13] According to this view, the Social Sources Thesis does not hold that the truth of the proposition 'In Argentina murder is forbidden' requires the existence of a social convention for the truth of such proposition. Rather, it says that the truth of the proposition 'In Argentina murder is forbidden' depends upon a social convention for the existence of a *rule* in Argentina forbidding murder or, better, a social convention for *the criteria of identification of a rule* forbidding murder as belonging to Argentine legal system.[14] Thus, what is needed to avoid the conclusion Dworkin attributes to Legal Positivism is not the rejection of the principle of bivalence, but to distinguish clearly between legal rules and propositions about them, something that is impossible in the previous reconstructions of the argument because the symbol *p* was being ambiguously used to represent both norms and normative propositions.[15]

By taking seriously this distinction, and replacing *p* as a means to represent a legal proposition like 'In Argentina murder is forbidden' by "'Fm' ∈ LS" (the rule 'Murder is forbidden' belongs to legal system LS), it is possible to reconstruct the premises of the argument as follows:

(1″)	'Fm' $\in$ LS $\leftrightarrow S_{LS}$ 'Fm'	Social sources thesis
(2″)	'Fm' $\notin$ LS $\leftrightarrow \sim S_{LS}$ 'Fm'	By transposition in (1″)
(3″)	'~Fm' $\in$ LS $\leftrightarrow S_{LS}$ '~Fm'	By substitution of 'Fm' by '~Fm' en (1″).

[11] The same idea is explicitly defended by José Juan Moreso in his *Legal Indeterminacy and Constitutional Interpretation, Dordrecht, Kluwer Academic Publishers,* 1998, Chap. 2.

[12] The argument has already been suggested by Dworkin as a possible way out for Legal Positivism (*supra* note 7). Dworkin examines two versions of the rejection of logical bivalence concerning legal propositions. According to the first, two propositions like 'The contract signed by *x* and *y* is valid' and 'The contract signed by *x* and *y* is not valid' may be both false because the latter would not be the negation of the former, as there could be intermediary categories. According to the second, we would assume that one of the two propositions is the negation of the other, but reject that one of them necessarily holds as a consequence of the rejection of the bivalence principle.

[13] See W. V. O. Quine, 'Two Dogmas of Empiricism', in *The Philosophical Review*, 60, 1951, pp. 20–43.

[14] For simplicity, in what follows I will use the former understanding of the Social Sources Thesis.

[15] Dworkin clearly commits this mistake when he states (*supra* note 7) that the structure of positivism as a type of legal theory may be presented this way "…if '*p*' represents a proposition of law, and '*L(p)*' expresses the fact that someone or some group has acted in a way that makes (*p*) true, then positivism holds that (*p*) cannot be true unless L(p) is true" (p. 131).

According to this reading of the Social Sources Thesis, the proposition that in legal system LS murder is forbidden is equivalent to the existence of a social source in LS for the rule 'murder is forbidden'. The claim that in legal system LS there is not a rule forbidding murder is equivalent to the absence of a social source in LS for the rule 'murder is forbidden'. And to say that in legal system LS there is a rule not forbidding (permitting) murder is equivalent to asserting the existence of a social source in LS for the rule 'murder is not forbidden'. When we distinguish norms from normative propositions it is possible to notice there are two different senses in which an action may be said to be permitted: a mere negative sense (there is no forbidding norm) and a positive sense (there is a permissive norm). The absence of a social convention for the identification of the norm 'murder is forbidden' as belonging to legal system LS (as in (2″)) is not equivalent to the existence of a social convention for the identification of the norm 'murder is not forbidden' as belonging to LS (as in 3″)). Hence, Legal Positivism is able to avoid the counterintuitive consequence that its basic thesis implies the necessary completeness of legal systems without any commitment to the antirealist thesis that rejects the principle of bivalence regarding the truth conditions of legal propositions.[16]

In spite of all the light this distinction between norms and normative propositions is capable to shed on the analysis of legal systems, there are certain shortcomings in this simplified approach. A first problem has been presented by Tecla Mazzarese, who argues that norm-propositions lack truth-values.[17] Her skeptical view rests on the following theses:

1. A norm-proposition is not the meaning of a single statement, but of a disguised conjunction of at least two statements: (1) an interpretative statement ('Norm-formulation NF expresses the norm N') and (2) a validity statement ('Norm-formulation NF has been validly created').
2. Neither interpretative statements nor validity statements can be conceived of as descriptive statements.
3. Neither interpretative statements nor validity statements can be conceived of as true or false statements.

[16]The importance of the distinction between norms and normative propositions and, correlatively, of a logic of norms and a logic of normative propositions, for the analysis of the ambiguity lying behind the principle 'what is not legally forbidden is legally permitted' and the postulate of the necessary completeness of law was first stressed in the seminal Carlos E. Alchourrón and Eugenio Bulygin, *Normative Systems*, Wien-New York, Springer Verlag, Chap. 7. Joseph Raz examines the problem in 'Legal Reasons, Sources and Gaps', in Joseph Raz, *The Authority of Law. Essays on Law and Morality*, Oxford, Clarendon Press, 1979, pp. 53–77, and though he there cites the work of Alchourrón and Bulygin, he does not seem to take any advantage of their ideas. For a critical view on Raz's thesis, see José Juan Moreso, Pablo E. Navarro and Cristina Redondo, *supra* note 8 and Eugenio Bulygin, 'On Legal Gaps', in P. Commanducci and R. Guastini, *Analisi e Diritto 2002–2003*, Torino, Giappichelli, 2004, pp. 21–28.

[17]See Tecla Mazzarese, *Logica Deontica e Linguaggio Giuridico*, Cedam, Padova, 1989, pp. 135–167; 'Norm-proposition: Epistemic and Semantic Queries', in *Rechtstheorie* 22, 1991, pp. 39–70.

In Mazzarese's view, on the one hand, validity statements involve an evaluation of the act of promulgation of a certain norm-formulation, so they cannot be purely descriptive assertions. On the other hand, interpretative statements assign a certain meaning to norm-formulations. But Mazzarese also claims that there is not a unique interpretation that can be considered 'correct' or 'true' of any norm-formulation. Therefore, the process of identifying the norm expressed by it would never render a unique result, and thus interpretative statements cannot be purely descriptive either.

I believe that Mazzarese's arguments do not allow deriving such a strong conclusion as the one she has in mind (that *all* norm-propositions lack truth values). Notwithstanding, her ideas stress an important aspect of an intuition held by many legal philosophers: that legal science has a normative dimension exceeding the fact that it deals with norms. The tasks of legal science are complex and, with no doubt, not all—and not even the majority—of its statements can be assimilated to normative propositions in the sense explained above. Therefore, it is undeniably true that most statements of legal science are not susceptible of truth or falsehood. And this is so because two of the most important tasks of legal science are the ascription of a certain interpretation to problematic norm-formulations and the evaluation of compatibility of certain norms with higher-ranked norms, and both activities have an indisputable evaluative content, as Mazzarese remarks.

6.3 The Problematic Status of Legal Statements

It is impossible to examine here in detail the many different approaches that have been defended in legal philosophy concerning the nature of legal statements. Moreover, they are widely and sufficiently known. My concern here is only to stress that the two aspects of the problem indicated above, the different conceptions on legal interpretation and on legal validity, allow introducing a certain classificatory order over these approaches. Oversimplifying things, on one extreme of the scale we might place those scholars that hold, on the one hand, that interpretation of legal rules is a non-cognitive activity that always involves an authoritative decision, and on the other hand that legal statements are purely descriptive in character. Alf Ross and other defenders of legal realism would be representative of this perspective. Ross, for instance, claims that legal statements do not describe valid norms but norms *in force*, and to say that a certain norm is in force in a legal system is a purely factual statement: it means that the norm in question will in fact be used by judges to justify their decisions in the cases within its scope.[18] On the opposite extreme of the scale we might place those scholars that hold a cognitivist conception of legal

[18] See Alf Ross, *On Law and Justice*, London, Stevens & Sons Ltd., 1958. Actually, in the English version of the book the term 'validity' is ambiguously used to express the normative idea of valid norms and the factual idea of norms in force. See the comments on the topic by Genaro Carrió in his Spanish translation, *Sobre el derecho y la justicia*, Buenos Aires, Eudeba, 1963.

interpretation, according to which there is always a right answer to any legal case, but at the same time they claim that statements on the validity of legal rules have the same character as the object to which they refer, i.e., they are normative and not descriptive. Dworkin and many Natural Law theorists may be taken as representing this point of view.

A great number of intermediate positions are conceivable in the ample space lying between these two extremes. Because of its significance, I would like to make some brief remarks on Kelsen's account of the problem. Kelsen has always defended the separation of 'is' (*Sein*) and 'ought' (*Sollen*). This idea has been influenced by two different philosophical trends that lead to a strong and a weak version of it. First, in his earlier works, he presents the idea of a 'world of ought' as a category of understanding, different from—and not reducible to—the 'world of is', that stems from the Kantian tradition. From this perspective, Kelsen holds that the is/ought distinction cannot be explained further: '*...we are immediately aware of the difference*'.[19] In this version of the distinction, there are two realms or worlds entirely different, the 'world of is' and the 'world of ought', each of them ruled by a logic of its own. In the 'world of is' rules the *principle of causality*, whereas in the 'world of ought' rules the *principle of imputation*. The relations we find in nature would be cause and effect relations, connected according to the principle of causality. In contrast, the science of law does not describe its object in the same way: when describing a normative order we apply a different principle, called *imputation* or *attribution*. This principle, though analogous to causality, is nevertheless characteristically different from it. Such a principle is similar in that it has a function in legal statements that equates the function of the principle of causality in the laws of nature: It connects two elements. However, the relation expressed in legal statements has a different meaning from the one expressed in laws of nature. They do not express that when A is, B *is*; but that when A is, B *ought* to be.[20] The difference stems from the fact that the connection described in legal statements between the antecedent fact and the legal consequence is brought about by the legal authority, i.e., by a rule created by an act of will, whereas the connection in the laws of nature is independent from such a human intervention.

Kelsen offers in his later works a weaker version of the same idea. The distinction appears now in terms of two different uses of language: prescriptions and descriptions, each one of them with a logic of its own, with the consequence that from a set of purely descriptive statements a set of prescriptive statements cannot be inferred and vice versa. Thus, Kelsen subscribes to the idea that there is no logical bridge between is and ought, and therefore condemns the naturalistic fallacy.[21] However, still in this second version of the distinction there are residues of a much stronger one, one that transcends a mere difference in the uses of language.

[19] Hans Kelsen, *Pure Theory of Law*, translation from the second (revised and enlarged) German edition [1960] by Max Knight, New Jersey, The Lawbook Exchange Ltd, 2008, p. 5.

[20] See Hans Kelsen, *supra* note 19, p. 77.

[21] See Hans Kelsen, *supra* note 19, p. 12, n. 3.

These residues are reflected in Kelsen's approach to the so-called 'legal statements' (*Rechtssätze*), i.e., statements describing legal norms (*Rechtsnormen*), an issue closely connected with the Kelsenian conception of legal science.

Kelsen maintains that legal science is 'normative', an idea with an evident Kantian influence. On this basis, Kelsen builds his distinction between factual (causal) and normative social sciences, between legal sociology and legal science. The difference between them rests on the kind of propositions they use in describing their objects. Legal science is normative not only in the sense that it describes norms, but also in the sense that its propositions are themselves *normative* in a peculiar sense.

The difference between 'legal statements' and legal norms was not at all clear in the earlier works of Kelsen, were he seems to confuse both ideas. However, at least since the *General Theory of Law and State*[22] he seems to distinguish between true or false legal statements ('rules of law', as he calls them) and legal norms, which lack truth values:

> [The] statements, by means of which the science of law represents law, must not be confused with the norms created by law-making authorities ... The legal norms enacted by law creating authorities are prescriptive; the rules of law formulated by the science of law are descriptive.[23]
>
> Rules of law (in a descriptive sense), on the other hand, are hypothetical judgments stating that according to a national or international legal order, under the conditions determined by this order, certain consequences determined by the order ought to take place. Legal norms are not judgments, that is, they are not statements about an object of cognition. According to their meaning they are commands; they may be also permissions and authorizations; but they are not instructions as is often maintained when law and jurisprudence are erroneously equated. The law commands, permits, or authorizes, but it does not 'teach'.[24]

However, Kelsen states that, though legal statements are true or false, they are *ought* statements, not only because they refer to legal norms, but also because they identify a norm as *valid*, and in the Kelsenian framework validity is a normative concept: to say that a certain norm is valid is tantamount to saying that one ought to do what that norm prescribes.[25] That is the reason why Kelsen thinks that legal statements not only ascertain empirical facts but also have a normative dimension: they are 'ought' statements, but descriptive ought statements.

The Kelsenian idea that legal statements are 'ought' statements, that do not express prescriptive but descriptive duties, seems nothing but the product of a confusion deriving from the ambiguity that systematically affects deontic terms, which are liable to be read both descriptively and prescriptively. Alf Ross and Herbert Hart, among others, have criticized this idea in extent. According to Ross, legal statements cannot be ought statements if they have truth values. Kelsen's use of the

---

[22] Hans Kelsen, *General Theory of Law and State*, Cambridge, Harvard University Press, 1945.

[23] Hans Kelsen, supra note 22, p. 45.

[24] Hans Kelsen, *supra* note 19, p. 71.

[25] A thorough analysis of the notion of validity is crucial for a critical evaluation of these Kelsenian ideas. However, for the sake of brevity, I will leave aside the point.

concept of validity as binding force, similar to the one we find in Natural Law theorists, entails that the propositions of legal science have a normative character not compatible with a positivistic theory of law for they refer to the validity of legal norms.[26]

Hart has objected the Kelsenian idea of 'descriptive' ought statements with the aid of the distinction between use and mention of words.[27] He says that when the lawgiver enacts a law she *uses* certain words, while when the legal theorist tells us what the law means she *mentions* the very same words, and thus the word 'ought' would be mentioned but not used in the statements of legal science. However, Kelsen's explicit rejection of this reading pushed Hart into reconsidering the point. He proposed an analogy with the relationship between a speaker of a foreign language and his interpreter. Suppose a foreign commander in a prisoner camp issues an order, translated by the interpreter as 'Stand up!'. The interpreter's statement is neither an order, because she is not an authority, nor a second order statement that mentions the original words and correlates them with a certain meaning. The interpreter's statement tries to *reproduce* the order: it is a special use of language, and we could say with Kelsen that here the use of the grammatical imperative was 'descriptive' and not 'prescriptive'. Nevertheless, Hart points out that logic has received substantial development in the last centuries—particularly in the realm of logical analysis of normative discourse—to be satisfied with this problematic category of 'descriptive oughts'.

Hart's distinction between statements formulated from an *internal* and from an *external point of view*, as well as Raz's category of *detached legal statements*, may be seen as an attempt to elucidate the problematic character Kelsen assigns to legal statements. Hart distinguishes legal statements formulated by those who accept the rules and use them to evaluate their own and other people's conduct, from those formulated by an external observer, who does not need to accept the rules, and may limit herself to register mere regularities of conduct of those who follow such rules, or may also take into consideration the attitudes of acceptance of those who follow the rules.[28] Only this latter kind of external statements, i.e., those taking account of the internal point of view of the acceptants, would constitute an adequate tool for a proper description of a legal system. Now, the simple fact that these statements register attitudes of acceptance of rules does not give them any 'normative' character, so they may be considered apt to truth values.

[26]See Alf Ross, *supra* note 18, 9–10; 'El concepto de validez y el conflicto entre el positivismo jurídico y el derecho natural', in *Revista Jurídica de Buenos Aires*, IV, 1961, reproduced in S. Paulson, *Normativity and Norms. Critical Perspectives on Kelsenian Themes*, Oxford, Oxford University Press, 1999.

[27]See H. L. A. Hart, 'Kelsen Visited', in *UCLA Law Review* 10, 1963. Hart cites on this point Martin P. Golding, "Kelsen and the Concept of 'Legal System'", in *Archiv für Rechts-und Sozialphilosophie* 47, pp. 355–364.

[28]See H. L. A. Hart, *The Concept of Law*, 2nd edition, Oxford, Oxford University Press, 1994, pp. 89 ff. and note at p. 291.

The status of Raz's detached legal statements is more problematic. According to Raz, legal scholars can use normative language to describe the law and make legal statements without endorsing law's moral authority.[29] This kind of statements makes use of normative terms and the speaker formulates them from the point of view of those who accept the rules, but this point of view is not necessarily shared by her, the speaker does not necessarily assume any commitment with what the rules require. Those statements can be exemplified by advises given by an expert on a certain system of rules, who does not endorse such rules, to someone that accepts them and has doubts on what they require regarding certain situations. As Bayón has pointed out, the possibility of formulating detached legal statements or statements formulated from a point of view, allows accounting for the way in which normative language can be used to describe a legal system without assuming any axiological commitment to it.[30]

Discussing this kind of statements Raz claims that they are 'normative',[31] though he also states that they can be true or false.[32] Similarly, Hart maintains that they are normative statements but can be used to describe the law.[33] According to this, it seems that we have not gone far beyond Kelsen's 'descriptive oughts'. And so it could be argued that the 'normativity' of detached statements, or statements from a legal point of view, is no more than the result of using deontic expressions in them, like 'ought', 'duty' or 'obligation'. However, as we have already seen, deontic expressions can be used to express either genuine norms or normative propositions. Thus, if detached legal statements are deemed true or false, they will express normative propositions.[34]

I believe, however, there is a way to conceive of the character of detached legal statements that gives a more faithful account of the platitude they are meant to grasp, and it consists in assimilating them to what von Wright calls *directives* or *technical norms*[35] and Schauer calls *instructions*.[36] Detached legal statements, like directives, have a standard conditional formulation in whose antecedent there is mention of some wanted thing and in whose consequent there is mention of something that must or must not be done. An example would be 'If you want to comply

---

[29] See Joseph Raz, *The Authority of Law*, Oxford, Oxford University Press, 1979, pp. 156–7.

[30] See Juan Carlos Bayón, *La normatividad del derecho. Deber jurídico y razones para la acción*, Madrid, Centro de Estudios Constitucionales, 1991, pp. 28.

[31] See Joseph Raz, *supra* note 29, p. 202.

[32] See Joseph Raz, *Practical Reason and Norms*, 2nd edition, Princeton University Press, 1990, p. 177.

[33] See H.L.A. Hart, 'Commands and Authoritative Legal Reasons', in *Essays on Bentham. Jurisprudence and Political Theory*, Oxford, Clarendon Press, 1982, p. 154.

[34] See Juan Carlos Bayón, *supra* note 30, p. 28.

[35] See Georg Henrik von Wright, *supra* note 5, pp. 9–11.

[36] See Frederick Schauer, *Playing By the Rules: A Philosophical Examination of Rule-Based Decision-Making in Law and in Life*, Oxford, Clarendon Press, 1991, pp. 3–4.

with this systems of rules, you should…'.[37] Here the antecedent mentions the end to be attained, i.e., the fulfillment of the obligations derivable from a system of rules, the attainment of which depends upon the agent's will. And the consequent mentions the action that must or must not be done to comply with the system. Directives or technical norms are neither true nor false, but there is a logical connection between them and certain descriptive statements to the effect that the action recommended is a necessary condition for the attainment of the end, expressing what von Wright calls *anankastic propositions*.

In similar terms, Schauer claims that instructions are optional in two ways. First, because they are applicable only if the agent wishes to succeed in the pertinent task—in our case, to obey a system of rules. They are hypothetical, containing an explicit or implicit 'if' clause limiting its application. Second, because their force to motive our conduct depends on our assessment of the likelihood they will produce the desired result. If, on the contrary, we believe that, at least in this case, the instruction will not lead to that result, the rule's force evaporates and we will feel free to ignore it. According to Schauer, the reason is that instructions work as *rules of thumb*, providing useful guides for ordinary cases, but not taken even by those who accept them as exerting any normative pressure *qua* rules if we believe that, in spite of following the guide they offer, the desired goal will not be attained. This is tantamount to von Wright's idea that the efficacy of directives depends upon the truth of the anankastic propositions presupposed by them; were they false, the efficacy of the directive would disappear or, what is the same, their force to motivate our conduct evaporate.[38]

Under this interpretation, detached legal statements are not by themselves true or false. What would be true or false is the information presupposed by them regarding the rules of the legal system. And they are 'normative' statements in the peculiar sense of normativity attributable to rules of thumb. Whether the information they presuppose concerning legal rules is correct, they are apt to bring about a practical difference for the addressee. Nevertheless, they actually do not provide genuine reasons for action, but rather reasons to believe on the existence of reasons for action.[39]

Many statements formulated by legal scholars can be interpreted in this way. As I said before, the tasks of legal science are complex, and many of its statements are not susceptible to truth or falsehood. Nevertheless, if we reject a radically

[37]Raz explicitly rejects this interpretation: he says that statements from a point of view cannot "*…be interpreted as conditionals: 'If you accept this point of view then you should* etc.'". However, he immediately adds: *'Rather, they assert what is the case from the relevant point of view as if it is valid or on the hypothesis that it is … but without actually endorsing it'* (see Joseph Raz, *supra* note 29, p. 157). I really cannot see the difference between asserting something under a certain condition and asserting something on the hypothesis that condition verifies.

[38]See Georg Henrik von Wright, *supra* note 5, pp. 160–163; 'Norms, Truth and Logic', in *Practical reason. Philosophical Papers, Volume I*, Oxford, Basil Blackwell, pp. 199–209.

[39]See Juan Carlos Bayón, 'Razones y Reglas. Sobre el concepto de 'razón excluyente' de Joseph Raz', in *Doxa* 10, 1991, p. 29.

skeptical conception of interpretation—one according to which the law is absolutely indeterminate, and accept that there is at least one sense of 'validity' according to which qualifying a norm as valid merely indicates that it belongs to a certain normative system, then we should admit the possibility of asserting at least *some* true normative propositions about the content of law.

6.4 Conceptions of Norms and Logical Consequences

A second problem with the distinction between norms and normative propositions is that its viability depends on the conception of norms we adopt. At least at first sight we may say that there are three different ways to characterize norms according to their relation with language[40]:

1. A *syntactic* conception, where norms are identified with linguistic entities, i.e., sentences in which certain normative expressions, such as 'obligatory', 'forbidden', 'permitted', etc. are used. Von Wright reserves the term 'norm-formulation' to refer to these entities.[41]
2. A *semantic* conception, where norms are conceived of as the meaning of certain linguistic expressions (norm-formulations). In this sense norms are proposition-like entities: they are the meaning of prescriptive sentences, just like propositions are the meaning of descriptive sentences.
3. A *pragmatic* conception, where norms are the outcome of the prescriptive use of language. The same proposition may be the object of different linguistic acts: it may be asserted, conjectured, questioned, ordered, etc., and each of those different acts would produce different results: an assertion, a conjecture, a question, an order, etc. From this point of view, the possibility of distinguishing norms from other entities is neither at the syntactic level nor at the semantic level. It would require taking into account the different uses of language.

Of these three alternatives, there is a powerful argument to reject the first, i.e., the syntactic conception. Norms cannot be identified at a mere syntactic level because, as has already been said, the very same linguistic expression can be used to express either a norm (if enacted by an authority) or a normative proposition (if uttered by someone who is not an authority).[42] Thus, von Wright maintains that whether a

[40] See José Juan Moreso and Pablo Navarro, *Orden jurídico y sistema jurídico. Una investigación sobre la identidad y la dinámica de los sistemas jurídicos*, Madrid, Centro de Estudios Constitucionales, 1993, pp. 30–31. In fact Moreso and Navarro take into account another possibility: what they call a syntactic-semantic conception, according to which norms are conceived of as linguistic entities under a certain interpretation. From this point of view, norms are neither merely linguistic formulations nor their meaning, but rather the correlation of the latter to the former. Nevertheless, at least for the sake of the analysis that follows, I believe this alternative can be taken as a sophisticated version of the semantic conception.

[41] See Georg Henrik von Wright, supra *note* 5, p. 109.

[42] See Georg Henrik von Wright, *supra* note 5, p. 109.

given sentence is a norm-formulation or not can never be decided on 'morphic' grounds, i.e., depending on signs alone.[43] We are left then with the semantic and the pragmatic conceptions. Alchourrón and Bulygin have respectively called these two alternatives the *hyletic* and the *expressive* conception of norms. And they have shown that the option we favor between these two different ways of characterizing norms has important consequences on the kind of relations we may accept among norms, particularly on the question of the admissibility of logical relations among them.[44]

This possibility of accepting a logic of norms requires to offer an answer to a primary difficulty which forces to reconcile certain preanalytic intuitions that seem to be in conflict. On the one hand, it seems natural to think that norms lack truth values. But, on the other hand, logic has been traditionally associated with the notions of truth and falsehood, in the sense that the concept of logical consequence as well as that of contradiction, and the meaning of logical connectives, have been defined in terms of truth. Consequently, it seems that the scope of logic is limited to descriptive statements. Yet, it is common to derive certain norms from others, and a clear example of this seems to be the common obligation over judges to justify their decisions in general norms. Indeed, they use arguments where at least one of their premises is one or more general norms, and from them, jointly with a description of the facts of the case at hand, they derive a particular norm as a conclusion. Moreover, there seems to be no substantial difference in the use of the logical connectives from descriptive to prescriptive discourse.[45]

Jorgen Jørgensen presented this problem in the form of a dilemma, and it may be said that the different answers offered to it mark the historical evolution of deontic logic.[46] The dilemma is this: Under the assumption that norms are neither true nor false, there are only two possible alternatives concerning the applicability of logic to normative discourse. Either the notion of logical consequence and the logical connectives are defined in terms of truth, in which case there is no possibility for a logic of norms, or a logic of norms is possible, but then the scope of logic has to be wider than descriptive discourse, and the notion of logical consequence, as well as the logical connectives, should not be defined in terms of truth, what contradicts a firmly established tradition.

---

[43] See Georg Henrik von Wright, *supra* note 5, p. 102.

[44] See Carlos E. Alchourrón and Eugenio Bulygin, *Sobre la existencia de las normas jurídicas*, Valencia (Venezuela), Universidad de Carabobo, 1979, pp. 37–41; 'The Expressive Conception of Norms', in R. Hilpinen (ed.), *New Studies in Deontic Logic*, Dordrecht-Boston-London, Reidel, 1981, pp. 95–124.

[45] See Eugenio Bulygin, 'Lógica deóntica', in C. Alchourrón, C.E. Méndez y R. Orayen (eds.), *Enciclopedia Iberoamericana de Filosofía, vol. 7, Lógica*, Madrid, Trotta-CSIC, 1995, pp. 129–142.

[46] See Jorgen Jørgensen, 'Imperatives and Logic', in *Erkenntnis* 7, 1938, pp. 288–296. For a thorough analysis of the different alternatives to overcome Jørgensen' dilemma, see Arend Soeteman, *Logic in Law*, Dordrecht-Boston-London, Kluwer Academic Publishers, 1989, Chaps. 3 and 4.

Alchourrón and Bulygin argue that among the supporters of the semantic conception there are those who defend that norms have truth values, and therefore accept a logic of norms, but also those who reject the former idea. In this second view it would still be possible to justify a logic of norms, but to support this possibility it would be necessary to assume that logic exceeds the realm of truth. And for any of these two different perspectives it would be possible to distinguish a genuine logic of norms from a logic of normative propositions.[47] By contrast, Alchourrón and Bulygin consider that the supporters of the pragmatic conception can only accept a logic of normative propositions, because within this view norms are facts—acts of prescription—and between facts there are no logical relations.[48]

I partially disagree with these ideas, but to explain my differences a closer examination of these two different conceptions of norms is needed. Using the well known idea introduced by Elizabeth Anscombe,[49] it may be said that when language is used to describe, it has a word to world *direction of fit*, what is tantamount to saying that in case of a discrepancy the problem is not in the latter but in the former. By contrast, when language is used prescriptively, the direction of fit goes in the opposite direction, so when the subject of the prescription does not act as required, the problem is not in language but in the world.

This is the explanation of norms and their differences with other entities which characterizes the pragmatic conception of norms. From this perspective, the difference between the assertion that *p* is the case and the prescription that *p* ought to be the case rests on the different propositional attitude adopted by the speaker. Norms are instances of a prescriptive use of language, were the direction of fit is from world to language.

The supporters of the semantic conception of norms need to offer an alternative reconstruction of the difference between propositions and norms. The most promising way of doing this seems to rely on a possible worlds semantics: one can say that, while what determines the truth value of the assertion that a certain proposition *p* is the case is something that occurs in the actual world, what determines the truth value of the assertion that *p* is obligatory is something that occurs, not in the actual world, but in those possible worlds which are normatively ideal with respect to the actual world. Hence, the norm 'obligatory *p*' would be true in the actual world if *p* were true in every possible world which is normatively ideal regarding the actual world.[50] Of course, presenting the difference between descriptive statements and norms in this way involves accepting that norms are capable of truth values.

---

[47] See Carlos E. Alchourrón, 'Logic of Norms and Logic of Normative propositions', in *Logique et Analyse* 12, No 47, 1969, pp. 242–268; Carlos E. Alchourrón and Eugenio Bulygin, *supra* note 16.

[48] See Carlos E. Alchourrón and Eugenio Bulygin, 'The Expressive Conception of Norms, *supra* note 44.

[49] See G. E. M. Anscombe, *Intention*, Oxford, Basil Blackwell, 1957, p. 56. See also John Searle, *Intentionality. An Essay in the Philosophy of Mind*, Cambridge, Cambridge University Press, 1983, p. 7.

[50] See, for instance, Hugo Zuleta, *Normas y Justificación. Una investigación lógica*, Madrid-Barcelona-Buenos Aires, Marcial Pons, 2008, p. 82.

It is important to notice that possible worlds semantics needs not necessarily assume the controversial claim that norms are proposition-like entities. For instance, one can say that prescribing that *p* is obligatory in the actual world is tantamount to *preferring* as normatively ideal with respect to the actual world those possible worlds in which *p* is true.[51] But if we opt for this alternative explanation, the difference between the assertion that *p* is the case and the prescription that *p* ought to be the case would be pragmatic and not semantic.

In other words, only one of the following two alternatives is possible. We may understand that the direction of fit of the sentence expressing a norm, like 'obligatory p', is from word to world. In that case the sentence will try to register what happens in certain normatively ideal worlds, and will be true or false depending on its success in doing so. The alternative option is that the direction of fit of such sentence is from world to language. In that case the sentence itself will determine which worlds the speaker deems normatively ideal, and norms will lack truth values. Accordingly, either we adopt the semantic conception of norms, and simultaneously accept that they are capable of truth values, or we follow the pragmatic conception. There seems to be no conceptual room for assuming the semantic conception and rejecting the attribution of truth values to norms.

On the other hand, from the pragmatic standpoint it seems at first sight that a genuine logic of norms is unacceptable. Logical relations would only be admissible among normative propositions, i.e., among descriptive statements about the existence of norms.[52] Now, the challenge for this point of view consists in offering a system of logic for normative propositions which does not presuppose logical relations among norms themselves.[53] However, as von Wright has demonstrated in one of his

---

[51] For an approach to the logic of norms based on preferences, see Sven Ove Hansson, *The Structure of Values and Norms*, Cambridge, Cambridge University Press, 2001, p. 146.

[52] Alchourrón and Bulygin explored the possibility of adopting the pragmatic conception of norms and facing Jørgensen's dilemma from its first horn, fundamentally in the works cited *supra* in note 44 and also in 'Pragmatic Foundations for a Logic of Norms', in *Rechtstheorie* 15, Berlin 41, Dunker & Humblot, 1984, pp. 453–464. However, after such explorations the authors returned to the semantic conception in virtue of some of the difficulties involved in the pragmatic approach, particularly for the representation of conditional norms. See Carlos E. Alchourrón and Eugenio Bulygin, *Análisis lógico y derecho*, Madrid, Centro de Estudios Constitucionales, 1991, pp. XXVII and XXVIII; David Makinson, 'On a Fundamental Problem of Deontic Logic', in P. McNamara y H. Prakken (eds.), *Norms, Logics and Information Systems. New Studies on Deontic Logic and Computer Science*, Amsterdam, IOS Press, 1998, pp. 29–53.

[53] In the system of logic for normative propositions as presented by Carlos E. Alchourrón in 'Philosophical Foundations of Deontic Logic and the Logic of Defeasible Conditionals', in J. Meyer y R. Wieringa, *Deontic Logic in Computer Science: Normative System Specification*, Chichester-New York-Brisbane-Toronto-Singapore, Wiley & Sons, 1993, pp. 43–84, the following are taken as axioms of a logic of normative propositions:

(A1) $\vdash O_\alpha(p \wedge q) \leftrightarrow (O_\alpha p \wedge O_\alpha q)$

(A2) $\vdash O_\alpha p \rightarrow P+_\alpha p$

(A3) $\vdash P+_\alpha(p \wedge q) \rightarrow P+_\alpha p$

None of these expressions are simply derivable from propositional logic.

last papers, such system will be nothing but a simple application of propositional logic, in the sense that there will not be any specific laws for normative propositions.[54] Therefore, on this view, either we accept that the realm of logic is wider than truth, and consequently we admit the existence of logical relations among norms, or we have to reject even the possibility of a logic of normative propositions, unless we are ready to give such a dubious title to a mere instance of propositional logic.[55]

The ultimate reason that justifies these conclusions is that I suspect that behind the distinction between the semantic and the pragmatic conception of norms there are in fact two different views on meaning: one according to which meaning is explained exclusively in terms of truth conditions, and the other in which the pragmatic aspects of language participate in meaning.[56] From the first point of view, norms will have a direction of fit from the language to the world and will be capable of truth values; from the other, norms will have a direction of fit from world to language and lack truth values.

Under the first approach Jørgensen's dilemma is avoided and it is easy to justify the possibility of logical relations among norms, but only because within this perspective norms are conceived of as proposition-like entities, and therefore, are capable of truth and falsehood. Now, an important corollary of this point of view is that, precisely because of this characteristic, the distinction between norms and normative propositions cannot be maintained, because norms themselves are *propositions about what ought to be the case*. The only distinction we may draw here is between the assertion that *p* is obligatory according to the norms of a certain normative system, and the assertion that p is obligatory *simpliciter*, i.e., between *relative normative propositions* (relative to what ought to be the case according to a certain set of norms) and *absolute normative propositions* (all things considered).[57]

By contrast, under the second approach the idea of norms having truth values is unacceptable. From this perspective, it is certainly possible to maintain the distinction between norms and normative propositions, but either we reject the existence of logical relations among norms, or we have to face Jørgensen's dilemma through its second horn and, contrary to the traditional view, justify that the scope of logic is not limited to truth.

---

[54] See Georg Henrik von Wright, 'On Norms and Norm-Propositions. A Sketch', in W. Krawietz et al. (eds.), *The Reasonable as Rational? On Legal Argumentation and Justification. Festschrift for Aulis Aarnio*, Berlin, Duncker & Humblot, 2000, pp. 173–178.

[55] For a more exhaustive justification of these ideas, see Jorge L. Rodríguez, 'Naturaleza y lógica de las proposiciones normativas. Contribución en homenaje a G. H. von Wright', en *Doxa* 26, 2003, pp. 87–108. In a similar line, see Ota Weinberger, 'The Expressive Conception of Norms—An Impasse for the Logic of Norms', in *Law and Philosophy* 4, 1985, pp. 165–198.

[56] For a brief comment on the objections directed against the traditional limits among syntax, semantics and pragmatics, following ideas of Wittgenstein, Austin and Sellars, and their consequences on legal interpretation, see Damiano Canale y Giovanni Tuzet, 'On Legal Inferentialism. Toward a Pragmatics of Semantic Content in Legal Interpretation?', in *Ratio Juris*, vol. 20, No. 1, 2007, pp. 32–44.

[57] The distinction between absolute and relative norm-propositions was suggested to me by Jan- R. Sieckmann in personal comunication.

Let's return now to the analysis of legal statements. If the ideas presented above are sound, then it is possible to show a different kind of difficulty in the projection of the distinction between norms and normative propositions to the legal domain. To illustrate the point, let me go back one more time to Kelsen and his view on legal statements. In his main works, Kelsen defended a non-cognitivist conception of norms, according to which they lack truth values. It is debatable whether this is due to Kelsen's adoption of the pragmatic conception of norms, though it seems apparent that in his latest writings Kelsen seems very close to it.[58] In the second edition of the *Pure Theory of Law* he affirms that logic cannot be applied directly to norms. However, logical principles, and the notion of contradiction, are in his view *indirectly* applicable to legal norms through their application to the legal statements that describe them.[59] However, Kelsen also states that, according to what he calls the *static principle* of derivation, the content of a certain norm can be derived from another norm, because it *'can be traced back to a norm under whose content the content of the [norm] in question can be subsumed as the particular under the general'*.[60] Kelsen contrasts this principle with the *dynamic principle*, according to which a norm can be traced back to another, not because of its content, but because the latter determines certain formal aspects of its enactment. In the same line, he distinguishes between static and dynamic systems.[61] And though there seems to be an evident tension between these two notions of a normative system, Kelsen asserts that the static and the dynamic principles may be combined in the same system, and therefore a normative system can be at the same time static and dynamic:

> The static and dynamic principles may be combined in the same system if the presupposed basic norm, according to the dynamic principle, merely authorizes a norm creating authority, and if this authority (or one authorized by it in turn) not only establishes norms by which other norm-creating authorities are delegated, but also norms in which the subjects are commanded to observe a certain behavior and from which further norms can be deduced, as form the general to the particular.[62]

---

[58] Alchourrón and Bulygin attribute to Kelsen the pragmatic conception of norms in 'The Expressive Conception of Norms', *supra* note 44. More cautiously, Bulygin claims that in his latest works Kelsen turns back to the expressivism he had originally defended. See Eugenio Bulygin, 'Norms and Logic. Kelsen and Weinberger on the Ontology of Norms', in *Law and Philosophy*, No. 4, pp. 145–163; 'Sobre el problema de la aplicabilidad de la lógica al derecho', in H. Kelsen and U. Klug, *Normas jurídicas y análisis lógico*, Madrid, Centro de Estudios Constitucionales, 1988, pp. 9–26. For a critical comment on this attribution to Kelsen of the pragmatic conception of norms, see Stanley Paulson, "On Ideal Form, Empowering Norms and 'Normative Functions'", in *Ratio Juris*, vol. 3, No 1, 1990, pp. 84–88, and Riccardo Guastini, 'Norme, giudizi di validità, e scienza giuridica nell'ultimo Kelsen', in Riccardo Guastini, *Distiguendo*, Turin, Giappichelli, 1996, pp. 101 ff., who distinguishes between the Kelsen of the classical period, that seems to defend the hyletic conception, and the late Kelsen, that seems to opt for the expressive conception.

[59] See Hans Kelsen, *supra* note 19, p. 74.

[60] See Hans Kelsen, *supra* note 19, p. 195.

[61] See Hans Kelsen, *supra* note 19, p. 197.

[62] Hans Kelsen, *supra* note 19, pp. 197–198.

This idea of a static system is incompatible with the rejection of logical relations among norms. In later works, Kelsen goes further and rules out the possibility of an indirect application of logic to norms. In fact, he also abandons the distinction between static and dynamic systems. But in spite of these variations, it is clear that Kelsen definitely opts for the first horn of Jørgensen's dilemma: norms are not capable of truth values and so there are no logical relations among them. Yet, the problem with this idea is that the analysis of what the law requires, at least in certain cases, makes it necessary to take into consideration not only the content of those norms that have been explicitly enacted by certain authorities, but some of their logical consequences as well.

The expression 'legal system' is used many times to refer to the reconstruction of the set of norms that are relevant for solving a certain case. This reconstruction seeks to determine the consequences that follow from a certain set of norms regarding a certain theoretical or practical legal problem, i.e., it tries to identify the kind of operation that legal scholars perform when they examine the solutions deriving from the law in force regarding a real or hypothetical case. Here the logical consequence relation is what determines the systematic structure of the set.[63]

To illustrate this I will use once more a recent decision made by the Argentina's Supreme Court. In 2004, in the 'Aquino'[64] ruling, the Court declared unconstitutional article 39.1 of the Labor Risk Act (number 24.557), which excluded in labor accidents the possibility of claiming from the employer full compensation even in cases of severe negligence, because the employee's system of fixed and limited compensations through assurance companies established in article 15.2 of the same Act produced in the case at hand a result that was insufficient to cover the damages suffered by Mr. Aquino, in violation of constitutionally entrenched rights.

The arguments used by the Court seem to indicate that article 39.1 of the Act by itself was not taken to be incompatible with the constitution in abstract terms, because if the assurance system of compensation were wider and not restricted to the limited items it took into account—material damages and an evaluation of the age and salary of the employee, it would be reasonable to substitute the employer's responsibility for a more simple and efficient system. And the same goes for article 15.2 of the Act, because if the victim of a labor accident were allowed to demand from her employer for full compensation in cases of serious deviation, as it happened in 'Aquino', the fixed compensation assurance system would not by itself conflict with the constitution. These ideas held by the Court generated an extended controversy among legal scholars in Argentina, which have been discussing up to present days on the exact scope of the decision.

---

[63] I have tried to defend that under other senses of the expression 'legal system'—e.g., the one associated with legal dynamics—it is neither necessary nor convenient to assume the logical closure of legal systems. See Jorge L. Rodríguez, 'La tensión entre dos concepciones de los sistemas jurídicos', in *Análisis Filosófico*, volumen XXVI, número 2, 2006, Homenaje a Carlos Alchourrón II, pp. 242–276.

[64] CSJN, *Fallos* 304:415, 421, 2004.

In my view, what clearly follows from the Court's remarks is that neither article 39.1, nor article 15.2 of the Act, when considered in isolation, was in conflict with constitutionally entrenched rights. The problem was generated by a consequence of the conjunction of both norms, and the controversy produced by this ruling is nothing but the result of the indeterminacy generated by the incompatibility with higher ranked norms of a consequence of a set of other norms, each one of them compatible with those superior in the hierarchy. The analysis of complex cases like this makes it necessary to take into account not only explicitly enacted norms but also the consequences that can be derived from them.

To sum up, I have tried to show that the distinction between legal norms, that lack truth-values, and true or false statements about the content of the law, requires committing oneself to a conception of norms within which justifying the existence of logical relations among norms proves very difficult. Nevertheless, statements of legal scholars are in many cases not relative to what enacted legal norms provide, but to their logical consequences. Indeed, the derivation of all the consequences that follow from enacted legal norms seems to be another important task of legal science. Still, in order to give due account of this intuition, an answer should be given to the problem of the foundations of a logic of norms when they are conceived of as lacking truth values. But this problem is, of course, far beyond the limits of this paper.[65]

[65] Carlos E. Alchourrón has defended the idea that logic does not limit its scope to descriptive discourse, and that the thesis that its fundamental concepts have to be defined in terms of truth and falsehood would be but the result of a traditional prejudice with no genuine justification. From this perspective, he suggested the possibility of designing a logical system independent of the notions of truth and falsehood on the basis of an abstract notion of logical consequence. See Carlos E. Alchourrón and Antonio Martino, 'Logic without Truth', in *Ratio Juris*, 3, 1990 and Carlos E. Alchourrón, 'Concepciones de la lógica', in C. Alchourrón, C.E. Méndez y R. Orayen (eds.), *Enciclopedia Iberoamericana de Filosofía, vol. 7, Lógica*, pp. 11–48. Recently, Hugo Zuleta has objected that the specific system of deontic logic presented in the first of those papers would face decisive shortcomings. See Hugo Zuleta, *supra* note 50. Nonetheless, the arguments used by Zuleta do not invalidate the general suggestion put forward by Alchourrón. A similar approach to face Jørgensen's dilemma is offered by Ota Weinberger in 'The Logic of Norms Founded on Descriptive Language', in *Ratio Juris*, vol. 4, No. 3, 1991, pp. 284–307.

Chapter 7
Juristenrecht: Inventing Rights, Obligations, and Powers

Riccardo Guastini

Scientific neutrality is [...] a habit of life, [...] our way of taking part in political struggle

Norberto Bobbio

7.1 Expository Versus Censorial Jurisprudence

The very beginning of every discussion about neutrality, meant as "Wertfreiheit", in the legal domain—it seems to me—is Jeremy Bentham's distinction between expository and censorial jurisprudence: "A book of jurisprudence can have but one or the other of two objects: (1) to ascertain what the law is; (2) to ascertain what it ought to be. In the former case it may be styled a book of *expository* jurisprudence; in the latter, a book of *censorial* jurisprudence: or, in other words, a book on the *art of legislation*".[1]

Bentham's distinction is echoed by John Austin in the following way: "The existence of law is one thing, its merit or demerit is another, whether it be or be not is one enquiry; whether it be or be not conformable to an assumed standard, is a

"La neutralità scientifica è [...] un abito di vita, [...] il nostro modo di partecipare alla lotta politica": N. Bobbio, "Lettera a Nicola Matteucci" (1963), a cura di C. Margiotta, in *Materiali per una storia della cultura giuridica*, XXX, n. 2, 2000, p. 418.

[1] J. Bentham, *An Introduction to the Principles of Morals and Legislation*, ed. by J.H. Burns and H.L.A. Hart, Clarendon Press, Oxford, 1996, pp. 293 f.

R. Guastini (✉)
Department of Law, University of Genoa, Via Balbi, 30, 16126 Genoa, Italy
e-mail: guastini@unige.it

J. Ferrer Beltrán et al. (eds.), *Neutrality and Theory of Law*,
Law and Philosophy Library 106, DOI 10.1007/978-94-007-6067-7_7,

different enquiry. A law, which actually exists, is a law though we happen to dislike it, or though it vary from the text, by which we regulate our approbation and disapprobation".[2]

The same attitude is shared by Hans Kelsen too: his "pure theory of law" purportedly responds to "the required separation of legal science from politics"[3]; the pure theory "is being kept free from all the elements foreign to the specific method of a science whose only purpose is the cognition of law [...]. A science has to describe its object as it actually is, not to prescribe as it should be or should not be from the point of view of some specific value judgments. The latter is a problem of politics, and, as such, concerns the art of government, an activity directed at values, not an object of science, directed at reality".[4]

Both Bentham and Austin, as well as Kelsen, aimed at distinguishing the value-free knowledge of the law from (a) the moral or political criticism and/or approval (or justification) of the existing law as well as (b) legal policy (viz., directives *de lege ferenda* addressed to the legislature).

Notice that if law is conceived of as a language—the language of law-giving authorities[5]—then both expository and censorial jurisprudence are second-order languages whose object-language is the law itself. Both concepts (expository and censorial jurisprudence) suppose a sharp logical distinction between the language of the law and the language of lawyers.

Nonetheless, Bentham's, Austin's, and Kelsen's characterization of expository jurisprudence as pure cognition of the law as it *is*—hence a purely cognitive, value-free, enterprise—cannot be taken as a satisfactory description of the actual practice of academic lawyers—i.e., in French juristic language, "la doctrine". Rather, it should be understood as a normative model of "legal science", since almost every book or essay usually claiming to be and actually considered as a piece of legal cognition ("expository jurisprudence", knowledge of the law in force) cannot be reduced to a merely cognitive enterprise.[6]

---

[2] J. Austin, *Lectures on Jurisprudence or The Philosophy of Positive Law*, 4th ed. by R. Campbell, John Murray, London, 1879, I, p. 220. Cf. also at pp. 33 and 176 f.: "General jurisprudence [...] is concerned with law as it necessarily *is*, rather than with law as it *ought* to be; with law as it must be, *be it good or bad*, rather than with law as it must be, *if it be good*"; "The *science of jurisprudence* [...] is concerned with positive laws [...] as considered without regard to their goodness or badness".

[3] H. Kelsen, *Introduction to the Problems of Legal Theory* (1934), ed. by B. Litschewski Paulson and S.L. Paulson, Clarendon Press, Oxford, 1992, p. 3.

[4] H. Kelsen, *General Theory of Law and State*, Harvard U.P., 1945, Cambridge (Mass.), p. XIV.

[5] N. Bobbio, "Scienza del diritto e analisi del linguaggio" (1950), in U. Scarpelli (ed.), *Diritto e analisi del linguaggio*, Comunità, Milano, 1976.

[6] I refer to legal writings such as textbooks, monographs, commentaries, etc., with a special look to continental legal scholarship.

7.2 The Issue Restated: Legal Science Versus Legal Scholarship

In the common usage of continental jurisprudence the ordinary juristic work is frequently labelled as "legal science",[7] "legal doctrine",[8] or "legal dogmatics".[9] Nonetheless, all such phrases can be understood as pointing to (at least) two quite different intellectual enterprises which ought to be distinguished:

1. On the one hand, *legal science* properly so called—the "science of law" (Kelsen), the "science of jurisprudence" (Austin)—i.e., the scientific (neutral, value-free) description of the law in force [10];
2. On the other hand, what I shall call *legal scholarship*,[11] i.e., the usual academic investigation into the law, especially into those normative texts which are regarded as the official sources of law.

What should the science of law exactly amount to, can be questioned, e.g., it may be questioned whether it should confine itself to describing the so-called "law in books" (this is often the case in continental jurisprudential style) or it should take

---

[7]German "Rechtswissenschaft", Italian "scienza giuridica", French "science juridique", Spanish "ciencia jurídica", etc.

[8]Cf., e.g., A. Peczenik, *Scientia Juris. Legal Doctrine as Knowledge of Law and as a Source of Law*, vol. 4 of E. Pattaro (ed.), *A Treatise of Legal Philosophy and General Jurisprudence*, Springer, Dordrecht, 2005, Chap. 1. See also A. Ross, *On Law and Justice*, Stevens & Sons, London, 1958, *passim* (in particular pp. 9, 19, 46), about what he calls the "doctrinal study of law".

[9]German "Rechtsdogmatik", Italian "dogmatica giuridica", French "dogmatique juridique", Spanish "dogmática jurídica", etc. The phrase "legal dogmatics" is not familiar to Anglo-American jurisprudence, but is commonly used in continental juristic parlance. Cf. e.g. A. Aarnio, *On Legal Reasoning*, Turun Yliopisto, Turku, 1977, pp. 266 ff.; R. Alexy, *A Theory of Legal Argumentation* (1978), trans. by R. Adler and N. MacCormick, Clarendon Press, Oxford, 1989; E. Bulygin, "Legal Dogmatics and the Systematization of Law", in T. Eckhoff, L.M. Friedman, J. Uusitalo (eds.), *Vernunft und Erfahrung im Rechtsdenken der Gegenwart*, Duncker & Humblot, Berlin, 1986 (*Rechtstheorie*, Beiheft 10), pp. 193–210; A. Aarnio, *The Rational as Reasonable*, Reidel, Dordrecht, 1987, Chap. 3; A. Peczenik, *Scientia Juris. Legal Doctrine as Knowledge of Law and as a Source of Law*, cit., esp. Chap. 1.

[10]D.M. Walker, *The Oxford Companion to Law*, Clarendon Press, Oxford, 1980, p. 754: "*Legal science*. Systematized and organized knowledge [...] of and about law. [...] The term 'legal science' may also be limited to systematic thinking and writing about law, as distinct from law making and application of law to practical problems, what might be better described as legal scholarship".

[11]D.M. Walker, *The Oxford Companion to Law*, cit., p. 750: "*Legal scholarship*. Systematic research into and thinking and writing about any division or subdivision of legal science. It is mainly the function of the legal scholar or jurist. [...] Its purpose may be highly theoretical or severely practical, to elucidate some abstract matter or to reduce to order and make understandable and usable the prescriptions of a particular statute. This activity is sometimes called 'legal science', though that phrase seems more appropriate for the total body of knowledge, understanding of which is advanced by legal scholarship".

into account judicial decisions (case-law) as the very core of "law in action". The first line of inquiry is (at least apparently) suggested, e.g., by Hans Kelsen; the second one is recommended namely by American Realists as well as the Scandinavian realist scholar Alf Ross. But this issue is immaterial in the present context.[12]

Legal science (strictly understood) and legal scholarship are different matters. The main difference between them, however, is not the same as between describing and evaluating and/or prescribing. Sure, from time to time academic lawyers do evaluate—criticize or approve (or justify)—the law in force; sometimes they also make statements *de lege ferenda*, i.e. directives belonging to the realm of the "art of legislation" (in Bentham's terms) or "art of government" (in Kelsen's language). In such circumstances, however, they do not usually claim to act as genuine "scientists". The non-neutral character of legal scholarship lies elsewhere and is the specific subject of this paper.

7.3 The Main Components of Legal Scholarship

In common juristic usage, the legal academic work as a whole is often labelled as "interpretation" without any further specification. However, such a use of the term "interpretation" is definitely too large. Its main fault is overshadowing the variety of intellectual operations actually accomplished by legal scholars. Since interpreting, properly understood, is but a part—and not the most important, I dare say—of actual juristic work. Side by side with interpretation, jurists accomplish a great deal of other operations too. I propose to label them "juristic construction".

1. Interpretation *stricto sensu* consists in ascribing meaning to normative texts (such as statutes, the constitution, etc.). The standard form of an interpretive sentence, I assume, is: "T means M" (where T stands for the interpreted text and M for the ascribed meaning).
2. Juristic construction, in the sense I am going to use the phrase, mainly consists in shaping unexpressed rules, i.e. rules that no normative authority ever formulated—rules that cannot be ascribed to any definite enacted text as its meaning-content or direct (logical) implication.

In most cases the grounds of such rules are juristic "theories" or "doctrines",[13] such as the theory of parliamentary government, the theory of written constitutions, the theory of the relationships between European Community law and the domestic legal systems of the member states, the doctrine of incorporation of rules of international

[12] Cf., however, the concluding remark of this paper.

[13] D.M. Walker, *The Oxford Companion to Law*, Clarendon Press, Oxford, 1980, p. 371: "*Doctrines of Law*. Systematic formulations of legal principles, rules, conceptions, and standards with respect to [...] fields of the legal order, in logically interdependent schemes, whereby reasoning may proceed on the basis of the scheme and its logical implications".

law in municipal legal systems, the opposite doctrine of transformation (according to which international rules only form part of municipal law if accepted by statutes), the competing theories of civil liability, the different conceptions of equality, and so on.

Such theories are, on the one hand, products of juristic construction and, on the other hand, powerful tools for further construction. In particular, they are used as arguments for asserting the existence or validity of unexpressed rules. Generally speaking, the framing of unexpressed rules is aimed at filling (real or supposed) gaps in the law.

But, of course, both interpretation and construction need some further analysis.

7.4 Interpretation

In common usage, "interpretation" refers sometimes to an act of knowledge, sometimes to an act of decision, sometimes to a genuine act of rule-creation. Therefore we should distinguish between "cognitive", "adjudicative", and "creative" interpretation.[14]

1. Cognitive interpretation consists in identifying the ("frame" of) various possible meanings of a legal text—the meanings admissible on the basis of shared linguistic (syntactic and semantic) rules, accepted methods of interpretation, and existing juristic theories—without choosing anyone of them.
2. Adjudicative interpretation consists in settling one definite meaning, chosen among the meanings identified (or identifiable) by means of cognitive interpretation, and discarding the others.
3. Creative interpretation consists in ascribing the text a "new" meaning not included in the frame of meanings identified (or identifiable) by means of cognitive interpretation.

Suppose a legal provision P is ambiguous or otherwise indeterminate in such a way that it could be interpreted as expressing either the rule R1 or the rule R2. Well, cognitive interpretation will take the form of a sentence stating "P can mean either

[14]The ground of the following distinction is the simple statement of fact that (almost) every "legal norm has two or more meanings", and "there is no juristic reason to prefer one of the various meanings to another. [...] The view [...] that the verbal expression of a legal norm has only one, 'true', meaning which can be discovered by correct interpretation is a fiction, adopted to maintain the illusion of legal security, to make the law-seeking public believe that there is only one possible answer to the question of law in a concrete case. [...] The view that it is the function of interpretation to find the 'true' meaning of the law, is based on an erroneous concept of interpretation. [...] The choice of interpretations [...] is determined by political motives. Authentic interpretation [i.e., interpretation performed by law-applying authorities] may even attribute to a legal norm a meaning which non-authentic interpretation could never dare to maintain. That is to say, by authentic interpretation a legal norm may be replaced by another norm of totally different content" (H. Kelsen, "On Interpretation", Preface to H. Kelsen, *The Law of the United Nations. A Critical analysis of Its Fundamental Problems*, Stevens & Sons, London, 1950, pp. XIII ff).

R1 or R2"; adjudicative interpretation, in turn, will be expressed by a sentence stating either "P means R1" or "P means R2"; creative interpretation, in turn, will consist in saying, e.g., "P means R3" (notice that, by hypothesis, R3 is not one of the admissible meanings of P, as identified by cognitive interpretation).

Take this very simple example. Article 40 of the Italian constitution states: "The right to strike will be exercised in compliance with the statutes which regulate it". Now, suppose that no statute actually exists regulating the exercise of such a right. Well, cognitive interpretation of this constitutional provision could run, more or less, like this: article 40 of the constitution can be ascribed three different meanings—(a) the right to strike may not be exercised until some statute does regulate its exercise; (b) lacking any statutory regulation, the right to strike may be exercised with no limits at all; (c) even in absence of any statute regulating the issue, the right to strike may be exercised although within limits, viz., its "natural" limits deriving from the balance of it with other fundamental rights and constitutional values.[15] Adjudicative interpretation, in turn, would consist in choosing one of such competing meanings.

As a good example of creative interpretation, I shall mention the following. Article 72 of the Italian constitution requires a certain legislative procedure for the enactment of any "statute on constitutional matters". No need to say that "constitutional matters" is an open-textured concept, which allows for a great deal of interpretive discretion. The phrase "statute on constitutional matters", however, is not ambiguous—in ordinary juristic language, it univocally denotes *ordinary* (i.e. non-constitutional) statutes bearing upon issues of constitutional significance (paradigmatic example: statutes concerning the electoral system of the Chambers). Nevertheless, according to the Constitutional Court's opinion, it should be interpreted as meaning the same as "constitutional statutes", i.e., statutes adopted by the special procedure required for constitutional amendments. Such a meaning of the phrase clearly falls outside the range of meanings—in the present case the one and only meaning, in fact—identifiable by cognitive interpretation.[16]

Cognitive interpretation is a purely scientific operation devoid of any practical effect—it belongs to the realm of legal science properly understood. Adjudicative and creative interpretations, in turn, are "political" operations—they do not point at ascertaining the existing law; rather, they point at shaping it.

However, as far as I can see, creative interpretation, as defined above, is somewhat unusual. In most cases creative interpretation takes a slightly different form—it consists in deriving from a legal text some unexpressed ("implicit", in a large, non-logical, sense) rules either by means of a great variety of non-deductive arguments (e.g., *a contrariis*, *a simili*, etc.) or on the basis of some *a priori* juristic theory.[17] Well, deriving ("constructing" or framing) unexpressed rules, strictly speaking, is

[15] The three interpretations listed above were actually maintained in recent Italian constitutional history.

[16] Corte costituzionale, decision 168/1963.

[17] Jurists treat such rules as "implicit" in view of hiding the creative import of their constructions.

not an "interpretive" act—it is a genuine form of so-called "interstitial legislation" by interpreters. And this last remark leads us to juristic construction.

7.5 Juristic Construction

Legal scholars' books and papers are crowded by theoretical assumptions, previous to the interpretation of any particular legal provision—assumptions that have no direct relationship with normative texts.[18] Such assumptions:

1. First, inevitably condition interpretation, either orienting it in a definite direction or excluding certain interpretive decisions otherwise possible;
2. Second, most of all, are grounds for deriving a great deal of unexpressed rules.

Let me provide some examples.

(a) According to the European Court of Justice,[19] "the European Economic Community constitutes a new legal order of international law [...] which comprises not only member states but also their nationals. Independently of the legislation of member states, Community law not only imposes obligations on individuals but is also intended to confer upon them rights which become part of their legal heritage. These rights arise not only where they are expressly granted by the Treaty, but also because of the obligations which the Treaty imposes in a clearly defined way upon individuals as well as upon the member states and upon the institutions of the Community. [...] According to the spirit, the general scheme and the wording of the EEC Treaty, article 12 must be interpreted as producing direct effects and creating individual rights which national courts must protect".

In other words, the Court assumes the European Community Treaty to be neither an ordinary international act (governing relationships among states) nor a constitutional act (governing relationships between citizens and the state), but an entirely new kind of legal act with a mixed nature, half international, half constitutional. This "theoretical" assumption leads the Court to interpret several provisions of the Treaty as creating rights and obligations not only in the relationships among states but even in the relationships between each state and its citizens.

(b) According to Alexander Hamilton,[20] "a limited constitution" is a constitution "which contains certain specified exceptions to the legislative authority", i.e.,

[18] As far as I know, this is especially true for continental legal scholarship.

[19] European Court of Justice, February 5, 1963, Case 26/62, *Van Gend & Loos*. According to the Court of Justice, April 8, 1976, Case 43/75, *Defrenne*, the mandatory articles of the Treaty apply not only to the action of public authorities but also to independent agreements concluded privately or in the sphere of industrial relations, such as individual contracts and collective labour agreements.

[20] *Federalist Papers*, n. 78.

a constitution limiting the competence of the legislature, and "limitations of this kind can be preserved in practice no other way than through the medium of courts of justice, whose duty it must be to declare all the acts contrary to the manifest tenor of the Constitution void. Without this, all the reservations of particular rights or privileges would amount to nothing".

Hamilton's reasoning—a piece of "art of legislation" in Bentham's terms—is quite simple: the Constitution states a number of limits to the legislative power; the only way to make such limits effective is declaring any legislative act contrary to the constitution void; such a declaration cannot be entrusted but to the courts. No need to say that such a power of the courts goes far beyond the explicit provisions of the Federal Constitution of the U.S.A.

Hamilton's theory of limited constitutions, however, is echoed and expanded by Justice Marshall, in *Marbury* (1803)[21]: "a legislative act contrary to the constitution is not law [...]. Certainly all those who have framed written constitutions contemplate them as forming the fundamental and paramount law of the nation, and, consequently, the theory of such government must be that an act of the legislature, repugnant to the constitution, is void. [...] So if a law be in opposition to the constitution; if both the law and the constitution apply to a particular case, so that the court must either decide that case conformably to the law, disregarding the constitution; or conformably to the constitution, disregarding the law; the court must determine which of these conflicting rules governs the case. [...] If, then, the courts are to regard the constitution, and the constitution is superior to any ordinary act of the legislature, the constitution, and not such an ordinary act, must govern the case to which they both apply".

Justice Marshall, in other words, assumes that, according to the intention of the framers, the Constitution is superior to (more valued than) legislative acts, and derives from such a "theoretical" assumption two outstanding normative consequences—first, any legislative act contrary to the constitution is void; second, the Court is entitled to declare such an act void. Both consequences are but unexpressed rules, that the Supreme court is adding to the Constitution.

(c) The Italian Constitution of 1948 has framed a "parliamentary government", since the Executive is subject to the confidence of the Chambers and, in case of a vote of censure, is (supposedly) under the obligation to resign. Now, Italian constitutional lawyers (more or less unanimous on this point) maintain that, under the supposed "general theory" of parliamentary government, the President of the Republic is not the "head" of the Executive: he or she is rather a "neutral" power—something like Benjamin Constant's *pouvoir neutre*—whose function is just "guaranteeing" the constitution, i.e. assuring the normal functioning of the ordinary political-constitutional process.

Such a "theoretical" assumption has a great normative import. For example: the President is granted a veto-power over legislative acts; however, he or she may not exercise such a power on political grounds, since the function of the

[21] *Marbury v. Madison*, 5 U.S. (1 Cranch) 137, 2 L.Ed. 60.

veto-power is allowing the President to exercise an *a priori* control over the constitutionality of statutes (quite different from the *a posteriori* control assured by the Constitutional Court); in particular, the President may use his/her veto-power (only) against statutes whose unconstitutionality is self-evident. Another example: the acts of the Executive, although settled by the Council of Ministers, are enacted by the President, i.e. they are, properly speaking, presidential (not governmental) acts; the President, however, may not refuse his/her signature except when facing acts clearly unconstitutional. And so on. In other words, the "general theory" of parliamentary government allows legal scholars to add a great deal of rules—limiting presidential powers—to those expressly stated by the Constitution.

(d) The Italian Constitutional Court assumes—without providing any argument—that the constitution contains (or implies) a number of "supreme principles", which are allegedly superior to the remaining constitutional provisions, and concludes that such principles may not be suppressed, derogated, or changed in any way—not even by means of the procedure of constitutional amendment. As a consequence, the Court empowers itself to declare null and void any constitutional amendment purporting to subvert the supreme principles.[22] Notice that in no way does the existing constitutional text allow for such theses.

7.6 Unexpressed Rules

An unexpressed rule is a rule that no normative authority ever formulated—a rule which cannot be ascribed to any legal text as its meaning-content.

Every unexpressed rule is the result of an argument, in which (usually) some expressed rule is one of the premises and the unexpressed one is the conclusion. But it has to be stressed that in most cases such arguments, first, are not logically valid and, second (most of all), include premises which are not expressed rules, but arbitrary juristic conceptual constructs and theories. At least three different kinds of reasoning and three different corresponding classes of unexpressed rules can be distinguished.

1. Some unexpressed rules are derived from explicit rules by means of a logically valid argument, in which all the premises are but explicit rules.

   For example, a first explicit rule states "All citizens have the right to vote"; a second explicit rule, in turn, states "Everyone procreated by citizen-parents is a citizen". From such premises one can deductively infer the implicit rule: "Everyone procreated by citizen-parents has the right to vote".

   Unexpressed rules of this kind, however, are of no interest in the present context, since, although not formulated by normative authorities, they are logically

[22] Corte costituzionale, decision 1146/1988.

entailed by explicit rules (without adding any further premises). Their juristic formulation is the result of a merely cognitive operation.

2. Other unexpressed rules are derived from explicit rules by means of logically invalid arguments—e.g., *argumentum a simili*, *argumentum a contrariis*, etc.

   For example, a constitutional provision grants all "citizens" the right to vote; arguing *a contrariis*, one could maintain that such a provision implies the unexpressed rule according to which non-citizens are positively (although implicitly) excluded from the exercise of such a right (in such a way that a statute granting them the same right would be unconstitutional). Another example: a statutory provision grants "big corporations" a tax-break; arguing *a simili*, one could maintain that, in the light of a supposed *ratio legis* (e.g., economic development during a financial crisis), big corporations are essentially "similar" to medium-size companies and, therefore, the provision at hand implies the further rule to the effect that the same tax-break is to be applied to such companies too. In both cases (*a contrariis*, *a simili*), a new unexpressed rule is added to the legal system.

3. Moreover, a lot of unexpressed rules are derived—deductively or not, this is not really important—either from explicit rules plus some theoretical assumption, or directly from a theoretical assumption alone.

I already gave some examples of it in the preceding section. Consider however some examples more.

(a) According to the "classical" constitutional theory of the Enlightenment, the function of every constitution is limiting political power[23]; this view implies that constitutional rules are addressed (only) to the supreme state organs and in no way subject to judicial application. Nowadays, on the contrary, most constitutional lawyers think that the function of the constitution is (also or even essentially) moulding social relationships among citizens[24]; from this view they draw the conclusion that constitutional rules should be directly applied by any judge in any controversy (what is called "Drittwirkung" in German jurisprudence).[25]

(b) Article 139 of the Italian Constitution prohibits whatever revision (even by means of constitutional amendment) of the "republican form" of the state. Most constitutional lawyers, however, assume that a republican state is, by definition, a democratic one, and conclude that no revision of the democratic form of the state is allowed. No need to say that this conclusion, whose only ground is a

[23] See article 16 of the *Déclaration des droits de l'homme et du citoyen*: "Toute société dans laquelle la garantie des droits n'est pas assurée, ni la séparation des pouvoirs déterminée, n'a point de constitution".

[24] G. Bognetti, "Teorie della costituzione e diritti giurisprudenziali", in Associazione italiana dei costituzionalisti, Annuario 2002, *Diritto costituzionale e diritto giurisprudenziale*, Padova 2004.

[25] See, e.g., G. Zagrebelsky, *Il diritto mite. Legge, diritti, giustizia*, Einaudi, Torino 1992.

disputable juristic concept of "republic", has the outstanding effect of excluding from constitutional amendment nearly the whole constitutional text.

(c) The Court of Justice of the European Community assumes, on the one hand, that the European Community law and the law of the member states form a unified legal system and, on the other hand, that European law is superior to state law, and draws the conclusion that state legislation is invalid (or, at any rate, non-applicable) when incompatible with Community law.[26] No need to say that both assumptions have no textual counterparts in the EEC Treaty.

(d) The Italian Constitutional court assumes, on the contrary, that the European Community law and the law of the member states are independent legal systems, and draws the conclusion that Community law cannot derogate or invalidate incompatible state legislation.[27] This assumption too has no textual basis in the Treaty.

Generally speaking, formulating unexpressed rules is often aimed at concretising principles. The concretisation of principles, in turn, is often a means to fill up real or supposed gaps in the law.[28]

---

[26]European Court of Justice, July 15, 1964, Case 6/64, *Costa*: "By contrast with ordinary international Treaties, the EEC Treaty has created its own legal system which [...] became an integral part of the legal systems of the member states and which their courts are bound to apply. [...] The integration into the laws of each member state of provisions which derive from the Community and more generally the terms and the spirit of the Treaty, make it impossible for the states, as a corollary, to accord precedence to a unilateral and subsequent measure over a legal system accepted by them on a basis of reciprocity. Such a measure cannot therefore be inconsistent with that legal system. The Law stemming from the Treaty, an independent source of law, could not because of its special and original nature, be overridden by domestic legal provisions, however framed, without being deprived of its character as Community law and without the legal basis of the Community itself being called into question. The Transfer by the states from their domestic legal system to the Community legal system of the rights and obligations arising under the Treaty carries with it a permanent limitation of their sovereign rights". Cf. also European Court of Justice, March 9, 1978, Case 106/77, *Simmenthal*.

[27]Corte costituzionale 170/1984.

[28]*Supposed* gaps, in most cases. Take the following example. Article 87 of the Italian constitution states (among many other things) that the President of the Republic enacts (certain) governmental acts. Most constitutional lawyers, however, are not satisfied with such a simple provision. They wonder about the limits of this presidential power—in particular, they ask in what circumstances the President is authorized to refuse the enactment and, since the constitution gives no answer to such a question, they conclude for the existence of a gap in the constitutional text and try to fill it (see, e.g., M Luciani, "L'emanazione presidenziale dei decreti-legge. (Spunti a partire dal caso E.)", *Politica del diritto*, 3, 2009). They do not even suspect that since the constitution states no limits hence no *constitutional* limits exist. Should we really consider as a gap any case that the constitution simply does not take into account? The supposed gap does not depend on the fact that the constitution fails to regulate the case although taking it into account—it depends on the juristic assumption that the constitution *ought to* regulate the case. In other words, the gap in question is an "axiological" one.

7.7 Concretising Principles

Framing unexpressed rules amounts to “apocryphal” legislation by interpreters. And, as a matter of fact, it constitutes the main and most significant part of legal scholars’ work. This is especially true as far as constitutional interpretation—or, rather, constitutional “construction”—is concerned.

It is a well known feature of most European constitutions of the twentieth century that they include a great deal of “principles”, i.e. provisions affected by a high degree of indeterminacy (open circumstances of application, defeasibility, etc.)—provisions, in particular, that because of their indeterminacy cannot be applied without previous “concretisation”.

On the one hand, principles, because of their peculiar form of indeterminacy, cannot be used as direct justifications of judicial decisions of individual cases. For example, the principle “Defence is an inviolable right at every stage and instance of legal proceedings” (article 24 of Italian Constitution) says nothing about the presence or absence of the advocate to the police interrogation of the accused person; to decide whether the advocate ought to be present or not, the principle must be “transformed” into a (relatively) precise rule.[29] The principle “National sovereignty belongs to the people” (article 3 of French Constitution) says nothing about the right to vote of immigrants from inside the European Union in the elections of city councils; to decide whether such immigrants are entitled to vote or not, one has to derive, from the principle, a definite rule.[30]

On the other hand, in most cases the judicial review of legislation requires comparing (not two rules, but) a rule and a principle.[31] Rules and principles, however, are logically heterogeneous sentences. As a consequence, such a comparison is simply impossible without previous concretisation of the principle at stake. How to compare a statutory rule which does not provide the presence of the advocate to the police interrogation with the constitutional principle of the defence as an inviolable right? How to compare the principle of national sovereignty with a statute or a treaty entitling European immigrants to vote in the elections of city councils? Once more, principles need concretisation.

Concretising a principle means “extracting” from it one or more unexpressed rules. Such a concretisation amounts to an argument where the premises are the principle at hand coupled with one or more arbitrary “theoretical” assumptions. For example: “Defence is an inviolable right at every stage and instance of legal proceedings”; the police interrogation of the accused person is a part of the legal proceedings; hence the advocate ought to be present.[32]

---

[29] See Corte costituzionale, decision 190/1970.

[30] See Conseil constitutionnel, decision 92–308 DC.

[31] G. Zagrebelsky, *La giustizia costituzionale*, 2nd ed., Il Mulino, Bologna 1988, pp. 125 ff.

[32] The example shows a logically valid argument, but in most cases juristic reasoning is not deductive.

7.8 Production of Rules by Means of Rules

Generally speaking, legal scholarship amounts to shaping the legal system in two connected ways[33]:

1. First, determining by means of adjudicative interpretation the meaning-contents of the enacted texts;
2. Second, producing (new) rules by means of (pre-existing) rules, i.e.—echoing a happy formula by J. L. Mackie—"inventing right and wrong"[34]: more precisely, inventing rights, powers, obligations, and other "jural relations".

In Bentham's, Austin's, and Kelsen's view, law is a language—the set of sentences enacted by the lawgiving authorities—and "expository jurisprudence" is depicted as a *second-order descriptive* language whose object-language is the normative language of the law.[35] This view of the "science of law" is a normative model on which one can easily agree. But it cannot be considered as a reliable description of actual legal scholars' practice.

In actual legal scholars' language, at least three kinds of sentences can be distinguished:

(a) "Normative propositions" ("Rechtssätze", "propositions of law", etc.), i.e. true or false sentences describing the law in force;
(b) Adjudicative interpretive statements, which are not propositions at all, since they do not describe, but ascribe meaning;
(c) Normative formulations, which do not describe anything at all, but settle new (unexpressed) rules.

There is no possible confusion between the revolving of the earth around the sun and the astronomical science which describes it, since the moving of planets is no language-entity (while astronomical science obviously is). As far as the relationship between legal scholarship and the law is concerned, on the contrary, such a confusion is possible and actually obtains. This is so since both law and legal scholarship are but languages. In other words, no clear-cut distinction can be established between the language of law and the language of lawyers—they are subject to a continuous osmotic process. Lawyers' language does not "bear upon" the language of the law—rather, legal scholars do mould and continuously enrich their subject-matter of study.

This amounts to say that interpretation and juristic construction are not the "legal science"—as academic lawyers usually claim—but a part of the law itself and therefore a part of the subject-matter of legal science. In other words, describing the law in force requires taking into account legal scholarship as a significant part of it.[36]

---

[33] The formula of the title obviously echoes Piero Sraffa's *Production of Commodities by Means of Commodities. Prelude to a Critique to Economic Theory*, Cambridge U. P., Cambridge 1960.

[34] J. L. Mackie, *Ethics. Inventing Right and Wrong* (1977), Penguin Books, Harmondsworth, 1978.

[35] By the way, criticism and approval of existing law, too—i.e., "censorial jurisprudence"—amount to a second-order (evaluative) language about the law.

[36] Provided, as a matter of course, that the rules framed by legal scholarship come into force through the decisions of law-applying organs.

Chapter 8
The Demarcation Problem in Jurisprudence: A New Case for Skepticism

Brian Leiter

For more than 200 years, legal philosophers have been preoccupied with specifying the differences between two systems of normative guidance that are omnipresent in all modern human societies: law and morality. In the last 100 years, what I will call the "Demarcation Problem"—the problem of how to distinguish these two normative systems—has been *the* dominant problem in jurisprudence and the theory usually denominated "legal positivism" has offered the most important solution.[1] Legal positivists such as Kelsen, Hart, and Raz claim that the *legal validity* of a norm cannot depend on its being *morally valid*, either in all or at least some possible legal systems (the range of the scope operator here marks the distinction between "Hard" and "Soft" versions of positivism).

Originally published at Oxford Journal of Legal Studies, (2011), pp. 1–15. The editors are grateful to Oxford Journal of Legal Studies for their permission to reprint this paper.

This paper owes its existence to a conversation with Larry Laudan many years ago. An earlier version benefitted from the discussion at the international conference on "Neutrality and the Theory of Law" at the University of Girona, May 20–22, 2010. I can recall particularly helpful questions or comments on that occasion from Eugenio Bulygin, Pierluigi Chiassoni, Luis Duarte D'Almeida, Dan Priel, Veronica Rodriguez-Blanco, Stefan Sciaraffa, and Scott Shapiro. I am also grateful to Frederick Schauer for written comments on that draft. The penultimate version was improved by astute criticisms of an anonymous referee for OJLS and by questions from an audience at the international conference on "The Nature of Law," sponsored by McMaster University in Hamilton, Ontario on May 12–15, 2011; I can recall particularly helpful questions or comments on that occasion from Matthew Kramer, Mark Murphy, Giovanni Ratti, and Kevin Toh.

[1]See Leslie Green, "Legal Positivism," *Stanford Encyclopedia of Philosophy* (January 3, 2003), available at http://plato.stanford.edu/entries/legal-positivism/, for a recent clean statement of the view.

B. Leiter (✉)
University of Chicago, 1111 E. 60th Street, 60615 Chicago, IL, USA
e-mail: bleiter@uchicago.edu

J. Ferrer Beltrán et al. (eds.), *Neutrality and Theory of Law*,
Law and Philosophy Library 106, DOI 10.1007/978-94-007-6067-7_8,

Kelsen tells us on the first page of the *Pure Theory* that the theory "attempts to answer the question what and how the law *is*, not how it ought to be"[2] and the second chapter on "Law and Morals" sets out to establish that the "science of law"—the science of the legal validity of norms—is not to be confused with "ethics," the science of the social norms denominated "moral" (59). "[L]aw and morals" must be "recognized as different kinds of normative systems" (62), Kelsen says, a difference he locates in the fact that law involves "a socially organized coercive" sanction, while morals lacks such sanctions, substituting "merely the approval of the norm-conforming and the disapproval of the norm-opposing behavior" (62).

The first sentence of *The Concept of Law* states Hart's aim "to further the understanding of law, coercion, and morality as different but related phenomena."[3] He famously identifies as one of the three main issues driving jurisprudential inquiry the question, "How does legal obligation differ from, and how is it related to, moral obligation?" (13). That issue looms so large because "law and morals share a vocabulary so that there are both legal and moral obligations, duties, and rights" and "all legal municipal legal systems reproduce the substance of certain fundamental moral requirements" (7). This, of course, leads positivism's most important competitor, natural law theory, to claim "that law is best understood as a 'branch' of morality or justice." Positivists, of course, deny this. Finally, and as is well-known, Hart devotes an entire chapter of *The Concept of Law* to the relationship between "Law and Morals," noting that positivists deny that "the criteria of legal validity of particular laws used in a legal system must include, tacitly if not explicitly, a reference to morality or justice" (185) and that, in consequence, "it is in no sense a necessary truth that laws reproduce or satisfy certain demands of morality, though in fact they have often done so" (185–186).

Raz, similarly, devotes fully half of his classic collection of essays, *The Authority of Law*, to "criticiz[ing] various attempts to establish a conceptual connection between law and morality" (x) and the seminal chapter on "Legal Positivism and the Sources of Law" makes clear that the identification of law "is a matter of social fact" thus independent of its "moral merit" (37).

If it is familiar and uncontroversial that the Demarcation Problem has been central to legal philosophy, it perhaps requires more emphasis what kind of answer to the Demarcation Problem jurisprudents have demanded. Hart himself says we want to understand "the nature (or the essence) of law" (6). But what is it to understand the *nature* or the *essence* of law? Julie Dickson, following Raz, says that,

> A successful theory of law…is a theory which consists of propositions about the law which (1) are necessarily true, and (2) adequately explain the nature of law….I am using "the

[2]Hans Kelsen, *Pure Theory of Law*, trans. Max Knight (Berkeley: University of California Press 1967), p. 1. Further citations are included by page number in the body of the text.

[3]H.L.A. Hart, *The Concept of Law*, 2nd ed. (Oxford: Clarendon Press 1994), p. vi. All further references will be included in the body of the text.

nature of law" to refer to those essential properties which a given set of phenomena must exhibit in order to be law.[4]

She is echoed more recently by Scott Shapiro, who says that in inquiring into "the fundamental nature of law" we want to "supply the set of properties that make (possible or actual) instances of [law] the things that they are"[5] and offers the example of water being H_2O: "Being H_2O is what makes water *water*. With respect to law, accordingly, to answer the question 'What is law?' on this interpretation is to discover what makes all and only instances of law instances of *law* and not something else."[6] In addition, says Shapiro (here again echoing Dickson who is following Raz), "to discover the law's nature" is also "to discover its necessary properties, i.e., those properties that law could not fail to have."[7]

Legal philosophy has, unsurprisingly, always been hostage to its philosophical climate—jurisprudents are rarely, if ever, innovators in philosophy. They, instead, are the jurisprudential Owls of Minerva, bringing considered philosophical opinion in its maturity (sometimes, alas, on its death bed) to bear on theoretical questions that arise distinctively in the legal realm. Thus, Kelsen's jurisprudence bears the stamp of NeoKantianism and the moral anti-realism common among logical positivists, while Hart's jurisprudence reflects the methodological influence of ordinary language philosophy and the substantive influence of post-World War II Oxford-style non-cognitivism. The early Kelsen and Hart had (or at least often appeared to presuppose) what seems to me to be the correct meta-ethical position (broadly anti-realist and non-cognitivist), but did not, perhaps, fully appreciate its import with respect to their central jurisprudential concerns. What is particularly striking is that, even at the dawn of the twenty-first-century, legal philosophers set conditions for a successful analysis of the Demarcation Problem—to identify the "necessary" and "essential" properties of law that distinguish it from morality in all cases—that would strike most philosophers in other fields, even 30 years ago, as wholly incredible. The persistence of the Demarcation Problem means that the most recent jurisprudential Owl of Minerva has not yet taken flight. I hope here to set this venerable philosophical bird on her path and to lay the Demarcation Problem to rest.

---

[4] Julie Dickson, *Evaluation and Legal Theory* (Oxford: Hart Publishing 2001), p. 17. Dickson faithfully follows Raz's lead here, though he has not always been so immodest. Thus, in the earlier essay "Legal Positivism and the Sources of Law," reprinted in his *The Authority of Law*, 2nd ed. (Oxford: Oxford University Press 2009), Raz notes that it is no part of the argument for the Sources Thesis "that a similar conception of legal systems is to be found in all cultures and in all periods." Id. at 50. That is only one kind of theoretical modesty, for one might still think that it is possible to state necessary truths that explain the essential nature of a culturally and temporally bounded human practice; as noted in the text, our experience in the philosophy of science in the twentieth-century invites skepticism.

[5] Scott J. Shapiro, *Legality* (Cambridge, Mass.: Harvard University Press 2011), pp. 8–9.

[6] Id. at p. 9.

[7] Id.

The concept of law is the concept of an *artifact*, that is, something that necessarily owes its existence to human activities intended to create that artifact.[8] Even John Finnis, our leading natural law theorist, does not deny this point.[9] I certainly do not understand Kelsen, Hart, Raz, Dickson, or Shapiro to deny this claim. Those who might want to deny that law is an artifact concept are not my concern here; the extravagance of their metaphysical commitments would, I suspect, be a subject for psychological, not philosophical investigation.

Artifact concepts, even simple ones like "chair," are notoriously resistant to analyses in terms of their essential attributes, both because they are hostage to changing human ends and purposes, and because they cannot be individuated by their natural properties—unlike say natural phenomena like "water," which just *is* H_2O. Chairs can be made of stone or wood or metal. Their apparent function—providing support for those who sit—can be discharged by boxes, tortoises, car seats, and steps. Moreover, some chairs have as their actual function ornamental decoration, not sitting; some serve primarily as shelves for stacking papers or books. Some chairs have arm rests, some do not; some have back rests, some do not. Because human ends and purposes shift, the concept of a "chair" has no essential attributes.[10]

Now the question of whether an artifact concept has an extension that can be picked out in terms of necessary and essential properties is not one unfamiliar to twentieth-century philosophy. Karl Popper, Rudolf Carnap, and Carl Hempel, to name three luminaries of twentieth-century philosophy, were interested in a version of the Demarcation Problem—not how to demarcate law from morality, to be sure, but how to demarcate epistemically reliable forms of inquiry from epistemically unreliable ones, that is, how to demarcate science from pseudo-science or nonsense. Like the legal philosophers, they sought to identify the essential properties of a human artifact (namely, science). They failed, and spectacularly so. Perhaps there is a lesson for legal philosophers in this story?

---

[8]Human beings are not artifacts on this account, since they do not *necessarily* owe their existence to human action intended to create them.

[9]Finnis, after all, admits that positivism gives the correct account of "what any competent lawyer… would say are (or are not) intra-systematically valid laws, imposing 'legal requirements.'" John Finnis, "On the Incoherence of Legal Positivism," *Notre Dame Law Review* 75 (2000), p. 1611. Finnis complains instead that positivism does not have an adequate answer to questions it was not asking, such as when there is a moral obligation to obey the law. See the critical discussion in Brian Leiter, *Naturalizing Jurisprudence* (Oxford: Oxford University Press 2007), pp. 163–164, and also pp. 193–194.

[10]It might be objected that someone like Hart, who is more metaphysically cautious than, e.g., Dickson or Shapiro, only claims to be analyzing the concept of law used by someone familiar with the "modern municipal legal system." Can we salvage the *essentialist* project with these kinds of temporal bounds? Perhaps so, but that is a question that can only be resolved *a posteriori*. The inductive case for skepticism developed below does not, in any case, depend on assuming that the account on offer is atemporal. Notice, of course, that this kind of move—deflating the ambitions of the analysis by bounding it temporally, perhaps culturally and geographically as well—makes mysterious the standard rhetoric of those committed to the Demarcation Problem. It also makes it puzzling why this is a philosophical topic, as opposed to an anthropological or sociological one.

In philosophy of science, the Demarcation Problem was the problem of figuring out which kinds of human inquiry were *epistemically special*, that is, which had epistemic properties or characteristics that warranted the inference that the conclusions of such inquiry were likely to be true. Those epistemically special forms of inquiry were to be deemed *scientific*, and so deserving of credence, while all others were not. Permit me to quote from Larry Laudan's seminal treatment of the rise and fall of the Demarcation Problem,[11] which he characterizes as follows:

> [W]e expect a demarcation criterion to identify the *epistemic* or *methodological* features which mark off scientific beliefs from unscientific ones. We want to know what, if anything, is special about the knowledge claims and the modes of inquiry of the sciences...[A]ny philosophically interesting demarcative device must distinguish scientific and non-scientific matters in a way which exhibits a surer epistemic warrant or evidential ground for science than non-science. If it should happen that there is no such warrant, then the demarcation between science and non-science would turn out to be of little or no philosophic significance. (Laudan, p. 118)

Attempts to solve the scientific Demarcation Problem were, in turn, precisely efforts to specify the "conditions which are both necessary and sufficient" for some form of inquiry to be scientific (Laudan, p. 119).

The history of the search for such a criterion is quite a long one, going back to antiquity (though the artifact Aristotle wanted to understand is different than ours, not surprisingly) (Laudan, pp. 112–113). In the nineteenth-century, there were attempts to specify the distinctive "method" of scientific inquiry (Laudan, pp. 115–117), but the solutions to the scientific Demarcation Problem most familiar to us now were those associated with the Logical Positivists and Karl Popper. "Verificationist" theories held that scientific propositions were genuinely meaningful, that is, empirically verifiable. These theories, however, ran into trouble because, on the one hand, as Laudan observes, "many statements in the sciences [are] not open to exhaustive verification (e.g., all universal laws)" (p. 120), while many false statements—like "the Earth is flat"—are verifiable (though false!) since "we can specify a class of possible observations which would verify" the statement (p. 121). Popper's alternative, eschewing verification in favor of falsifiability, ran into different problems: it could not explain the scientific status of most "singular existential statement[s]" (p. 121) (e.g., "there exists a Black Hole") and it deems "scientific" "every crank claim which makes ascertainably false assertions" (p. 121).[12]

---

[11] Larry Laudan, "The Demise of the Demarcation Problem," in R.S. Cohen & L. Laudan (eds.), *Physics, Philosophy and Psychoanalysis* (Dordrecht: D. Reidel 1983). Cited hereafter by page number in the text.

[12] Other objections were raised to Popper's falsificationism. Paul Feyerabend called attention to the commitment of natural scientists to theories some of whose predictions had actually been falsified. The so-called Duhem-Quine thesis about the underdetermination of theory by evidence suggests that no theoretical claim can ever be falsified, since there is always a choice, when confronted with recalcitrant evidence, to reject *either* the claim being tested *or* the background assumptions underlying the test. (Laudan, however, is a critic of the Duhem-Quine thesis: see, e.g., his *Science and Relativism* [Chicago: University of Chicago Press 1990].)

As Laudan observes, we cannot "prove that there is no conceivable philosophical reconstruction of our intuitive distinction between the scientific and the non-scientific" (or we might add, between the "legal" and the "moral") (p. 124). But we can conclude, as Laudan does, that "none of the criteria which have been offered thus far promises to explicate the distinction" (p. 124). We should, therefore, ask *why solving the Demarcation Problem* matters? For what philosophical or practical purposes do we need a solution to the Demarcation Problem?

In the case of science, the solution mattered for explicitly *practical* reasons. As Laudan remarks, "demarcation criteria are typically used as *machines du guerre* in a polemical battle between rival camps" (p. 119). So, for example, "Popper was out to 'get' Marx and Freud" (p. 119) by showing that their theories were not falsifiable. Popper, alas, had no real understanding of either Marx's or Freud's views,[13] but that is tangential to our concerns here. What matters, as Laudan notes, is that,

> The labeling of a certain activity as 'scientific' or 'unscientific' has social and political ramifications which go well beyond the taxonomic task of sorting beliefs into two piles.... Precisely because a demarcation criterion will serve as a rationale for taking a number of *practical* actions which may well have far-reaching moral, social and economic consequences, it would be wise to insist that the arguments in favor of any demarcation criterion we intend to take seriously should be especially compelling. (120)

In other words, the Demarcation Problem was thought to matter because *knowledge* matters, because what we *know* affects what we think ought to be done. As Laudan remarks, "It remains as important as it ever was to ask questions like: When is a claim well confirmed? When can we regard a theory as well tested? What characterizes cognitive progress?" (124). What the failure in philosophy of science to solve the Demarcation Problem shows is that we cannot take a shortcut to answer these questions by simply dividing forms of inquiry into the "scientific" and "non-scientific" based on some necessary and essential properties distinguishing the two forms of inquiry.

So what then about the Demarcation Problem in jurisprudence? I do not need to rehearse for this audience the doubts about the positivist analysis of law, the most powerful and successful analysis of law we have. Many of these doubts may be, as I am inclined to think, misguided, yet who can deny that there are genuinely hard cases for the positivist to explain?[14] Hart says that the "necessary and sufficient conditions" (p. 116) for a legal system require that citizens generally obey the valid primary rules and that the officials of the system accept the secondary rules of the system from an "internal point of view," that is, they view them as imposing obligations upon them. Can there not then be a legal system in which the officials are motivated by merely self-interested concerns, e.g., they enforce the secondary rules because it advances their professional career or spares them from political retribution? Can the idea of a rule of recognition really account for the reasoning of

[13] See generally, Brian Leiter, "The Hermeneutics of Suspicion: Recovering Marx, Nietzsche, and Freud," in B. Leiter (ed.), *The Future for Philosophy* (Oxford: Oxford University Press 2004).

[14] I focus on versions of positivism associated with Hart and his heirs.

common-law courts interpreting precedents? Hart says the "rule of recognition" is merely a social rule, so its content is fixed by whatever the practice of officials in a particular legal system happens to be.[15] Raz says the practice cannot include appeal to moral criteria of legal validity consistent with the law's claim to authority.[16] Shapiro says it cannot include such appeals consistent with the law's claim to guide conduct.[17] Waluchow argues the law's claim to authority is compatible with an official practice of employing moral criteria of legal validity if authoritative directives are merely weighty, rather than exclusionary, reasons for action.[18] And so on.

If, in the history of philosophy, there is not a single successful analysis of the "necessary" or "essential" properties of a human artifact, why should we think law will be different? If hundreds, perhaps thousands, of philosophers in the last century—both the innovators like Carnap and Popper, and the legions of less well-known philosophical laborers—could not specify the essential and necessary features of *science*, perhaps the most important and transformative human artifact of recorded history, should we really hold out hope that an analysis of *law* will yield "necessary" and "essential" criteria, that is, criteria that will classify every norm in either the "legal" or the "non-legal" camp?

A skeptical induction over past failure is not a conclusive refutation, just as the failure to solve the Demarcation Problem in philosophy of science does not prove that there is no account of the *essential* and *necessary* properties of an inquiry that is scientific. But, rather than belabor the no-doubt familiar disputes about the Demarcation Problem in jurisprudence, let us follow Laudan's lead and ask a different question: namely, *why does solving this problem matter*?

In surveying the writings of the great writers on the Demarcation Problem in jurisprudence—I here mean Kelsen, Hart, and Raz—it seems that two practical concerns (sometimes implicit, sometimes explicit) explain the importance for these writers, and those who follow them, of demarcating *legal* from *moral* norms[19]:

1. First, the fact that a norm is *legally valid* does not mean it is *morally obligatory* (or even *morally attractive*).
2. Second, the fact that a decision by a legal official would be *morally attractive* does not mean it is *legally obligatory*.

In other words, legal positivists—those who have insisted that the Demarcation Problem can be solved—are keen to emphasize that *legality does not entail morality*

---

[15]See Hart's discussion in "The Postscript" to *The Concept of Law*, esp. pp. 250–254.

[16]Joseph Raz, "Authority, Law, and Morality," reprinted in his *Ethics in the Public Domain* (Oxford: Oxford University Press 1994).

[17]Scott J. Shapiro, "On Hart's Way Out," *Legal Theory* 4 (1998), pp. 469–507.

[18]W.J. Waluchow, *Inclusive Legal Positivism* (Oxford: Oxford University Press 1994).

[19]I do not mean to deny that these writers also have a purely theoretical concern, i.e., figuring out what they take to be true of the concept of law. But since I am arguing that there is no reason to think this is a sensible theoretical project—unless ethnographically and temporally bounded in ways that are not obviously congenial to their original ambitions—it seems useful, following Laudan's lead, to think about its import for practical reasoning.

and, conversely, that *morality does not entail legality*. You will notice, of course, that the need to draw this distinction, to solve the Demarcation Problem, turns on the assumption that the *moral validity* of a norm entails a practical consequence, i.e., it entails acting in accordance with the norm. If we grant that assumption, then confusing law and morality has serious practical consequences indeed: it means that if the *legal validity* of a norm is equivalent to its moral validity, then every law *ought to be obeyed*. And, conversely, it means that if a norm is morally valid, then a legal actor *ought to apply it*.

The Demarcation Problem in philosophy of science was meant to solve a normative problem about theoretical rationality, about what we ought to believe. But, as Laudan correctly observed, its solution had consequences for practical reason, for what *ought* to be done, and it was these that motivated the ultimately futile search for a theoretical short-cut. The Demarcation Problem in jurisprudence also purports to resolve a theoretical dilemma: what to believe about the nature of law. But the connection of an answer to this question to matters of practical import is even more apparent.[20] Perhaps we can defuse interest in the Demarcation Problem in jurisprudence if we tackle its underlying assumption—namely, that the *moral validity* of a norm is overriding in practical reasoning?

Suppose it were agreed that the *moral validity* of a norm was *not* overriding in practical reasoning. Suppose morally valid norms merely give defeasible (even easily defeasible) reasons for acting, just like legally valid norms and norms of instrumental rationality. That a norm was legally valid might, in some cases, also mean it is morally valid, but what if that did not change reasoning about what ought to be done? That a norm was morally valid might be an interesting fact for a judge to note, but it would not require from the judge one decision rather than another. In such a world, would solving the Demarcation Problem in jurisprudence matter? It is hard to see why.

Kelsen and Hart, as everyone knows, were both metaphysical anti-realists about moral norms: that is, they denied that such norms had any objective existence, they denied that the best metaphysical account of what the world contains would include facts about what is morally right and wrong. This might suggest that the *normativity* of morals—its ability to give people reasons to act—should be understood in exclusively psychological terms, i.e., as a psychological fact about what particular people believe and feel when they learn that, "It is morally wrong to do X" or "It is morally right to Y." I believe the most charitable reading of Hart should understand him as accepting something like this view, since, unlike Kelsen, his was an "impure" theory of law, in which anti-realism about norms was conjoined with non-cognitivism about the semantics of normative judgment: to judge that doing X is morally (or legally) wrong is just to express a certain kind of attitude or feeling,

---

[20] Some writers draw the connection explicitly: e.g., Shapiro says that "analytical jurisprudence [meaning a solution to the Demarcation Problem] has profound practical implications for the practice of law…." *Legality*, p. 25.

presumably one tied—psychologically—to motivation and action.[21] Hart did, of course, reject the view he associated with Alf Ross, namely, that legal *validity* consisted in "a verifiable hypothesis about future judicial behavior and its special motivational feeling."[22] For Hart, of course, to say that a legal rule is *valid* is just to say that it satisfies the criteria of legal validity in the Rule of Recognition. But nothing in my reading is meant to deny Hart's conceptual point about legal validity, namely, that it is not reducible to predictions about behavior. Rather, the point at issue here concerns what an anti-realism about *norms*, which Hart accepts, entails about motivation and action. On the view I am proposing, to the extent an agent's judgment that X is *morally right* has normative force for the agent, that normative force is explicable in terms of certain psychological facts about the agent. It is possible Hart did not always understand this, as when he says that "the internal character of [normative legal judgments, like, 'You must stop at the red light'] is not a mere matter of the speaker having certain 'feelings of compulsion'; for though these may indeed often accompany the making of such statements they are neither necessary nor sufficient conditions of their normative use in criticizing conduct, making claims and justifying hostile reactions by reference to the accepted standard."[23] On one reading, all Hart might mean is that agents manifest the 'internal point of view' simply in virtue of using the right kind of normative language and making the right kinds of justificatory or critical comments about, respectively, conforming or deviant behavior vis-à-vis some rule. But to the extent the 'internal point' of view of the actor making the legal judgment is *normative* for that agent, i.e., motivates him to act, then that just is a psychological fact about the agent, about his 'feelings' as it were. If Hart really meant to deny that, then he was, alas, just confused about how his implicit metaphysical picture of moral norms interacted with plausible assumptions about human psychology and motivation.

Insofar as Hart believed that people felt moral rightness demanded action, he had good reason to worry about the Demarcation Problem. The "purity" of Kelsen's theory—his reluctance to assimilate the normativity of law to psycho-social facts about behavior and attitudes—might seem to block the naturalization of the problem suggested by Hart's approach. So as not to be taken far afield, I shall simply declare, somewhat dogmatically, my allegiance to Hume, Nietzsche, and (I would hope) Hart in being skeptical that any sense can be given to the NeoKantian idea of the grounds of intelligibility of the application of norms apart

---

[21] See, e.g., Kevin Toh, "Hart's Expressivism and his Benthamite Project," *Legal Theory* 11 (2005), p. 115. See also, Kevin Toh, "Legal Judgments as the Plural Acceptance of Norms," in *Oxford Studies in the Philosophy of Law, Volume 1,* ed. L. Green & B. Leiter (Oxford: Oxford University Press 2011).

[22] H.L.A. Hart, "Scandinavian Realism," reprinted in *Essays in Jurisprudence and Philosophy* (Oxford: Oxford University Press 1983), p. 165.

[23] Id. at 167.

from a psychological one.[24] We need, accordingly, to approach the Demarcation Problem in that spirit.

If we understand the idea of the *morally obligatory* or *morally attractive* in purely psychologistic terms—which is precisely how we should, I have argued, read Hart—then the practical import of solving the Demarcation Problem changes. What is legally valid is not necessarily morally obligatory, and what is morally attractive is not necessarily legal obligatory: those are the two key (often implicit) contentions of proponents of the positivist answer to the Demarcation Problem. But this only seems important to emphasize because *people actually think the moral is overriding in practical reasoning*. In a world in which people, for example, viewed *moral obligation* as on a par in practical reasoning with "would feel pleasant," it is hard to see why the Demarcation Problem would matter. Perhaps legal norms are *morally obligatory*, but that does not answer the question what should be done. And perhaps certain norms are morally attractive: that does not decide, at all, the question whether a judge should apply them.

Admittedly, the world as the moral philosophers imagine it is one in which morality is overriding in practical reason. We may bracket, for the moment, Nietzschean and Thucydidean skepticism about whether this is the real world.[25] The point that bears emphasizing is that the solution to the Demarcation Problem is supposed to answer a practical question about *what ought to be done*, one that is reducible to a psycho-social question about the attitudes people have about morality and legality. Thus we may ask whether there is any reason to think a *theoretical* solution to the Demarcation Problem will affect the actual psychological attitudes of persons?

Defenders of legal positivism, the dominant answer to the Demarcation Problem in the last 200 years, are surely familiar with the contention that a solution to the Demarcation Problem has far-reaching consequences for practice. This was, after all, the central thought behind Lon Fuller's famous 1957 attack on H.L.A. Hart,[26] which has been a target of philosophical derision ever since for its odd mischaracterizations of the claims of legal positivists, including Hart. Fuller thought, simply put, that the blame for the moral depravity of Nazi judges could be laid at the door of their "positivism," i.e., their view that they were bound to apply the legally valid norms of their immoral system (cf. p. 649). According to Fuller, positivism's "definitions

[24] I am also fairly confident (*contra* Quine's naturalism, with its unprincipled commitment to psychological behaviorism even in the face of the *a posteriori* failure of that research program) that our best explanatory theory of the world will need to presuppose the reality of the mental states of persons, though it will not need to make explanatory appeal to moral norms. See my "Moral Facts and Best Explanations," reprinted in *Naturalizing Jurisprudence*.

[25] See my, "In Praise of Realism (and Against 'Nonsense' Jurisprudence)," *Georgetown Law Journal* 100 (forthcoming 2012).

[26] "Positivism and Fidelity to Law—A Reply to Professor Hart," *Harvard Law Review* 71 (1957), pp. 630–672. Further citations will be by page number in the body of the text.

of 'what law really is' are not mere images of some datum of experience, but direction posts for the application of human energies" (p. 632) and he reminds us that "words have a powerful effect on human attitudes" (p. 649). Thus, Fuller deems it worth asking "whether legal positivism, as practiced and preached in Germany, had, or could have had, any causal connection with Hitler's ascent to power" (p. 658) and concludes that, due to the ideas of legal positivism, the "German lawyer was therefore peculiarly prepared to accept as 'law' anything that called itself by that name" (p. 659), even, of course, when the law was morally abhorrent.

Fuller's attack has been criticized for its many misstatements of Hart's views, for example, when he claims that Hart believes there is an "amoral datum called law, which has the peculiar quality of creating a moral duty to obey it" (p. 656). That Hart's version of the positivist theory of law had none of the implications that Fuller described is not the issue.[27] What requires notice here, however, is that the main practical rationale for solving the Demarcation Problem we have identified appears to be the mirror image of Fuller's attack on positivism: namely, that the correct or incorrect view about legality will affect action! To be sure, many legal philosophers might object that their only concern is a theoretical one, namely, figuring out what is *true* about law. Since we have never found any truths about any artifact concepts that would satisfy the desiderata legal philosophers like Raz and Dickson and Shapiro regularly announce, it is hard to see why we should take seriously the idea that there is a theoretical reason for solving the Demarcation Problem. That leaves us, then, only with the practical reasons, and they are real enough, assuming one thinks that confusions about *morality* and *legality* have consequences in political practice.

Let us suppose that they do, much as Fuller did. *But why, then, think that a jurisprudential solution to the Demarcation Problem would resolve them*? That is the key question. If I am right about the perceived practical importance of solving the Demarcation Problem in jurisprudence, then positivism confronts a psycho-social phenomenon: people think that *morally obligatory* means *overriding* in practical reasoning, and they think *legally valid* means *morally obligatory*. Does anyone seriously believe Kelsen's *Pure Theory of Law* or Hart's *The Concept of Law* are the manifestos to counteract these psycho-social phenomena? To think so would be to commit Fuller's mistake, but in reverse.[28]

Fuller sought to lay at the door of positivism the reprehensible behavior of Nazi legal officials.[29] A positivist solution to the Demarcation Problem would, by

---

[27] See, e.g., my "The Radicalism of Legal Positivism," *National Lawyers Guild Review* 66 (2009), pp. 165–172.

[28] Not the mistake of misunderstanding legal positivism, but the mistake of thinking a certain legal theory (denominated "positivist") constitutes the actual explanation for why Nazi judges did abhorrent things. (Thanks to Matt Kramer for clarification on this issue.)

[29] I am assuming, of course, that Fuller's speculation is preposterous. That he adduced no actual evidence on its behalf is only one of many reasons for thinking it silly.

contrast, teach the Nazis that legal obligations are defeasible, since they are not moral obligations—or so the anti-Fullerian positivist must suppose. But if Fuller was mistaken, not only in his characterization of positivism but in his claim that it had some "causal connection with Hitler's ascent to power" (Fuller's words), then why should there be any practical reason to try to solve the Demarcation Problem in jurisprudence?

Law and morality, as we noted at the start, are pervasive normative phenomena in modern societies. We generally believe that judges have a defeasible obligation to apply the law; we also generally believe that judges, like other persons, ought to do what is morally right. These two normative demands can conflict, and then there can be a hard practical questions to answer. The idea that a putative solution to the Demarcation Problem gives us the answer—which seems to be what Fullerians and anti-Fullerians think—is an illusion.

Even though we cannot demarcate science and non-science, we still need to assign degrees of epistemic credence to differing claims about what the world is like. And even if we cannot precisely demarcate law and morals, we still need to decide what it is we ought to do, and what it is we have an obligation to do. Solutions to Demarcation Problems, if they worked, would give us shortcuts. But if they do not work, then we have to tackle the practical questions directly. In philosophy of science, that has meant concentrated attention on the epistemology of the various sciences, from physics to biology to psychology, and whether their distinctive claims are well-supported by the available evidence. In philosophy of law that would mean focusing on *particular* legal systems and the practical demands they make upon officials. To take a very American example, the question is *not* whether the original public meaning of the Constitution is the criterion of legal validity in the U.S. legal system—as, for example, the far right Supreme Court Justice Antonin Scalia believes—the question is whether applying the original public meaning in resolving concrete controversies could be morally justified. Even if Justice Scalia were right about the legal meaning of the Constitution, the right conclusion might be that the legal meaning should be discounted.

Two objections to the preceding now demand explicit attention. Am I not already supposing a distinction between law and morality? After all, I have conceded that judges have a defeasible obligation to apply the law and that judges, like other persons, ought to do what is morally right. This statement already supposes that the two source of norms, law and morality, are different. But of course they are *obviously* different in many cases, and many contexts! It is a mistake to assume that a distinction, to be useful for *many* purposes, has to be made in terms of *essential* properties that will demarcate *all* cases for all purposes, the way the molecular constitution of water definitely settles the status of all clear potable liquids. But it has been precisely the claim of jurisprudents who offer solutions to the Demarcation Problem that they have identified the criterion that cuts the normative world at the legal and non-legal joints.[30] Even after the almost-universal admission that philosophers

[30]This is explicit in Raz, Dickson, and Shapiro, and in Hart's use of the language of "necessary and sufficient" conditions. Perhaps their ambitions, suitably deflated, survive the criticisms developed here.

failed to solve the Demarcation Problem in philosophy of science, philosophers, and the "folk," can still happily recognize that chemistry is a fairly good bet for telling us what the world is like, and astrology is not, even though there is no criterion that will tell us the scientific status of any and all propositions about the world. For most purposes, we operate quite well with the method of paradigm cases, and analogies to those cases; for those purposes, legal positivism does better than any competitors, or so it seems to me and many others. But the practical problems the Demarcation Problem might solve rarely arise in the ordinary cases, but in the extraordinary ones, where the demands of what seems paradigmatically to be law pull in one direction and the demands of what seem paradigmatically to be moral considerations pull in the other. Does the Eighth Amendment of the U.S. Constitution, prohibiting "cruel and unusual punishments," prohibit, in particular, the imposition of the death penalty? Some traditional jurisprudents think a solution to the Demarcation Problem would help.[31] But given what is at stake, how could it? Why would we think the state is justified in terminating the life of a citizen just because it turns out to be *constitutional* on one reading of the constitutional provision? Perhaps the death penalty is a *legally valid* punishment in the United States; it is hard to see why that would change the fact (if it is a fact) that it is morally abhorrent to empower the state to deprive citizens of their life. A legal positivist might agree that the death penalty in the U.S. is *legally valid*, but deem it so morally abhorrent a penalty that equitable considerations require judges to override their valid legal obligations. An anti-positivist who thinks the immorality of the death penalty means it is not legally obligatory will reach the same conclusion. In each case, the *key* question is *what is the moral status of the death penalty*?[32] The rest is just jurisprudential window-dressing.

A second worry about the argument of this paper also naturally arises at this point. Has not my posture here brought me surprisingly close to the position of Ronald Dworkin in his recent work.[33] For has not Dworkin chastised legal positivists for attempting to divorce legal philosophy from political philosophy, to divorce questions about what the law is from questions about what it ought to be, and what judges out to do? Indeed, he has, but for reasons wholly unrelated to the considerations adduced here. Dworkin thinks that solving the Demarcation Problem leads to answers to the practical questions, that the two kinds of questions stand and fall together. Thus, Dworkin claims that the positivist solution to the Demarcation Problem entails claims about how judges should decide particular cases—though as I, and others have noted, this reading involves such a wild fabrication of the positivist

---

[31] Cf. Shapiro, *Legality*, pp. 28–30.

[32] The hypothetical positivist here will get one extra question, to be sure: namely, does the law require the immoral decision? And that question *could* affect the practical reasoning of the positivist judge depending on her view of the moral weight of legal validity. But notice, then, that the extra question for the hypothetical positivist judge is also a *moral* one. In the end, it is hard to see how the overriding consideration could not be the seriousness of the moral inequity of the death penalty. (Thanks to an anonymous referee for pressing this issue.)

[33] See, e.g., "Hart's Postscript" and "30 Years On" in *Justice in Robes*.

position that Fuller looks like a paragon of interpretive charity by comparison.[34] For positivists, the fact that a norm is legally valid certainly creates a *prima facie* legal reason to decide in accordance with the legal norm, but one that is defeasible by other equitable considerations. And, conversely, Dworkin thinks his own theory of law as integrity both solves (or should we say, "dissolves") the Demarcation Problem *and* tells judges how to decide concrete cases.

The skeptical argument developed here is different. It suggests we abandon the Demarcation Problem in favor of arguing about *what ought to be done*, whether by judges confronted with novel cases, or citizens confronted with morally objectionable laws. This is the practical consideration that animates interest in the Demarcation Problem, but since human artifacts never admit of successful analysis in terms of their essential characteristics—the inductive lesson to be learned from twentieth-century philosophy, especially philosophy of science—why not address the practical considerations directly? The lesson, frankly, seems well-confirmed by the increasingly baroque attempts by legal positivists to solve the Demarcation Problem after the valiant and seminal efforts of Kelsen, Hart, and Raz. And it seems equally well-confirmed by the efforts of natural law theorists like John Finnis and Mark Murphy, who *really* want theorists to focus on *morally good* law or *practically reasonable* legal systems, but who insist on claiming that their transparent change of the subject is *really* an answer to the Demarcation Problem, *really* a case of saying what "non-defective" law is or what the "focal" cases of law are.[35] The professionalization of philosophy, including legal philosophy, guarantees, I fear, continued attention to the Demarcation Problem, since specialization always run the risk of generating both an audience and performers for ultimately pointless disputes. In the spirit of Marx's second Thesis on Feuerbach, let me suggest that a "dispute…that is isolated from practice is a purely *scholastic* question." I can see why Kelsen, Hart, and Raz might have thought that a solution to the Demarcation Problem was both possible and might be relevant to practice. I think we no longer have an excuse for believing this today.

[34] See my "The End of Empire: Dworkin and Jurisprudence in the 21st Century," *Rutgers Law Juornal* 36 (2004), esp. pp. 175–177.

[35] See, e.g., the useful survey piece by Mark Murphy on "Natural Law Theory," in *The Blackwell Guide to Philosophy of Law and Legal Theory*, ed., M. Golding & W. Edmundson (Oxford: Blackwell 2005).

Chapter 9
Normative Legal Positivism, Neutrality, and the Rule of Law

Bruno Celano

> *Neutrality is not vitiated by the fact that it is undertaken for partial (...) reasons. One does not, as it were, have to be neutral all the way down (Waldron 1989, 147).*
>
> *Like other instruments, the law has a specific virtue which is morally neutral in being neutral as to the end to which the instrument is put. It is the virtue of efficiency; the virtue of the instrument as an instrument. For the law this virtue is the rule of law. Thus the rule of law is an inherent virtue of the law, but not a moral virtue as such.*
>
> *The special status of the rule of law does not mean that conformity with it is of no moral importance. [...] Conformity to the rule of law is also a moral virtue (Raz 1977, 226).*

9.1 Introduction

Usually, in jurisprudential debates what is discussed under the rubric of 'neutrality' is the claim that jurisprudence is (or at least can, and should be) a conceptual, or descriptive—thus, non-normative, or morally neutral (these are by no means the

Earlier versions of this paper were presented at the Seminar on legal philosophy, University of Palermo, at the DI.GI.TA., University of Genoa, and at the conference "Neutrality and Legal Theory" (Girona, Spain, 21–22 May 2010). I am grateful for their comments and criticisms to Federico Arena, Mauro Barberis, Clelia Bartoli, Marco Brigaglia, Pierluigi Chiassoni, Paolo Comanducci, Elena Consiglio, Isabel Fanlo Cortés, Riccardo Guastini, Giulio Itzcovich, Pau Luque Sanchez, Giorgio Maniaci, Realino Marra, José Luis Martí, José Juan Moreso, Nicola Muffato, Giorgio Pino, Francesca Poggi, Jahel Queralt, Cristina Redondo, Serena Romano, Aldo Schiavello, Isabel Trujillo, Francesco Viola.

B. Celano (✉)
Dipartimento di studi su politica, diritto e società, University of Palermo,
piazza Bologni 8, I-90139 Palermo, Italy
e-mail: bruno.celano@unipa.it

J. Ferrer Beltrán et al. (eds.), *Neutrality and Theory of Law*,
Law and Philosophy Library 106, DOI 10.1007/978-94-007-6067-7_9,

same thing)—inquiry: a body of theory having among its principles and its conclusions no substantive normative claims, or, specifically, no moral or ethico-political claims; and that the concept of law, as reconstructed in jurisprudential analysis proper, is not a normative or morally-laden concept—not the concept of how the law ought, or morally ought, to be. 'Neutrality', in short, designates a requirement, or a condition, to the effect that jurisprudential inquiry should be value-free, or non-normative, or morally neutral.

I do not know whether this requirement, in its most significant forms, can be met, but, be that as it may, I am going to discuss neutrality in an altogether different sense, namely, neutrality as an ethical, or ethico-political, ideal. Mine will be an essay in legal theory as a substantive, normative inquiry, pursuing neutrality as an ethico-political ideal the law should meet.

My starting point is normative legal positivism, or the claim that it is a good and desirable thing that the laws have easily identifiable, readily accessible non-controversial social sources (Sect. 9.2). What justifies normative legal positivism, I shall claim, is the value—or the ideal—of neutrality, suitably understood. I.e., what is desirable about laws being such as normative legal positivism claims they ought to be is, in a sense to be specified, their neutrality.

What, then, is the relevant concept of neutrality? And why is neutrality, so understood, a value? Answers to these questions, I shall argue, can be found when we consider the idea of the Rule of Law.

By the 'Rule of Law' I mean, as has now become usual among legal theorists, a set of formal and institutional features the law may possess in varying degrees (Sect. 9.3). These features define an ideal, which laws have traditionally been expected to live up to. Normative legal positivism, I claim, envisages neutrality through the Rule of Law. There are two connections, one regarding the Rule of Law generally, the other regarding a particular version of the Rule of Law (I shall call it 'Enlightenment Rule of Law'; Sect. 9.5). The first connection is through stability of mutual expectations (Sect. 9.4). The second connection stems from what I will call the 'inherent neutrality' of prescriptions (Sect. 9.6). Under both respects, it turns out, "observance of the rule of law is necessary if the law is to respect human dignity" (Raz 1977, p. 221).

9.2 Normative Legal Positivism

There are various—more or less thick—versions of normative legal positivism (hereinafter NLP) available. NLP may involve a commitment to the separation of powers and fidelity to the constitution (Scarpelli 1965); it may involve a commitment to democracy (Campbell 1996; J. Waldron's arguments, too, often point in this direction, cf. e.g. Waldron 2009, pp. 689, 698, 700). My understanding of NLP is very thin, one could say skeletal ('minimal' NLP). By 'normative legal positivism' I understand the thesis that the separation of law and morality, the separation of the grounds of legal judgment and the grounds of moral judgment, is a good thing, something to be valued and encouraged.[1]

I distinguish two versions of NLP, an epistemic and a substantive one. Substantive NLP claims that "law should be restricted as to its moral content" (MacCormick 1985, p. 37). There are sound moral reasons why the law should reproduce and enforce only a very limited portion of the content of morality—how the relevant portion is to be circumscribed is a matter for discussion.[2] Epistemic NLP concerns the desirability of non-moral, so far as possible trivially factual, non-controversial and readily applicable, criteria—or tests—of legal validity (i.e., of membership in a legal system). Laws, epistemic NLP claims, should be recognizable and identifiable as such, and their content capable of being determined, on the basis of (so far as possible easily accessible, readily identifiable, non-controversial) social facts, or sources, independently of moral or other evaluative considerations. In its epistemic version, in short, NLP says that it is desirable that the existence and content of the laws be capable of being determined "by reference to social facts"—to non-controversial, easily identifiable social facts—and "without relying on moral considerations" (Raz 1979, p. 53).

Epistemic NLP's main claim echoes J. Raz's sources thesis. It is, however, a different claim, under two respects. First, what NLP claims is that it is desirable that the law could be identified and its content determined on the basis of 'non-controversial, easily identifiable, readily accessible' social facts. This clause is not part of Raz's sources thesis. Second, and most important, Raz's sources thesis is meant as a claim about what the law is. NLP's main claim—we might dub it the 'normative sources thesis'—is a claim about what the law ought to be. It says that it would be good, desirable etc., that the laws be such as Raz's sources thesis claims them to be. I will say that, when it meets epistemic NLP's central requirement, the law 'satisfies the sources thesis' (that it 'satisfies ST'). This should be understood as a term of art.

In what follows, I shall be concerned with the epistemic version of NLP only (unless otherwise specified, 'NLP' will designate this position).

NLP raises some issues. I will only list some of them here, deferring a detailed treatment to another occasion.

(1) Is NLP a jurisprudential position? Jurisprudence, it is often argued, is a purely conceptual inquiry, and NLP—better, the kind of theorizing NLP may be taken to

---

[1] I am here paraphrasing Waldron (2001, p. 411), defining NLP as "the thesis that [the] separability of law and morality, [the] separability of [the grounds of] legal judgment and [the grounds of] moral judgment, is a good thing, perhaps even indispensable (from a moral, social, or political point of view), and certainly something to be valued and encouraged". The label is to some extent unfortunate, since the phrase 'normative legal positivism' has been used, in recent times, to designate "the version of legal positivism that identifies law with norms" (Waldron 2001, p. 411). For a discussion of the terminological issue, and of the reasons for preferring the phrase 'normative legal positivism' to the alternative 'ethical legal positivism' (Campbell 1996); cf. Waldron 2001, pp. 411–412.

[2] According to MacCormick (1985, p. 32) the law should only enforce duties of justice; in the name of the sovereignty of conscience, or of respect for autonomous agency, it should abstain from attempting to enforce "matters of aspiration and supererogation", our self-regarding duties, and duties of love.

be the result of—is not. NLP is a normative position, resting on moral grounds. It is the result of substantive normative—specifically, moral—inquiry.

This is true. The premise of this argument may perhaps be doubted—some philosophers doubt whether the divide between, on the one hand, a purely conceptual inquiry and, on the other hand, normative, or moral, theorizing may be maintained all the way down. But I will not go into these matters. Whether you wish to call it 'jurisprudence' or not is immaterial to my present purposes.

(2) Is NLP in fact a form of *positivism*? Positivism, it is sometimes argued, claims that the concept *law* can and should be defined independently of any moral assumptions. Apparently, NLP does not satisfy this condition.

But, it may be replied, NLP, as defined, does not purport to provide a definition of the concept *law*. It merely claims that it would be a good thing if the law had a certain property (i.e., if it satisfied ST). This reply, however, sets the stage for a further, deeper objection.

(3) NLP presupposes proper jurisprudential, conceptual analysis, and is parasitic on it. Before you can claim that it would be a good (or, for that matter, a bad) thing if law satisfied ST, you have to know what law is—you have to gain an adequate understanding of the concept *law*. And, it is added, positivism is a position in jurisprudence, so understood. Thus, NLP is neither a position in jurisprudence nor, *a fortiori*, a form of positivism. It rather presupposes a positivistic analysis, or reconstruction, of the concept of law.

According to some defenders of NLP the concept *law* itself is normative, and morally-laden. These philosophers cast doubt on the assumption that the concept *law* may, or may interestingly, be defined independently of any moral assumptions. For these people, NLP is, in fact, a position in jurisprudence proper; conceptual inquiry into the concept *law* is not, at bottom, free from moral assumptions. And it is, in fact a variety of positivism (once 'positivism' is suitably redefined, abandoning the untenable assumption that the concept *law* should be defined independently of moral assumptions, and that this is what identifies legal positivism). I do not follow this path here. That the concept *law* be itself normative, or morally-laden, is not part of NLP, as here understood. For my purposes, nothing depends on the label 'positivism'. If you wish to withdraw from the position the label 'legal positivism', you may do it.[3] Nothing in my argument depends on hanging on to this label.

(4) A problem arises as regards the presuppositions of NLP. According to what we understand NLP as presupposing, we may distinguish two further versions of NLP; I will call them the 'Panglossian' and the 'contingency' version respectively.

[3]If you wish, you may call defenders of NLP "positivity-welcomers", maintaining that "insofar as legal noms are valid on their sources, rather than their merits, this fact [endows] legal norms with some redeeming merit even when they are (in any other respect) unmeritorious norms" (Gardner 2001, pp. 204–205). (NLP, however, does not exactly coincide with the position Gardner describes here, for reasons which are irrelevant in the present context.)

It is a necessary condition for NLP's main claim to be a sound principle of political morality that (a) the law *can* satisfy ST. If the laws could not satisfy ST, the question whether they should satisfy it or not would not even arise. But, what about the further condition (b) that it also be possible that the law does *not* satisfy ST?

Perhaps it is a matter of fact that law, as such, satisfies ST—perhaps it is a conceptual necessity that it does—*and* it is a good and desirable thing, something to be welcomed, that this is so.[4] Happily, the law—as such—in fact is, under this respect, as it ought to be. This is Panglossian NLP: luckily, we happen to live in the best (under the relevant respect) of all possible legal worlds.

Do we wish to endorse Pangloss' optimism? Arguably, for NLP to be a sensible ethico-political position, condition (b), too, has to be met. In other words, it has to be contingent that the law satisfies ST.

There are a number of ways in which the law may fail to satisfy ST. Some of them are obvious—but by no means unimportant. It may happen that the tests for identifying the laws, or for determining their content, are not, as required by NLP, easily applicable, or such that the upshot of their application is non-controversial. The relevant social facts may not be easily identifiable, or readily accessible. In such cases what the law is will be difficult to discern, controversial, or indeterminate. But the idea that the law does not satisfy ST may also be understood in a stronger way—and this seems a more interesting reading in the present context. It may be understood as allowing for the possibility that there is indeed law, well-determined law, on a given issue, but it is not—or at least not directly—source-based.

And here's the rub. In what ways should we take it to be possible that the law does not satisfy ST, on this strong reading of 'not satisfying ST'? For positivists, the most obvious possibility will be that the law, by virtue of its sources, incorporates moral standards. Accordingly, the contingency version of NLP claims that it is possible for the law, by virtue of its sources, to incorporate moral standards, and that it is better (and possible) that it doesn't.[5]

So understood, the contingency version of NLP presupposes the possibility of the incorporation of morality by law—it presupposes the falsity of exclusive legal positivism. Some will want to deny this possibility. Suppose we deny that condition (b), so understood, can be satisfied. I can think of three hypotheses.

(i) Satisfaction of (b) is impossible, because there are no moral facts for the law to incorporate. Ethical non-cognitivists will want to argue this way. To rebut thus objection, it suffices that there are criteria of correctness in (some) moral argument;

---

[4]This is, in J. Gardner's terminology (2001, p. 205), a position similar to that of those 'positivity-welcomers' who are also 'legal positivists' proper. (It is not the same position, however, because, in Gardner's taxonomy, inclusive positivists count as endorsing the relevant notion of a norm's positivity—its being valid in virtue of a source. According to the text, they don't; the relevant notion of positivity is, rather, satisfaction of ST.) Cf. also Green 2003, 4.3.

[5]Cf. Waldron 2001, pp. 411, 413–414: NLP "*assumes* (…) negative positivism"—i.e., it presupposes "the inclusive possibility"—"but *prescribes* something like exclusive positivism".

it suffices, that is, that it be conceded that it makes sense to argue about (some) moral issues.

(ii) The very notion of incorporation (of morality by law) is misconceived. Rather, what we actually have in cases of apparent incorporation of morality by law is, in fact, the non-exclusion of, or modulation of the application of, morality (Raz 2004). This, in fact, concedes the point. In this hypothesis, condition (b) will be held to be satisfied, not by virtue of incorporation, but by virtue of the non-exclusion, or modulation of the applicability, of morality by law. It will be contingent *in this sense* that the law satisfies ST.

(iii) Incorporation is impossible (inclusive legal positivism is false), but people mistakenly believe it to be possible, and this belief is non-dispensable. This leads to an error theory of the law. In cases of apparent incorporation there is, in fact, no law—although people mistakenly believe there is law, and this belief cannot be dispensed with. I find this hypothesis puzzling.

(5) I said that it is a necessary condition for NLP to be a sound principle of political morality that the law *can* satisfy ST. If the laws could not satisfy ST, the question whether they should satisfy it or not would be futile. Now, the idea that the existence and content of the laws may be capable of being determined on the basis of social facts alone—more so, on the basis of trivially factual, non-controversial and readily applicable tests—sounds naïve. It apparently flies in the face of what goes on in legal interpretation and legal reasoning (Chiassoni 1990; Diciotti 1999; Guastini 2004).

What NLP presupposes is not that it is possible that the law as a whole, *all* legal norms, be capable of being identified, and their content determined, on the basis of readily accessible non-controversial social facts. NLP, however, does presuppose the possibility that at least some laws—and not a negligible or insignificant part of the law as a whole—satisfy ST. This is incompatible with (a) the claim that all law—or even the bulk of, or the most important portions of, the law—is (always, necessarily) indeterminate; (b) a sceptical view of legal interpretation and legal reasoning.

(6) NLP claims that it is a good and desirable thing that laws satisfy ST. This claim should be understood as non-absolute, in two respects. First, defenders of NLP (in its contingency version) may, and—if sensible—should, grant that it is under certain social, political or economic conditions that it is a good thing that law satisfies ST. A fully developed NLP theory should specify which these conditions are. Second, defenders of NLP may, and—if sensible—should, claim that it is only *pro tanto* (or *ceteris paribus*, etc.) good that the laws satisfy ST. Whatever reasons there may be in favour of laws satisfying ST, or of complying with such laws, they are in principle overridable (cf. Moreso 2005).

So, NLP, in my favoured version, claims that it is (contingent and) desirable that the existence and content of the laws satisfy ST. But, we should ask, *why* can this be thought to be a good thing? What can be desirable about law's satisfying ST?

One possible answer is the following. If the law is to have legitimate authority it must be like that. In other words: the law should have legitimate authority (cf. e.g. Raz 2003, p. 180); for it to have legitimate authority, it is a necessary condition that it satisfies ST; thus, the law should satisfy ST.

A few comments on this argument. (1) The second premise is in the spirit of J, Raz's service conception of authority (Raz 1985, 1986, Chap. 3).
(2) The second premise, I think, can and should be weakened, in two ways: (a) satisfying ST is, not a necessary condition but, the main way in which law can be capable of having legitimate authority; (b) for the law to have legitimate authority, it is required that it, to the extent that it is reasonable, satisfies ST. Neither qualification is in the spirit of Raz's theory.
(3) The inference. like all inferences of this form, has to be taken carefully; it does not allow detachment. It is not the case that, whenever it ought to be the case that p, and q is a necessary condition of p, then it ought to be the case that q, period. But there is, under this respect, nothing peculiar to our argument.
(4) I am not claiming that law has legitimate authority, nor that since it necessarily claims that, it has to be such as to satisfy the sources thesis (apparently, this is Raz's argument, leading to his version of exclusive legal positivism; cf. Raz 1985).[6]

So this is one possible reason supporting NLP. Whatever the merits of this argument, in what follows I will explore an altogether different line of argument. What justifies NLP is the value—or the ideal—of neutrality (suitably understood). That the law be separated from morality—that the existence and content of the laws may be determined on the basis of easily identifiable, readily accessible, non-controversial social facts—is desirable, because when it satisfies this condition the law is, in a sense to be specified, neutral.

How should the word 'neutrality' be understood, here? And why is neutrality, in the relevant sense, a value? In order to answer these questions, I submit, we have to turn our attention to the Rule of Law (hereinafter RoL).

NLP, I shall argue, envisages neutrality through the RoL, in two ways. The first connection is via stability of mutual expectations (below, Sect. 9.4). Neutrality surfaces here in two forms: (1) indifference; (2) reciprocity and fairness. The second connection stems from what I will call the 'inherent neutrality' of prescriptions (below, Sect. 9.6).

[6]Note, however, that Waldron (2001, pp. 412, 432) ascribes Raz, albeit hesitatingly, to the NLP party. It all depends, in his view, on whether Raz is understood as claiming that law claims authority, or that it is a good thing that society be organized through a system of directives claiming authority (cf. e.g. Raz 1996a, p. 115).

9.3 The Rule of Law

There are many different ways of understanding the phrase 'the Rule of Law'.[7] Here I adopt the one which has become common in contemporary jurisprudence in the last 40 years or so.[8] Accordingly, by 'the Rule of Law' I understand a loose cluster of (1) formal features of the laws (prospectivity, publicity, relative generality, relative stability, intelligibility and relative clarity, practicability,[9] consistency), plus (2) institutional and procedural desiderata (such as, for instance, that the making of singular norms, applying to individual cases, be guided by general rules; and, further, so-called principles of 'natural justice': that the resolution of disputes be entrusted to somebody not having an interest at stake in the judgment, and not being otherwise biased; the principle *audi alteram partem:* and so on).[10] Items on the list partly vary according to the accounts given by different authors. The core, however, is stable.[11]

Some of these are features that the law may possess in varying degrees. Most of them specify, more or less directly, what is instrumentally required in order to achieve an end—namely, the end of guiding human behaviour through rules.[12] In other words, they are features the laws must possess if they are to be capable of being followed and obeyed.[13] So understood, the features constituting the RoL are

[7]For a survey cf. Waldron 2002a, pp. 155–157; Id. 2004, pp. 319–320; Bennett 2007, pp. 92–94. According to some (including Waldron; see 2002a, pp. 157–159), the concept of the RoL is an "essentially contested concept", in W. B. Gallie's sense. This claim will not be discussed here.

[8]Accounts in this family have the form of "a sort of laundry list of features that a healthy legal system should have. These are mostly variations of the eight desiderata of Lon Fuller's 'internal morality of law'" (Waldron 2002a, p. 154). Cf. ibid., 154–155, for a survey of some of the main accounts in this vein (L. L. Fuller, J. Raz, J. Finnis, J. Rawls, M. Radin).

[9]I.e., conformity to the principle *'ought' implies 'can'*.

[10]For a list of these institutional and procedural requirements see e.g. Raz 1977, pp. 215–218 ("the making of particular laws (particular legal orders) should be guided by open, stable, clear, and general rules"; "the independence of the judiciary must be guaranteed"; "the courts should have review powers over the implementation of the other principles"; "the courts should be easily accessible"; "the discretion of the crime-preventing agencies should not be allowed to pervert the law"). On principles of natural justice cf. Hart 1961, pp. 156, 202. For similar lists of the RoL requirements see Fuller 1969, Chap. 2; Finnis 1980, pp. 270–271; Marmor 2004, 5ff. For sorting out principles constituting the RoL in formal and procedural ones see Waldron 2008a (but cf. also Raz 1977, p. 218).

[11]As noted by Waldron (2002a, p. 155), the accounts given by these authors (Fuller, Finnis, Raz, Rawls, Radin)—their partly differing "laundry lists"—"seem quite congenial to each other; they are filling in the details of what is more or less the same conception in slightly different ways".

[12]In L. L. Fuller's phrase, "the enterprise of subjecting human conduct to the governance of rules" (1969, p. 106).

[13]According to Raz (1977, p. 214) the "basic idea" underlying RoL requirements ("the basic intuition from which the doctrine of the rule of law derives") is "that the law must be capable of guiding the behaviour of its subjects" ("if the law is to be obeyed *it must be capable of guiding the behaviour of its subjects*. It must be such that they can find out what it is and act on it", ibid., my emphasis). Cf. also Marmor 2004, p. 5.

features an instrument (laws) must possess in order to perform its function (guiding human behaviour) well—they are analogous to the good-making properties entailed by the meaning of any functional term. RoL requirements are analogous to the sharpness of a knife (Raz 1977, p. 225; cf. also Marmor 2004, p. 7).

RoL features define an ethico-political ideal, which laws are usually expected to live up to.[14] But, I emphasize this, this view of the RoL has nothing to do with ideologically-driven views, widely spread in contemporary (non-jurisprudential) literature, that oppose the RoL to social and economic legislation, which—it is complained—"interfere[s] with market processes, limit[s] property rights, or make[s] investment in the society more precarious or in other ways less remunerative".[15] Such conceptions of the RoL I take as spurious.[16] I side with traditional, formal *cum* institutional and procedural, understandings of the RoL.

9.4 Neutrality (I): Stability of Mutual Expectations

NLP, I said, envisages neutrality through the RoL. There are two connections. In this section, I will lay out the first.

Consider the following train of thought (I shall call this 'the common measure myth'). Thanks to law-making satisfying NLP's main desideratum, some standards of conduct become the law of the land: by virtue of their satisfying ST, they are singled out as unique in being the rules of the group as a whole. Different individuals or different groups of individuals in the society may have different views about how to act in given circumstances, about the best or proper way of pursuing a common goal, about what course of action to settle on in case of a felt need for a common decision,[17] etc. Laws satisfying ST, so the story goes, settle these uncertainties, thus resolving such quandaries. The many private judgments of individuals and groups are replaced by a source-based—in principle, readily accessible and applicable—common measure: a single public judgment, counting as the judgment of the group (its 'public reason', supplanting the many conflicting 'private' reasons of individuals).

This is, as it stands, a myth. The mere fact that a directive is enacted as source-based law, by itself, does not solve disagreements, nor does it create a common

[14] The much debated question whether the features constituting the RoL are part of the very concept *law* I simply leave aside here. Cf. e.g. Bennett 2007; Waldron 2008a, Id. 2008b; Viola 2008.

[15] I borrow this characterization from Waldron 2007, p. 92.

[16] Cf. generally Waldron 2007.

[17] "We may say (…) that the felt need among the members of a certain group for a common framework or decision or course of action on some matter, even in the face of disagreement about what that framework, decision or action should be, are the *circumstances of politics*" (Waldron 1999a, p. 102 cf. also Id., 1999b, p. 154, and 2000, p. 1849). Some disagreements or conflicts are such that not all parties involved would prefer the adoption of a common course of action to doing, each one of them, what they prefer (Gaus 2002; Benditt 2004; but cf. Waldron 2000, pp. 1840, 1844).

measure, expressing a purported public judgment of the group as a whole. Of course, if the law is backed by an effective coercive apparatus there may be self-interested reasons for members of the group to comply with it. But talk of such laws as the 'public reason' of the community as a whole, or as expressing a 'public judgment' and 'common measure', which replaces the many diverse and conflicting private judgments of individuals,[18] does not contribute to clarity. Directives enacted as law claim legitimate authority. They become the common measure of the group—expressing what *ought* to count as the judgment of the group as a whole—only if they in fact have legitimate authority.[19]

There is, however, a grain of truth in the common measure myth. Directives enacted as source-based law are, in a sense, neutral. And this is, *ceteris paribus*, something valuable about them.

There is, first, a trivial sense in which this is true, Consider normative ST: it is a good and desirable thing that the existence and content of the law may be determined without recourse to moral argument. 'Neutrality', here, is exemplified, trivially, in the following way: what the law is on a given matter (i.e., what the law requires, or permits) may be determined on the basis of morally neutral considerations. Among people who endorse different and conflicting ethical views, what counts as law is something that can be determined in a neutral way (with regard to these different views). This may bring obvious advantages.

But, it seems to me, the grain of truth in the common measure myth goes deeper. Laws satisfying ST—directives enacted as source-based laws—may work as neutral social interaction devices, in that they may become the common focus for relatively stable mutual expectations. This may happen in two ways.

(1) Laws may afford the resolution of coordination problems proper (I mean coordination problems in the strict, game-theoretical sense), by singling out one coordination equilibrium among many. By hypothesis, each party is (almost) indifferent as to which among the different equilibria available is selected, and will do

[18]This is a permanent temptation in talk of law as Hobbesian "public reason" (Gauthier 1995).

[19]Cf. Raz 1979, pp. 50–51: "social life requires and is facilitated by various patterns of forbearances, co-operation, and co-ordination between members of the society or some of them. The same is true of the pursuits of goals which the society or sections in it may set themselves. Different members and different sections of a society may have different views as to which schemes of co-operation, co-ordination, or forbearance are appropriate. It is an essential part of the function of law in society to mark the point at which a private view of members of the society, or of influential sections or powerful groups in it, ceases to be their private view and becomes (i.e., *lays a claim to be*) a view binding on all members notwithstanding their disagreement with it. It does so and can only do so by providing publicly ascertainable ways of guiding behaviour and regulating aspects of social life. Law is a public measure by which one can measure one's own as well as other people's behaviour" (my emphasis). Cf. also Raz 1996a, pp. 100–104, 107–110. This is not to deny that, under some conditions, efficacy (or, specifically, public efficacy) may play a decisive role in endowing directives—e.g., some legal directives—with legitimate authority (cf. Raz 1986, Chap. 3, 1996a, p. 115, and 2006, p. 158; cf. also, for a related argument, Waldron 1999a, pp. 104–105, and 2000, pp. 1839–1840, 1847). In such cases, however, the story will have to be much more complicated than the common measure myth suggests.

his part in it provided he expects that the others will do theirs. Being singled out by law-making institutions, one equilibrium becomes salient, and the parties converge on it.

In such cases, the common measure myth is, in fact, no myth. In coordination problems proper, there is no question of authority (Ullmann-Margalit 1981; Green 1988, pp. 111–115): it is enough that one pattern of coordination is publicly selected, so as to become salient in the eyes of the parties. Coordinative agencies need not have authority (i.e., issue preemptive, protected reasons) in order to accomplish this task.[20]

Neutrality, here, is indifference. The choice of a particular equilibrium is neutral, in the sense that, by hypothesis, it is (almost) indifferent to the parties which, among the many equilibria available, will be the chosen one.[21]

In such cases, laws do indeed qualify as a common measure. These are, however, marginal cases, of limited import. Arguably, real-world interaction problems do not often exhibit this simple pattern. And, in any case, critical interaction problems—those where disagreement and conflict loom large, and where the need for a common decision is most acutely felt—are not coordination problems (in this restricted sense).[22]

(2) In the case of strategic interaction problems of different, more intractable sorts (Battles of the Sexes, Prisoner's Dilemmas, problems of collective action of various kinds) the law may purport to afford a unique resolution of conflicts, answering to the felt need for a common decision or course of action. In such cases, however, unless the law enjoys legitimate authority, the common measure myth is, indeed, a myth.[23] I.e., unless the law enjoys legitimate authority, purported 'solutions' of the relevant problems only qualify as such in so far as they are backed by an effective coercive apparatus, rendering compliance with enacted directives in the self-interest

[20]The law performs, here, the function of a mere indicator. What it affords to the parties, is the possibility of forming shared, or mutual, expectations, of various orders, about what course of action will be followed by the others. The course singled out by the law will appear as salient to each of the parties (i.e., it will appear such that it appears salient to each of the parties, and it will thus *be* the salient option). And this, given the structure of the problem, is sufficient reason for the parties to converge on it.

[21]A related case is that of Assurance Games (Elster 1983). In AG's there is no indifference. But the law may work in the same way.

[22]This is a widely acknowledged point. Cf. e.g. Waldron 2000, pp. 1838, 1844.

[23]This is not incompatible with J. Waldron's view (1999a, pp. 104–105, cf. also 2000, pp. 1839–1840, 1848) that some issues—especially issues concerning details or, generally, the *determinatio* of general norms—may have a structure such that it is preferred—strongly enough—by each of the parties that the issue be somehow settled (rather than that it be settled in the way he prefers it to be settled), so that the fact that the law can select a particular decision becomes a reason for all to accept it and to comply with it. Issues having this structure are Battles of the Sexes the law can solve; it follows trivially that the law can solve them. It does not follow, as Waldron notes (1999a, p. 104), that the law, as such, generally solves Battles of the Sexes, and that "this is why we should respect it". More generally still, wherever it matters a lot that an issue be somehow settled, and "univocality, determinacy, decisiveness" (Waldron 2002b, p. 368) are to be highly prized, the law may play a decisive role.

of the parties and changing, in fact, the shape of the problem (by altering the pay-off matrix). It may plausibly be argued, moreover, that many real-world disagreements and conflicts between people endorsing different conceptions of the good life, or different religious views, are not amenable to game-theoretical or public choice modeling.[24] In the case of such conflicts talk of legal directives, as such, as a common measure is mere rhetoric.

There is, however, a connection between law's purported resolution of conflicts in these kinds of cases and the idea of neutrality. In such cases, directives publicly enacted as laws—specifically, laws satisfying ST—may afford stability of mutual expectations. It is common knowledge that, probably, people will comply with them[25]; and this allows each of the parties to form expectations about how the others will act, on the basis of expectations about how the others will expect him to act, about how the others will expect him to expect them to act, and so on. Interlocking mutual expectations of this sort will enable individuals to make reasoned choices, and to plan their future.[26]

And it is here that the RoL comes into play. RoL requirements define an ethico-political ideal. It is one political ideal among many (I mean many other respectable ideals: democracy, justice, equality, human rights, and so on), not to be confused with any one of them (Raz 1977, p. 211). It is, moreover, a modest ideal. Not in the sense that it is easily attainable, but in the sense that it is compatible with gross injustice, and in general with gross violations of other ideals.

However modest, the ideal defined by RoL requirements is crucially important in the present connection. For the following reason.

Apparently, we could argue this way: source-based laws generally tend to afford stability of mutual expectations; stability of mutual expectations, however, is most firmly secured where RoL requirements are met;[27] therefore, the relevant sort of

---

[24] And, *a fortori*, not amenable to a simple Battle of the Sexes matrix (Gaus 2002; Benditt 2004; but cf. Waldron 2000, pp. 1840, 1844).

[25] On the notion of common or mutual knowledge see respectively Lewis 1969, 52ff.; Schiffer 1972, 30ff.

[26] Of course, the relevant expectations may also concern the ways in which the law will be modified (i.e., they may be grounded in the rules—themselves legal rules—according to which legal norms are created, changed, or repealed). More generally, secondary rules, too, may become the common focus for stable mutual expectations.

[27] This, I suggest, is how we should understand what is involved in the RoL requirement of publicity. When it is required that laws should be public, what is meant by this is not only that each one of the addressees should know what the law is, but also that everybody should know that everybody knows… (and so on, up through a chain of suitable mutual beliefs) what the law is. (Think of a regime in which laws are made known to their addressees by sending each one of them sealed envelopes. Everybody knows what the law is. But, would in this case the RoL requirement of publicity be met?) Cf. the discussion of a related point in Marmor 2004, p. 17, and Celano forthcoming. (So understood, the RoL condition of publicity corresponds to Rawls' first level of publicity of the principles of justice in a well-ordered society; cf. e.g. Rawls 1999, pp. 292–293, 324. Thanks to José Juan Moreso and Jahel Queralt for reminding this to me.)

neutrality is most firmly secured where the laws, apart from satisfying ST, also satisfy RoL requirements.

The connection, however, is tighter than that. When we find ourselves inclined to say that source-based law generally tends to afford stability of mutual expectations, it is in fact source-based law meeting, to some degree, at least some of the RoL requirements that we are thinking of.[28] It is laws that satisfy ST *and* meet, at least to a minimal degree, some of the RoL requirements (prospectivity, intelligibility, publicity, relative generality, regular application by unbiased judges) that work as neutral social interaction devices, affording stability of mutual expectations.

And, where RoL requirements are met, we can clearly see what is valuable in stable mutual expectations. RoL requirements imply that the expectations the law will give rise to will be—in so far as the law itself is concerned—*reliable* expectations. In affording the rise of mutual expectations, the law will not work as an "entrapment" device, encouraging expectations that it will afterwards frustrate (Raz 1977, p. 222). Laws meeting RoL requirements will, in sum, give rise to a stable, reliable system of interlocking mutual expectations, thus guaranteeing a measure of trustworthiness, fairness and reciprocity in the interaction of rulers and ruled (Fuller 1969, pp. 39–40; Finnis 1980, pp. 272–273; MacCormick 1985, p. 26), and of law's subjects with each other. This, I submit, is a form of neutrality: neutrality as fairness.

So understood, neutrality is, of course, compatible with gross injustice and discrimination. Where source-based laws are in place, e.g., the slave knows what he can expect from his master, because he knows what the master expects from him, and so on. Their dealings conform, however, to a stable, mutually reliable pattern.[29]

In both cases—coordination problems proper, and deep forms of social conflict and disagreement—, then, laws satisfying NLP's main desideratum, and the RoL, will more likely achieve the relevant aim (stability of mutual expectations), and instantiate the relevant value (respectively, neutrality as indifference, and neutrality as fairness).

9.5 Enlightenment Rule of Law

I now come to the second connection between NLP and neutrality (via the RoL). This connection concerns a particular version of the RoL. The building blocks of this version of the RoL have been developed, very roughly, in European legal culture in the eighteenth and nineteenth centuries; it is associated, *inter alia*, with

[28] Witness some kinds of sources which afford stability of mutual expectations only to a very limited extent: ordeal, drawing lots, divination by authorized soothsayers (I owe this point to Francesca Poggi), e.g. it is common knowledge that a certain dispute will be resolved by drawing lots; it is unknown, however, what the outcome will turn out to be.

[29] A putative counterexample is given by laws such as 'Whenever they wish, members of the ruling elite may seize and kill members of group X'. Such counterexamples are, however, ad hoc. These rules are general in their logical form only. They are not general in the way required by the RoL.

(Poggi, e.g.) J. Bentham's understanding of the formal features laws should possess. In this understanding, what is central to the RoL is the activity of legislating—i.e., the issuing of prescriptions.

Prescribing, as a kind of purposive human activity (roughly, trying to make people do something by telling them to do it), and prescriptive relationships (i.e., the kind of relationship which comes into being, by virtue of the happy issuing of a prescription, between a prescriber, or lawgiver in a wide sense, on the one hand, and those to whom her prescription is addressed, on the other hand) have many formal features. As with any other purposive, goal-oriented activity (and functional terms generally) some of these features express the requirements that the activity has to meet, in order to achieve—and to achieve well—its constitutive purpose. Some of these features aptly instantiate elements of the RoL ideal. So, for instance, prescribing is a procedure openly and publicly directed at the issuing of public directives.[30] And, as we have seen, publicity of the relevant standards of behaviour is one of the requirements of the RoL. Thus, where prescriptions are involved, not only the standard itself, but also its mode of birth, are laid out in the open.[31] Further, prescriptions typically have to be prospective, and intelligible; if they are to be capable of achieving their purpose (i.e., guiding human behaviour), they have to be laid out in advance, and clear enough for their addressee to understand them (cf. Marmor 2004, pp. 19–20, 26–27). Further still, the activity of prescribing is subject to rational pressure in favour of conformity to the principle *'ought' implies 'can'*, and the avoidance of conflicts (so called 'antinomies').[32] The latter, too, are, as we have seen (above, Sect. 9.3), among the requirements of the RoL—respectively, practicability, and consistency.

This legislative twist to the RoL should not be surprising. After all, most of the requirements of the RoL follow, as I have remarked, from what is instrumentally required when we want to subject human behaviour to the guidance of rules

---

[30] For a detailed discussion of this point see below, Sect. 9.6.

[31] Cf. Waldron 2007, p. 99: the legislature "is an institution set up explicitly to make and change the law. (…) Law-making by courts is not a transparent process; law-making in a legislature by contrast is law-making through a procedure dedicated publicly and transparently to that task" (the "transparency" of legislation). See also Waldron 2009, p. 693.

[32] These are all features that prescriptions *typically* exhibit, and pressures prescriptions are *standardly* subject to. The possibility of non-standard prescriptions is not ruled out (cf. e.g. below, n. 56). These will be cases of abuse of the institution of prescribing. So, for instance, one assumption which makes possible the issuing of prescriptions, and the coming into existence of prescriptive relationships, is that the lawgiver wants the addressee to do what she tells him to do (von Wright 1963, pp. 7, 119; Id., 1983, I, 8; Celano 1990, p. 127). This is a defeasible presumption. It is, however, standardly true; and an explicit denial of this condition would prevent a prescription from coming into being ('I hereby order you to do A, but I don't care whether you do it or not'; cf. Searle 1969, pp. 60, 64ff.). In the light of this presumption, the principle *'ought' implies 'can'* applies to prescriptions (so, e.g., a prescription enjoining an action explicitly acknowledged to be physically impossible would sound odd). Likewise, purported logical relations between prescriptions may be interpreted, via the assumption that whoever prescribes somebody to do something wants the addressee to do it, as criteria of a rational lawgiving will (von Wright 1983; Bobbio 1971; Celano 1990, pp. 268–282).

('subjecting human conduct to the governance of rules'; above, Sect. 9.3). And, of course, prescribing just *is*, in a straightforward sense, trying to subject human behaviour to the guidance of rules (trying to make somebody do something by telling them to do it).[33] True, prescribing is not necessarily the issuing of *general* directives, or of 'rules' proper. Under this, and perhaps other, respects the requirements of the RoL do not apply to prescribing, as such. But let us abstract from these, and focus on the respects listed above, in which prescribing does indeed instantiate the kind of activity RoL requirements apply to. When we see things in this light, a particular version of the RoL emerges, comprising the conditions which a certain form of guidance of human behaviour has to satisfy, if it has to succeed; comprising, i.e., what is in fact involved in a particular method of social control, which consists primarily in the issuing of prescriptions, that is, of directives communicated to persons, who are then expected to understand and to conform to these directives.[34] This includes, of course, orders backed by threats; it is not, however, limited to these. It encompasses (with some qualifications, to be spelt out along the way) all cases of *telling somebody what she should do.*[35] Henceforth, I shall call this version of the RoL 'Enlightenment RoL' (ERoL), due to its embodying some more or less utopian, eminently rationalistic (see below, Sect. 9.6) and, perhaps, simplistic desiderata. ERoL gives pride of place, in law's development and operation, to legislation.

A few comments about the role of legislation in ERoL are in order. (1) Some conceptions of the RoL celebrate it as a spontaneous, non-manufactured, unintended, gradually evolving order of human interaction whose administration and piecemeal development is entrusted to the collective, 'artificial' reason of the judiciary. But, as J. Waldron notes, such views forget "the rule of law difficulties of the Common Law—its opacity, the ad hoc character of its development, its unpredictability, its inherent retroactivity".[36] There is no need for us, here, to adjudicate this controversy. It is enough that we establish the credentials of a 'legislative' version of the RoL.

[33] Waldron (2007, pp. 109–110) rightly observes that L. L. Fuller's treatment of the subject in Fuller 1969, Chap. 2, "illustrates a strong (...) tendency to associate the rule of law with formal features of legislation, as opposed to other modes of law and law-making". Cf. also Viola 2008, p. 159.

[34] I am here paraphrasing Hart (1961, p. 202, speaking of "any method of social control" consisting primarily of "general standards of conduct" addressed to "classes of persons").

[35] Two clarifications are needed here. (1) In order to make room for power-conferring rules (and, especially, for rules conferring to private individuals the power to achieve some ends of theirs: 'If you wish to do this, this is the way to do it', Hart 1961, p. 28), this phrase, as I use it here and in what follows, should be understood as including cases of *telling people how to pursue the goals they want to achieve* (or *telling people how to do what they want to do*). (Cf. Raz 1977, p. 215: "power-conferring rules are designed to guide behaviour".) 'Prescribing', so understood, covers both the issuing of mandatory directives, and the issuing of power-conferring rules. (2) 'Telling' people what they should do, as I mean it here, refers to cases of *issuing* prescriptions, not to 'detached' statements of what the addressee should do according to a given set of prescriptions (Raz 1979, pp. 153–157).

[36] Waldron 2007, p. 95; cf. also Bobbio 1961, pp. 91–96. *Contra*, cf. Viola 2008, pp. 159–164.

(2) The notion of a legislation-oriented RoL—ERoL—runs counter the well-established contrast between the RoL and 'the rule of men'. But this is a mythical contrast.[37] Traditionally, formal and procedural or institutional aspects of the RoL have played a central role in the ideal; and "in both cases, the importance of these features in the rule of law tradition belies any claim that legislation is incompatible with or repugnant to the rule of law".[38]

I do not mean to rule out the possibility of giving a definite meaning to the 'Rule of Law' vs. 'rule of men' antithesis. So, e.g., a non-mythical way of understanding the contrast is the one suggested by F. Schauer (2003, 276). Generalizations—thus, treating unlike cases alike—, Schauer notes, are ubiquitous in legal practice (witness decision-making by rules, reliance on precedent, and the practice of giving reasons). And, Schauer argues

> when the 'rule of law' is contrasted with the 'rule of men', the core idea is that individual power, creativity, initiative and discretion have their dark side. The rule of men would be fine if all men were good, but when many men are not so, and when a degree of risk-aversion is justified, we may often prefer to lose the most positive efforts of the best of men in order to guard against the most negative efforts of the worst of them. (…) [L]aw may be the institution charged with checking the worst of abuses even if in doing so it becomes less able to make the best of changes (ibid.)

And, we may add, there is such a thing as limited (constitutional) government. or 'government under the law'. But, unless by 'law' we mean, here, natural law, room has to be made, in these ways of understanding the traditional antithesis, for the idea that it is men that make the laws. So, when men rule 'under the law', it is man-made law that the government rules under. And, in fact, Schauer's understanding of the traditional antithesis implies that the rules and generalizations constraining the discretion of individual officials are themselves made by men. So understood, the contrast is about the allocation of decisional power, i.e., the desirability, as regards certain classes of decisions to be made by certain classes of decision-makers, of decision-making on the basis of entrenched generalizations (themselves framed, it is assumed, by other human decision-makers), or of "rule-based particularism", rather than (purely) particularistic decision-making (Schauer 1991, Chap. 7). Taken literally, I think, there is no such a thing as 'the rule of laws, not men'.[39]

---

[37] Cf. Raz 1977, p. 212; Bobbio 1983; Marmor 2004, pp. 2–3; Waldron 2007, pp. 101–104.

[38] Waldron 2007, p. 104. Cf. also ibid.: "traditional rule of law theorists" (e.g., Fuller) have emphasized "procedural requirements, like due process in legislation and the separation of powers, and formal requirements, like generality, publicity, prospectivity, constancy and so on"; "these standards implicitly acknowledge that law is an instrument wielded by men; the traditional view concedes that men rule; it just insists that their rule be subject to the formal and procedural constraints of legality".

[39] Or, alternatively, *all* legal systems are cases of the 'rule of laws, not men' (Kelsen 1945, p. 36; cf. Celano 2000; and see also Raz 1977, p. 212).

(3) There may be various, more or less weighty ethico-political reasons for endorsing, as an ideal, a conception of the RoL which—just like ERoL—emphasizes the role of legislation in law's development and operation.[40] Its connection with neutrality (below, Sect. 9.6) is only one of these.
(4) In focusing on the activity of prescribing, and on prescriptive relationships, considered in themselves, I am abstracting from the complex, articulated procedural and institutional aspects of legislation proper, as it occurs in developed legal systems. These, too, may be interpreted as instantiating the RoL, or as dictated by RoL considerations,[41] but I shall not follow this path here. Prescribing is legislation at its minimum, so to speak. True, issuing prescriptions may also be the instrument of ad hoc decisions. The aspects of prescribing I shall focus on, and which constitute its distinctive sort of neutrality, however, are not peculiar to the ad hoc issuing of decrees.

So, I assume that the very simple fact of someone trying to make someone else do something by telling him to do it (and the relationship that comes into being as a consequence of this fact) is a suitable model for understanding what goes on in legislation proper (although it certainly does not give us an exhaustive picture of it). This is by no means obvious, or undisputed (cf. e.g. Hurd 1990, part II). Under many respects, the activity of a legislature in a modern democracy cannot be assimilated to that simple model (Waldron 1999a, part I; Id., 1999b, pp. 26–28). But I shall not try to defend this assumption here.

9.6 Neutrality (II): The Inherent Neutrality of Prescriptions

The second connection between NLP and neutrality (via the RoL) stems from the 'inherent neutrality' of prescriptions.

Laws meeting RoL requirements may have almost any content. But, I suggest, what is peculiar, as regards the RoL, is the *form* that the exercise of power takes. The RoL is, in the first instance, a specific mode of the exercise of power.

It is certainly not unusual to characterize the RoL as "a particular mode of the exercise of political power". When it is so characterized, the RoL, understood as "governance through law", is usually contrasted with "managerial governance or rule by decree".[42] Or it is contrasted with 'arbitrary' power, meaning by this public power wielded in the pursuit of private interests (Raz 1977, pp. 219–220). These contrasts are not mistaken, of course. But, I suggest, in order to understand what is

[40] See e.g. Waldron 2007, pp. 99–100 ("in general, legislation has the characteristic that it gives ordinary people a stake in the rule of law, by involving them directly or indirectly in its enactment, and by doing so in terms of fair political equality", ibid., 100). What Waldron has in mind, here, clearly is *democratic* legislation.

[41] Cf. Waldron 2007, p. 107.

[42] The quoted phrases are taken from Waldron 2008a, p. 78.

peculiar to the RoL (and to ERoL), and to see what is neutral about it, we have to widen the scope of the comparison. We have to contrast the RoL (specifically, ERoL) with other modes of the exercise of power over human beings—modes that are by no means anomalous, rare or bizarre, but often go unnoticed in these debates.[43] Power exercised by *telling* people to behave in the desired ways—thus, power exercised by issuing laws meeting ERoL requirements—has to be distinguished from power exercised through different means, or through linguistic means used differently. Thus, it has to be distinguished from symbolic, charismatic, and pastoral[44] power; from power exercised through manipulation, indoctrination, propaganda, or various forms of deceit (such as, e.g., power exercised through lying, or by modifying, unknown to the agent, the options that are available to him); and, finally, from persecution, disciplinary power (*pouvoir disciplinaire*; Foucault 1975, pp. 159–227), mute punishment, and sheer physical interference. What distinguishes it from these forms of power is the combination of two features: (1) it is rational; (2) it is public, transparent, out in the open. Let me explain.

When the government treats its subjects in accordance with the ERoL, it treats them as adults, capable of making their own decisions on the basis of their own preferences and their own understanding of the relevant facts. It tells them explicitly 'I want you to behave in such and such a way; these will be the consequences—I shall inflict you such and such a harm—in case you don't; now it's up to you'. Let us contrast this mode of exercising power over a human being with the way in which children are often treated. In order to make children do what we want them to do we sometimes tell them lies ('Candy shops are closed now'); we fake non-existing unpleasant consequences ('The wolf will come and get you'); in various ways, we distort reality. Or we try unknown to them directly to manipulate the environment, or their preferences, by working behind their back, so to speak. Or, again, we rely, in trying to make them do what we want them to do, on an aura of parental authority, or on symbols. In acting in these ways, we do not recognize children the dignity of responsible agents, capable of autonomous choice; we do not treat them as autonomous agents capable of—and entitled to—making their own choices on the basis of preferences and beliefs which are in fact their own (on the basis, thus, of their awareness of the way things in fact are, or of the way they see things, rather than on the basis of a mistaken understanding of reality, that we have induced on purpose).[45]

Let us try to spell out what is involved in this contrast. We are considering a simple situation: X issues a prescription addressed to Y—for instance, X orders Y to do something, and his order is backed by the threat of visiting her with an evil

[43] But cf. Raz's discussion of "enslavement" and "manipulation" in Raz 1977, 221; and A. Marmor's (2004, 15–16) discussion of "subliminal advertising".

[44] On "pastoral" power cf. Foucault 1981.

[45] What matters. here, is not that their preferences and beliefs are not the upshot of some form of conditioning or other disreputable process. It is, rather, that *we* are not responsible for these processes.

in case of non-compliance. The latter is what Hart (1961) famously referred to as 'the gunman situation'. In what follows, I shall use this label, because I think it is important to stress, in the present context, that it is also this kind of situation that I am focusing on. But it should be remembered throughout that the gunman situation is only one among different kinds of prescriptive relationships. What I am interested in is, generally (albeit with some qualifications), the mode of power exercised in trying to make somebody do something by telling her to do it.

The gunman situation has two basic features: it relies on the rational agency of the parties, and it is fully public. (These are features that prescriptions *typically* exhibit, and defeasible presumptions. Non-standard prescriptions are possible.)

(1) *Rationality*. In the gunman situation, appearances notwithstanding, rationality is pervasive. The gunman situation is, conspicuously, a form of *rational* interaction—i.e., a kind of situation an adequate description of which is premised on the assumption that the parties involved possess, and are capable of exercising, distinctively rational abilities, and that their attitudes, choices and actions meet standards of minimal rationality (Celano 2002, 2.1). True, in the gunman situation X exerts a kind of causal influence over Y. But, contrary to what happens in cases, e.g., of sheer physical force, or of straightforward manipulation of the agent's preferences, or of symbolic influence, the influence being exerted on the subject's behaviour is mediated by (thus, it depends on, and requires) the exercise, on the part of the individual whose behaviour is being affected, of a varied set of complex rational skills and abilities.

(a) The individual whose behaviour is affected by the gunman's order is presumed by the gunman to be a rational agent. 'Rationality', here, designates in the first instance the ability to understand the utterance of a sentence, to grasp its meaning and force. The act of issuing an order backed by a threat is a communicative linguistic act: the order is a message addressed to somebody of whom it is assumed that he is able to understand a message, and to act in one or the other of two alternative ways on the basis of this understanding. (This is why it is usually assumed—a plausible assumption—that it would make no sense to address an order backed by a threat to a stone, a colour, or a number.)

The gunman situation is, thus, a situation whose description (when adequate) entails that the individual whose behaviour is affected is endowed with highly developed communicative competences—specifically, linguistic competence. The relevant competence includes the mastery of—i.e., the ability to grasp and to apply correctly—concepts.

Moreover, an order backed by a threat is issued, typically, with a certain intention, and its workings rest on a complex set of interrelated intentions, and their successful expression and detection (Grice 1957; Strawson 1964, pp. 256–257; Schiffer 1972, p. 19; Celano 1990, pp. 127–151, 205–213; cf. also Raz 1996b, p. 283). Typically, the lawgiver has, first, the intention to make the addressee perform a certain action; and, second, he intends to make the addressee perform a certain action as a consequence of his uttering a sentence. Third, he intends to make the addressee perform a certain action (as a consequence of his uttering a sentence) by virtue of the recognition, by the addressee, of these very same intentions. It is not enough, for a prescription to come into existence, that the aim of the lawgiver be that the addressee act the way he desires, and that this should happen as a consequence of his uttering a sentence. It is necessary, further, "that the speaker should intend the person addressed to recognize that this is his purpose in speaking",[46] and to recognize this intention. In issuing a prescription the lawgiver assumes his addressee to be capable of detecting—and of expressing her detection of—a complex set of nested intentions. The addressee is presumed to be capable of understanding (1) that the speaker wants her to behave in a certain way; (2) that he wants to make her behave in the desired way; (3) that he wants to produce this outcome as a consequence of his uttering a sentence; (4) that he wants to produce this outcome by virtue of her recognition of this whole set of intentions, (1) to (4). Thus, for a prescription to affect its addressee's conduct in the way it is intended to, it is necessary that the addressee understand that her understanding of the prescription—this very understanding—is a necessary condition for it to produce the desired outcome.

So, in claiming that the gunman situation is a case of rational interaction, what I mean by 'rationality' is, first, an individual's ability to understand a non-naturally meaningful message addressed to her—an ability which, in turn, involves the mastery of concepts, and the ability to have, to recognize and to express the recognition of, complex intentional structures of the required sort. As a consequence, the influence exerted by the lawgiver on the addressee may be said to be a kind of 'causal-*cum*-rational' influence: in order for the addressee's conduct to be affected in the desired way, she has to understand that it is being affected in this way, and what this way consists in. A prescription is a kind of tool that works (in the way it is intended to work) only if the object it causally affects understands that it is so working. Under this respect, it is a kind of tool very different from tools whose operation relies on physical processes only. (Imagine a hammer which works in pinning down nails only if the nail understands (1) that it is being pinned down, and (2) the physical laws according to which the hammer's blows cause its being progressively pinned down.) The addressee's understanding of the process leading her to act in the relevant way is a necessary step in this very same process.

(b) But how can understanding an utterance of the relevant sort lead an individual to act in a given way rather than another?

X orders Y to perform action A, and he threatens her with the infliction of a sanction—something unpleasant—in case Y does not comply. If Y understands the order (and the annexed threat), and if X is in fact capable of, and is willing to (or, if Y believes he is)[47] visit her with the threatened evil in case of non-compliance, it may happen that Y decides, on the basis of her understanding of the order, and of her desire to avoid the unpleasant consequence X has threatened, to do what X ordered her to do. This illustrates a further sense in which the influence a prescription

[46] Hart 1961, p. 235, cf. also Id. 1982, pp. 250–252. This is the set of intentions constitutive of what H. P. Grice (1957) has called "non-natural meaning".

[47] I shall leave this complication aside here.

produces on its addressee's conduct may be said to be a form of 'causal-cum-rational' influence. The influence which is being exerted on the addressee's behaviour depends on, and is grounded in, a piece of reasoning—drawing the conclusion of an inference—on the addressee's part (e.g., 'Unless I do A, I shall incur in sanction S; I do not wish to incur in S; thus, I ought to do A').[48]

Orders backed by threats, thus, 'work'—i.e., they manage to produce their intended outcomes—by relying on their addressees' ability to perform practical inferences, and to act according to the latter's conclusions. A prescription's characteristic mode of operation is, in short, mediated by its addressee engaging in a piece of practical reasoning.[49]

Let us take stock. A prescription is addressed to an individual of whom it is assumed that she can understand the utterance of a sentence, and is, further, capable of deciding, on the basis of this understanding, to act in a certain way rather than another—is, i.e., capable of making choices on the basis of the weighing of reasons for and against compliance. The kind of—causal—influence a prescription is meant to exert on an individual, thus, may be said to be a kind of rational influence in so far as the working of a prescription—Y's conduct being affected by X's uttering a sentence—(1) is premised on Y's (and, of course, X's) ability to speak a language—thus, on their mastering concepts, and their ability to form, express, and detect complex intentional structures of a Gricean sort; (2) is grounded in Y's—and X's—performing the relevant pieces of practical reasoning—and, crucially, on X's anticipating Y's practical reasoning (including Y's representation, in her practical reasoning, of X's practical reasoning, and of this very anticipation); and (3) under both

[48] On this variety of practical inferences cf. von Wright 1962. This is only one among many possible forms, of course.

[49] Specifically, orders backed by threats work (when they do work) by altering the addressees' preference ordering. A given option (e.g., giving one's purse to a stranger)—an option the agent, if rational, would not have chosen, given his current preference ordering, had the order not been issued—becomes, by virtue of the order, and the associated threat, the preferred one, so that (on a simple maximizing conception of practical rationality) choosing it is, now, rationally mandated (i.e., it has now become what a rational agent, given his newly shaped preference ordering, should do). Behaviour in accordance with the order is the object of a choice; this choice is, in turn, the outcome of a piece of practical reasoning. The order does indeed affect the preference ordering of its addressee; it does so, however, in a peculiar way, very different from the one involved in manipulating the agent's preferences by acting 'behind his back'-e.g., by pouring, unknown to him, a drug in his tea, or through brainwashing. In the latter cases, X operates 'behind Y's back' in the following sense: X produces the desired outcome—making a given option Y's preferred one (thus, altering Y's preference ordering)—by exerting a purely causal influence. Typically, the agent will remain unaware of the way in which her preference ordering has been modified. In the case of an order backed by a threat, on the contrary, the agent is made to face a choice. Her being aware of the mechanism through which X tries to make her behave in a certain way, her taking this mechanism's workings into account, is part and parcel of its very same workings. An order backed by a threat is a device, which works only if the individual on which it exerts its influence understands that, ad how, it is exerting its influence. When an order backed by a threat has success, its addressee chooses, decides to comply (*coactus tamen voluit*).

respects, it relies on Y's understanding of this working itself. It is in virtue of these features that, I think, the gunman situation may be characterized as a form of rational interaction—a kind of situation an adequate description of which entails, or presupposes, that the parties involved be endowed with rationality.[50]

(2) *Common knowledge*. The mode of power we are discussing is a kind of power whose exercise takes place out in the open between lawgiver and prescription-addressee.

In order for the lawgiver to achieve his aim, it is necessary for him to make his intention—the intention of making the addressee perform a certain action through the utterance of a given sentence—known to the addressee. This is not, however, sufficient for his utterance to count as a prescription. If odd or deviant ways of influencing others' behaviour through linguistic means have to be ruled out (Strawson 1964, pp. 256–257, 263; Schiffer 1972, p. 30), a condition of common knowledge has to be satisfied. In prescribing, the lawgiver intends to make the addressee perform a given action by virtue of the recognition, by the addressee herself, of this very same intention (cf. above). Thus, an utterance may count as a prescription only if the addressee believes that the lawgiver has the relevant intentional structure, if she believes the lawgiver to believe that she believes he has it, and so on. Likewise, it is necessary that the lawgiver believes that the addressee recognizes this structure, he believes her to believe that he believes this, and so on. In short, a prescription only has been issued—and a prescriptive relationship between X and Y only comes into existence—if a suitable system of interlocking mutual beliefs comes into place: only if it is common (or mutual) knowledge between lawgiver and addressee that it has been issued.

This is, once again (above, Sect. 9.4) the idea of publicity. Legislation—i.e., the issuing of prescriptions—egregiously qualifies as a way of meeting this requirement.

Thus, the mode of power exercised in trying to make somebody do something by telling her to do it has two basic features: it relies on the rational agency of the parties, and it is fully public. When power is exercised in this way—thus, when ERoL requirements are satisfied—I suggest, a kind of neutrality is achieved. Lawgiving neutralizes some of the differences between lawgiver and addressee, levelling, in a sense, their respective positions. By this I mean two things.

(1) In a prescriptive relationship, lawgiver and addressee are put in a position of reciprocity: they interact as rational agents, in the light of an appropriate set of mutual beliefs concerning, *inter alia*, their status as rational agents. I.e., they presume each

[50] J. Austin was well aware of this; see Austin 1832, at 18, 20; this is also Bentham's view (see Hart 1982, pp. 244, 251). Cf. also Raz 1977, p. 222: "a legal system which does in general observe the rule of law (...) attempts to guide [people's] behaviour through affecting the circumstances of their action. It thus presupposes that they are rational (...) creatures and attempts to affect their actions and habits by affecting their deliberations".

other to be endowed with the relevant rational abilities. To this—limited, of course—extent, their respective positions are levelled. They face each other as equally engaged in communicating with each other.

(2) In a prescriptive relationship, the subject to whom the relevant prescription is addressed is kept at a distance, so to speak. She is not regarded by the lawgiver as an appendix to, or an extension of, his own body, as merely a tool, or as one commodity among others at his disposal, or again as something in the environment to be manipulated. Causal efficacy on her conduct is mediated by her own understanding of its being exerted, and how—and this is common knowledge between the two.

All this may look overstated. Orders backed by threats are sometimes harsh, brutal. They may be addressed by a master to his slave. The operation of requests may rest on sweeping forces and all too powerful incentives, such as, e.g., parental love, or the implicit threat of their withdrawal. (Some 'offers' simply 'cannot be refused'.[51]) The two features I have listed, however, concern the form, or structure, of the relationship (at least when conditions are satisfied, designed to rule out 'offers that cannot be refused').[52] When we contrast the issuing of a prescription with recourse to sheer physical force, or to silent manipulation of the subject's environment, I think we can see this twofold difference.[53] Under both respects, I think, one distinctive feature of prescriptive relationships is that rulers regard their subjects, literally, as addressees—i.e., as subjects capable (and worthy; see below) of being addressed. To borrow a phrase from Strawson, their dealings with them, as addressees, are not premised on "objectivity of attitude": a "purely objective view of the agent as one posing problems simply of intellectual understanding, management, treatment and control".[54]

---

[51] Thanks to José Juan Moreso for reminding me this point.

[52] Think, for a related case, of threats having a 'Your money or your life' structure. These do not exemplify the structure described in the text: they do not offer the subject a choice. In case the subject complies, the gunman will get her money. In case she doesn't, the gunmen will get *both* her life and her money. This is, in fact, no (well-formed) alternative. The latter hypothesis includes the former—they are not logically independent.

[53] Doesn't charismatic power, too, work by *telling* people what to do? Not in the way described here. Charismatic power does not, by hypothesis, offer the subject a choice—it does not rely on the subject's weighing reasons for and against doing what the leader wants her to do. Rather, it works by virtue of some sort of magnetism (however this may then be explained) a person exerts on another person—and this is, precisely, why the former may properly be said to be the 'leader', rather than a lawgiver.

[54] Strawson 1962, p. 87. "To adopt the objective attitude to another human being is to see him, perhaps, as an object of social policy; as a subject for what, in a wide range of sense, might be called treatment; as something certainly to be taken account, perhaps precautionary account, of; to be managed or handled or cured or trained" (ibid., 79). Strawson writes that "if your attitude towards someone is wholly objective, then though you may fight him, you cannot quarrel with him, and though you may talk to him, even negotiate with him, you cannot reason with him" (ibid.). But this, it seems to me, downplays what is involved, by way of reasoning with someone, in *talking* to him.

Lawgiving, thus, in a sense neutralizes asymmetries between lawgiver and addressee, levelling their positions. Prescriptions are, in this sense, inherently neutral devices for the exercise of power. This is not substantive neutrality—not taking sides in favour of any particular subject, or group of them. As far as their content is concerned, laws meeting ERoL conditions have, as such, nothing neutral in them.[55] What I have called their inherent neutrality concerns their form: the kind of communicative attitude involved in their workings.

Prescriptions satisfying ST will egregiously exemplify this model. In fact, prescriptions as such are, typically, source-based: directives enacted as prescriptions, as such, typically satisfy ST. But, does this kind of 'neutralization' have anything of value in it?

Once again, the RoL—and, specifically, ERoL— is a modest ideal. It is compatible with violations of other ideals. But, when we consider the inherent neutrality of prescriptions, we see that there is something valuable in ERoL.

When the government treats its subjects in accordance with the ERoL, it treats them as rational agents, capable of (1) mastering concepts, and of detecting, grasping, forming, expressing and generally finding their way in, complex structures of communicative intentions; (2) making their own decisions on the basis of their own preferences and their own view of the relevant facts. By treating them in this way, government recognizes them the dignity of beings worthy of being publicly, openly addressed, and of being guided through their understanding of the way in which power is being exerted on them.

So, when treating its subjects in accordance with ERoL requirements government recognizes people the dignity of responsible agents, capable of autonomous choice; it addresses them openly, and tries to guide their behaviour through their very understanding of what it is trying to do, and how. In short, it treats them with, and shows them, *respect*. (Recall the contrast with manipulation, indoctrination. propaganda, deceit, persecution, *discipline*, mute punishment.) This way of exercising power, I said, is very different from the way in which people sometimes try to guide children's behaviour—distorting reality, or trying to manipulate the environment or their preferences, by working behind their back; relying on the efficacy of symbols or charisma. These, of course, are ways in which even adult men and women are often treated—and sometimes wish to be treated (or have to be treated). But they are not, I submit, respectful ways.[56]

---

[55] I hope it is clear enough from what I have said so far that my claim is not that law is—or should be—value-neutral, or morally neutral. This claim is simply untenable. Cf. e.g. Raz 1996a, p. 112, n. 17; Green 2003, 4.3: "law is not value-neutral. Although some lawyers regard this idea as a revelation (and others as provocation) it is in fact banal. The thought that law could be value neutral does not even rise to falsity—it is simply incoherent. Law is a normative system, promoting certain values and repressing others. Law is not neutral between victim and murderer or between owner and thief. When people complain of the law's lack of neutrality, they are in fact voicing very different aspirations, such as the demand that it be fair, just, impartial, and so forth. A condition of law's achieving any of these ideals is that it is not neutral in either its aims or its effects".

[56] Remember that we are dealing, here, with standard cases. Abuses are possible. So, for instance, one interesting way of acquiring and exercising power over human beings is by inducing in them strong feelings of guilt, or the sense of their constitutive insufficiency, or weakness—and setting ourselves as their healers (either because we are uniquely authorized to guarantee them forgiving

Individuals are, to the extent that they are all addressed as the addressees of prescriptions, treated with *equal respect.*[57] (Remember that this concerns the form of the relationship only, not the prescription's content.[58]) This is compatible with all sorts of disrespect and unjust discrimination, of course. But it positively is, it seems to me, a valuable feature of laws satisfying ST and meeting ERoL desiderata.

9.7 Conclusion

My conclusion, then, is that, if you have some sense that the law ought to be neutral, and if you are looking for a way of giving a definite, respectable meaning to this distressingly vague and generic thought, then you have a good reason for claiming that the law should satisfy ST, and conform to ERoL requirements (you have, then, good reasons for endorsing NLP).

I have tried to flesh out this claim by explaining some of the ways in which the idea that the law ought to be neutral can sensibly be understood and, correspondingly, to explain why conformity to the RoL—and, specifically, ERoL—requirements, and to ST, warrants neutrality, in the relevant sense, or senses.[59] Laws satisfying ST

for their faults, or because we know how, and are able to, supplement them in their insufficiency or weakness). One way of doing this is by issuing prescriptions we know they will not be able to comply with—setting a standard we (and they) know they will not be capable of living up to. I.e., by flouting the requirement that whoever prescribes wants the addressee to do what he prescribes her to do (see above, n. 32), and tries, by issuing a prescription, to make her perform the desired action. In such cases, we do not actually want the addressees do what we (seem to) require from them; it is thanks to their (expected) *non*-compliance that we (mean to) acquire power over them.

[57] This, I think, is the point of Bentham's criticism of the Common Law as "Dog Law" (cf. e.g. Bentham 1970, p. 184, and Postema 1986, p. 277). Cf. also MacCormick 1985, pp. 24–27.

[58] There is, however, a continuum ranging from, at one extreme, prescriptions as a vehicle of respect for their addressees and, at the other extreme, prescriptions wielded as weapons by people intending only to make other people do certain things—or positively aiming at humiliating them. Orders may be barked at night by armed guards to deprived, terrorized people at their arrival at the concentration camp, so as to make them reach as soon as possible their barracks, or the gas chamber. If prescriptions are to work as vehicles of respect, such cases have to be ruled out, by imposing additional conditions. One such condition is, I think, that meaningful options should be open to the addressee in case he acts as he is ordered to. (On the other hand, I have already hinted at a condition ruling out 'offers that cannot be refused'; more generally, if prescriptions are to work as vehicles of respect meaningful options have to be open in case of non-compliance.) Or, again, we should allow for the possibility that, in some circumstances, treating somebody as the addressee of a prescription (thus implying that he enjoys the dignity of a rational being) may be a peculiarly effective way of shaming him (thanks to Nicola Muffato for this point). It should also be noted that the utterance of sentences in the imperative mood—or, generally, sentences standardly used for issuing prescriptions—may simply trigger a conditioned reflex, or work through symbolic properties. Prescriptions, as discussed in the text (and as envisaged in ERoL) as the prime instrument of government, are an ideal communicative type.

[59] 'Neutrality' has no definite meaning. I have tried to set out relevant specifications of this—admittedly vague and generic—idea. They may also be understood, however, as different—though related—meanings of an equivocal term. (Thanks to Pierluigi Chiassoni and Frencesco Viola for pressing this point on me.) Further, there are some ways of understanding the thought that the law

and meeting RoL desiderata may achieve neutrality as indifference (in the case of coordination problems proper) and neutrality as fairness (via reliability of mutual expectations, in the case of interaction problems and patterns of disagreement where conflict is serious). Further, laws meeting ERoL desiderata may achieve, via the inherent neutrality of prescriptions, neutrality as equal respect.

In ERoL, these two perspectives combine: the first connection combines with the second. Where the law satisfies ST and meets ERoL requirements, fairness and respect for persons are instantiated in the structure of the law. Or, in Raz's words, "observance of the rule of law is necessary if the law is to respect human dignity" (Raz 1977, p. 221).[60]

References

Austin, J. 1832. In *The province of jurisprudence determined*, ed. W.E. Rumble. Cambridge: Cambridge University Press. 1995.

Benditt, T.M. 2004. Acting in concert or going it alone: Game theory and the law. *Law and Philosophy* 23(6): 615–630.

Bennett, M. 2007. '"The rule of law" means literally what it says: The rule of the law': Fuller and Raz on formal legality and the concept of law. *Australian Journal of Legal Philosophy* 32: 90–113.

---

ought to be neutral that are expressed by some of the RoL requirements themselves. So, e.g. the idea that laws should be general (as to their subjects and to the acts required), or the desideratum that their administration be entrusted to an impartial judiciary (thanks to Mauro Barberis, Paolo Comanducci and Riccardo Guastini for this).

[60] Reciprocity and fairness (as realized in the operation of laws as neutral interaction devices stabilizing mutual expectations; above, Sect. 9.4), too, involve—and express—respect for human beings as responsible agents, entitled to make autonomous choices. As noted by many, this is true of the RoL ideal as such. Cf. e.g. Fuller 1969, pp. 162–163; Finnis 1980, pp. 272–273; MacCormick 1985, p. 26; Marmor 2004, p. 21 (on prospectivity), 32 (on practicability); Waldron 2008a, p. 76 (thanks to conformity to the principles of legality—i.e., the requirements of the RoL—laws attain *both* "efficiency from the point of view of the ruler" (Hart's 'craft of poisoning' analogy; efficiency at making people do what the ruler wants them to do) *and* "efficiency for the subjects" ("the purpose of advancing not the ruler's own aims, but of making room in the ruler's calculations—*respectful* room—for the purposes of the individuals who live under his power", my emphasis)). It is worth here to quote at length Raz's statement of this point. According to Raz (1977, pp. 221–222) "observance of the rule of law is necessary if the law is to respect human dignity. Respecting human dignity entails treating humans as persons capable of planning and plotting their future. Thus, respecting people's dignity entails respecting their autonomy, their right to control their future". There are, Raz argues, two main ways in which disregard for the RoL "violates human dignity": by generating uncertainty and by frustrating expectations the law itself has encouraged (a kind of "entrapment": this expresses "disrespect", "disrespect for people's autonomy"). "A legal system which does in general observe the rule of law treats people as persons at least in the sense that it attempts to guide their behaviour through affecting the circumstances of their action. It thus presupposes that they are rational autonomous creatures and attempts to affect their actions and habits by affecting their deliberations". I have tried to make explicit various aspects of this, and have argued that laws satisfying ST and meeting ERoL requirements are more likely to display these features to a high degree.

Bentham, J. 1970. In *Of laws in general*, ed. H.L.A. Hart. London: University of London/The Athlone Press.
Bobbio, N. 1961. *Il positivismo giuridico*. Torino: Giappichelli. 1996.
Bobbio, N. 1971. Le bon législateur. *Logique et Analyse* 14: 59.
Bobbio, N. 1983. Governo degli uomini o governo delle leggi? In Id., *Il futuro della democrazia*. Torino: Einaudi. 1984.
Campbell, T. 1996. *The legal theory of ethical positivism*. Aldershot: Dartmouth.
Celano, B. 1990. *Dover essere e intenzionalità. Una critica all'ultimo Kelsen*. Torino: Giappichelli.
Celano, B. 2000. Kelsens's concept of the authority of law. *Law and Philosophy* 19(2): 173–199.
Celano, B. 2002. *Introduzione alla teoria del diritto di H. L. A. Hart*. Dispense del corso di Teoria generale del diritto, Facoltà di Giurisprudenza, a.a. 2001–2002, Dipartimento di studi su politica, diritto e società, Università degli studi di Palermo.
Celano, B. Forthcoming. Publicity and the rule of law. In *Oxford Studies in Philosophy of Law*, vol. 2, ed. L. Green and B. Leiter. Oxford: Oxford University Press.
Chiassoni, P. 1990 *L'interpretazione della legge: normativismo semiotico, scettiismo, giochi interpretativi*. In AA. VV., *Studi in memoria di Giovanni Tarello*, vol. II, Giuffrè, Milano.
Diciotti, E. 1999. *Interpretazione della legge e discorso razionale*. Torino: Giappichelli.
Elster, J. 1983. Rationality. In Id., *Sour grapes. Studies in the subversion of rationality*. Cambridge: Cambridge University Press. 1983.
Finnis, J.M. 1980. *Natural law and natural rights*. Oxford: Clarendon.
Foucault, M. 1975. *Surveiller et punir. Naissance de la prison*. Paris: Gallimard. 2002.
Foucault, M. 1981. Omnes et Singulatim: Towards a criticism of 'Political reason'. In *The Tanner lectures on human values*, ed. S. McMurrin. Salt Lake City: University of Utah Press.
Fuller, L.L. 1969. *The morality of law*. New Haven: Yale University Press.
Gardner, J. 2001. Legal positivism: 51/2 myths. *American Journal of Jurisprudence* 46: 109–227.
Gaus, G.F. 2002. The legal coordination game. *American Philosophical Association Newsletter on Philosophy and Law* 1: 122–128.
Gauthier, D. 1995. Public reason. *Social Philosophy and Policy* 12(1): 19–42.
Green, L. 1988. *The authority of the state*. Oxford: Oxford University Press.
Green, L. 2003. Legal positivism. In *The Stanford encyclopedia of philosophy*, ed. E.N. Zalta. http://plato.stanford.edu/entries/legal-positivism/#Rel.
Grice, H.P. 1957. Meaning. In Id., *Studies in the way of words*. Cambridge: Harvard University Press. 1989.
Guastini, R. 2004. *L'interpretazione dei documenti normativi*. Milano: Giuffrè.
Hart, H.L.A. 1961. *The concept of law*. Oxford: Clarendon.
Hart, H.L.A. 1982. *Essays on Bentham. Studies in jurisprudence and political theory*. Oxford: Clarendon.
Hurd, H.M. 1990. Sovereignty in silence. *Yale Law Journal* 99: 945–1028.
Kelsen, H. 1945. *General theory of law and state*. Cambridge: Harvard University Press.
Lewis, D. 1969. *Convention. A philosophical study*. Oxford: Blackwell.
MacCormick, N. 1985. A moralistic case for a moralistic law? *Valparaiso Law Review* 20: 1–41.
Marmor, A. 2004. The rule of law and its limits. *Law and Philosophy* 23: 1–43.
Moreso, J.J. 2005. Positivismo giuridico e applicazione del diritto. *Materiali per una storia della cultura giuridica* 35: 225–244.
Postema, G.J. 1986. *Bentham and the common law tradition*. Oxford: Clarendon.
Rawls, J. 1999. *Collected papers*, ed. S. Freeman. Cambridge: Harvard University Press.
Raz, J. 1977. *The rule of law and its virtue*, in Raz 1979.
Raz, J. 1979. *The authority of law. Essays on law and morality*. Oxford: Clarendon.
Raz, J. 1985. Authority, law and morality. In Id., *Ethics in the public domain*. Oxford: Clarendon. 1994, 1996^2.
Raz, J. 1986. *The morality of freedom*. Oxford: Clarendon.
Raz, J. 1996a. *On the nature of law*, in Raz 2009.
Raz, J. 1996b. *Intention in interpretation*, in Raz 2009.
Raz, J. 2003. *About morality and the nature of law*, in Raz 2009.

Raz, J. 2004. *Incorporation by law*, in Raz 2009.
Raz, J. 2006. *The problem of authority: Revisiting the service conception*, in Raz 2009.
Raz, J. 2009. *Between authority and interpretation. On the theory of law and practical reason.* Oxford: Oxford University Press.
Scarpelli, U. 1965. *Cos'è il positivismo giuridico*. Milano: Comunità.
Schauer, F. 1991. *Playing by the rules. A philosophical examination of rule-based decision-making in law and in life*. Oxford: Clarendon.
Schauer, F. 2003. *Profiles, probabilities, and stereotypes*. Cambridge: Harvard University Press.
Schiffer, S. 1972. *Meaning*. Oxford: Clarendon. 1988.
Searle, J.R. 1969. *Speech acts. An essay in the philosophy of language*. Cambridge: Cambridge University Press.
Strawson, P.F. 1962. Freedom and resentment. In *Studies in the philosophy of thought and action*, ed. P.F. Strawson. Oxford: Oxford University Press. 1968.
Strawson, P.F. 1964. Intention and convention in speech acts. In Id., *Logico-linguistic papers*. London: Methuen. 1971.
Ullmann-Margalit, E. 1981. Is law a co-ordinative authority? *Israel Law Review* 16: 333–349.
Viola, F. 2008. Il "Rule of Law" e il concetto di diritto. *Ragion pratica* n. 30.
von Wright, G.H. 1962. Practical inference. In Id., *Practical reason*. Oxford: Blackwell. 1983.
von Wright, G.H. 1963. *Norm and action. A logical enquiry*. London: Routledge & Kegan Paul.
von Wright, G.H. 1983. Norms, truth and logic. In Id., *Practical reason*. Oxford: Blackwell.
Waldron, J. 1989. Legislation and moral neutrality. In Id., *Liberal rights*. Cambridge: Cambridge University Press. 1993.
Waldron, J. 1999a. *Law and disagreement*. Oxford: Oxford University Press.
Waldron, J. 1999b. *The dignity of legislation*. Cambridge: Cambridge University Press.
Waldron, J. 2000. Lex Satis Iusta. *Notre Dame Law Review* 75: 1829–1858.
Waldron, J. 2001. Normative (Ethical) positivism. In *Hart's postscript. Essays on the Postscript to The concept of law*, ed. J. Coleman. Oxford: Oxford University Press.
Waldron, J. 2002a. Is the rule of law an essentially contested concept (in Florida)? *Law and Philosophy* 21(2): 137–164.
Waldron, J. 2002b. Legal and political philosophy. In *The Oxford handbook of jurisprudence and philosophy of law*, ed. J. Coleman and S. Shapiro. Oxford: Oxford University Press.
Waldron, J. 2004. The rule of law as a theatre of debate. In *Dworkin and his critics*, ed. J. Burley. Oxford: Blackwell.
Waldron, J. 2007. Legislation and the rule of law. *Legisprudence* 1: 91–124.
Waldron, J. 2008a. Hart and the principles of legality. In *The legacy of H. L. A. Hart. Legal, political, and moral philosophy*, ed. M. Kramer et al. Oxford: Oxford University Press.
Waldron, J. 2008b. The concept and the rule of law. *Georgia Law Review* 43: 1–61.
Waldron, J. 2009. Can there be a democratic jurisprudence? *Emoy Law Journal* 58: 675–712. 2008–2009.

Chapter 10
On the Neutrality of Charter Reasoning

Wilfrid Waluchow

10.1 The Central Problem

Judicial review under a charter or bill of rights[1] is not an easy practice to justify in a liberal democracy, particularly one marked by the "fact of reasonable pluralism."[2] It appears to be an unavoidable feature of modern, liberal democracies that reasonable people of good will and integrity, faced with what John Rawls calls "the burdens of judgment," will continue to disagree fundamentally about moral and political matters, even after what looks like an exhaustive, good faith investigation of all relevant reasons and arguments.[3] Even if there is a truth of the matter with respect to the important questions of political morality that concern us in liberal democracies, to a very large extent, it seems, that truth is epistemically inaccessible to us. And if it's epistemically inaccessible to us, we have no way of discovering which, among the various reasonable answers offered to the questions posed, are

---

[1] Henceforth I will refer to this practice as "charter review." Charter review comes in a wide variety of forms, but for purposes of this paper, I will assume a form such as one finds in Canada and the United States. In these systems judges are empowered to strike down official government acts, most notably acts of congress or parliament if, in the best judgment of the court, such acts violate rights of political morality to which their charter and bill of rights (respectively) make reference. I have in mind rights to such things as "due process," "freedom of expression," "equality," "equal protection" and "fundamental justice."

[2] John Rawls, *Political Liberalism* (New York: Columbia University Press, 1996), 36. How one distinguishes reasonable from unreasonable views is, of course, an important, difficult and highly contentious issue. It's also one that I will leave unexplored in this paper.

[3] *Ibid.*, pp. 54–58.

W. Waluchow (✉)
Department of Philosophy, McMaster University,
1280 Main Street West, Hamilton, Ontario L8S 4K1, Canada
e-mail: Walucho@Mcmaster.ca

J. Ferrer Beltrán et al. (eds.), *Neutrality and Theory of Law*,
Law and Philosophy Library 106, DOI 10.1007/978-94-007-6067-7_10,

correct or most justified.[4] No way of telling who has it right, or whose answer is best—or even better. This is particularly so when we reach the level of comprehensive moral and religious doctrines, where deep differences emerge between Kantians and utilitarians, Christians and Muslims, and between theists and atheists. Despite this predicament we more often than not need to settle on a set of answers, some "way of formulating [our] plans, of putting [our] ends in an order of priority and of making [our] decisions accordingly."[5] One of the claimed virtues of the ordinary, majoritarian procedures one typically finds in established democracies is that they facilitate shared settlements, and do so in a manner that is prima facie fair to all who have a stake in the relevant matter. One person, one vote ensures, it is said, that each participant in the process participates on an equal footing and has an equal chance of having her admittedly controversial answer carry the day.[6] It also ensures that the answer chosen can be legitimately described as "our decision," not the decision of whatever faction happens to have had enough power or influence to win the day. Democracy, it is said, allows all of us to take ownership of the laws that regulate our lives and restrict our liberties, even those with which we fundamentally disagree. In short, it respects our autonomy.

But things seem very different when charter review enters the picture. It adds a new element to our decision-making processes, one that seems seriously to disrupt the path to ownership and legitimacy I just described. This is because charter review arguably takes away citizens' power of decision and authorizes judges to make controversial moral and political decisions instead. According to some of its most ardent critics, charter review enables judges to impose their own partisan moral views on the rest of us, citizen and legislator alike, whether or not we agree with those views, and whether or not we've had a fair opportunity to influence, let alone contribute to, the decisions the judges end up imposing. Given the facts of reasonable pluralism, many of us will, of course, inevitably disagree—and profoundly so—with the moral bases upon which the judges' decisions are made. Sometimes, of course, that disagreement will be

[4]In saying that truths of political morality seem epistemically inaccessible to us, I do not mean to deny that many people believe that they know the truth. Neither do I wish to deny that many people have perfectly respectable justifications for their claims, nor that some of those claims are true. What I mean to deny is that there are few, if any, truths of political morality which can be demonstrated or established to the satisfaction of all reasonable persons, regardless of their differing moral perspectives.

[5]*Ibid.*, p. 212.

[6]Whether reality matches theory in this respect is, of course, highly debatable. For instance, when corporations and other organizations with deep pockets are able freely to contribute to electoral campaigns, political power can become concentrated in ways that seriously threaten the notion that one person—one vote embodies equal political power. Various attempts, in the United States, to correct for this kind of power imbalance, via campaign financing regulations, were recently declared unconstitutional by the US Supreme Court. See *Citizens United v FEC* 558 U.S. (2010).

clearly ill-founded, perhaps even unreasonable. It is yet another unavoidable feature of modern, liberal democracies that the moral and political views of ordinary citizens and their elected representatives are sometimes uninformed, irrational, or unduly motivated by factors like fear, unmitigated partisanship, selfishness or sheer prejudice. In at least some such instances, especially when someone's fundamental moral rights are being threatened by a democratic process gone astray—a plausible case can be made that allowing judicial decisions to help settle matters might not be such a bad thing to have, even within a liberal democracy. Perhaps judges are able, in such circumstances, to save us from ourselves, to make the decisions that we would have made had we not been subject to the various improper influences we seem unable fully to avoid or suppress. Perhaps, that is, charter review can serve to enhance, not reduce or eliminate, our moral autonomy. But quite often our disagreements cannot be so readily dismissed. On the contrary, they seem perfectly reasonable. But if that's true, then how can one possibly meet the burden of justifying a practice like charter review in such cases? How can we possibly take ownership of the decisions reached through such a process, and of the significant legal consequences that often follow from them?

In previous work, I have tried to meet the rather hefty burden of answering these questions.[7] I argued for a conception of charter review under which the principal role of a judge is not to adjudicate on the basis of his or her own convictions in regard to issues of political morality such as equality, fundamental justice and the right to life, liberty and security of the person, but to hold the community to its own fundamental moral commitments on such matters. These commitments, I argued, are expressed or represented in what I called "the community's constitutional morality" (CCM).[8] As I conceive it, CCM is not the personal morality of any particular person or institution, e.g. the Catholic Church, the Republican Party, or a judge who helps decide a constitutional case. Nor is it the morality decreed by God, inherent in the fabric of the universe, or residing in Plato's world of forms. Rather, it a kind of community-based, positive morality consisting of the fundamental moral norms and convictions to which the community has actually committed itself and which have, in one way or another, acquired some kind of formal legal recognition. It is the political morality actually embedded in (or endorsed or expressed by) a community's legal practices in much the same way as particularized principles of corrective justice are, if Jules Coleman is correct, embedded in (or endorsed or expressed by)

[7]See in particular *A Common Law Theory of judicial review: The Living Tree* (Cambridge: Cambridge University Press, 2007).

[8]On this see *ibid.* See also "Constitutional Morality and Bills of Rights" in ed. Grant Huscroft, *Expounding the Constitution: Essays in Constitutional Theory* (Cambridge: Cambridge University Press, 2008) p. 77, from which the following characterization of CCM is drawn.

the tort law of Anglo-American legal systems.[9] So construed, CCM is a subset of the wider set of moral norms which enjoy some (not insignificant) measure of reflective support within the community (however that is identified). Some members of this wider set lack any kind of legal recognition whatsoever. Even if there are, within the community moralities of most contemporary western societies, norms of positive morality governing non-political matters like friendship, gratitude, marital fidelity, charitable giving, as well as norms governing political matters like the responsible, but legally unregulated, exercise of political power,[10] these are not, in the main, part of the CCM of those societies because they lack appropriate legal recognition. Distinct (and as between different communities) different principles of equality and fundamental justice are, on the other hand, characteristic elements of the CCMs of those communities. In the United States and Canada, and in many of the countries of the European Union, legal recognition of CCM norms includes (though it is not limited to) enshrinement in a bill or charter of rights and the legislative history and jurisprudence that combine to flesh out the local, concrete understandings or Thomistic "determinations" of those principles for that particular community.[11]

---

[9] I have deliberately framed my characterization of CCM in such a way as to remain neutral among rival theories about the nature of law. I am particularly interested in remaining neutral as between inclusive positivism, as defended by, e.g., Hart, Coleman, Kramer and Waluchow, and exclusive positivism as defended by, e.g., Raz, Green, Giudice, Marmor and Gardner. An inclusive positivist is prepared to say that the norms of CCM can actually be part of the law. A defender of the exclusive version, on the other hand, would likely insist on situating those norms outside the law, as norms of positive morality upon which judges may (or must) draw when deciding whether to introduce changes into the law, as when they decide whether to change the law by eliminating one of its hitherto binding legal standards, i.e., by striking it down. (I say "likely insist" because an exclusive positivist might be prepared to subsume the norms of CCM under the category of customs, which have a social source.) In any event, the phrase 'legal recognition' is meant to be neutral as between different theories concerning the nature of law. Works that defend inclusive positivism include Hart, *The Concept of Law*, 2nd edn. (Oxford: Clarendon Press, 1994), especially the Postscript; Coleman, Jules, "Negative and Positive Positivism" *The Journal of Legal Studies* 11 (1982), p. 139; Waluchow, W.J., *Inclusive Legal Positivism* (Oxford: Clarendon Press, 1994); Kramer, Matthew, *Where Law and Morality Meet* (Oxford: Oxford University Press, 2004). Works defending exclusive positivism include Joseph Raz, *The Authority of Law* (Oxford: Clarendon Press, 1979) and "Authority, Law and Morality" *The Monist* 68 (1985), 295; Leslie Green, "Legal Positivism" in N. Zalta (ed.) *The Stanford Encyclopedia of Philosophy* (Spring 2003 edn). URL = http://plato.stanford.edu/archives/spr2003/legal-positivism/; Michael Giudice, "Existence and Justification Conditions of Law" *Canadian Journal of Law and Jurisprudence*, vol. 16, no. 1 (2003), pp. 23–40 and "Unconstitutionality, Invalidity, and Charter Challenges" *Canadian Journal of Law and Jurisprudence*, vol. 15, no. 1 (2002), pp. 69–83; Andrei Marmor, *Positive Law and Objective Values* (Oxford: Clarendon Press, 2001); John Gardner, "Legal Positivism: 5½ Myths" *American Journal of Jurisprudence* 46 (2001), p. 199. On Coleman's theory concerning the principles of corrective justice embedded in modern tort law, see his *Risks and Wrongs* (Cambridge: Cambridge University Press, 1992).

[10] An example of the kind of thing I have in mind here is the responsibility of a Prime Minister not to exercise his or her prerogative powers for purely partisan political reasons.

[11] On Aquinas' theory of "determination of common notions," see his *Summa Theologica*, I–II, Q. 95, AA. 1–4. See also, John Finnis, *Natural Law and Natural Rights* (Oxford: Clarendon Press, 1980), pp. 281–290; and Waluchow, *The Dimensions of Ethics* (Peterborough, Ontario: Broadview Press, 2003), pp. 111–116.

With this conception of constitutional morality in hand, I set out to defend charter review against many of its most ardent critics, particularly those, like Jeremy Waldron, who view the practice as fundamentally at odds with democratic principle. Put simply, my thesis was that CCM, owing to its social origin, is a source of moral norms upon which judges can draw in charter review without compromising democratic legitimacy. A key premise in my defense of this thesis is the claim that charter review includes (though it is by no means limited to) the task of ensuring that acts of parliament or congress do not, in ways that could not have been reasonably foreseen by legislators, and which they would have wished to avoid had they had the opportunity to do so, infringe the fundamental moral norms of CCM. If this is the role a judge plays in a particular instance of charter review, then democratic legitimacy is not compromised. The judge is, in effect, helping to implement, and render effective, the democratic will. Furthermore, many of the critics' other concerns can be successfully parried as well. For example, one prominent complaint is that charter review foolishly asks judges to serve as philosopher kings and queens, asks them to discover Platonic moral truth in respect of matters of justice and equality and to enforce their understanding or interpretation of that elusive truth against the acts and erroneous interpretations of our democratically elected legislators. Given the fact of reasonable pluralism, together with the fact that judges, no less so than the rest of us, suffer the burdens of judgment in matters moral, having them perform such a task asks judges to accomplish the impossible. Not only that, it transforms the judicial task into something completely different from the role judges have traditionally been thought to serve—by most everyone except, perhaps, proponents of the various forms of critical legal theory and other similarly minded skeptics. It is to give up even the pretense of supposing that, in charter cases, the role of the judge is to engage—or at the very least make a good faith attempt to engage—in the impartial, neutral application of binding legal standards, (largely) set elsewhere—that is, to play the role she is supposed to play in everyday, run of the mill legal cases.[12] It is instead to ask judges to decide on the basis of what ends up being *their own* (possibly purely partisan) moral opinions about an ever elusive Platonic morality. And no matter the high regard in which we hold our judges, such a practice simply

[12]Considerable philosophical controversy exists regarding the meaning and import of the terms 'impartial' and 'neutral.' I hope to remain above this fray by simply assuming a more or less intuitive understanding of these two terms according to which (a) they are more or less equivalent in meaning; and (b) mean something like the following. To be neutral or impartial is to make a decision that is based exclusively on relevant reasons and which displays no bias towards any particular point of view on the relevant matter, or any person or persons holding such a view. A useful analysis along these lines is proposed by Bernard Gert who posits that "*A* is impartial in respect *R* with regard to group *G* if and only if *A*'s actions in respect *R* are not influenced at all by which member(s) of *G* benefit or are harmed by these actions." See his "Moral Impartiality," *Midwest Studies in Philosophy* XX: 102–127. On this reading impartiality (or neutrality) is a property of a set of decisions made by a particular agent, directed toward a particular group. For our purposes, this would be a group sharing a particular view on some question of political morality arising in a charter case. For a survey of the literature concerning the concepts of impartiality (and neutrality), see Troy Jollimore, "Impartiality" at http://plato.stanford.edu/entries/impartiality/#MorImp.

cannot be tolerated in a liberal democracy. But if I am right that judges in exercising charter review are not seeking—and inevitably failing—to apply Platonic moral truth, but are instead seeking to hold the democratic community to its own constitutionally grounded moral commitments; and if, in addition to this, I am correct in thinking that that set of commitments can often be discovered through a kind of morally neutral, impartial reasoning, then the sting of this powerful argument can be largely avoided. We can restore the possibility of judicial impartiality and neutrality, a possibility which seems central to the legitimacy of legal decision-making within a liberal democracy. Judges are not, on this view, being asked to decide on the basis of *their own* best judgments concerning the demands of moral truth. Rather they are being asked to decide on the basis of their best judgments as to the *democratic community's* best judgments concerning the demands of moral truth. Judges can be said, in such circumstances, to be doing nothing more contentious than doing their best to apply, in a fair, impartial and neutral manner, standards that originate from an entirely legitimate source, namely, the community's own fundamental moral beliefs and commitments.[13]

If only matters were this straightforward. But of course they are not. As some of my critics have pointed out,[14] we seem reasonably to disagree not only about the demands of Platonic moral truth. There is considerable room for disagreement about the demands of CCM as well, especially in the controversial legal cases in which disputes about its concrete requirements come fully to the fore. Of course, the sheer fact of disagreement in no way implies that there is no fact of the matter in such cases, and that CCM is therefore incomplete or indeterminate, and hence unavailable to a court as a ground for its decisions. This no more follows than that there are no determinate answers available when there is reasonable disagreement about the nature of black holes, or about whether the defendant exercised reasonable care to ensure the integrity of his neighbour's property when he set about chopping down his (the defendant's) tree. But there is no getting round the fact that such disagreement threatens to undermine the practical possibility of neutral decision-

[13]That the norms of CCM can be largely discovered via a process of reasoning that can plausibly be described as 'impartial' and 'morally neutral' is also, of course, a highly contentious claim, It is also one that I cannot explore or defend here. Were I to do so, my argument(s) would be similar to those advanced by Joseph Raz in his discussion of "detached judgments" and by Julie Dixon in her splendid book *Evaluation and Legal Theory*. See Raz, *The Authority of Law* (Oxford: Clarendon Press, 1979), pp. 153–157 and Dixon, *Evaluation and Legal Theory* (Oxford: Hart Publishing, 2001), *passim*, but especially her discussion of the agnostic observer of the Roman Catholic mass, pp. 68–9. For my own, somewhat under-developed thoughts on the matter, see my *Inclusive Legal Positivism* (Oxford: Clarendon Press, 1994), pp. 19–30.

[14]See, e.g., B. Miller, "Review Essay: A Common Law Theory of Judicial Review" 52 *American Journal of Jurisprudence*, pp. 297–312; N. Struchiner and F. Shecaira, "Trying to Fix Roots in Quicksand: Some Difficulties With Waluchow's Conception on the True Community Morality," *Problema Anuario de Filosofía y Teoría del Derecho*, no. 3 (2009); Imer. B. Flores, "The Living Tree Constitutionalism: Fixity and Flexibility," *ibid.*; Natalie Stoljar, "Waluchow on Moral Opinions and Moral Commitments," *ibid.*; and Larry Alexander, "Waluchow's Living Tree Constitutionalism," 29 *Law & Philosophy* 93 (2010).

making and hence legitimacy. How can the decision to apply a CCM norm in a particular way be properly described as impartial or neutral if there is so much partisan disagreement about its proper understanding or interpretation? Will judges not be forced, in the end, to base their choices on their own personal views about the demands of Platonic moral truth? What else could they do in such circumstances, short of simply declining to make a decision at all?

Once again in previous work, I have argued that things are not quite as bleak as might appear at first blush for defenders of charter review. In a good many CCM cases there is much more of a basis for agreement and consensus than initially meets the eye. In other words, the limits of justification do not extend only so far as we find explicit agreement. Drawing on the notion of reflective equilibrium, most closely associated with the political philosophy of John Rawls, I argued that our considered judgments concerning the commitments of CCM can often (or can at the very least sometimes) be brought into a kind of reflective equilibrium with one another. When this happens, we can be led to see that we actually agree (or are *committed* to agreeing, if one prefers that way of phrasing the point) on more than we think we do. We can, in other words, be led to recognize an implicit basis for explicit agreement on the meaning and implications of the relevant CCM norms when initially this might not have seemed possible. I argued that the judge's role in a charter case—enforcing the commitments of CCM—will often lead her to draw on these bases of agreement and to decide accordingly. When such a basis is found, and a decision is made on its footing, the fact of disagreement will sometimes be replaced by reasonable agreement. This was the case, I suggested, with respect to the question of same-sex marriage in Canada.[15]

Despite all this there is no getting round this further point: it is distinctly possible that in a good many cases arising under CCM, especially those in which passions and controversy run deepest, and where differences are rooted in significantly different comprehensive doctrines,[16] there is no uniquely correct answer to be found—just answers. What, one might reasonably ask, are judges to do if they encounter a case in which this appears so? In my view, judges should—and in fact often do—engage in a type of moral reasoning traditionally associated with the common law. They should creatively develop or construct the norms of CCM, in an incremental, case-by-case way, in much the same manner as common law judges have historically developed, incrementally, and in a case-by-case manner, the principles of negligence, and the concepts of foreseeability and the reasonable use of force.[17] In so doing, I suggest, they often engage in Thomistic determinations of common

[15]Some commentators have criticized this assertion, suggesting that, notwithstanding various courts' decisions on entitlements for unmarried same-sex couples and on various forms of discrimination, sex-based or otherwise, the question whether banning gay marriage is consistent with Canada's CCM remains an open question. In other words, there continues to be reasonable disagreement on which construction of Canada's constitutional norms of equality is better than which. On this see, Brad Miller, *supra* note 14.

[16]Abortion and same-sex marriage are obvious examples of this possibility.

[17]On this see *A Common Law Theory of Judicial Review*: *The Living Tree*, Chaps. 5 and 6.

notions, deciding among available solutions, none of which is uniquely determined by, but each of which is fully consistent with, the relevant moral notion and with previous efforts by judges and legislators to shape it through the process of determination. Such previous attempts we might think of as having set "CCM precedents." Judges will, in such cases, no doubt be exercising discretion to choose from among non-excluded solutions. But there is, in my view, no better way to proceed in these circumstances.[18]

Now if we acknowledge that a process of determination is indeed what should be (and perhaps is) going on in many such cases, then we once again encounter our threat to democratic legitimacy. The threat, and the reason we face it yet again, should be fairly obvious by now: in developing CCM in this way, judges can no longer straightforwardly be viewed as attempting to *follow*, in a fair, impartial and neutral manner, standards previously set by others with the democratic authority to do so. On the contrary, it is they who will themselves be *setting* the relevant standards. At the very least they will be deciding what authoritatively established standards shall be taken to mean and imply for the particular kind of situation in which a charter question has arisen. They will, in short, be involved in the creation, not the discovery, of law. Or to put it in terms perhaps more familiar to constitutional lawyers, they will be engaged in construction not interpretation.[19]

So admitting what appears all but certain, that CCM is not always fully determinate, threatens to reintroduce our original concern that charter review cannot possibly be justified in a liberal democracy. It appears to assign judges a role, the creative construction of CCM, that renders us no longer masters in our own houses. We can, it seems, no longer maintain ownership of each and every one of the laws that regulate our lives and restrict our liberties. Handing over such a significant power cannot be justified on the usual ground: that judges are simply applying, in a more or less neutral and impartial manner, standards authoritatively set earlier on, through one or more of the democratic procedures we encounter in liberal democracies. Of course we must never lose sight of the fact that even in run of the mill cases not involving the construction of CCM, judges do not always succeed in displaying, to an acceptable degree, these same judicial virtues of fairness, impartiality and neutrality.

---

[18]It might be thought that there is at least one other option worth considering here: we could return such questions for authoritative settlement by elected legislators. There are many reasons for thinking that this is not, in the end, an attractive option to pursue. See my discussion of "the circumstances of rule making" in *A Common Law Theory of Judicial Review: The Living Tree*, *passim*, but especially pp. 203–215 and 259–270. See also Denise Reaume, "Of Pigeonholes and Principles: A Reconsideration of Discrimination Law," *Osgoode Hall L.J.* 40 (2002), p. 113. See also, my discussion below (p. 220 ff.) of the uncertain borderlines between hard and easy cases, that is, between cases in which discretion is (or at least seems) necessary and those in which it is not. For the time being, we will assume that there are cases in which it is reasonably clear that discretionary choice is necessary. And our question is: how to reconcile the exercise of discretionary choice with the fundamental requirements of democracy.

[19]Henceforth I will use the term "construction," and mean by it the creative or discretionary development of a moral principle or concept in the manner suggested by Aquinas when he referred to the "determination of common moral notions."

And in such cases the usual justification will be not be available either.[20] But in all such cases there is at least the theoretical possibility that the judges will succeed in displaying the required virtues. And we at least have an intelligible basis for criticism and complaint when that possibility is not actualized in a particular judicial decision. But nothing remotely like this seems available when the judge's decision requires her creatively to construct the relevant elements of CCM using her discretion. There simply is no such justification and no such basis for assessment and critique.

If, despite what I have just conceded, we continue to ask judges to make the kinds of discretionary determinations that sometimes seem necessary when CCM is in play, then we appear left with two options. First, we can abandon all pretense of reconciling charter review with the demands of democratic legitimacy. We can, that is, attempt to justify it by way of competing values, for example justice, or values closely associated with the rule of law.[21] Alternatively, we can develop a more nuanced account of what it is that judges should be up to when and if they engage in the discretionary construction of CCM by way of common law reasoning. It is this latter option that I propose to pursue in the remainder of this paper. My question is this. Is there a way of engaging the process of CCM construction, via a kind of case by case reasoning modeled on the common law, that still allows for the possibility of impartial, neutral decision making? If there is, then we may yet have a means of reconciling discretionary charter review with liberal democratic principle. We may yet be able to maintain ownership of all the laws and legal decisions that regulate our lives and restrict our liberties, even those discretionary decisions with which we fundamentally disagree—to see them as, in one very important sense, *our* decisions not those of the judges.

What follows is a preliminary sketch of what such an account might look like. I argue that discretionary constructions of CCM can be rendered consistent with liberal democracy if we place significant restrictions on the *kinds* of reasons upon which judges may legitimately draw when they engage that process. The restrictions I have in mind are inspired by the theory of public reasons developed in a number of places by John Rawls, but most notably Lecture VI of *Political* Liberalism. Rawls' view has also been adopted and adapted by Larry Solum in "Public Legal

[20] Among the most noteworthy instances is perhaps *Bush v Gore*, where the United States Supreme Court decided on what appeared to many observers to be purely partisan political grounds. See *Bush v. Gore*, 531 U.S. 98 (2000). In the view of many, *Citizens United v. Federal Election Commission*, 558 U.S.(2010) provides yet another example.

[21] I have in mind values like predictability, finality of decision, and so on. Another route might be to argue that alternative political practices, e.g. legislative debate, fail miserably to live up to democratic ideals and are therefore, on balance, even worse in this respect than charter review. Those who favour the abandonment (of charter review) option include Grant Huscroft, Jeremy Waldron and Tom Campbell. See, e.g., Huscroft, "The Trouble with Living Tree Interpretation" (2006) 25 U *Queensland LJ*, pp. 3–23; Waldron, "The Core of the Case Against Judicial Review" *The Yale Law Journal*, (2006) 1346; and Campbell, "Slaying the Hydra: Living Tree Constitutionalism and the Case for Judicial Review of Legislation", 3 *Problema*, 2009, pp.17–30. For purposes of this paper, I will assume that some form of charter review is, on balance, desirable in a constitutional democracy and that our aim is to see how the practice might be justified.

Reason" and by Ronald Den Otter in *Judicial Review in the Age of Moral Pluralism.*[22] In what follows, I attempt to show how, were we to restrict judges to reasons of the kind endorsed by Rawls, Solum and Den Otter, the discretionary development of CCM can be rendered faithful to the fundamental commitments of liberal democracy. The sketch I provide is, I hasten to repeat, quite preliminary. But my hope is that it is detailed and plausible enough to convince even the most ardent skeptic that there just might be something of value in the line of argument it would have us pursue.

So on what kinds of reasons should judges be expected to draw when and if they are asked to engage in the discretionary construction of CCM in a liberal democracy? Putting it another way, what kinds of restrictions can we, members of a democratic community, legitimately place upon judges' discretionary decisions and the kinds of reasons upon which they draw in making them, so as not to abandon completely our claim to being masters in our own house? Let's begin by dismissing one misguided thought: that limits are simply out of the question here because the concept of discretion implies the complete *absence* of restriction, and hence the *absence* of any possibility of rational development, assessment and critique. Were this true, then permitting judges to engage in discretionary constructions of CCM norms would, in effect, be demanding no more than that they render a decision, or that they make a decision based on some reason or other, whatever that might be—including the purely partisan moral reasons that raise so much difficulty for defenders of charter review. This would be to flirt with abandoning our moral autonomy altogether.

But the concept of discretion carries no such implication. As Ronald Dworkin once remarked, to say that a decision maker has (what Dworkin called) strong discretion on some matter is not to grant her open license. Even when her decision is "not controlled by a standard [or reason] furnished by the particular authority we have in mind when we raise the question of discretion," we retain the possibility of legitimate critique for failure to meet appropriate standards of good decision-making. "The strong sense of discretion is not tantamount to license, and does not exclude criticism. Almost any situation in which a person acts (including those in which there is no question of decision under special authority, and so no question of discretion) makes relevant certain standards of rationality, fairness, and effectiveness."[23] Presumably, we can add further restrictions here, restrictions arising from the special role judges play in liberal, constitutional democracies. It would, I take it, be a clear violation of a judge's responsibility in *any* legal case, including one in which the construction of CCM norms is involved, were he to decide on the basis of a coin flip (chance), on his daily horoscope (a scientifically discredited mode of

---

[22] John Rawls, *Political Liberalism. Supra* note 2; Larry Solum, "Public Legal Reason", *Virginia Law Review*, Vol. 92, p. 1449 (2006); Ronald Den Otter, *Judicial Review in an Age of Moral Pluralism* (New York: Cambridge University Press, 2009). I wish to acknowledge, in particular, the degree to which my account accords with and draws upon Den Otter's. His excellent book came to my attention only after I had conceived and sketched the main arguments of the present paper.

[23] Ronald Dworkin, *Taking Rights Seriously* (London: Duckworth, 1977), p. 33.

ascertaining truth), or on which lawyer was least annoying in presenting her case (irrelevant facts about the presenter, not the case being presented). It would be wrong were he to decide on the basis of who provided the larger bribe (personal advantage), on which decision was more likely to further the judge's own personal ambitions or partisan political agenda (ibid.), or for the reason that he disliked the cut of the defendant's jib (personal taste). It would be equally wrong were the decision biased in some way. It would be wrong, for example, were it blatantly homophobic, racist, misogynist, or nepotistic. At least this would be true in any of the liberal, constitutional democracies with which I am concerned in this paper.

But of course dismissing the misguided thought that discretion entails open license does not get us very far, even with these sorts of additions, because it isn't discretion alone that leads to our fundamental difficulty. It's discretion coupled with the fact of reasonable pluralism in matters moral. Our main worry is not that judges might end up constructing CCM on the basis of reasons that everyone would agree are bad ones. The fear is that there are far too many *plausibly good* reasons for different constructions of CCM norms, and no means of adjudicating among them in a way that appears neutral. In other words, it's not that that there is no way at all to distinguish good from bad reasons—clearly, the fact that a lawyer has been the least annoying in presenting her case in favour of construction C(1) is a bad reason; and the fact that construction C(2) can be justified on the basis of a principle acceptable to all reasonable citizens within the relevant jurisdiction, and recognized in a long line of judicial determinations of that principle, is a rather good one. On the contrary, the main worry is that there is an *overabundance* of moral reasons and the constructions of CCM they appear to support. And all of these will seem perfectly good, plausible or convincing to some reasonable person or other within the community. The problem is only exacerbated by the fact that, for each of these constructions, there will likely be some significant segment of the relevant jurisdiction—defined, perhaps in terms of their commitment to a particular comprehensive doctrine, say, Catholicism or libertarianism—who would like nothing better than to see that particular construction win the day. Indeed, it is quite possible that members of the community who find themselves within that particular segment will be able to mount a reasonable—though by no means decisive—case for the claim that their preferred construction is actually the only one consistent with CCM and the jurisprudence which has hitherto shaped its particular contours within that particular community. And the same might well be true of other segments of the population and the comprehensive doctrines that unite them.[24] How, it might be asked, is a judge to adjudicate in the midst of all these options? And most importantly for our purposes, how is she to do so in a way that can plausibly be characterized as neutral or impartial? It is here, I suggest, that the notion of public reasons might prove helpful. So what are public reasons, and how might these be used by courts in such a way as to legitimate their discretionary constructions of CCM?

---

[24] I will return to this last point, and its significance for debates on the legitimacy of charter review, in the final section of this paper. See note 46 and surrounding text.

10.2 Public Reasons

According to Larry Solum, a good deal of contemporary scholarship assumes that the notion of public reason originated with Rawls. But as Solum points out, the idea has a long pedigree stretching at least as far back as early modern times. Hobbes, Rousseau and Kant each discussed the idea, though their conceptions of public reason differed from one another.[25] According to Hobbes, public reason is the reason or judgment of the sovereign which, for familiar Hobbesean reasons, must hold sway over private exercises of reason in all matters concerning public life. For Hobbes, then, what distinguishes public from non-public reasons is not the type of reasons applicable in each domain but rather the person or persons through whom reason or judgment is exercised. Reason becomes public whenever it is exercised by the sovereign power, whomever or whatever that might be, and for whatever reasons he/she/it deems appropriate. For Rousseau, on the other hand, public and private reason are distinguished, not in terms of the agent through whom reason is exercised, but in terms of the kinds of reasons to which appeal is made: partisan reasons of self interest, for example, versus reasons pertaining to the common good and which are supposedly expressible via the general will.

As with Rousseau, Rawls' theory of public reason draws the line between public and nonpublic reason (and reasoning) in terms of the kinds of reason to which each appeals. These can be distinguished, according to Rawls, in terms of a number of key features. First, "the limits imposed by public reason do not apply to all political questions but only to those involving what [Rawls] call[s] "constitutional essentials" and questions of basic justice."[26] Thus, questions concerning the scope of free expression fall within the domain of public reason; questions concerning the most efficient means of ensuring a competitive auto industry do not. What precisely Rawls means by "constitutional essentials" and questions of "basic justice" is not altogether clear. But however that issue is resolved, the resolution will surely be such as to subsume, under the domain of public reason, the kinds of morally charged, fundamental questions with which courts are typically concerned when they engage in charter review. These include questions like the coercive regulation of hate speech, pornography and campaign financing, the banning or regulation of abortion and euthanasia, and the right of child soldiers incarcerated in foreign detention facilities, and subjected to torture and interrogations that flagrantly flout constitutional principles, to the protection and assistance of their government.[27] If these are not concerned with constitutional essentials and issues of basic justice, it is hard to imagine what might be.

---

[25]Thomas Hobbes, *Leviathan*, (Richard Tuck, ed., 1991), p. 306; Jean-Jacques Rousseau, "Discourse on Political Economy" in *Political Writings* (Cress ed. & trrans., 1987), pp. 111–113; Immanuel Kant, "An Answer to the Question: 'What is Enlightenment?'" in *Political Writings* (Reiss & Nesbitt trans., 2nd enlarged ed. 1991), pp. 54–55.

[26]*Political Liberalism*, 214.

[27]For a Canadian case in which the latter question was recently addressed, see *Canada* (*Prime Minister*) *v Kadhr* 2010, SCC 3, retrievable at http://scc.lexum.umontreal.ca/en/2010/2010scc3/2010scc3.html.

A second key feature of public reason for Rawls is that it is the common reason of a liberal democratic society, "its way of formulating its plans, of putting its ends in an order of priority and of making its decisions accordingly."[28] It "is characteristic of a democratic people: it is the reason of its citizens, of those sharing the status of equal citizenship. The subject of their reason is [as in Rousseau] the good of the public…"[29] Nonpublic reasons, on the other hand, include the reasons of churches and universities and of many other associations in civil society."[30] They include the highly contentious, moral and political premises characteristically found within various comprehensive doctrines, such as Christianity, Islam, utilitarianism, Kantian deontology, Aristotelian virtue ethics, libertarianism and communitarianism. These may legitimately be appealed to by private citizens in discussions pertaining exclusively to their private affairs and the affairs of the various private institutions and associations to which they belong. That it has been so decreed by the Pope is a legitimate nonpublic reason for Catholics when debating some contentious matter of Catholic theology, even those bearing on questions of basic justice, for instance the morality of abortion or euthanasia. It is not, however, a public reason to which citizens can legitimately appeal "when they engage in political advocacy in the public forum, and thus for members of political parties and for candidates in their campaigns, and for other groups who support them. It holds equally for how citizens are to vote in elections when constitutional essentials and matters of basic justice are at stake."[31] As Rawls stresses, citizens often engage in decidedly political dialogue outside of public forums, and hence they are not *always* restricted to public reasons when conversing about political questions broadly construed, including those pertaining to constitutional essentials and questions of basic justice. Not so public officials. Whenever they are acting *as officials* a complete ban on appeal to non-public reasons applies. "It applies in official forums and so to legislators when they speak on the floor of parliament, and so to the executive in its public acts and pronouncements."[32] More importantly,

> it applies also in a special way to the judiciary and above all to a supreme court in a constitutional democracy with judicial review. This is because the justices have to explain and justify their decisions as based on their understanding of the constitution and relevant statutes and precedents. Since acts of the legislative and the executive need not be justified in this way, the court's special role makes it the exemplar of public reason.[33]

---

[28]*Ibid.*, p. 212.

[29]*Ibid.*, p. 213.

[30]*Ibid.*, p. 213.

[31]*Ibid.*, p. 215.

[32]*Ibid.*, p. 216.

[33]*Ibid.* Whether citizens and legislators should be restricted to public reasons when they debate issues within public forums is a highly controversial issue. It is also one on which I hope to remain neutral since my focus here is on charter cases. My claim is only that, in adjudicating cases under CCM, judges can justifiably be limited to public reasons. For attempts to relax Rawls' ban on nonpublic reasoning by citizens and legislators see, for example, Jeremy Waldron, "Religious Contributions to Public Deliberation," 30 *San Diego Law Review* (1993); Richard Bellamy, *Liberalism and Pluralism: Towards Politics of Compromise* (New York: Routledge, 1998); Robert P. George & Christopher Wolfe, eds., *Natural Law and Public Reason*, (Washington, D.C.: Georgetown University Press, 2000).

It is worth stressing that, for Rawls (and others who draw a similar distinction) public and nonpublic reason do overlap with one another in many ways. Both include, for example, elementary rules of inference and agreed rules governing the evaluation of evidence. What principally distinguishes the two domains in this regard is that public reason is restricted to premises enjoying widespread support within the community. These include "presently accepted general beliefs…and the methods and conclusions of science when these are not controversial."[34] But, crucially, they also include what Rawls calls a "political conception of justice." This is a shared conception of justice on which all reasonable people within a particular liberal democratic society, regardless of their other deep differences, could reasonably be expected to agree as a common basis upon which to conduct public life. It is a conception which each person, from the vantage point of his or her own partisan, comprehensive conception could reasonably accept as a reasonable basis upon which the coercive power of the state is to be exercised on her behalf and that of her fellow free and equal citizens.

As Rawls stresses, there is no uniquely justified (or most justified) political conception of justice: these can vary from one society to the next, and presumably from time to time within one and the same society.[35] More importantly, though a particular conception might be acceptable to each person as a reasonable basis upon which political power is to be exercised, it almost invariably demands some degree of compromise from everyone. Different citizens with differing comprehensive doctrines will almost always prefer the political conception closest to the one judged ideal from the vantage point of their own comprehensive doctrine. But each, recognizing the fact of reasonable pluralism, will also realize that garnering the benefits of civil society almost inevitably requires that (most) everyone must settle for less than their ideal choice. Each will also acknowledge the requirement that an acceptable compromise from her vantage point must also be, for no doubt different reasons and perhaps to a greater or lesser degree, an acceptable compromise for others whose comprehensive doctrines suggest a quite different order of preference. This, Rawls claims, is a requirement of the *duty of civility*, which is recognized in all reasonable comprehensive doctrines within a liberal democracy and serves as the basis for agreement on a shared political conception. Commenting on the concern that a political conception, because it involves so much compromise and must therefore be couched in terms acceptable to all, will be unacceptably "shallow," Rawls writes:

> ..we think we have strong reasons to follow [an accepted political conception] given our duty of civility to other citizens. After all, they share with us the same sense of its imperfection, though on different grounds, as they hold different comprehensive doctrines and believe different grounds are left out of account. But it is only this way, and by accepting that politics in a democratic society can never be guided by what we see as the whole truth, that we can realize the ideal expressed by the principle of legitimacy: to live politically with others in the light of reasons all might reasonably be expected to endorse.[36]

---

[34] *Ibid.*, p. 224.

[35] In this respect, a political conception of justice is similar to a CCM. Indeed, a society's CCM is perhaps best viewed as identical with, or at least a part of, a society's public conception of justice.

[36] *Ibid.*, pp. 242–243.

Later, Rawls nicely summarizes this crucial feature of public reason and its appeal as an ideal for social deliberation within a liberal democracy as follows.

> The ideal…expresses a willingness to listen to what others have to say and being ready to accept reasonable accommodations or alterations in one's own view. Public reason further asks of us that the balance of those values we hold to be reasonable in a particular case is a balance we sincerely think can be seen to be reasonable by others. Or failing this, we think the balance can be seen as at least not unreasonable in this sense: that those who oppose it can nevertheless understand how reasonable persons can affirm it. This preserves the ties of civic friendship and is consistent with the duty of civility. On some questions this may be the best we can do.[37]

Rawls reflections suggest a way of determining whether or not a reason is public and hence can serve as a legitimate basis for the proper exercise of political power, including, importantly for our purposes, discretionary constructions of CCM in charter cases.[38] They are not necessarily the reasons that the community happens widely to accept at any particular point in time as a common basis for public justifications. There are a number of reasons why this cannot be the appropriate standard. Among these is the fact that people do not always hold reasonable, well-founded beliefs. On the contrary, they sometimes hold what I elsewhere call "mere moral opinions," beliefs that are, e.g., rooted in false empirical claims and/or stereotypes, insufficiently thought out, or are deeply inconsistent with other, more fundamental, well-thought-out beliefs and commitments.[39] A second reason is that even when unfounded moral opinions are purged from the resources upon which courts may draw, what usually remains is reasonable disagreement. So actual, explicit agreement is far too stringent a test of acceptable public reasons. Were we to restrict judges to moral reasons to which everyone (or most everyone) within the community explicitly agrees, then public reason would be far too shallow a pool from which they could draw in fashioning their CCM constructions. Hence the lesser standard of reasons we *could* all accept as reasonable—or at the very least, as Rawls puts it, not unreasonable. But how, in practical terms, is that standard to be applied?

---

[37] *Ibid.*, p. 253.

[38] In this paper I have, for purposes of analysis, treated public reasons as though they were a type or class of reasons distinct from the reasons constituted by CCM. The former are characterized as a distinct set of reasons upon which judges might draw in rendering the norms of CCM more determinate. In truth, the norms of CCM are probably best viewed as a *part* of public reason, that part which is distinctly linked to the community's authoritatively expressed constitutional commitments (e.g., the provisions of its constitutional charter or bill of rights). In short, *all* the reasons upon which judges legitimately draw in deciding constitutional cases are instances of public reasons. Viewed in this way, the argument of this paper is meant to show that discretionary construction of CCM norms is warranted because and to the extent that judges draw from the same bank of reasons—public reasons—as they do in cases involving the application of CCM. I owe this point to Brian Burge-Hendrix.

[39] In my previous defenses of charter review, I argue that one of the primary roles of courts when engaged in that practice is to hold the community to its fundamental moral commitments in instances where democratic procedures, responding to unfounded moral opinions within the community, threaten to lead to their violation. On this see *A Common Law Theory of Judicial Review: The Living Tree*, *passim*.

Den Otter provides a useful test that helps ensure that exercises of public power are at the very least sensitive to the reasonable views of everyone: public reasons are "those that an ideal reasonable dissenter would consider good enough."[40] They are not necessarily the reasons everyone would (reasonably) prefer under ideal conditions of deliberation. Nor are they reasons which every reasonable person in such circumstances would consider particularly strong, or ideally worthy of support but for the fact of reasonable pluralism. Rather they are reasons, as Rawls would have it, that such persons would all judge to be at the very least "not unreasonable," in the sense that those who oppose them can understand how reasonable persons could affirm them in justifying an exercise of public power. In drawing exclusively from such reasons, judges "must cast their constitutional arguments in ways that might appeal to reasonable dissenters…a person who is willing to be persuaded by the better argument, assumes that reasonable moral disagreement will characterize difficult constitutional cases, and will conclude that [the act] in question is publicly justified only when the state has produced sufficiently public reasons on its behalf."[41] Public reasons, so construed, are "typically…as neutral as possible with respect to the wide range of reasonable conceptions of the good and normative political ideologies that currently exist in the [community]. They should be uncontroversial, which means that an ideal reasonable person could not reasonably reject them."[42] Nonpublic reasons, on the other hand, are usually "based on perfectionist standards of human flourishing, on contested theories of political morality, or on controversial empirical claims."[43] As Bruce Ackerman notes, an argument "that incorporates a premise that a particular way of life is sinful, unpopular, unnatural, unconventional, misguided, silly, or idiotic is exactly the kind of argument that the state must eschew. An argument that contains a premise that a particular way of life is superior to others or that certain people are by nature inferior is also insufficiently public."[44]

10.3 Why Public Reason?

So the appropriate standard, I would like to suggest, is this: A reason is sufficiently public, and hence a legitimate basis upon which a court can draw when engaging in discretionary constructions of CCM, when it is a reason to which no reasonable dissenter could reasonably object, given the duty of civility. It is one that such a

[40] Ronald Den Otter, *supra* note 22, p. 10. Den Otter notes that he has borrowed the idea of reasonable rejectability from T.M. Scanlon's "Contractualism and Utilitarianism," in *Beyond Utilitarianism*, ed. Amartya Sen and Bernard Williams (New York: Cambridge University Press, 1984), p. 110.

[41] *Ibid.*, p. 11.

[42] *Ibid.*

[43] *Ibid.*

[44] *Ibid.*, drawing on Bruce Ackerman, *Social Justice in the Liberal State* (New Haven: Yale University Press, 1980), pp. 10–11.

dissenter could, despite his differences, accept as "good enough," as, at the very least, "not unreasonable." So how can the employment of such reasons be brought to bear on questions concerning the justification of charter review? Let's begin by recalling what brought us to this point. I began with an admission. As many critics of charter review have pointed out, that practice is hard to reconcile with the fundamental principles of democracy, especially in a society marked by the fact of reasonable pluralism. It appears to take the power of decision away from citizens and their democratically chosen representatives and place it in the hands of a small group of democratically unaccountable judges. It is they, not the people and/or their elected agents, who ultimately end up setting the fundamental standards of political morality governing the exercise of public power. Now (a) were it true that, in settling such questions, judges were simply determining the requirements of moral norms ultimately set or accepted by the people themselves, in an easily identifiable CCM; (b) were it clear, perhaps upon due reflection but clear nevertheless, what those norms require in all cases; and (c) were it true that judges are, for some reason, better able or better situated to engage in the kind of reasoning and reflection required to answer such questions; then it would be fairly clear how one might go about trying to justify charter review in a liberal, constitutional democracy. Judges would not be doing anything significantly different from what we expect of them in ordinary, run of the mill cases. They would be applying, in a fair, impartial and neutral manner, standards authoritatively established elsewhere in ways that seem perfectly consistent with the fundamental ideals of democracy. Or at least that's what we could reasonably demand of them, and we would have a rational basis for criticizing them for any failure to live up to our expectations. But things are different when CCM proves inadequate to the task. In any case in which its demands appear indeterminate, judges seem forced to exercise discretion, to creatively determine or construct the norms of CCM that they then set about applying to the cases that come before them. In other words, they appear forced to engage in the creation of norms, not their (it is hoped) fair, impartial and neutral application. And this, it was acknowledged, brings us right back to our original worry—that charter review cannot possibly be justified in a modern, liberal democracy.

We are now, I hope, in a position to see that restricting judges to public reason in such cases allows us a promising means of warding off democratic concerns about CCM constructions. Such constructions are consistent with liberal democratic principles because and insofar as they appeal to reasons to which no reasonable dissenter could object, given the duty of civility which features in his comprehensive doctrine, as well as the reasonable comprehensive doctrine of every other reasonable member of a liberal democratic community marked by the fact of reasonable pluralism. Such a dissenter could no more object to a decision based on such reasons than he could object to a decision, properly taken by a properly constituted democratic, majoritarian decision procedure, with which he disagrees. In both cases, our dissenter might prefer that a different decision have been made. But in each case, he must be prepared to recognize the legitimacy of the decision actually taken, despite his displeasure with its substance. So appeal to public reasons in justifying the discretionary construction of CCM norms allows each citizen, including those who strongly, but reasonably, dissent from that development, to take ownership of it nevertheless, to see it as the product of a process of decision which appeals to reasons to which they could not reasonably object.

10.4 Indeterminacy Yet Again?

So restricting judges to public reasons seems to present a promising way of answering the concerns of those worried about the democratic legitimacy of charter review. But of course our critic will not likely be satisfied with this manoeuvre. Theories of public reason have been subject to numerous criticisms, at least one of which threatens to undermine completely the plausibility of my account.[45] Public reasons, given their shallowness—they must be shallow or abstract enough to attract the support of all reasonable people—very seldom seem to lead to one and only one reasonable conclusion. On the contrary, different constellations of such reasons often lead to contradictory results, and even when we restrict ourselves to one such constellation, different weightings of the included reasons can have much the same result—no uniquely correct solution. In short, public reasons seem to suffer from the very kind of uncertainty and indeterminacy that has concerned us from the start. In most any case involving charter review, any number of public reasons will seem relevant and these can almost always be weighed differently: reasons of equality, for example, often compete against reasons of liberty, as is typically the case in affirmative action cases, or cases involving polygamous marriage. Security of the person sometimes competes with reasons of liberty in cases lying at the edges of life, e.g., those dealing with abortion and euthanasia. It also competes in the many cases involving national security that have become an all too prevalent feature of modern life. Yet if there is no single set of relevant public reasons in such cases, or no uniquely correct way of balancing them even when there is, there will be no uniquely correct answer to the question a judge might attempt to answer by invoking them. No uniquely correct answer to the question whether, e.g. a particular affirmative action program, or a practice sanctioning and regulating voluntary euthanasia, can be publicly justified in a particular modern, liberal democracy. No way of determining whether, and if so when, habeas corpus may legitimately be suspended in times of national emergency. If this is so, then instructing a court to appeal to them in deciding difficult charter cases in which the construction of one or more CCM norms seems required, might seem of little help. The court will once again be forced to exercise discretion, the sovereign prerogative of personal choice. It will be forced to choose a reasonable, *but at the same time reasonably contestable*, balance among the relevant public reasons and to decide accordingly. In short, we seem once again to have taken away the community's right to determine, for itself, the fundamental norms by which it is governed.

---

[45]For very helpful surveys of the various objections made to theories of public reason, together with valuable efforts to address them, see Den Otter and Solum, *supra* note 22.

So my analysis gives rise to this troubling question: How can one seemingly indeterminate source of guidance, public reason, be at all helpful in dealing with similar problems of indeterminacy lurking in a different source of guidance, CCM. We seem right back where we started—with no means of answering those worried about the democratic legitimacy of charter review. In answer to this particular objection, I would like to draw attention to a number factors. First, it should be stressed that if discretionary choice ends up being necessary when public reasons are invoked, it is only after all the other relevant sources of determinate guidance have been exhausted. In other words, it is only after all the explicit legal decisions, and norms and judgments of CCM have been considered and reconciled in an attempt to reach reflective equilibrium; and only after the further dictates of public reason, such as they are, have been examined and given due measure, that a court will be called on to exercise discretionary judgment. Only then will a court be called on to choose from among options arguably left open to it. But more importantly, if the court does make such a choice, and does so responsibly, it will end up choosing an option that everyone, dissenter included, will have to acknowledge to be at the very least *not unreasonable—and quite possibly the only one actually consistent with public reason*. This last point—the standing possibility that someone might actually be correct in her belief that she has what turns out to be the uniquely correct balancing of the relevant public reasons in a Charter case, despite her inability to convince everyone else of this fact, leads me to a further consideration that I would like to spend the final part of my paper exploring.

It is tempting to think of charter cases as falling into one of two distinct categories: those in which it is clear that the relevant norms provide determinate guidance and those in which it clearly does not. (As an aside, this sort of picture is quite often lurking in the background in contexts in which the possibility of discretionary choice under binding norms is in play. Attempts to justify or discredit discretion as a mode of decision-making in such contexts often assume that we actually know *when* the limits of determinate, authoritative guidance have been reached. And then the question is: On what type of grounds must the (appropriate) decision-maker decide, if at all? But this is almost never the case, a point to which I'll return in a moment.) Let's assume, for the time being, that a particular case, Case 1, does clearly fall into the first category. In other words, it seems clear to all reasonable people that public reason justifies one and only one construction of the relevant norms of CCM, a construction according to which the legislation in dispute is constitutionally invalid. Let's further assume that the arguments I have advanced here and elsewhere are sufficient to justify the court's having the power to construct the norm in such a way as to render the statute constitutional invalid.[46] There is, I would like to suggest, no violation of democratic principle in such a case. Now consider a second case, Case 2, that falls into the second of my two categories. It seems clear

[46] In addition to the argument developed here, which focuses primarily on the question of democratic legitimacy, I would draw on the various arguments advanced in *A Common Law Theory of Judicial Review: The Living Tree*, most notably those deriving from what I call "the circumstances of rule-making." See note 19 above.

to everyone that public reason is incapable of ruling out all but one competing construction of the relevant CCM norms. It's equally clear that at least one of these constructions supports a construction warranting a declaration of constitutionality, and also clear that at least one other construction supports the opposite conclusion. It's very tempting to argue that the court should, in Case 2, be required to defer to the elected legislators and leave the disputed legislation untouched. Since the relevant public reasons seem clearly to have run out, the court might be said to lack a democratically legitimate warrant to construct the relevant CCM norm so as to underwrite a declaration of invalidity. Hence, the court should simply leave matters as they stand.[47] It should, in other words, leave the legislation untouched.

There are, however, a number of things to be said in response to this particular line of argument. First, we should once again bear in mind that if it's uncertain whether a norm or set of reasons yields a uniquely correct solution to a question, it does not follow that it certainly does not. This no more follows than it follows from the fact that it's uncertain whether Tom is bald that he certainly has a full head of hair. Hence, the legislation in question might in actual fact *be* invalid despite the fact that it's not clearly so. Suppose our critic accepted this point. He might then go on to reply that I have simply ignored here the importance of context and associated burdens of proof. Returning to Tom and his questionable head of hair, consider a context in which the burden is on whomever wishes to declare Tom bald. And suppose that, for some reason or other, that burden dictates that Tom is not to be considered bald unless it can be proved that he is in fact so. In other words, if we cannot conclusively establish that he is bald, then he must be treated as if he is not. Might we not say analogous things about judges and the context in which they deal with hard constitutional cases? For reasons having to do with the archetypal role of judges in a constitutional democracy, one might be tempted to assert that the burden of proof always lies on courts to establish, before issuing a declaration of invalidity, either that the impugned legislation clearly violates a CCM norm and is therefore unconstitutional, or failing this, that public reason clearly warrant one and only one result: that the relevant CCM norm should be extended in such as way as to render it unconstitutional. In other words, one might be tempted to argue that courts really are under obligation to defer to the legislature unless they can decisively show that the relevant constitutional norms (such as they are, or as constructed in the only reasonable way sanctioned by public reason) have been violated by their enactments. Unless they can demonstrate that the relevant norms have been violated, then the case must, in effect, be treated as one in which it is certain that they have not.

[47] I have framed this objection in terms of public reasons but the argument actually applies to any of the norms and reasons upon which a court might draw in exercising charter review, including for our purposes the norms of CCM. It is seldom, if ever, clear whether or not a court is in fact faced with indeterminate CCM norms. Someone might argue that in any such case the court should always defer to the legislature. It should not, in other words, draw on further public reasons to create a discretionary construction upon which the court then relies to declare the relevant legislation unconstitutional. My reasons for thinking that this would not be a good option in the case of further indeterminate public reasons apply equally here.

This latter argument is problematic, I believe, for at least two reasons—which brings us back to the way in which the original objection was framed. First, and foremost is a fact to which I drew attention above: that cases do not come neatly packaged into my two clearly defined categories—those in which it is clear that the relevant norms and reasons are determinate [Case 1] and those in which they are clearly not [Case 2]. In short, there is almost never a clear borderline between hard and easy cases. Rather, we find what might be called an "epistemically uncertain borderline" between the two. Putting it another way, it is often epistemically uncertain whether we are faced with what, for want of a better term, I'll describe as "normative indeterminacy."[48] If so, then there is no escaping the fact that, for virtually every case in which the possibility of normative indeterminacy looms large—i.e. virtually every controversial charter case—a difficult decision will have to be made as to which of the two categories is in play. And this will be one with which reasonable people could reasonably disagree, one person believing that the relevant norms and/or public reasons yield a determinate answer to the relevant question, the other thinking that they do not. In short, the decision that a case does or does not require discretionary choice among CCM constructions, or among weighted clusters of further public reasons bearing on that choice, seems *itself* to be one upon which reasonable people will reasonably disagree. Should a judge simply place all epistemically uncertain (i.e. controversial) cases into the category of cases in which indeterminate normative guidance is to be found, and then defer to the legislature's views of its constitutional responsibilities, then someone's reasonable view will be *automatically* rejected. More to the point, it will be rejected in a way that ignores the fact of reasonable pluralism and arguably does violence to the duty of civility. Someone whose perfectly reasonable view is that the case actually falls into the category of normative determinacy, and hence actually does involve a determinate violation of his constitutional rights, or of the only reasonable extension or construction of them, would have every right to complain. He would have every right to complain that the court had abdicated its responsibility to attempt, to the best of its abilities, to hold the legislature to its constitutional responsibilities. He would also have every right to complain that the court had failed to take his constitutional rights seriously.

So a simple policy of judicial deference in all cases where it is unclear whether the relevant CCM norms or further public reasons provide determinate guidance seems unacceptable. Judges cannot avoid the hard calls, which brings me to my final point, one that returns us, once again, to the nature of public reasons and the role they play within a liberal democratic community. The proposals defended in my paper hardly add up to a recipe for unbridled judicial activism of a sort that is incompatible with the fundamental tenets of democracy. A decision with respect to which a sincere attempt is made to offer justification in terms of CCM, or failing that, in terms of a CCM construction justified by way of some reasonable balance of

[48] By 'normative indeterminacy' I mean the absence of a uniquely right answer to the question "What does this norm actually require in this particular case with these particular facts?" In such a case, it isn't just uncertain what the right answer it; there is no right answer.

further relevant public reasons, should not be viewed as an alien force compelling us to act independently of our convictions. And this is true even when the decision is one with which many of us deeply disagree. Rather it should be viewed by each and every one of us as an exercise of public power to which none of us, reasonable dissenters included, could object, given our commitment to the duty of civility, a duty of vital importance in any democratic society marked by the fact of reasonable pluralism. It will be a decision to which we can all sign on, so to speak. To repeat, this is not to say that we will always agree with the decision made, including the decision that a discretionary construction of CCM norms was called for. Nor will we always agree with the balance of public reasons on which a court might have relied in justifying the construction it chose to act on. Nor, for that matter, will we all agree with a court's judgment as to the relevant public reasons, thinking, perhaps, that what the court took to be a public reason is in actual fact a partisan, non-public reason that has no place in constitutional adjudication. But insofar as, and to the extent that, the decision is based on a good faith attempt to strike a reasonable balance of what are sincerely taken to be the relevant public reasons, and given that this step is taken only after all other resources have, in the opinion of the court, been exhausted, it is one which all reasonable citizens can accept as good enough. Each can view the decision as one that allows her to continue to maintain ownership of each and every decision regarding the proper exercise of public power in her democratic community—including, importantly, decisions taken by judges in the exercise of charter review.[49]

[49]I wish to thank a number of individuals for their very helpful comments on earlier versions of this paper. These include: Matt Grellette, Stefan Sciaraffa, Fabio Shecaira, Noel Struchiner, Wayne Sumner, Lorraine Weinrib, Grant Huscroft, Brad Miller, Natalie Stoljar, Brian Burge-Hendrix and Imer Flores. I also wish to acknowledge the helpful comments of all those others who contributed to discussions of the paper when it was presented to the Faculty of Law, University of Toronto; at the "First Annual Graduate Conference in the Philosophy of Law," McMaster University, May 5–7, 2010; at "Living Tree Constitutionalism: Democracy and the Rule of Law", April 22, 2010 at The Institute for Legal Research at the National Autonomous University of Mexico (UNAM); and at "Neutrality and Theory of Law", Girona Spain, May 22, 2010.

Chapter 11
Between Positivism and Non-positivism? A Third Reply to Eugenio Bulygin

Robert Alexy

Serious criticism honours and challenges an author. Eugenio Bulygin offers me, now for the third time, the great benefit of his critique,[1] and I am delighted to have occasion here to respond.

11.1 Normative Arguments and the Concept of Law

In *The Argument from Injustice. A Reply to Legal Positivism* I defend the non-positivistic connection thesis which says that law necessarily includes moral elements, and I claim that the supporting arguments for this thesis can be divided into two groups: analytical and normative.[2] On this basis, I propose to call a connection supported by normative arguments 'normatively necessary'.[3] Normative necessity is explained in the following way: 'That something is normatively necessary means

I should like to thank Stanley L. Paulson for suggestions and advice on matters of English style.

[1]For the first two rounds see Eugenio Bulygin, 'Alexy und das Richtigkeitsargument', in: Aulis Aarnio, Stanley L. Paulson, Ota Weinberger, Georg Henrik von Wright, and Dieter Wyduckel (eds.), *Rechtsnorm und Rechtswirklichkeit. Festschrift für Werner Krawietz zum 60. Geburtstag* (Berlin: Duncker & Humblot, 1993), 19–24; Robert Alexy, 'Bulygins Kritik des Richtigkeitsarguments', in: Ernesto Garzón Valdes, Werner Krawietz, Georg Henrik von Wright, and Ruth Zimmerling (eds.), *Normative Systems in Legal and Moral Theory. Festschrift for Carlos E. Alchourrón and Eugenio Bulygin* (Berlin: Duncker & Humblot, 1997), 235–250; Eugenio Bulygin, 'Alexy's Thesis of the Necessary Connection between Law and Morality', *Ratio Juris* 13 (2000), 133–137; Robert Alexy, 'On the Thesis of a Necessary Connection between Law and Morality: Bulygin's Critique', *Ratio Juris* 13 (2000), 138–147.

[2]Robert Alexy, *The Argument from Injustice. A Reply to Legal Positivism* (first publ. 1992), trans. Bonnie Litschewski Paulson and Stanley L. Paulson (Oxford: Clarendon Press, 2002), 20.

[3]Ibid., 21.

R. Alexy (✉)
Department of Law, University of Kiel, Leibnizstraße 6, 24118 Kiel, Germany
e-mail: alexy@law.uni-kiel.de

J. Ferrer Beltrán et al. (eds.), *Neutrality and Theory of Law*,
Law and Philosophy Library 106, DOI 10.1007/978-94-007-6067-7_11,

nothing other than that it is commanded'.[4] Bulygin argues that this 'idea of a normative necessity' is 'extremely doubtful'.[5] The use of the term 'necessary' instead of terms like 'obligatory' or 'binding', he maintains, 'can only lead to linguistic confusions', and he poses the question of 'who is it that can command the connection thesis'.[6] His conclusion:

> All this sounds extremely strange. If there are conceptual connections between law and morality, then there is no need to resort to normative arguments. Either the element of morality is included in the concept of law, or it is not. If it is included, then normative arguments are superfluous; if it is not included, they are useless.[7]

My reply to this is that there exists, indeed, a conceptually necessary inclusion of morality into the concept of law, but this makes normative arguments by no means superfluous, as Bulygin suggests. On the contrary, it makes normative arguments necessary.

In *The Argument from Injustice* I describe the relation between analytical and normative arguments as a relation of supplementation and strengthening.[8] In order to meet Bulygin's objection, I have to add to this a relation of inclusion. The argument from inclusion consists of two parts, and the first part is this. It is a conceptual necessity that law raises a claim to correctness. The second part of the argument is that this claim to correctness necessarily leads to an inclusion of non-authoritative normative—that is, moral—elements, not only at the level of the application of law but also at the level of determining the nature and defining the concept of law.[9]

Eugenio Bulygin remarks that the necessity of the claim to correctness is a topic that has given rise to a long discussion between us and that—with the exception of two additional remarks—he does not wish to take up this theme still another time.[10] I shall follow him on this point, confining myself to comments on his two additional remarks. This, however, shall be taken up later. For the present, I will presuppose that law necessarily raises a claim to correctness, that is, I will take the first part of the argument from inclusion as given. This means that my position, as presented here, acquires a hypothetical character. It will be an answer to the question of whether, if law necessarily lays a claim to correctness, normative arguments can be employed in the determination of the nature and the definition of the concept of law.

Law's claim to correctness refers not only to the question of whether the application of law in a concrete case is correct but also to the question of whether it is correct at all to apply law. The first concerns the concrete dimension, the second the abstract dimension of the claim to correctness.

---

[4]Ibid., 21, n. 40.

[5]Eugenio Bulygin, 'Alexy between Positivism and Non-positivism', in: Jordi Ferrer Beltrán, José Juan Moreso, and Diego M. Papayannis (eds.), *Neutrality and Theory of Law* (Dordrecht: Springer, 2013), 2.

[6]Ibid.

[7]Ibid.

[8]Alexy, *The Argument from Injustice* (n. 2, above), 22.

[9]On the relationship between the concept and the nature of law, see Robert Alexy, 'On the Concept and the Nature of Law', *Ratio Juris* 21 (2008), 281–299, at 290–292.

[10]Bulygin, 'Alexy between Positivism and Non-positivism' (n. 5, above), 8.

The abstract claim to correctness, for its part, also has two dimensions: a real dimension and an ideal dimension. The most abstract principle of the ideal dimension is justice. The idea of justice as such—that is, morality *simpliciter*—does not, however, suffice to resolve the problems of social co-ordination and co-operation.[11] The moral costs of anarchy can be avoided only by law understood as an enterprise that strives to realize the value or principle of legal certainty. For that reason, law's claim to correctness refers not only to justice but also to positivity as defined by authoritative issuance and social efficacy.[12] This is what I have termed the real dimension of the claim to correctness. In this way, the claim to correctness necessarily connects both the principle of justice and the principle of legal certainty with law. This is an expression of the dual nature of law.[13]

If justice as well as legal certainty are necessarily connected with law, a participant in the legal system, confronted with unjust law, must ask himself whether justice as necessary connected with law requires that he consider the unjust law as invalid law. If the principle of justice were the only relevant principle here, the answer would be easy. The dual nature of law, however, requires also that he consider the principle of legal certainty. This is to say that in order to determine the borderline between valid law on the one hand and invalid law on the other, he has to strike a balance. The determination of this line, however, is a question that concerns the concept and the nature of law.

Elsewhere I have argued that the correct result of this balancing is that the principle of legal certainty precedes justice in all cases of injustice except for the case of extreme injustice.[14] This corresponds to Radbruch's formula.[15] Four points are of interest. Here balancing—and this is the first point—concerns the problem of the concept and the nature of law. The second is that the arguments applied in this balancing are normative or moral arguments. The third point is that these normative or moral arguments are, owing to the claim to correctness, necessarily connected with the concept of law. This necessary connection implies that it is impossible for a participant in a legal system to say what law is without saying what law ought to be.[16] And this, in turn, answers Bulygin's question of 'who is it that can command the connection thesis'.[17] It is the claim to correctness taken seriously by the participant. By contrast with the observer's 'is', the participant's 'is' includes an 'ought'.[18]

[11]Robert Alexy, 'The Nature of Arguments about the Nature of Law', in: Lukas H. Meyer, Stanley L. Paulson, and Thomas W. Pogge (eds.), *Rights, Culture, and Law. Themes from the Legal and Political Philosophy of Joseph Raz* (Oxford: Oxford University Press, 2003), 3–16, at 8.

[12]On this concept of positivity, see Alexy, *The Argument from Injustice* (n. 2, above), 3–4, 14–19.

[13]See Robert Alexy, 'The Dual Nature of Law', *Ratio Juris* 23 (2010), 167–182, at 173–174.

[14]Ibid., 175, 177, n. 14.

[15]See Robert Alexy, 'A Defence of Radbruch's Formula', in: M.D.A. Freeman (ed.), *Lloyd's Introduction to Jurisprudence*, eighth edn. (London: Sweet & Maxwell and Thomson Reuters, 2008), 426–443, at 427–428.

[16]Robert Alexy, '*An Answer to Joseph Raz*', in: George Pavlakos (ed.), *Law, Rights and Discourse. The Legal Philosophy of Robert Alexy* (Oxford: Hart, 2007), 37–55, at 52.

[17]Bulygin, 'Alexy between Positivism and Non-positivism' (n. 5, above), 2.

[18]Alexy, 'On the Concept and the Nature of Law' (n. 9, above), 297.

Finally, the fourth point concerns Bulygin's thesis that normative arguments are 'superfluous' once 'the element of morality is included in the concept of law'.[19] In referring to justice, the claim to correctness contains moral elements, and it is included in the concept of law. The inclusion of the claim to correctness, however, does not as such imply that the principle of justice becomes superfluous as an argument supporting the definition of the concept of law. The claim to correctness, taken by itself, does not have sufficient content to carry out this task. For this reason, the principles or values to which it necessarily refers are indispensible.

11.2 The Observer's Perspective

The distinction between the perspective of the observer and the participant has played an important role in the considerations adumbrated above on the relation between the concept of law and normative arguments. The distinction is, indeed, a central element of the non-positivistic theory of law. This leads one to expect that the distinction will be seen critically by positivists.[20] Bulygin's first point concerning this issue is that 'the dichotomy between observers and participants is not so sharp as Alexy seems to believe. Most observers are at the same time participants and all participants are also observers'.[21]

I wish to begin with comments on this by noting that the distinction at issue is not one between persons but between perspectives. The participant's perspective is defined by the question: What is the correct legal answer?, the observer's by the question: Which legal decisions have actually been made, are actually being made, and will actually be made? The version of legal non-positivism that I wish to defend defines law by means of three elements: authoritative issuance, social efficacy, and correctness of content. Authoritative issuance and social efficacy concern the real or factual dimension of law, correctness of content its ideal or critical dimension. This implies—what cannot come as a surprise—that non-positivism includes positivistic elements. This inclusion of positivistic elements, in turn, implies that the participant's perspective necessarily includes the observer's perspective. To this extent, Bulygin is, then, right in maintaining that 'all participants are also observers'.[22] In this case, however, the observer's perspective is subordinate to the participant's perspective. The answer given to the observer's question, as hard cases make clear, is not necessarily the final answer—as it would be in case of a pure observer. This is also the crucial point where Bulygin's thesis that '[m]ost observers are at the

[19] Bulygin, 'Alexy between Positivism and Non-positivism' (n. 5, above), 2.

[20] See Joseph Raz, 'The Argument from Justice, or How Not to Reply to Legal Positivism', in: Joseph Raz, *The Authority of Law*, 2nd edn. (Oxford: Oxford University Press, 2009), 313–335, at 319–323, and, in reply thereto, Alexy, 'An Answer to Joseph Raz' (n. 16, above), 45–8.

[21] Bulygin, 'Alexy between Positivism and Non-positivism' (n. 5, above), 3.

[22] Ibid.

same time participants' is concerned.[23] This might be read as follows: There are many fewer pure observers than participants.

Bulygin's main argument against my description of the observer's perspective is that it gives rise to a contradiction:

> There is a clear contradiction between the thesis that the non-positivistic concept of law necessarily includes moral elements and Alexy's assertion that even an extremely unjust system as the governor order is nevertheless a legal system. What moral elements does this order contain?[24]

My reply is that it by no means gives rise to a contradiction. In order to establish a non-positivistic concept of law one has to defend the connection thesis, which says that there is a necessary connection between law and morality or, more precisely, between legal validity or legal correctness on the one hand and moral correctness on the other. The connection thesis requires not more than just one connection of this kind. Such a connection exists, in any case, in the participant's perspective, and this perspective is the fundamental perspective. Law is impossible without participants, but it would be possible without pure observers. The necessary connection in this necessary perspective suffices to establish a non-positivistic concept of law. If, alongside this, there were no necessary connection in the observer's perspective, this would not affect the non-positivistic concept of law.

This by itself would be enough to dismiss Bulygin's reproach of contradiction. It can be added to this that a necessary connection exists even from the observer's perspective. A system of rules that does not lay claim to correctness is not a legal system, even from the point of view of an observer.[25] The claim to correctness, however, necessarily raised by law, implies a necessary connection between law and morality. Bulygin's reproach of contradiction is, therefore, wrong for two reasons.

Bulygin links this reproach to another objection. The existence of a legal system requires only that the claim to correctness be raised. The claim need not be met. Thus, from the observer's perspective, a system of rules can be considered as a legal system even if it is extremely unjust, provided that the claim to correctness is raised.[26] Now Bulygin argues that such a hypocritical claim is, from a moral point of view, 'considerably worse than an openly predatory order'.[27] For this reason, he maintains, the thesis that the claim to correction transforms a bandit's order into a legal system—one might call it the 'transformation thesis'—'is certainly incompatible with the assertion that the concept of law necessarily includes moral elements'.[28] It is, that is to say, incompatible with the connection thesis.

I agree with Bulygin that extreme injustice along with hypocrisy is morally worse than extreme injustice without hypocrisy. I do not think, however, that this leads to

---

[23] Ibid., 4.

[24] Ibid.

[25] Alexy, *The Argument from Injustice* (n. 2, above), 34.

[26] Ibid.

[27] Bulygin, 'Alexy between Positivism and Non-positivism' (n. 5, above), 4.

[28] Ibid.

any incompatibilities between the transformation thesis and the connection thesis. The opposite is true. Tyrants, despots, and dictators usually strive to acquire legitimacy in order to avoid open suppression. For this reason they mask the suppression by means of a legal façade. The necessity of the claim to correctness implies in this case the necessity of hypocrisy, and public hypocrisy endangers legitimacy. Show trials, for instance, are an attempt to eliminate opponents in a legitimate way; they are, however, owing to hypocrisy, at the same time a risk for legitimacy. The fact that the claim to correctness never allows tyrants to attain more than hypocritical legitimacy does not refute the connection thesis. It corroborates it.

11.3 The Participant's Perspective

The observer's perspective is a perspective rather favourable to positivism. The case is different with the participant's perspective. Bulygin nevertheless argues that positivism also fits in the case of the participant's perspective best—especially the perspective of a judge.

His argument is based on the distinction between plain and hard cases. A plain case is at hand when 'the existing legal rules determine a univocal and clear solution of the case'.[29] According to Bulygin, '[i]n such [a] situation only the observer's perspective is relevant also for the judge'.[30] Here one must object. To be sure, in many cases the authoritative material, especially statutes and precedents, dictate a univocal answer. Nevertheless, the ostensible clarity of plain cases is not a simple matter. One who asserts that the solution is clear is to be understood as asserting that there are no arguments that might give rise to serious doubts. Such arguments, however, are always conceivable. Bulygin alludes to such arguments when he says that

> it is possible that the judge decides not to apply the existing norm and to resort to another norm (eventually created by himself) that does not belong to the system at the time of his decision.[31]

This shows that the categorization of a case as 'plain' includes a negative judgment with respect to all possible counter-arguments.[32] These possible counter-arguments comprise moral reasons. This negative judgment transcends, therefore, the observer's perspective. It is conceivable only as an act performed from the participant's perspective. For this reason it is never the case that 'only the observer's perspective is relevant also for the judge'.[33]

---

[29]Ibid., 5.

[30]Ibid.

[31]Ibid., 5.

[32]Robert Alexy, *A Theory of Legal Argumentation. The Theory of Rational Discourse as Theory of Legal Justification* (first publ. 1978), trans. Ruth Adler and Neil MacCormick (Oxford: Clarendon Press, 1989), 8.

[33]Bulygin, 'Alexy between Positivism and Non-positivism' (n. 5, above), 5.

Positivists and non-positivists generally agree that every positive law has, as Hart remarked, an open texture.[34] This is necessitated, *inter alia*, by the vagueness of legal language, the possibility of a conflict between norms, the gaps that exist in the law, and the possibility of deciding a case contrary to the language of a statute in special cases. Cases within the scope of this open texture are hard cases.

Like Kelsen and Hart, Bulygin argues that no argument against positivism can be grounded on the existence of hard cases. In such cases, the judge has to be seen as creating new law on bases other than legal standards and according to his own discretion, much as in the case of an legislature.[35] The positivistic concept of law, Bulygin stresses, is in no way affected by this:

> In which way can these facts influence the concept of law? Does it mean that the judge uses another concept of law than the external observer that wants to describe it? I don't think so. When the judge does not apply a valid norm because in his opinion its application would lead to great injustice and instead applies another norm, eventually created by him, this cannot be described as modification of the concept of law. What is modified in such cases are the norms or rules of a legal system, not the concept of law.[36]

I agree with Bulygin that the *contra legem* decision of the judge cannot be described as a modification of the concept of law by this judge. What the judge thinks he is doing or says he is doing, is not decisive.[37] What is decisive is what he really does and what the law necessarily requires him to do. This is a question of the correct description of legal decision-making. Bulygin describes legal decision-making in hard cases as a law-making act that transforms moral considerations into law. I think that this description is insufficient. The first point of my argument is, again, the claim to correctness. A judge necessarily raises this claim. The second point is that this claim refers, like Raz's claim to 'legitimate, moral, authority',[38] not only to positive law but also to justice, that is, to morality.[39] Bulygin's argument might be interpreted as saying that the avoidance of 'great injustice' is only a personal or subjective concern of the judge, and not something that is objectively required by law's claim to correctness. If this subjective interpretation should reflect Bulygin's intention, then our respective descriptions take altogether different paths already at this point. But a positivist can grant the point that law's claim to correctness comprises a claim to moral correctness, and nevertheless contest the claim that this amounts to a necessary connection between legal validity or legal correctness and morality. This third point seems to be the decisive one.

My thesis is that a necessary connection, once one has arrived at the third point, is indispensible. One might imagine a case in which the positive law allows for two

[34] H.L.A. Hart, *The Concept of Law*, 2nd edn. (Oxford: Clarendon Press, 1994), 128.

[35] Hans Kelsen, *Reine Rechtslehre*, 2nd edn. (Vienna: Franz Deuticke, 1960), 350–351; Hart, *The Concept of Law* (n. 33, above), 126, 135, 204–205; Bulygin, 'Alexy between Positivism and Non-positivism' (n. 5, above), 6.

[36] Ibid.

[37] Bulygin, ibid., 6, however, ascribes the opposite opinion to me. Naturally, it is possible that the judge is doing what he says he is doing. In this case one can also refer to what he says.

[38] Joseph Raz, 'On the Nature of Law', *Archives for Philosophy of Law and Social Philosophy* 82 (1996), 1–25, at 6.

[39] Robert Alexy, 'Law and Correctness', *Current Legal Problems* 51 (1998), 205–221, at 216.

different interpretations: I_1 and I_2. I_1 is just, I_2 unjust. In this case, law's claim to correctness requires I_1. Perhaps, positivists and non-positivists may agree up to this point. Disagreement begins where the question has to be answered of what happens when I_2, that is, the unjust interpretation, is chosen. According to positivism the decision is a legally perfect decision with moral defects. According to non-positivism the decision is not only morally defective but also legally defective.[40] It is legally defective, for not only is morality's claim to correctness violated in the case of a morally defective legal decision, but law's claim to correctness is violated, too. This leads to a necessary qualifying or ideal connection between law and morality.[41] With this, the claim to correctness implies that law necessarily comprises an ideal dimension as well as a real or authoritative dimension. That defects in either dimension are legal defects can, however, be adequately grasped only by means of a non-positivistic concept of law. This is the theoretical aspect of the problem. A practical aspect has to be added. If the defect were only a moral one, it would be difficult to explain why a higher court should have the power to set aside unjust decisions of a lower court in cases in which a just decision is as compatible with the positive law as the unjust decision.

11.4 Construction: Thrust and Parry

In *The Argument from Injustice* I presented two cases with an eye to demonstrating the practical significance of the debate over positivism. The first concerns the application of Radbruch's formula to the Eleventh Ordinance, 25 November 1941, issued pursuant to the Statute on Reich Citizenship of 15 September 1935, which stripped emigrant Jews of German citizenship and property on ground of race.[42] The second case concerns the permissibility of a development of law by judges that is contrary to the literal reading of a statute—the permissibility, in other words, of a *contra legem* decision.[43] Both decisions express a non-positivistic understanding of law. Bulygin argues that the non-positivistic arguments put forward in these cases are no more than 'rhetorical devices' by means of which judges attempt to conceal 'that they [are] really changing the law'.[44] For this reason one has to distinguish 'between what judges say that they do and what they are doing really'.[45] The German Federal Constitutional Court declared that the Eleventh Ordinance was null and void, that is, invalid from the outset, because '[i]ts conflict with justice reached … an intolerable degree'.[46] Bulygin objects that the Eleventh Ordinance was in fact 'a valid norm of

[40] Alexy, 'On the Concept and the Nature of Law' (n. 9, above), 295–296.

[41] Alexy, *The Argument from Injustice* (n. 2, above), 26.

[42] Ibid., 5–7. See also Alexy, 'A Defence of Radbruch's Formula' (n. 15, above), 428–429.

[43] Ibid., 8–10.

[44] Bulygin, 'Alexy between Positivism and Non-Positivism' (n. 5, above), 7.

[45] Ibid.

[46] Decisions of the Federal Constitutional Court, vol. 23 (1968), 98–113, at 106—quoted from Alexy, *The Argument from Injustice* (n. 2, above), 6.

the German law during … Nazism'.[47] What the Court really did was to annul the ordinance '*ex tunc*, i.e. retroactively.'[48] Something similar applies, according to Bulygin, to the *contra legem* case. The German Federal Constitutional Court simply empowers judges 'to create new norms in critical cases'.[49]

Now Bulygin is right in maintaining that one has to distinguish between what judges say they are doing and what they really are doing. But this distinction does not imply that judges are always doing something different from what they say they are doing. In order to show this, one has to analyze their arguments. Bulygin simply substitutes for the non-positivistic construction a positivistic construction. The mere confrontation of the non-positivistic construction with a positivistic counterpart does not suffice, however, as a rejection of the non-positivistic construction. For this purpose it has to be shown that the positivistic construction of the cases is better than the non-positivistic counterpart. To show this is to show, *inter alia*, that positivism is better able to grasp the nature of law than non-positivism. But this is precisely the question at issue. Bulygin's criticism of the two decisions, therefore, presupposes what has to be established.

11.5 The Claim to Correctness: Two Points

In my second reply to Bulygin, I compared the following two sentences:

(10) Faulty legal systems are faulty

and

(11) Continental legal systems are Continental.

The result I arrived at was—how could it have been otherwise?—that both are trivial, and that the triviality is of the same kind in both cases. I then continued as follows:

> Nevertheless, there is a difference concerning the relation of the predicates 'faulty' and 'Continental' to the concept of a legal system. The difference stems from the fact that legal systems necessarily raise a claim to correctness, whereas they do not necessarily raise a claim to be, or not to be, Continental.[50]

Bulygin objects:

> But then the sentence (10) is not as trivial as (11) and consequently it is not an ordinary tautology. This sounds very rare.[51]

---

[47] Bulygin, 'Alexy between Positivism and Non-Positivism' (n. 5, above), 6.

[48] Ibid.

[49] Ibid., 7.

[50] Alexy, 'On the Thesis of a Necessary Connection between Law and Morality: Bulygin's Critique' (n. 1, above), 146.

[51] Bulygin, 'Alexy between Positivism and Non-Positivism' (n. 5, above), 8.

I agree with Bulygin that it would be rather strange to consider (10) as less trivial than (11). But this is not my point. The triviality of (10) and (11) stems from the relation between 'faulty' and 'faulty' on the one hand, and 'Continental' and 'Continental', on the other. The relation between 'faulty' and 'faulty' is the same as the relation between 'Continental' and 'Continental'. The difference, to which I referred—perhaps in a way that suggested misunderstandings—concerns the relation between the concept of a legal system on the one hand and the predicates 'faulty' and 'Continental' on the other. My point is that being Continental is not necessarily connected with the concept of a legal system, whereas there exists a necessary connection where faultiness is concerned. The necessary connection stems, first, from the necessity of the claim to correctness, and, second, from a negation. The claim to correctness is equivalent to the claim not to be faulty or defective, for correctness is non-faultiness or non-defectiveness. This implies that the necessity of the claim to correctness necessarily connects the concept of non-faultiness with law. When I said: 'It is the necessity of the claim to correctness which gives faultiness a special character',[52] I had this in mind.

According to Bulygin my argument is not only 'very rare', but also 'circular':

> The claim to correctness is necessary because normative systems that raise it without fulfilling it are faulty. And this faultiness has a special character because it is based on the necessity of the claim. So the necessity of the claim is at the same time a reason and a consequence of this claim.[53]

Indeed, I claim that the concepts of correctness and faultiness or defectiveness are analytically connected by means of negation. But I do not claim that this equivalence is a relation of substantive reason and substantive consequence, as it would have to be if the reproach of circularity were defensible.

Bulygin's second comment on the claim to correctness concerns the kind of connection that is established by this claim. In *The Argument from Injustice* I make a distinction between a weak and a strong version of the connection thesis:

> In the weak version, the thesis says that a necessary connection exists between law and *some* morality. The strong version has it that a necessary connection exists between law and the *right* or *correct* morality.[54]

Bulygin presents a formalization of these two versions, which employs '*L*' for law, '*M*' for morality, and '*I*' for the relation of inclusion. The weak version says:

$$(1)\ \forall x\big(Lx \rightarrow \exists y\big(My \wedge Ixy\big)\big),$$

---

[52] Alexy, 'On the Thesis of a Necessary Connection between Law and Moralitwy: Bulygin's Critique' (n. 1, above), 146.

[53] Bulygin, Alexy between Positivism and Non-positivism (n. 5, above), 9.

[54] Alexy, *The Argument from Injustice* (n. 2, above), 75.

whereas the strong version maintains:

$$(2)\ \exists y\big(My \wedge \forall x\big(Lx \rightarrow Ixy\big)\big).^{55}$$

Bulygin is entirely right in saying that the weak version causes no problem at all for positivists, for '[n]o positivist would deny that every law includes some moral principles'.[56] His argument is, therefore, directed solely to the strong version. Here he presents two objections:

> There are at least two objections that can be raised against this idea: In the first place it is by no means clear that there is something like **the** correct or true morality and secondly, one must distinguish between the correct morality and the **idea** of a correct morality. Even if there were one correct morality, there certainly are different ideas of it. In order to prove that the strong connection thesis is true one should be able to show that all persons have the same idea of a correct morality. This is extremely improbable. Is it the same what such people as Kant, Hitler, Stalin, Ghandi or Bush have understood by a correct morality?[57]

These two objections show that the concept of morality used in the strong connection thesis, that is, in (2), can be understood in quite different ways. The strongest interpretation would have '*M*' understood as representing, first, the one and only correct morality conceivable, second, as a system of moral norms that provides for a single right answer to each moral question, which, third, can be established in a real discourse. This shall be expressed by 'M_1'. Now it is easy to see that the thesis

$$(3)\ \exists y M_1 y,^{58}$$

is difficult to defend. There are many moral questions for which a single right answer cannot be established in a real discourse.[59] This suffices to preclude the possibility that (2), that is, the strong connection thesis, is to be interpreted by means of M_1. M_1 is too strong an interpretation of *M*.

Bulygin's second objection turns to the concept of the 'idea of a correct morality'.[60] In order to understand what Bulygin means by the 'idea of a correct morality', one has to look at the list of people he presents in connection with such an idea. His list comprises Kant, Hitler, Stalin, Ghandi, and Bush. This suggests that Bulygin simply

---

[55]Bulygin, Alexy between Positivism and Non-positivism' (n. 5, above), 9. I have made slight changes in the notation.

[56]Ibid, 9–10

[57]Ibid.

[58]If one wants to express that there exists exactly one morality one could also use the following formula:

$$(3')\ \exists x(Mx \wedge \forall y(My \rightarrow (x = y))).$$

(3′), however, is not identical with (3), for (3) says not only that there exists exactly one morality but also that this one morality provides for a single right answer to each moral question that can be established in a real discourse.

[59]Alexy, *A Theory of Legal Argumentation* (n. 32, above), 206–208.

[60]Bulygin, 'Alexy between Positivism and Non-positivism' (n. 5, above), 9 (emphasis removed).

wants to say that different people have different moral ideas. Morality (M) in (2) would then stand for a morality that is actually or really held. Such a morality shall be represented by 'M_2'. Now, the thesis

$$(4)\ \exists y M_2 y$$

is without any doubt true. But (2), that is, the strong version of the connection thesis, would be mistaken if one substituted M_2 for M. There exists no actually held morality that is included in all legal systems. For this reason, M_2 is too weak an interpretation of M.

The question is whether an interpretation of M is possible that is neither too strong nor too weak. It is, I think, possible. For there exists a third interpretation of M, 'M_3', that suffices as the basis of a defence of the strong connection thesis. This third interpretation leads to

$$(5)\ \exists y\left(M_3 y\right).$$

M_3 consists of two elements. The first element is a theory of basic human rights that can be established as discursively necessary.[61] This is an elementary form of the one and only correct or right morality, but it does not suffice to provide for a single right answer to each and every moral question. The second element consists of the rules and forms of rational practical argumentation or discourse.[62] The first element is substantive, the second procedural. To be sure, these two elements, even taken together, by no means guarantee a single right answer in each and every case. They define, however, a regulative idea that transcends the convictions of actual persons. It is an idea necessary for all rational beings. This idea defines the ideal dimension of law. Interpreted in this way, the strong connection thesis is true.

11.6 Inclusive Non-positivism

The title of Bulygin's article: 'Alexy between Positivism and Non-positivism' might give rise to the impression that there exists a third position or a third way between positivism and non-positivism. I think that this impression would be mistaken. One can only be a positivist or a non-positivist: *tertium non datur*. The decisive criterion is whether a necessary connection—of whatever kind—is assumed between legal validity or legal correctness on the one hand and moral correctness on the other.[63]

---

[61] Robert Alexy, 'Discourse Theory and Human Rights', in: *Ratio Juris* 9 (1996), 209–235, at 221–233.

[62] Alexy, *A Theory of Legal Argumentation* (n. 32, above), 188–206.

[63] Alexy, 'On the Concept and the Nature of Law' (n. 9, above), 285.

Bulygin maintains that my thesis 'that the positivistic separation thesis is essentially correct from the observer's perspective'[64] 'puts an end to the debate between positivism and non-positivism, at least concerning the concept of law, because positivism is interested not in the application of law, but in its identification'.[65]

This has to be rejected for three reasons. The first is that my statement about the correctness of the positivistic separation thesis from the observer's perspective does not simply say that the separation thesis is correct. It says that it is 'essentially correct'. This allows for restrictions. A highly important restriction stems from the fact that '[e]very legal system lays claim to correctness'.[66] This, indeed, has 'few practical consequences, for actually existing systems of norms regularly lay claim to correctness' however feebly justified the claim may be'.[67] It has, however, significant systematic consequences. Specifically, it excludes, from the concept of law, those systems of norms that do not raise the claim to correctness. In this way, 'it restricts the positivistic separation thesis a good bit even in the observer's perspective'.[68]

The second reason for rejecting Bulygin's thesis on the end of the debate between positivism and non-positivism is that the concept of law is by no means a concern solely of positivism. As just stated, even from the observer's perspective a necessary connection exists; it stems from the claim to correctness. Over and above this, from the participant's perspective normative arguments are necessarily included in the concept of law—as I have argued in the first part of this article, where I discuss the relation between normative arguments and the concept of law. These normative arguments establish a threshold of extreme injustice, as expressed by Radbruch's formula. This concerns—as I have attempted to show in the fourth part of this text, where I discuss the relation between construction and counter-construction—not only the application but also the identification of law. The formula does not say that 'extreme injustice should not be law' but, rather, that 'extreme injustice is not law'.

The third reason for rejecting Bulygin's end-of-the-debate thesis is that the claim to correctness has the effect—as elaborated in the third part of this article, where I discuss the participant's perspective—of transforming moral defectiveness into legal defectiveness. This, too, is an issue concerning the concept of law.

To be sure, the version of non-positivism that I defend contains strong positivistic elements. It by no means substitutes correctness of content for authoritative issuance and social efficacy. On the contrary, both are necessarily included. For this reason, the version of non-positivisms I wish to defend can be characterized as 'inclusive non-positivism'.[69] But this inclusion does not mean that law is reduced to the real dimension as defined by issuance and efficacy. The ideal dimension as

[64] Alexy, *The Argument from Injustice* (n. 2, above), 35.

[65] Bulygin, 'Alexy between Positivism and Non-positivism' (n. 5, above), 10.

[66] Alexy, *The Argument from Injustice* (n. 2, above), 34.

[67] Ibid., 35.

[68] Ibid.

[69] Alexy, 'On the Concept and the Nature of Law' (n. 9, above), 287–288.

defined by correctness is alive, too.[70] Bulygin suggests that this is no more than a 'metaphorical invocation'.[71] My reply is that the exclusion from the concept of law of those systems of norms that do not lay claim to correctness and of individual norms that are extremely unjust shows, along with the transformation of moral defectiveness into legal defectiveness by the claim to correctness, that this is not the case. This provides an answer, too, to Bulygin's final thesis 'that the discrepancy looks very like a verbal one'.[72] The dispute between positivism and non-positivism is not a verbal issue. On the contrary, it reaches to the essence of law.

[70] Alexy, 'The Dual Nature of Law' (n. 13, above), 173–174.

[71] Bulygin, 'Alexy between Positivism and Non-positivism' (n. 5, above), 11.

[72] Ibid.

Chapter 12
The Scientific Model of Jurisprudence

Dan Priel

Shortly after John Austin published *The Province of Jurisprudence Determined* to an indifferent world John Stuart Mill came to his former teacher's assistance and published a very congratulatory review. In the course of that review Mill offered a pithy summary of Austin's project:

> Jurisprudence … does not take any direct cognizance of the goodness or badness of laws, nor undertakes to weigh the motives which lead to their establishment: it assumes their existence as a fact, and treats of their nature and properties, as a naturalist treats of any natural phenomenon. It furnishes an analytical exposition, not indeed of any particular system of existing laws, but of what is common to all or most systems of law.
>
> …
>
> [I]f we are to strip off from the arrangement and technical language of each system of law, whatever is purely accidental, and (as it may be termed) historical, having a reference solely to the peculiar history of the institutions of the particular people: if we were to take the remainder, and regularize and correct it according to its own general conception and spirit; we should bring the nomenclature and arrangement of all systems of law existing in any civilized society, to something very nearly identical. (Mill 1984a: 55–56)[1]

Though neglected during his lifetime, Austin's work has gained in popularity after his death, so much so that when a century later H.L.A. Hart sought to revive interest in analytic jurisprudence it was to Austin's work that he turned as a basis for developing his own ideas. Though he subjected Austin's work to severe (and some say unfair) criticism, he seems to have adopted the Austinian approach to the nature

---

[1]In a review of Austin's posthumously published *Lectures on Jurisprudence*, published some 30 years later, Mill (1984b, p. 173) described another characteristic of Austin's project: though he started with Roman law, his aims were to describe the general features of law. And "[b]y stripping off what belongs to the accidental or historical peculiarities of the given system [i.e., Roman law], the elements which are universal will be more surely and completely arrived at…." This is remarkably similar to the conception of jurisprudence found in Raz (2009a, pp. 104–105).

D. Priel (✉)
Osgoode Hall Law School, York University, 4700 Keele Street, M3J 1P3 Toronto, ON, Canada
e-mail: dpriel@osgoode.yorku.ca

J. Ferrer Beltrán et al. (eds.), *Neutrality and Theory of Law*,
Law and Philosophy Library 106, DOI 10.1007/978-94-007-6067-7_12,

of the jurisprudential enterprise. And it is probably due to Hart's great influence that Austin's approach has remained dominant in (Anglophone) jurisprudential circles to this day. Indeed, what is most remarkable about the passages just quoted is how well they describe not just Austin's approach to jurisprudence, but what many people *today* take jurisprudence to be about.

Thus, Hart (1994 p. 239) characterized his effort in *The Concept of Law* as "general and descriptive"; Marmor (2006) defended the view that legal positivism is "descriptive and morally neutral"; Gardner (2001, p. 202) has argued that positivism is "normatively inert," and Green (2008, p. 1036) has criticized Fuller for failing to understand that Hart's project was not concerned with "giving advice" but rather with "trying to understand the nature of law." Other defenses of this view are abundant (e.g., Coleman 2007, pp. 597–608; Kramer 1999, p. 129), and less directly the view can also be discerned in familiar contemporary ideas such as the distinction between the question "what is law (in general)?" and "what is the law (in a particular place)?," or in the claim that identification of the conditions of legal validity constitutes the most fundamental (Marmor 2007) or even the only proper (Wolheim 1954, pp. 138–139) question of jurisprudence. It is probably best captured in the popular understanding of "general" jurisprudence as concerned with the "concept," "essence," or "nature" of law.

I will call this view the Scientific Model of Jurisprudence (SMJ). I chose this name because the resemblance between jurisprudence understood in this way and a certain kind of (eighteenth century) science is quite remarkable, although its origins are probably much earlier than that.[2] To get an idea of what I have in mind consider the following description of how Carl Linnaeus worked to identify species:

> The flowers and fruits … of a single species are to be described in detail; then from this description are to be removed all features found on comparison to vary from species to species; the result statement of features common to all species is the natural character of the genus. This was … Linnaeus's original procedure, and doubtless always his aim though not always his achievement…. (Stearn 1957: 37).

Just like the eighteenth century botanical taxonomist, the legal philosopher on this model seeks to identify the central features of law and in this way to distinguish it from other phenomena. Though the similarly between the two enterprises is considerable, I must add a qualification or else the term SMJ and the analogy with natural science are prone to mislead: most contemporary legal philosophers (including most contemporary legal positivists) have adopted an anti-naturalistic or anti-positivist (in the sense this term is used in the philosophy of science) (Priel 2012, pp. 301–307), so it may seem odd to suggest that legal philosophy is modeled after the sciences. To understand my claim, then, it would help to distinguish, as philosophers of science often do, between scientific aims, theories and methodologies (Laudan 1984: Chap. 3). In devising jurisprudential theories proponents of SMJ often reject the *methods* of the natural sciences while endorsing (certain) of their *aims*.

[2] "[T]he object of scientific knowledge [*epistemē*] is of necessity. Therefore it is eternal; for things that are of necessity in the unqualified sense are all eternal…." Aristotle (2009, p. 104).

The analogy with science helps us understand the appeal of SMJ: it looks like an innocuous activity with a respectable pedigree. It is uncontroversial that law is a phenomenon that exists in the world in some form, and it is also uncontroversial that it exists in different forms: there is criminal law and civil law; there is Roman law and Italian law; there is judge-made law and statutory law. Presumably there is something that unites all these together, and it is plausible to want to have an account of what that is. Nonetheless, in what follows I will argue that the philosophical project based on these plausible starting points is misguided. My strategy will be to spell out the assumptions underlying it and then argue that they are inconsistent.

12.1 What Is SMJ?

SMJ rests on four assumptions.

1. *The assumption of evaluative neutrality*. The aim of jurisprudential theory is to provide an account of law that is morally neutral about the subject of her inquiry. The legal philosopher adopting SMJ may be a philosophical anarchist thinking that law can never be justified, or, less radically, that the laws of her country are too complex, rigid, unjust, inefficient (or simple, flexible, just, and efficient), but none of this is relevant to the question of the nature of law, which is concerned with what features something has to have in order to be law.
2. *The assumption that legal philosophy is interested in the "deep" structure of law*. In explaining the nature of law legal philosophers distinguish their work from both linguistics and sociology. On the one hand "the philosopher is not explaining how the word 'law' is used," (Hart 1994, p. 213; to the same effect: Gardner 2004, pp. 168, 180; Raz 2009b, pp. 29, 48); on the other, she tries to avoid those accounts that tell us why or how the law developed in a particular time and place. Put differently, proponents of SMJ try to avoid both what might be called "superficial" accounts (as found in dictionary definitions) and parochial or contingent accounts. They are interested in what is necessarily true of law (Raz 2009a, pp. 104–105; Dickson 2001, p. 17; Moore 2000, pp. 306–308). This implies that the legal philosopher should focus on identifying the conceptual connections that underpin the law: the connections that exist (if they exist) between law, obligation, authority, guidance, social order, and so on. In this the legal philosopher is like the botanist who tries to classify what a fish is (or, if you wish, the nature of fish-hood) not according to superficial features like shape or habitat, but on the basis of less visible, "deep" features based such as shared ancestors or genetic similarity. Probably for this reason much of the work of the leading proponents of SMJ is devoid of all historical or cultural context.
3. *The assumption that different accounts are competing*. Hart spoke of "the" concept of law, and much contemporary writing says that the primary question of legal philosophy is the identification of "the" nature of law. And it is because of this belief that many of the debates among legal philosophers—between legal positivists and natural lawyers, between legal positivists and Dworkinians,

among different legal positivists of different stripes—only make sense if understood as competing accounts. To be sure, in recent years there have been several attempts to show that at least some of the competing views are reconcilable as they present different aspects of a complex phenomenon. But even these explanations (which are of course not accepted by everyone) do so from a standpoint of a theorist trying to identify the true nature of law, one that it is a major task of legal philosophers to describe in a manner consistent with the other assumptions discussed here.

4. *The assumption of agreement on object of inquiry*. According to this assumption in order for SMJ to be even possible we must have agreement over what *counts* as a sample of the object that we examine. If we are trying to discover what gold is, we must have some samples that are uncontroversially samples made of the substance we call (in English) "gold." There is no real disagreement about what gold is if it turns out that what one group of scientists calls "gold" refers to a sample the metal with atomic number 79 (Au) and what another calls "gold" is a sample of iron pyrite ("fool's gold," FeS_2). The same must be true of law.[3] This assumption is not frequently mentioned in jurisprudential debates, but only because it seems too obvious to state.

*

I hope that with the assumptions spelled out it is easier to see why I called this approach the Scientific Model. While conceptual legal theorists examine linguistic usage and intuitions as part of "conceptual analysis" of law—*methods* that no doubt are not central to modern science—the *aims* of jurisprudence quite closely resemble those of a scientist trying to discover, say, what water is. Such a scientist stands outside the examined phenomenon and tries to provide a *description* of its essential features while remaining neutral about whether it is a good thing or not. And just like what water is not determined by its superficial features (liquidity at room temperature, transparency etc.) but by its "deep" molecular structure, legal philosophers work on the assumption that the answer to the question "What is law?" is to be determined by looking at law's deep structure.[4] In the rest of the essay I will argue that, despite its superficial plausibility, SMJ is an indefensible research program.

---

[3]Sometimes a similarly sounding argument is used to argue for a certain substantive conclusion: the fact that two parties are engaged in what seems like a real argument shows that they are arguing about something real. In other words, genuine disagreement implies that skepticism about the domain is misguided. This has been a familiar argument made first by Dworkin, and then, ironically, leveled at Dworkin by his critics (Marmor 2001, p. 6). But this argument is mistaken. The point in the text is that for a disagreement to be genuine it has to be over the same thing; this does not imply that whenever an argument exists it follows that the disputants are talking about the same thing. Indeed, it is my point that proponents of SMJ fail to see that disagreements among legal philosophers may be the result of them talking about different things.

[4]Once again, things did not change much since Austin's day. Consider a similar analogy in another early review of Austin's work (Anonymous 1832, p. 107): "If we may be pardoned a simile, we would say that jurisprudence is to legislation what the science of chemistry is to the science of medicine; the one deals with necessary properties, the other with their application to a proposed end."

12.2 Assessing SMJ

12.2.1 The Challenges to SMJ

My strategy against SMJ can be quickly stated: *in the context of law* the four assumptions specified above contradict each other. Why should we think that? We surely do not think that they are inconsistent in the case of the natural sciences, so what makes law different? The gist of the argument is this: in order to explicate the nature of law the theorist must have an agreed object of inquiry, as required by the assumption of agreement on object of inquiry. The problem is how to determine what falls within this object of inquiry. As I see it a proponent of SMJ has to take one of three options: (a) to adopt the accepted usages of "law" by members of society, and then analyze the people's concept of law; (b) to attempt to provide an account of the origins of people's attitudes about law; or (c) to offer her own interpretation of those attitudes. A theorist adopting the first approach can only provide superficial definitions thus failing the assumption that the theorist is after the deep structure of law; if she adopts the second, she can provide deep analyses, but ones that are (by currently accepted standards) of little philosophical significance, and indefensible (even if true) because they lack adequate confirmation; and if the theorist adopts the third approach, she will have to adopt a particular understanding of the practice, which will require taking a stand on evaluative questions, thus violating the assumption of evaluative neutrality. In what follows I explore this trilemma more closely.

In order to provide an account of law there has to exist an agreement on what it is that it is to be explained. Without it we cannot know that when two theorists claim to disagree over the nature of law, and not from the fact that they are talking about different things. The problem is, however, that things don't usually come to the world clearly marked as what they are. Indeed, part of the motivation for SMJ seems to be the hope that jurisprudence could aid in the task of identifying law. But if we do not know in advance what it is that we are explaining, it may be that in deciding what counts as the object to be explained different theorists will already implicitly rely on different theoretical conceptions which will result in different views on what belongs to the object to be explained. This will result in seemingly competing accounts, each true on its own terms but false on others. Each will be believed by its proponents to be a decisive argument against competing accounts, but could be dismissed as mistaken by proponents of other accounts. And at their core they will be circular, because they will presuppose the conception of law they describe (Priel 2010).

To avoid this problem legal theorists must agree on a neutral way of identifying their object of inquiry thus guaranteeing that whatever disagreements remain are not based on different objects of inquiry. Natural scientists avoid this problem by developing an agreed method for determining what counts as "the same thing." If trying to provide an account of the nature of an object with physical existence—be it gold or a human being—this can be by fixing the object of inquiry by ostention.

Once certain samples have been agreed on, it is then possible to further develop a method for identifying classifying objects into categories. (This is not to deny that there may be some controversial marginal cases, but disagreements among scientists are usually not the result of disagreement over what belongs to the object to be explained.) This solution, however, is not available to legal philosophers: are the rules used by Nazi Germany belong to our object of inquiry or not? Or to take an issue that troubled many legal philosophers in the last two decades: are moral norms mentioned in legal sources part of the law? Legal philosophers tend to think this is a matter for them to decide according to theoretical arguments, but this is getting matters the wrong way around: what needs first to be established is whether these are cases of law which are part of the object to be explained. Any "descriptive" account that takes the object of inquiry as it is and seeks to explain it has to come afterwards.

Oddly, given the centrality of SMJ to contemporary jurisprudence, there is very little discussion on the matter. The implicit assumption in most jurisprudential work is that legal philosophers can rely on their knowledge as members of society and normal language users for a stock of examples of things that count as law, and that these are enough for identifying what law is in an uncontroversial manner *prior to theorizing*. Philosophers' appeal to intuitions at this stage may be thought a primitive method for gathering the relevant information for the theorist to develop his theories. Hart (1994, p. 3) was explicit on this point when he said that jurisprudential inquiry should begin with the attitudes of "educated people" about law. Counting himself among those Hart could then simply rely on his intuitive discriminations between law and non-law as the data on which to theorize.

There is an obvious problem with this approach: it assumes that all educated people have fairly similar attitudes on what counts as law, but this assumption may not be true. Indeed, as I will suggest below, there are good reasons for thinking that it is false. Further, even if it is true that the attitudes of educated people on what counts as law are similar, it is never explained why it is only their attitudes we should consider in fixing the object of inquiry, and not also those of, say, criminals who come in contact with the legal system, or, for that matter, those of uneducated people.

A more reliable method for discovering people's attitudes *for the sake of fixing the object of inquiry* would be to conduct surveys or obtain information on what people think belongs in the domain of law in some similar way. This will help guarantee that all theorists are offering competing accounts of the same thing and that the theoretical accounts offered by different theorists are not different because they describe different objects of inquiry. By themselves, however, such surveys would be of no philosophical significance. These surveys would, at best, discover some patterns of views, even perhaps a predominant view among people. Though such surveys might at first be resisted as the exact opposite of philosophical inquiry, such surveys might be thought a boon for the legal philosopher, because they would presumably not tell us much about what I called the deep structure of law. For a proponent of SMJ it is at this point that the theorist should come in and seek to identify the "folk theory" underlying people's attitudes as to what counts as law.[5]

Such an account looks at first as though it would fit the aim Raz and others have identified for jurisprudence: that of "helping people understand themselves" (Raz 1995, p. 237; Green 1996, p. 1717). Unfortunately, legal philosophers have not engaged in this kind of empirical inquiry for the sake of determining in a non-tendentious fashion what their object of inquiry is; and they do not seem particularly interested in the work of psychologists who have engaged in exactly such work (e.g., Tyler 1990).

Were philosophers to look into such work, all kinds of problems might emerge. For example, it is assumed by proponents of SMJ that there is a unique account of the nature of law, but it is not clear what a theorist would do if it turns out that people's attitudes turn out to be more or less evenly split between two or more views, or if it turns out that people's attitudes in one country are radically different from the attitudes of those people in another. In fact, we need not have such surveys to know that if surveys were to be conducted they would reveal different views. Among members of society some will be "legal positivists" believing that even immoral enactments are laws; there will also be some "natural lawyers" who will reject this view. (We *know* that this is so because the legal theorists themselves are members of society and so we know that we will find support for both these positions and presumably for others as well.) Proponents of SMJ treat this as a debate on the best way to understand the object of inquiry, but they have no basis for treating it this way when the alternative—that it reflects different attitudes as to what people take the object of inquiry to be—is also possible. To assume the former is not just to bias the argument in favor of the desired conclusion, it is to also to implicitly give SMJ a larger scope for inquiry than it should: for if it turns out that the question is one on which it is impossible to identify any clear view among members of society, this does not call for "conceptual" or "descriptive" debate. At best, such a result would suggest that the concept of law is indeterminate on the matter. Any attempt to make matters more determinate by means of conceptual analysis (as opposed to a normative argument) will not illuminate the object of inquiry, but rather obscure it.

---

[5] I think this is the case even in the case of natural kinds: even in those cases it is a societal "decision" to have a certain standard that may not be fully known to humans at the time they fix the reference and "baptize" it. We could have lived with a concept that covered every yellowish metal, instead of a concept that referred only to the metal with atomic number 79 and leaves it to scientists to tell us what its nature is.

The same is true of Moore's (2000) suggestion that law is a "functional" kind: whether he is right or not is ultimately a matter that cannot be determined by philosophical reflection, but rather by examining how the law is understood by the people engaging in it. This means that Moore can offer an account of *a* certain functional kind that has the same attributes Moore gave to what he calls "law." Such an account would not be in any way undermined by the fact that most people's concept of law does not match Moore's account. On the other hand, this means that Moore's account has no descriptive significance (although it may still have prescriptively valuable).

The typical way to deal with such differences about concepts in attitudes in time and place or between different individuals is the way sociologists, historians (and more recently, economists) go about it. They try to identify the factors that explain the divergence in attitudes, not to adjudicate between them as conceptually correct or incorrect. Such work is often of great interest and value for "helping people understand themselves," but it is not what counts as "philosophy," at least not as the term is currently understood and as currently practiced by proponents of SMJ.

How can the legal theorist avoid this predicament and provide a general account of the "nature" of law despite all the fundamental differences in attitudes about it? One way is to strip the account of all controversies and try and identify something that everyone could accept, in spite of, or before, all the differences. If properly done, such a definition may be able to provide us with an account that does not violate the assumption of agreement over object of inquiry, for it would be based on people's attitudes that would set the boundaries of the object of inquiry. But the cost of maintaining the assumption of agreement on object of inquiry and (perhaps) also the assumption of evaluative neutrality would be an account that does not satisfy the assumption that the aim of the inquiry is revealing the deep structure of law. The kind of account that most resembles this solution to the problem is what we find in dictionaries.

The way to get around this problem is for the theorist to take people's attitudes as to what counts as law and then provide an account that would satisfy the assumption of deep analysis. But I will argue there is no way of doing this without violating the assumption of evaluative neutrality. There are at least two reasons why. First, in order to explain the "nature" of law in this way the theorist will have to account for many different attitudes among members of society about the nature of law. The theorist will have to decide among those different views, for example by considering some to be more central or representative than those of others. If in doing this the theorist bases her judgment on a certain implicit view of what law is, then her account is bound to be fallacious for assuming the conclusion it reaches. To avoid this, the theorist will have to base her account not on a view of what law is, but on some normative judgments of the sort of goals law is to achieve, its role in society, its relationship with other institutions and so on. But these are, of course, evaluative judgments, and will thus result in violation of the assumption of evaluative neutrality.

Second, even if there are no differences among members of society about the nature of law, in order for the theorist to turn the "raw materials" of people's attitudes into a theory, he will have to resort to evaluative judgments. The move from data to theory is the stage at which the theorist provides "a map exhibiting clearly the relationships dimly felt to exist between the law they know and other things" (Hart 1994, p. 14). There are, however, many possible ways of turning the data, even after it has been purged off contingencies, into theory. Consider the following example: Hart's account of the nature of law, the union of primary and secondary rules, ignored the distinction between criminal law and tort law and more generally between criminal law and civil law, distinctions that lawyers (and often non-lawyers) treat as fundamental. Why did he do that? This question cannot be answered, of course, by saying that since both tort law and criminal law contain rules directed at the public, they are both made up of primary rules and they belong together. Not only is this statement not entirely accurate (Dan-Cohen 1984), it begs the question why it is that the identity of the rule-subjects should be the basis for distinguishing between types of rules. And then there are rules that do not sit comfortably in either category. Are what Calabresi and Melamed (1972) called "liability rules," the likes of which are easily found in many legal systems, primary or secondary rules?

Hart presumably thought that there is something illuminating in his distinction between primary and secondary rules, but not (for a general account of law) between criminal law and tort law, which is why his key to the science of jurisprudence highlighted the former but ignored the latter. But this is exactly what other theorists did when they eliminated the distinction Hart considered important between primary and secondary rules. They thought that we will gain further illumination by showing that secondary rules can reduced to primary rules. Still others thought that all rules can be illuminated by explaining them in terms of behavior, exactly because they removed from the explanation the obscure and unverifiable internal workings of the human mind. Hart, by contrast, thought such approaches were mistaken because in their search for "reduction" they resulted in "distortion" (Hart 1994, pp. 38–42, 89–91). Thus, the problem the theorist faces is how to distinguish between those cases in which reduction is illuminating and those in which it is distorting at exactly the stage of inquiry in which there are no more lay attitudes on which to rely.

All this does not show that Hart's account was mistaken. But it does show that just like those alternative accounts he criticized, his account contained a degree of reduction, unification, analysis and synthesis of what he took to be his object of inquiry. It is just that what he thought was illuminating was different from what, say, Bentham or Kelsen did. There is an element of choice here (as Hart essentially admits at in Hart 1994, p. 213), and so the question is how to decide between competing accounts. We might say "to each his own," and leave it at that, but this would imply that Hart's criticisms of other theories (criticisms nowadays widely thought to be correct) are mistaken for presupposing a right answer where there is none. At most we could say that at this point there is nothing more than intuition to tell us which account is correct.

In their different ways, however, both suggestions lead to the conclusion that there is little point in jurisprudential debate. We have seen before one use for intuitions. In that use intuitions were seen as an means for fixing the object of inquiry by means of introspection instead of surveys. By contrast, in the present context intuitions are used to decide between competing *theories*. The result would be (or rather, the result has been) that each theorist would develop the account that she finds intuitively illuminating, but there would be no way, *even in principle*, of telling who is right. Thus, this approach leads to violating the assumption that the theories are competing.

To avoid this outcome, legal philosophers will have to examine what it is that is behind their intuitions. I suppose some of those intuitions are going to be about what counts as a good explanation in general. But in part what counts as a good explanation will depend on what is being explained as well as certain evaluative judgments about what is significant about it. For example, the distinction between criminal law and civil law reflects attitudes on the right relation between different individuals and the relationship between individuals and state. (Libertarians, for example, may wish to expand the domain of private law "restorative justice" at the expense of the retributive justice of public criminal law: Barnett 1977.) Similarly, Hart's statement that contracts are "a relatively minor legal institution" (Hart 1968, p. 10), a statement which perhaps explains why contracts do not figure prominently in his theory of law, would be challenged by others who see contracts as the paradigm of individual autonomy and the only theoretical foundation for societal coercion. Deciding to remove these elements from one's account of the nature of law thus cannot be neutral. What we see, then, that once the intuitions on what to include and what to exclude from the account are brought to light, they violate the assumption of evaluative neutrality.

If my argument is correct, it should be by now clear that SMJ is indefensible. Let me summarize my reasons for thinking that: I began by articulating the sort of requirements necessary for providing a uniquely *philosophical* account of the *nature* of law in general, as distinct from sociological or historical accounts of the development of law in a particular place. I proposed three ways of articulating this idea, but all three ended in failure. The first interpretation of SMJ maintained the requirement of evaluative neutrality but could only lead to something like a dictionary definition, the kind of account that legal philosophers themselves have said they are not pursuing. The second interpretation avoided the problem of superficiality but only at the expense of providing an account that was historical or sociological (and thus necessarily particular) and so clearly different from what one finds in the leading examples of SMJ. The third interpretation avoided both problems, but it did so by offering an interpretation of legal practice which violated the assumption of evaluative neutrality.

12.2.2 Possible Objections

As something like the third interpretation is what I think legal philosophers have in mind as what they are doing, it should not come as a surprise that they have focused their efforts on ways of averting its problematic conclusions. Here I can only consider the two (related) ways that have found most support among defenders of SMJ.

12.2.3 Judgments of Importance

Following Raz's lead (1995, pp. 209, 235) many proponents of this view have conceded that any attempt at capturing the nature of law must be based on evaluative considerations of importance (Coleman 2001, pp. 177–178; Kramer 2004, pp. 158,

236; Green 1987, p. 15; Waluchow 1994, pp. 19–29; Dickson 2001; Hart 1987, p. 36; Marmor 2001, p. 156). We are told, however, that these are different from moral evaluations. On this view the assumption of evaluative neutrality is somewhat weakened: a proponent of SMJ (just like any scientist) must rely on certain values, but those are not moral values, only judgments of importance.

Though popular, this position is usually asserted rather than defended. Few legal theorists have considered seriously the way in which judgments of importance are to figure in their account and whether such judgments can be separated from other evaluative judgments. It is often assumed that the only role evaluative judgments play is in narrowing down the number of truths the theorist has found out. Even on these grounds this answer is unsatisfactory. Judgments of importance are subjective, and as such incapable of generating conclusions that can be the basis of rational disagreement. If this is the case, it would suggest that much of the disagreement among legal philosophers cannot be resolved, rendering most jurisprudential debates among proponents of SMJ pointless (Priel 2010).

We might not have been troubled by this fact had competing accounts been simply considered different and complimentary ways of accounting for the same phenomenon. But this is not what jurisprudential debates look like: they are usually presented as challenges to competing views. In other words, to present all competing account as the result of different judgments of importance would solve one problem but will do so at the cost of casting doubt on the very idea of SMJ. We would have to conclude that all legal theories are merely possible interpretations of the object of inquiry. Apart, perhaps, from errors of contradiction, any account would be immune from criticism as it would be considered illuminating in the eyes of its proponents.

This means that in order to make current debates intelligible there must be some way of assessing judgments of importance. But what is it that makes something important about law? Answering this question is particularly difficult for those proponents of SMJ who deny that law has any general purpose or function (e.g., Hart 1994, p. 243; Raz 2009b, pp. 374–375). Even then, however, it is possible to say that given certain empirical observations about what laws are used for (proscribe and prescribe behavior, create obligations and powers, express and communicate on moral matters, affect the social meanings of certain activities) it is plausible that at least some of the things that are important about law have to do with evaluative concepts like autonomy, responsibility, liberty, authority, community, and agency. Making judgments of importance would inevitably embroil the theorist with questions about these concepts. (I ignore here the fact that it may be that those values may change from time to time and place to place, even though this is, obviously, an additional serious problem for SMJ.)

At first, this may sound like good news for the proponent of SMJ. If there is an objective account of values, then judgments of importance based upon them will presumably be objective as well, and if this is true we can thus avoid the challenge that judgments of importance cannot be the basis for debate. But even if some true account of objective values exists, what those happen to be is a matter of great controversy and would effectively require abandoning the assumption of evaluative neutrality. Hence, resorting to the objectivity of values as a way of solving conflicts about judgments as to what is important about law is unlikely to prove a very promising strategy. Judgments of importance then are either subjective, in which case the assumption that the debates are conflicting will have to be dropped; or they are objective, in which case in all likelihood they depend on certain value judgments, which require rejecting the assumption of evaluative neutrality.[6]

12.2.4 Description of an Evaluation

A second possible way of trying to avoid the conclusions of the last section is the suggestion that it is possible to describe an evaluative stance without endorsing it. It is epitomized in the words of Hart (1994, p. 244) that "description remains a description even when what it describes is an evaluation," and it has been supported by many proponents of SMJ.

This claim is usually made independently of the argument just discussed about judgments of importance, but I think it is better understood as part of a single argument. (I will address it in this way, but my challenge to it general and as such applies to it whether made as part of another argument, or independently.) When taken together, this idea seems to provide a way out of the dilemma posed in the end of the last subsection[7]: in this way we may base our account of objective values of importance *seemingly without violating the assumption of evaluative neutrality* as the theorist would not need to make judgments of importance, only describe them.

That one may describe an evaluative position without endorsing it is by no means an uncontroversial view (McDowell 1998), but I will ignore this point here. The main difficulty with it is that even if true it does not help the proponent of SMJ, for judgments of value are made here not at the stage of the gathering of data; they are made at the stage of turning the data into theory. At this stage the theorist goes beyond existing attitudes, trying to articulate what she considers underlies them. For Hart, for example, this was guidance of conduct; for Dworkin, by contrast, it is encouraging political participation and the inculcation of a certain right-based view among citizens towards each other (Priel forthcoming).Both thought this is something that can be *found* in the practice, but for both this required an elaboration of

[6]Whether there is a way around this problem is discussed in the next subsection, but even if this answer is successful, the help it provides is limited. The role assigned to judgments of importance in this view is that of distinguishing important or interesting truths from unimportant and uninteresting ones. Recall, however, that one of the challenges to SMJ as currently practiced is that evaluative judgments are required for the sake of specifying what belongs in the object of inquiry. Whatever one may think of the claim that non-moral judgments of importance are sufficient for narrowing down the results of our inquiry, they are incapable of specifying the object of inquiry.

[7]Possibly another way out is Platonism about values. But this position is not only implausible, it would also require proponents of SMJ to add to their theory such heavy metaphysical baggage that the original appeal SMJ may have had would be completely lost.

the relation between individuals and the state, and relations among individuals. These were based on certain (different) judgments about personhood and morality. In Hart's case, for example, the Humean conception of morality he endorsed was not merely a description of prevailing attitudes, it was exactly in line with the relatively skeptical views he held about moral value, which are of course very different from Dworkin's, and are no doubt very different from those of other people. In relying on them for the sake of his theory Hart was not merely describing the evaluations of others, he was making his own evaluative judgments. And had Hart succeeded in accurately describing certain values, those would have been the values of a particular time and place, and the account of the nature of law dependent upon them correspondingly relative.

12.3 Does the Argument Prove Too Much?

If all this is true, does it not show that no description of any social practice or institution is possible? For what I said of law is arguably true of other social practices as well. And is it not absurd to suggest that we cannot give a descriptive account of notions like money, marriage, or property?

If that were the case, it would suggest that somewhere along the way something has gone wrong with the argument. But the conclusion is premature. It is possible, of course, to describe social practices; my challenge to SMJ is based on the way it is purported to be done. There are at least four different ways in which social practices may be described. The first is for the theorist to provide her own *definition*. As Humpty Dumpty has told us one may give words any meaning one wishes; but for the sake of fruitful conversation one would better define one's words in a manner that bears some similarity to the way others use the term. It is clear, however, that here—so long as the theorist is clear about her definitions—it is of little concern if her definitions depart from prevalent views. In any case, such definitions are only provided for the sake of further inquiry, not as an end in themselves. This, then, is not what proponents of SMJ are after.

A second way of describing social practices, already mentioned, is by providing the kind of descriptions found in dictionaries: here, the aim is to capture some superficial prevalent linguistic usage. Dictionary definitions are not always free from evaluative judgments, but they try to avoid them exactly by providing the kind of superficial descriptions that proponents of SMJ have insisted they are *not* concerned to provide.

A third and more interesting way of describing social practices is by analyzing the different attitudes of individuals as found in society. Such analyses usually aim to show the ways in which such attitudes differ according to factors like age, gender, wealth, education, ethnicity, nationality, and so on, and they do so for the sake of showing some kind of causal connection, or at least correlation, between some such factors and the resulting practice. Such an account might reveal, for example, that in a certain state the most people are "legal positivists" in thinking that legality is not determined by morality whereas in another the majority thinks differently; it will then try to trace this difference to, for example, the different political histories of the two states. Needless to say, this is quite different from the "general and descriptive" approach of Hart and other proponents of SMJ.

Finally, there is the *interpretive* approach which seeks to provide an interpretation of a practice in light of certain values that are thought to underlie it. There are different ways of specifying this approach, but on any formulation this approach depends quite explicitly on making certain evaluative judgments about the practice (Taylor 1985; Geertz 1973). The theorist on this view must take the "data" and interpret them to show what he thinks are the values the practice best serves. In the context of law, such interpretations will inevitably depend on moral values. It is hardly worth noting here that in the area of jurisprudence the best known proponent of this approach in recent decades, Ronald Dworkin, has also been a longstanding opponent of SMJ.[8]

All these are viable methods for explaining social practices in general and law in particular, and it is not difficult to name successful examples of each. To give just one example of an attempt to describe a social institution, Zelizer's (1994) work on the social meaning of money, which blends elements of the third and fourth approaches, may well contribute to our self-understanding, but it is very different from the work of analytic legal philosophers. In fact, outside jurisprudence it is very difficult to find other social practices subject to anything resembling SMJ.

12.4 Concluding Remarks

There is an interesting historical question as to why jurisprudence has taken this turn towards SMJ. In part the answer has to do with the dominance of legal positivism among legal philosophers. Though I did not discuss this matter here, there is no doubt that most proponents of SMJ are legal positivists, but when looking at figures like Hobbes or Bentham, thinkers who in various ways are harbingers of contemporary legal positivism, it is clear that their legal positivism had nothing to do with SMJ. Here, I suspect an important part of the story has to do with the immense influence Hart has had on Anglo-American jurisprudence. Hart felt more secure in the Austinian version of legal positivism than in Bentham's more openly political version, because unlike Bentham he was unsure about the foundations of morality and of his ability to engage in the kind of Benthamite project in which law is only part

[8]This essay is not concerned with defending Dworkin's views, so I will not consider at length the question whether his specific views avoid the criticism of SMJ. I will only note that I think his reliance on the "pre-interpretive stage" (Dworkin 1986, pp. 64–66), which many positivists have thought to be a fatal concession to their theory, does not implicate Dworkin's theory with SMJ. For his approach it is enough that the pre-interpretive stage captures the superficial understandings of law, which the theorist then interprets.

of a grander scheme. Making legal philosophy "descriptive" by separating it from political philosophy may have seemed to him, consciously or unconsciously, like an attractive way of doing philosophy without having to tackle these broader concerns. Hart's lead was then followed by others, even those who did not share his metaethical doubts.

Apart from Hart it may be that the other main theorist to entrench SMJ may have been, ironically, its leading contemporary detractor. As part of his critique of legal positivism Dworkin has made the claim, implicitly at first and explicitly in more recent writings, that there is no clear distinction between describing individual legal propositions and making a normative claim as to their correctness. This was part of a very thoroughgoing and not always carefully articulated rejection of what Dworkin called Archimedeanism (Dworkin 1996). In their eagerness to reject this position, legal positivists may have reacted by insisting on the significance of SMJ as the foundation of jurisprudential inquiry. If this is so, this may have been an overreaction, which missed a more nuanced position, namely that any philosophically significant account of law would depend on making some moral and political judgments as to the place of law in society and alongside other regulatory institutions while rejecting Dworkin's stronger claims about individual propositions of law.

References

Anonymous. 1832. Review of John Austin, the province of jurisprudence determined. *The Jurist* 3: 105–122.

Aristotle. 2009. *Nicomachean ethics*. Trans. W.D. Ross ed. Lesley Brown. Oxford/New York: Oxford University Press.

Barnett, R.E. 1977. Restitution: A new paradigm of criminal justice. *Ethics* 87: 279–301.

Calabresi, G., and A.D. Melamed. 1972. Property rules, liability rules, and inalienability: One view of the cathedral. *Harvard Law Review* 85: 1089–1128.

Coleman, J.L. 2001. *The practice of principle: In defence of a pragmatist approach to legal theory*. Oxford: Oxford University Press.

Coleman, J.L. 2007. Beyond the separability thesis: Moral semantics and the methodology of jurisprudence. *Oxford Journal of Legal Studies* 27: 581–608.

Dan-Cohen, M. 1984. Decision rules and conduct rules: On acoustic separation in criminal law. *Harvard Law Review* 97: 625–677.

Dickson, J. 2001. *Evaluation and legal theory*. Oxford: Hart Publishing.

Dworkin, R. 1986. *Law's empire*. Cambridge: Harvard University Press.

Dworkin, R. 1996. Objectivity and truth: You'd better believe it. *Philosophy and Public Affairs* 25: 87–139.

Gardner, J. 2001. Legal positivism: 5½ myths. *American Journal of Jurisprudence* 46: 199–225.

Gardner, J. 2004. The legality of law. *Ratio Juris* 17: 168–181.

Geertz, C. 1973. *The interpretation of cultures: Selected essays*. New York: Basic Books.

Green, L. 1987. The political content of legal theory. *Philosophy of the Social Science* 17: 1–17.

Green, L. 1996. The concept of law revisited. *Mich Law Rev* 94: 1687–1717.

Green, L. 2008. Positivism and the inseparability of law and morals. *New York University Law Review* 83: 1035–1058.

Hart, H.L.A. 1968. *Punishment and responsibility: Essays in the philosophy of law*. Oxford: Clarendon.

Hart, H.L.A. 1987. Comment. In *Issues in contemporary legal philosophy: The influence of H.L.A. Hart*, ed. R. Gavison, 35–39. Oxford: Clarendon.
Hart, H.L.A. 1994. *The concept of law*, 2nd ed. Oxford: Clarendon.
Kramer, M.H. 1999. *In defense of legal positivism: Law without trimmings*. Oxford: Oxford University Press.
Kramer, M.H. 2004. *Where law and morality meet*. Oxford: Oxford University Press.
Laudan, L. 1984. *Science and values: The aims of science and their role in scientific debate*. Berkeley: University of California Press.
Marmor, A. 2001. *Positive law and objective values*. Oxford: Oxford University Press.
Marmor, A. 2006. Legal positivism: Still descriptive and morally neutral. *Oxford Journal of Legal Studies* 26: 683–704.
Marmor, A. 2007. The nature of law. Retrieved from Stanford Encyclopedia of Philosophy: http://plato.stanford.edu/entries/lawphil-nature.
McDowell, J. 1998. *Mind, value, and reality*. Cambridge: Harvard University Press.
Mill, J.S. 1984a. Austin's lectures on jurisprudence. In *The collected works of John Stuart Mill*, vol. 21. Toronto: University of Toronto Press.
Mill, J.S. 1984b. Austin on jurisprudence. In *The collected works of John Stuart Mill*. Toronto: University of Toronto Press.
Moore, M.S. 2000. *Educating oneself in public: Critical essays in jurisprudence*. Oxford: Oxford University Press.
Priel, D. forthcoming. Are jurisprudential debates conceptual? Some evidence from democratic theory. *Osgoode Hall Law Journal* 50.
Priel, D. 2010. Description and evaluation in jurisprudence. *Law and Philosophy* 29: 633.
Priel, D. 2012. Jurisprudence between science and the humanities. *Washington University Jurisprudence Review* 4: 269-323.
Raz, J. 1995. *Ethics in the public domain: Essays on the morality of law and politics*, Rev. ed. Oxford: Clarendon.
Raz, J. 2009a. *The authority of law*, 2nd ed. Oxford: Oxford University Press.
Raz, J. 2009b. *Between authority and interpretation*. Oxford: Oxford University Press.
Stearn, W.T. 1957. An introduction to the species plantarum and cognate botanical works of Carl Linnaeus. In *Species plantarum: A fascimile of the first edition 1753*, vol. 1, ed. C. Linnaeus, 1–176. London: Ray Society.
Taylor, C. 1985. *Philosophy and the human sciences*. Cambridge: Cambridge University Press.
Tyler, T.R. 1990. *Why people obey the law*. Princeton: Princeton University Press.
Waluchow, W. 1994. *Inclusive legal positivism*. Oxford: Clarendon.
Wollheim, R. 1954. The nature of law. *Political Studies* 2: 128–141.
Zelizer, V. 1994. *The social meaning of money: Pin money, paychecks, poor relief and other currencies*. New York: Basic Books.

Chapter 13
Jurisprudential Methodology: Is Pure Interpretation Possible?

Kevin Walton

After the bombings on the public-transport system in London in July 2005, Thomas L. Friedman wrote:

> After every major terrorist incident, the excuse makers come out to tell us why imperialism, Zionism, colonialism or Iraq explains why the terrorists acted. These excuse makers are just one notch less despicable then the terrorists [...].[1]

This sort of opinion is common. People often denounce attempts to make sense of immoral conduct.[2] In doing so, they assume a connection between understanding and morality. They suppose that comprehension of human action implies moral evaluation of it. But is their assumption warranted? Can one explain behaviour *without* reference to moral norms?

More specifically, I wonder whether theorists of legal practice must rely on morality. This paper explores the possibility of a jurisprudential methodology that is morally neutral and thus 'pure'.[3] Largely by way of critical engagement with the recent and influential work of Julie Dickson, it denies the need for legal philosophers to view their subject through moral lenses.

[1] Friedman 2005. Compare Clark 2001.

[2] Recall, for instance, the controversy over the publication of Gitta Sereny's book on Mary Bell, who was convicted at the age of 11 of the manslaughter of two boys. See Sereny 1998.

[3] Although I borrow this label from Hans Kelsen, I do not consider here the other sort of purity on which he insists, namely, non-contamination by sociology. See, for example, Kelsen 1966: 2–3.

K. Walton (✉)
Sydney Law School, University of Sydney, Eastern Avenue, Sydney, NSW 2006, Australia
e-mail: kevin.walton@sydney.edu.au

J. Ferrer Beltrán et al. (eds.), *Neutrality and Theory of Law*,
Law and Philosophy Library 106, DOI 10.1007/978-94-007-6067-7_13,

13.1 Hart's Methodology

Much of the current debate about jurisprudential methodology involves disagreement regarding the way in which H.L.A. Hart defends his account of legal practice.[4] I start by considering this exegetical dispute, but I do not purport (and have no present reason for trying) to settle it. Instead, I use it to set out three distinct techniques between which a theorist of law must choose. I look more closely at these philosophical techniques in subsequent sections.

A number of theorists maintain that Hart's description of law merely reports the beliefs of legal actors as articulated, whether explicitly or implicitly, in their speech. According to Dworkin, for instance, Hart's theory is 'semantic'.[5] This mode of understanding comprises the single rule that a description of a practice should match the language of participants. It does not analyse the concept of which participants speak. By treating linguistic usage as decisive, it reduces philosophy to lexicography. One might cite the following extract from the preface to *The Concept of Law* as evidence for this reading of Hart's theory of law:

> Notwithstanding its concern with analysis the book may also be regarded as an essay in descriptive sociology; for the suggestion that inquiries into meanings of words merely throw light on words is false. Many important distinctions, which are not immediately obvious, between types of social situation or relationships may best be brought to light by an examination of the standard uses of the relevant expressions and of the way in which these depend on a social context, itself often left unstated.[6]

Jules Coleman, however, says that 'Hart's aim is not to report on usage, but to analyse the concept of law.'[7] And Hart himself emphatically denies that he makes sense of legal practice by simply recording the language of its participants: '[N]othing in my book or in anything else I have written supports such an account of my theory.'[8] Certainly, his reference to 'descriptive sociology', which Dworkin finds 'baffling',[9] cannot be understood as a commitment to ordinary-language philosophy given his implicit admission (in the quoted extract) that 'inquiries into the meaning of words' do not supplant his 'concern with analysis'. Although he insists that an appreciation of everyday speech is necessary, he appears to reject its sufficiency. He professes to do more than list the beliefs of those who take part in legal practice. Hart thus dismisses the allegation that he is in thrall to ordinary language.

---

[4] Hart aims to describes legal practice in general as opposed to that of a particular society: see Hart 1994: 239–240. This distinction has no impact on my argument, which does not depend on the extent of the practice that the theorist considers. For scepticism about the generality of Hart's account, see Tamanaha 2001.

[5] See Dworkin 1986: 34–35, 2006: 31, 165–166, 214. See also Lyons 1984: 64; Stavropoulos 2001: 59.

[6] Hart 1994: v.

[7] Coleman 2002: 213. See also Bayles 1990: 29, 1991: 360; Endicott 2001: 39–47.

[8] Hart 1994: 246.

[9] Dworkin 2006: 165. See also Dworkin 2006: 214.

Perhaps, then, analysis, not lexicography, is Hart's project. To analyse the concept of law, one must identify the significant (and maybe even the essential) aspects of legal practice. This requires evaluation, rather than mere narration, of the beliefs of legal actors. Such an assessment depends on criteria according to which one can discriminate between the opinions of those who accept legal rules. Some theorists declare—indeed, Stephen Guest is 'in no doubt'[10]—that Hart relies on moral norms. They say that his description of law results from interpretation that I (no doubt pejoratively) label 'moralistic'.

As apparent proof of Hart's dependence on morality, many of these theorists refer to his contention that his theory of legal positivism improves moral deliberation by 'preserving the sense that the certification of something as legally valid is not conclusive of the question of obedience'.[11] Stephen Guest, Matthew Kramer, Neil MacCormick and Frederick Schauer belong to this subgroup.[12]

Hart, though, is adamant that his theory 'is morally neutral and has no justificatory aims'.[13] He explicitly rejects moralistic interpretation. Even if the supposed consequences of legal positivism are morally valuable, Hart denies that his description of law is contingent on them. They are, he implies, merely a beneficial side-effect of legal positivism. At most, he would claim that he is, to borrow John Gardner's expression, a 'positivity-welcomer'.[14]

Although Hart dismisses moralistic interpretation, Stephen Perry is convinced that he 'applies such a methodology in *The Concept of Law* when he limits law to normative systems with a rule of recognition, thereby excluding social practices that consist of primary social rules alone.'[15] For Hart, a regime comprising only primary rules—namely, those that establish duties—suffers from certain defects: it lacks a way in which any doubt concerning the identity of its rules might be eradicated; it has no procedures for creating new and extinguishing current obligations; and it needs an effective mechanism for deciding whether specific rules have been infringed.[16] Hart says that these deficiencies are cured by 'supplementing the *primary* rules of obligation with *secondary* rules which are rules of a different kind.'[17] The latter 'specify the ways in which the primary rules may be conclusively ascertained, introduced, eliminated, varied, and the fact of their violation conclusively determined.'[18] According to Hart, a 'rule of recognition' solves the problem of uncertainty, 'rules of change' facilitate both the creation of new and the abolition of

[10] Guest 1996: 30.

[11] Hart 1994: 210. For further discussion, see Hart 1983: 72–78, 1994: 207–212.

[12] See Guest 1992: 27, 1998: 335; Kramer 2001: 683; MacCormick 1985: 10, 2008: 196–197, 209; Schauer 1998: 69–70.

[13] Hart 1994: 240. See also Coleman 2002: 336; Waluchow 1994: 98.

[14] See Gardner 2001: 205.

[15] Perry 1995: 118.

[16] See Hart 1994: 92–94.

[17] Hart 1994: 94.

[18] Hart 1994: 94.

existing duties and 'rules of adjudication' allow for the efficient resolution of disputes.[19] The introduction of these secondary rules, he says, 'convert[s] the regime of primary rules into what is indisputably a legal system.'[20] Given Hart's belief that law remedies the defects of a regime comprising only duty-imposing rules, Perry concludes that Hart 'delimit[s] the concept of law by appealing to the values of certainty, flexibility, and efficiency.'[21] Dworkin, contrary to his depiction elsewhere of Hart as a semantic theorist, also infers that Hart relies on these moral values to justify his legal theory.[22]

Yet the conclusion that Hart's description of law is the product of moralistic interpretation need not follow from his contention that a legal system effects certainty, flexibility and efficiency. These values need not be his motivation for including secondary rules in his theory. Indeed, Coleman says that Hart's discussion of the shift from a pre-legal regime to a legal system might be understood as 'a kind of social-scientific/functionalist explanation of law [that] reinforces the philosophical analysis of law as a union of primary and secondary rules, and makes the philosophical theory continuous with a standard social scientific explanation.'[23] Rather than using the values of certainty, flexibility and efficiency to justify his description of legal practice, in other words, perhaps Hart mentions them to explain its historical development.

The third methodology that several commentators attribute to Hart is also a form of interpretation. According to this mode of understanding, a description of a practice ought only to meet certain 'meta-theoretical' standards, such as clarity and consistency. Because it specifies criteria that are exclusively non-moral for analysing the beliefs of participants, I call it 'pure' interpretation. Coleman says that Hart 'quite clearly' adopts this means of comprehension when describing legal practice.[24] Dworkin, moreover, implies that Hart is a pure theorist when he attributes Hart's legal positivism to a desire for clarity.[25] Indeed, Hart himself seems to advocate pure interpretation in the following passage:

> [A legal theorist] must [...] be guided, in focusing on [some] features rather than others, by some criteria of importance of which the chief will be the explanatory power of what his analysis picks out. So his analysis will be guided by judgements, often controversial, of what is important and will therefore reflect such meta-theoretic values and not be neutral between all values.[26]

Yet Hart's apparent insistence on pure interpretation is complicated by his assertion that 'explanatory power' is the primary meta-theoretical value. Far from being

[19] See Hart 1994: 94–97.

[20] Hart 1994: 94.

[21] Perry 1995: 118.

[22] See Dworkin 1984: 255.

[23] Coleman 2002: 342. See also Coleman 2001: 207.

[24] See Coleman 2002: 335–336. See also Coleman 2001: 201; Dickson 2004: 117; Waluchow 1994: 98.

[25] See Dworkin 1984: 254–255.

[26] Hart 1987: 39. On 'explanatory power', see also Hart 1994: 81, 155.

a philosophical norm, explanatory power *results from* the application of such norms.[27] Whether a theory exhibits this quality, in other words, depends on the methodological criteria that it ought to satisfy. Hence, a theorist for whom philosophy is equivalent to lexicography would credit explanatory power to a description of a practice that simply records the language of participants. The same theorist would claim, moreover, that a moralistic or a pure interpretation of a practice lacks this capacity. Hart's reliance on explanatory power, then, simply begs, rather than answers, the question of the appropriate method for describing a practice.

In spite of disagreement about the means of comprehension that Hart employs, I express no definite opinion on whether he engages in philosophy as lexicography, moralistic interpretation or pure interpretation. I mention the controversy regarding his methodology only as a way of introducing some different philosophical techniques for making sense of law. I now consider each of these approaches in turn.

13.2 Philosophy as Lexicography

Should a description of a practice simply report the beliefs of those who take part in it? For some theorists, philosophy as lexicography is defeated by the fact that participants do not always agree about their behaviour. I argue here that a particular form of this objection succeeds. Having rejected philosophy as lexicography, I then comment on the need for interpretation.

If a description of a practice ought only to match the language of participants, then a theorist must simply report disagreements between them. Philosophy as lexicography cannot discriminate between the competing beliefs that participants hold about their practice. When faced with substantive debate—Dworkin calls it 'theoretical disgreement'[28]—an ordinary-language philosopher must copy the speech of all disputants. According to Michael Bayles, legal theories that reproduce arguments between lawyers concerning their practice are 'uninteresting'.[29] Matthew Kramer also criticises descriptions of law that record substantive disagreement. He bemoans their failure to 'yield a fully uniform account that could be associated with the internal perspective of the participant.'[30] Theories of non-legal practices that report substantive discord would presumably be subject to the same objections.

Yet these attacks do not defeat philosophy as lexicography. They assume, rather than establish, that a theorist should do more than record substantive disputes. Whether a theory is interesting depends on the methodological criteria that it ought to satisfy. That Bayles is not inspired by reports of arguments between legal actors follows from, rather than warrants, his rejection of philosophy as lexicography.

[27] For a similar argument, see Postema 1998: 334.

[28] See Dworkin 1986: 4–5. His label supposes a particular conception of philosophy, whose necessity I challenge in the final section.

[29] See Bayles 1990: 31, 38.

[30] Kramer 1999: 169.

Likewise, Kramer's insistence on a coherent description of a practice supposes the inadequacy of merely recording everyday speech. These theorists regard substantive disputes as fatal to philosophy as lexicography only because they rely on a methodology that aims to solve, rather than reproduce, disagreements of this type.

One cannot show that substantive conflict defeats philosophy as lexicography by assuming the superiority of another mode of understanding. But one might claim that substantive discord undermines philosophy as lexicography *from within*. My critique of this methodology is, therefore, internal. I argue that disagreement between *philosophers* about their practice contradicts philosophy as lexicography.

Because methodological rules state the means by which one ought to comprehend a practice, every methodology must be self-justifying. To defend philosophy as lexicography, then, one must report the language of philosophers. Yet this defence succeeds only if every philosopher believes in philosophy as lexicography. In fact, not all philosophers treat linguistic usage as decisive. They obviously disagree about the criteria that a description of a practice ought to satisfy. Since philosophy as lexicography must reproduce their dispute, it cannot support itself. Philosophical debate is thus fatal to philosophy as lexicography.

Given the existence of substantive conflict between philosophers, a theorist of any practice, including law, must interpret, rather than simply report, the beliefs of participants. The necessity of interpretation follows from the impossibility of philosophy as lexicography. When interpreting a practice, a theorist analyses the concept of which participants speak (and about which they almost certainly disagree). Such 'modest' analysis produces a *conception* of the concept.[31] This conception is an attempt to isolate that which is significant about the concept.[32]

Although philosophy as lexicography is defeated by the existence of substantive disagreement between philosophers, a theorist cannot ignore everyday speech. An interpretation of a practice must start from the language of those who participate in it.[33] Their use of words is the phenomenon that requires analysis. Before interpreting a practice, then, a theorist must report the everyday speech (and so the beliefs) of its participants. In Dworkin's words: '[T]here must be a "preinterpretive" stage in which the rules and standards taken to provide the tentative content of the practice are identified.'[34] Yet how far might conceptual analysis revise ordinary speech? Were no modifications possible, interpretation would be equivalent to philosophy as lexicography. Excessive departure from the normal use of words, however, would result in the creation of an imaginary (as opposed to a theory of an actual) practice. As Dworkin states: '[An interpretation] need not fit every aspect or feature of the standing practice, but it must fit enough for the interpreter to be able to see himself as

[31]On 'modest' conceptual analysis, see Jackson 1998. See also Farrell 2006: 999–1001. On the difference between concepts and conceptions, see Rawls 1999: 5.

[32]On this, see Coleman 2001: 179; Dickson 2001: 25; Finnis 1980: 17; Green 1996: 1713; Kramer 1999: 179, 2001: 688; Raz 1995: 235, 237, 2009a: 69, b: 41.

[33]See, for example, Morriss 1987: 3.

[34]Dworkin 1986: 65–66. See also Coleman 2001: 199–200, 2002: 336.

interpreting that practice, not inventing a new one.'[35] The extent to which a theorist might alter normal language is limited, therefore, by consideration of the distinction between interpretation and invention.

Although the need for interpretation does not allow one to ignore ordinary language, the defeat of philosophy as lexicography does require evaluation of the normal use of words. Numerous legal philosophers justify such an assessment on moral grounds. Their approach is the topic of the next section.

13.3 Moralistic Interpretation

A theorist who relies on moral criteria to defend an understanding of a practice provides a moralistic interpretation of it. Drawing on Julie Dickson's helpful examination of jurisprudential method, I consider some attitudes of legal philosophers towards moralistic interpretation and conclude by isolating the belief whose rejection is my aim in this paper.

Dickson identifies three distinct theses concerning moralistic interpretation to which a legal philosopher might subscribe: the 'moral-evaluation' thesis, the 'moral-justification' thesis and the 'beneficial-moral-consequences' thesis.[36] I consider each in turn.

The 'moral-evaluation' thesis states that a theorist cannot make sense of law without reference to morality.[37] As Dickson recognises, both Finnis and Dworkin embrace the moral-evaluation thesis. To understand law, says Finnis, a theorist must consult its focal meaning.[38] The (moral) requirements of 'practical reasonableness' determine the central case of law for him. He states that a legal philosopher must rely on these requirements.[39]

While Finnis holds that a legal philosopher must defend an understanding of law in terms of the requirements of practical reasonableness, Dworkin promotes the moral-evaluation thesis by insisting on the 'constructive interpretation' of every social practice, including law. Such interpretation 'is a matter of imposing purpose on an object or practice in order to make of it the best possible example of the form or genre to which it is taken to belong.'[40] A theory of a practice, says Dworkin, must fit the language of participants and explain 'why a practice of that general shape is worth pursuing, if it is.'[41] This requires a theorist to 'propose[...] value for the practice by describing some scheme of interests or goals or principles the practice can

[35] Dworkin 1986: 66. See also Raz 2009a: 74–75; Waldron 2002: 138.

[36] See Dickson 2001: 9, 29.

[37] For discussion, see Dickson 2001: Chap. 2.

[38] See Finnis 1980: Chap. 1.

[39] See Finnis 1980: 15.

[40] Dworkin 1986: 52.

[41] Dworkin 1986: 66. See also Dworkin 2006: 15.

be taken to serve or express or exemplify.'[42] Dworkin regards the justification of governmental force or, more succinctly, the value of 'legality' as the moral purpose (or the 'aspirational' concept) of law.[43] He says that a legal philosopher must describe law according to this goal. Dworkin thus adheres to the moral-evaluation thesis. He agrees with Finnis that a legal theorist must subject law to moral appraisal. 'The cutting edge of a jurisprudential argument,' declares Dworkin, 'is its moral edge.'[44]

Dickson also portrays Finnis and Dworkin as advocates of the 'moral-justification' thesis, which states that a legal theorist must treat law as morally justified.[45] She says that both of them explain their adherence to the moral-justification thesis using the same reasons as those for which they assert that a legal philosopher must morally evaluate law. According to Dickson, Finnis holds that a theory of legal practice cannot fail to satisfy the requirements of practical reasonableness,[46] whereas Dworkin's assent to the moral-justification thesis is 'driven by his view of the function of law.'[47]

Whether or not Finnis and Dworkin hold that a legal philosopher must treat law as morally justified—some commentators doubt that they do[48]—Dickson is right to deny that the moral-justification thesis follows automatically from the moral-evaluation thesis. She recognises that the former cannot be established simply by proving the latter when she notes that the moral-evaluation thesis 'is a methodological precept which could be accepted by a critical race theorist who believes that in many instances, law operates in a way which results in great injustice to persons of colour.'[49] Hence, the moral-justification thesis is merely a particular version of (and thus entails) the moral-evaluation thesis. While dismissal of the moral-evaluation thesis implies rejection of the moral-justification thesis, the converse is not true.

According to the moral-evaluation and moral-justification theses, moralistic interpretation of legal practice is necessary. The 'beneficial-moral-consequences' thesis, however, states only that a specific type of moralistic jurisprudence is *possible*. For philosophers who accede to this thesis, an understanding of law can be supported by the moral advantages (and, I presume, defeated by the moral disadvantages) to which it gives rise.[50] Some theorists defend legal positivism by claiming that their description of law improves moral deliberation. They believe that the moral effects of legal positivism might vindicate (and are not just an incidental

---

[42] Dworkin 1986: 52.

[43] See Dworkin 1986: 93, 2006: 5, 168–171. Compare Dworkin 1985: 160.

[44] Dworkin 2006: 178.

[45] For discussion, see Dickson 2001: Chap. 4.

[46] See Dickson 2001: 71–73.

[47] Dickson 2001: 107.

[48] See Kramer 2003: 211–213; McBride 2003: 663.

[49] Dickson 2001: 73.

[50] For discussion, see Dickson 2001: Chap. 5.

benefit of) their interpretations of law. These legal positivists are not easy to identify. According to Dickson, however, they include Neil MacCormick, Frederick Schauer and Liam Murphy.[51] She denies that Hart is among them.[52]

Lon Fuller says that legal positivism fails to bring about the moral advantages on which these philosophers depend.[53] Indeed, he regards its moral consequences as a reason for dismissing it (in favour of another description of legal practice). David Dyzenhaus repudiates legal positivism in the same way.[54] Insofar as their critique hinges on the moral results of legal positivism, Fuller and Dyzenhaus assent to the beneficial-moral-consequences thesis. Their dispute with the legal positivists whom Dickson cites is empirical, not philosophical. Whether legal positivism (or any other description of law) generates moral benefits is a (difficult) question of fact.[55] Rather than speculating on its answer, I wish to comment briefly on Dickson's rejection of the methodological proposition on which all of these theorists agree.

Dickson contends that the beneficial-moral-consequences thesis is false. She denies the possibility of justifying an interpretation of legal practice with reference to its moral effects. Such an argument, she says, 'runs in the wrong direction, *from* premises consisting of a claim about the beneficial consequences of espousing a certain theoretical understanding of law, *to* the conclusion that this way of understanding the law is therefore correct.'[56] Dickson accuses philosophers who subscribe to the beneficial-moral-consequences thesis of 'reduc[ing] legal theory to no more than an exercise in wishful thinking'.[57] In other words, she supposes that they invent, rather than interpret, legal practice.

But her assumption is not valid. There is no reason to think that an adherent to the beneficial-moral-consequences thesis cannot respect ordinary speech to the extent required for a theory of law to be an interpretation as opposed to an invention. An evaluation of legal practice based on its moral results need not be less compatible with the language of participants than any other sort of assessment. Dickson does not explain her claim that a philosopher who justifies an understanding of law in terms of its moral consequences 'fails to take seriously the enterprise of attempting accurately and adequately to characterise what is distinctive about law as an actually existing institution.'[58] She simply ignores the possibility that the distinctive aspects of law might be identified by the moral advantages to which they give rise. Hence, Dickson is mistaken: a description of law *can*, which does not mean that it must, be supported by the moral advantages that it produces.[59]

---

[51] See Dickson 2004: 145.

[52] See Dickson 2004: 149–150.

[53] See Fuller 1958: 657–661.

[54] Dyzenhaus 1991: 269–270. See also Dyzenhaus 1997.

[55] See Soper 1987: 32.

[56] Dickson 2001: 89. See also Waluchow 1994: 99.

[57] Dickson 2001: 90. See also Dickson 2004: 148–149.

[58] Dickson 2001: 92.

[59] For Schauer's response to Dickson's critique, see Schauer 2005: 493.

Nevertheless, Dickson provides a useful survey of moralistic jurisprudence by setting out three different theses to which a legal philosopher might assent. My quarrel is not with all of these propositions. To establish the possibility of pure theory, I need only deny the *necessity* of moralistic interpretation. My argument is, therefore, compatible with a belief in the *possibility* of offering moral support, whether consequentialist or otherwise, for an understanding of law. Nevertheless, it is at odds with the claim, which Dickson calls the moral-justification thesis, that a theorist cannot describe legal practice without treating the behaviour of its participants as morally justified. As a specific version of the more general proposition that a philosopher can only defend an understanding of law on moral grounds, this claim is inconsistent with my rejection of the need for moralistic jurisprudence. But why do I deny that a philosopher of law must cite moral norms in support of his or her theory?

13.4 Pure Interpretation

Given the failure of philosophy as lexicography, a theorist cannot make sense of legal practice without interpreting it. In the absence of a non-moral mode of analysis, however, moralistic jurisprudence is necessary by default, as Dworkin appreciates.[60] Hence, I must start my argument for the possibility of pure interpretation by describing a jurisprudential methodology in which morality has no place.

A number of theorists purport to evaluate legal practice without reference to moral criteria. They include Matthew Kramer,[61] Jules Coleman[62] and Joseph Raz.[63] For Dickson, 'Raz's stance exemplifies the correct sort of methodological position for a legal theorist to adopt'.[64] Of course, these philosophers must specify the non-moral values on which they claim to rely if their methodological assertions are not to be empty. Only by naming such ideals can they disprove the need for a theorist to consult morality when selecting the important aspects of legal practice. These philosophers cite different, albeit overlapping, sets of norms in support of their theories. In examining the criteria mentioned by them, I offer my own understanding of the methodology that they claim to practise.

Of the ideals to which they refer, but on the meaning of which they offer surprisingly little, I regard 'clarity',[65] 'consistency',[66] 'comprehensiveness'[67] and 'coherence'[68]

---

[60] See Dworkin 2006: 32.

[61] Kramer 1999: 179.

[62] Coleman 2001: 3.

[63] See Raz 1995: 235.

[64] Dickson 2001: 10.

[65] See Kramer 2001: 688.

[66] See Bayles 1990: 25; Green 1996: 1713.

[67] See Bayles 1990: 25; Kramer 2001: 688.

[68] See Coleman 2001: 3.

as primary. Whereas clarity requires the elimination of ambiguity from a concept, consistency demands the removal of contradiction. These two norms are distinct: the paradoxical nature of a conception might be obvious and a vague understanding need not be illogical. A description of a practice is comprehensive, meanwhile, insofar as it matches the beliefs of participants and it is coherent to the extent that it forms connections between those beliefs. According to the value of comprehensiveness, an interpretation should fit ordinary language as much as possible (and not only to the degree that separates interpretation from invention).[69] Yet the ideals of clarity, consistency and coherence might require modification of everyday speech. For example, an understanding of a practice whose participants express contradictory beliefs cannot be both wholly comprehensive and entirely consistent. Conflict between the norms of coherence and clarity is possible too, given that integration of the various aspects of a practice might depend on a failure to correct their ambiguity. The goals of coherence and consistency, though, are fully compatible. Since contradiction is detrimental to unity, a coherent understanding of a practice must be consistent. Yet the impossibility of conflict between the norms of coherence and consistency does not imply their equivalence. Although the eradication of paradox is necessary for coherence, it is not sufficient.[70]

Each of the other values that these legal philosophers mention either corresponds to one or more of the primary norms (and so is merely another way of expressing it or them) or is actually not a criterion by which a theory can be assessed. The extent to which an understanding of a practice is 'broad'[71] or 'in agreement with facts'[72] depends solely on its respect for the beliefs of participants and, therefore, its comprehensiveness. The ideal of 'precision',[73] according to which a conception ought not to be vague, is no different from that of clarity. The 'consilience'[74] of various elements of a practice appears synonymous with their coherence. Since contradiction, ambiguity and plurality generate complexity, the oft-cited goal of 'simplicity'[75]—which Kramer calls 'parsimony'[76]—is realised only insofar as a theory is consistent, clear and coherent. An understanding of a practice that displays the virtue of simplicity is also 'elegant'[77] or 'subtle'[78] to the degree that it is comprehensive (and crude inasmuch as it fails to account for the beliefs of participants). Finally,

[69] Dworkin also distinguishes between these minimal and maximal notions of fit: see Dworkin 1986: 230–231, 255–257.

[70] The absence of a link between two things—a desire to run a marathon and a preference for the colour blue, say—does not make them contradictory. On the difference between coherence and consistency, see MacCormick 1994: 106–107.

[71] See Coleman 2001: 119.

[72] See Bayles 1990: 25.

[73] See Kramer 2001: 688.

[74] See Coleman 2001: 3.

[75] See Bayles 1990: 25; Coleman 2001: 3, 119; Green 1996: 1713; Waluchow 1994: 19.

[76] See Kramer 2001: 688.

[77] See Coleman 2001: 3, 119; Kramer 2001: 688.

[78] See Kramer 2001: 688.

none of 'explanatory power',[79] 'depth of understanding',[80] 'charity'[81] or 'fecundity'[82] is a methodological norm. These qualities result from the application of philosophical standards and are not themselves values on which a description of a practice might be based.[83] The explanatory power of a theory, its depth, its generosity towards those who take part in the practice under scrutiny and its production of interesting hypotheses all depend on the methodological criteria that it ought to satisfy. After all, a moralistic philosopher would not regard an understanding of a practice that fails to discriminate between the beliefs of participants on moral grounds as deep.

In my opinion, then, a pure theorist analyses a concept with reference to the meta-theoretical norms of clarity, consistency, coherence and comprehensiveness. Although moralistic philosophers might (and actually do) accept some or all of these values, a pure theorist is concerned with them alone. A pure interpretation of a practice is based *exclusively* on these meta-theoretical norms.

Yet Julie Dickson objects to this mode of analysis.[84] She denies that reliance on clarity, consistency, coherence and comprehensiveness is a substitute for moralistic interpretation of legal practice. I dismiss her objection and argue that, when combined with her failure to identify other non-moral ideals to which a philosopher of law might refer, her rejection of meta-theoretical norms undermines her critique of the moral-evaluation thesis.

Dickson disputes the need for moralistic interpretation by claiming that a legal theorist can 'indirectly' assess law.[85] Whereas direct evaluation of legal practice involves moral appraisal of the beliefs of participants,[86] indirect evaluation merely classifies a particular aspect of law as significant.[87] An assessment of the latter kind need not be moral.[88] Yet on which other standards might such an evaluation of legal practice be based? Dickson denies that meta-theoretical norms are an alternative means of selecting the important elements of law. For her, these values relate solely to the effective communication of a theory: '[T]hey do not bear upon the truth of the particular substantive claims which a given theory makes, but are rather concerned with optimal ways of getting the message of the theory across, and are hence considerations which apply irrespective of what the content of that message might be.'[89]

---

[79] See Kramer 2001: 688.

[80] See Coleman 2001: 119.

[81] See Waluchow 1994: 19.

[82] See Green 1996: 1713.

[83] Recall both my criticism of Hart's apparent reliance on explanatory power as well as my rejection of the argument by Bayles and Kramer against theories that reproduce substantive disagreement.

[84] Inexplicably, Brain Bix thinks that she endorses it: see Bix 2003: 233.

[85] See Dickson 2001: Chap. 3.

[86] See Dickson 2001: 51–52.

[87] See Dickson 2001: 53. For criticism of this distinction, see Kramer 2003: 211.

[88] See Dickson 2001: 58.

[89] Dickson 2001: 34. Compare Raz 2009a: 31.

In rejecting meta-theoretical norms as potential grounds for treating certain features of law as significant, Dickson simply assumes that these values cannot support a theory because they relate to the efficacy of its communication. She offers no reason not to think that meta-theoretical norms might be relevant to both the successful communication and the validity of a theory. Even if she does not say so, perhaps a conviction that these two issues must never to be conflated prompts her to exclude this possibility. But it need not. Since effective communication depends on more than clarity, consistency, coherence and comprehensiveness—a shared language, for instance, is vital—a theory might satisfy meta-theoretical criteria and yet not be communicated successfully. Hence, Dickson's belief that ambiguity, contradiction, plurality and selectivity might impair communication does not preclude reliance on meta-theoretical norms as a substitute for moralistic interpretation.

Indeed, Dickson seems to concede as much when she offers her second argument against the possibility of a legal theory based entirely on these norms. Although not characterised by Dickson as separate, this further argument actually contradicts the first by implying that meta-theoretical criteria might vindicate analyses of *some* concepts. Whereas the first argument assumes that these values can never justify a theory, the second allows for reliance on them in various non-legal contexts. According to this alternative argument, the impossibility of a legal theory supported only by meta-theoretical norms follows from the distinctive nature of concepts such as law: 'I present [these norms] as insufficient because of the kind of concept that law is, [namely,] a concept people use to understand themselves and their social world.'[90] But Dickson provides no reason to suppose that a philosopher who seeks clarity, consistency, coherence and comprehensiveness must neglect the ways in which people use the idea of law to make sense of their lives.[91] If Dickson thinks that meta-theoretical values alone are often sufficient, then she must explain their inadequacy for analysing law and similar concepts. Given her failure to do so, her second argument is no more successful than the first.

Moreover, she does not propose any other ideals on which a pure theory of law might be based. Since her distinction between direct and indirect evaluation is contingent on the existence of non-moral values for selecting the important aspects of legal practice, Dickson's rejection of the moral-evaluation thesis is subject to her identification of norms to which a pure theorist can refer in defence of an understanding of law. Rather than specifying these values, however, she merely makes some vague remarks that either beg the question or suggest dependence on norms to which she objects.[92] Whereas her contention that 'the features of the law which are important to explain are those which best reveal the distinctive character of law as a special method of social organisation'[93] is empty—a moralistic philosopher, for example, would

[90] Dickson 2004: 137. See also Dickson 2001: 37, 40–44.

[91] For a similar point, see Leiter 2007: 172–175.

[92] For related criticisms, see Bix 2003: 236; Himma 2001: 569; Leiter 2007: 195–196; McBride 2003: 664.

[93] Dickson 2001: 58.

explain the distinctive character of law in moral terms—her claim that 'sometimes a legal theorist may judge that a given feature of the law is important to explain on the basis of the prevalence of certain beliefs concerning that feature on the part of those subject to the law'[94] seems to imply that a description of legal practice ought to fit with the attitudes of participants or, in short, be comprehensive. Dickson's tacit reference to the value of comprehensiveness is, of course, at odds with her dismissal of meta-theoretical norms as potential support for a pure theory of law. In addition, her assertion that 'certain [...] features [of the law] can be adjudged important to explain because they bear upon matters which are of practical concern to us in conducting our lives'[95] contradicts her aversion to teleological reasoning by legal theorists—her 'wishful-thinking' objection indicates her opposition to such arguments[96]—and her declaration that 'one reason why certain features of the law are important to explain is because an understanding of them is vital if we are to be able [...] to subject the law to moral scrutiny'[97] seems no different from the version of the beneficial-moral-consequences thesis that is endorsed by philosophers for whom a theory of law might be justified in terms of its positive impact on moral deliberation.

Dickson thus fails to specify non-moral values by which she thinks the significant elements of legal practice might be discerned. And, despite Kenneth Einar Himma's kind suggestion to the contrary,[98] her omission is far from minor: it is fatal to her critique of the need for moralistic jurisprudence. By rejecting meta-theoretical values as reasons for treating certain aspects of legal practice as important and by neglecting to identify other norms on which a pure theory of law might be based, Dickson cannot reject the moral-evaluation thesis.

By examining the non-moral values to which some legal philosophers refer and articulating my version of their methodology, I offer a substitute for moralistic jurisprudence. According to this alternative mode of analysis, a description of legal practice ought only to be clear, consistent, coherent and comprehensive. Moralistic interpretation is not, therefore, necessary by default. But my account of pure interpretation is not sufficient to disprove the need for a philosopher to justify an understanding of legal practice in moral terms. To show that moralistic jurisprudence is not essential, I must also reject all arguments against the feasibility of pure analysis. I consider three prominent ones now.

The first argument derives the necessity of moralistic interpretation from the claim that pure theorists always disagree.[99] It states that philosophical disputes about practices, including law, are never settled with reference to meta-theoretical norms alone and that, consequently, pure interpretation is impossible. But this

[94] Dickson 2001: 59.

[95] Dickson 2001: 60.

[96] See Dickson 2001: 89–90.

[97] Dickson 2001: 135.

[98] See Himma 2001: 569.

[99] For discussion, but not endorsement, of the jurisprudential form of this argument, see Coleman 2001: 173–174.

argument is problematic. Both its major premise—that philosophical consensus is a necessary consequence (as opposed to a welcome side-effect) of a theory—and its minor premise—that pure theorists disagree at all times—are at least dubious. Given the prevalence of moral discord, moreover, the introduction of morality is not likely to end philosophical debate. Hence, the allegation that pure theorists never agree does not establish the need to supplement meta-theoretical norms with moral criteria.

The second argument for the necessity of moralistic interpretation is based on the perception that pure theorists have no effect on the behaviour that they describe. Whereas the first argument assumes that a philosophical understanding of a practice must change the opinions of other theorists, this reasoning supposes that it must alter the beliefs of its subjects.[100] That these practical consequences are a methodological requirement is, however, far from obvious. Furthermore, there is no evidence that moralistic theories produce these results, while pure theories do not. The extent to which philosophical reflection modifies a practice depends on the power of a philosopher or philosophers over participants in it. Since the practical influence of a moralistic theorist need not exceed that of a pure theorist, the second argument for the necessity of moralistic interpretation also fails.

According to the third argument, pure theorists cannot make sense of practices with moral content. This argument is more limited than the previous two. It does not say that pure interpretation is never possible. Rather, it says merely that philosophers cannot rely exclusively on meta-theoretical norms when analysing concepts in which morality features. Despite its restricted scope, its success might nevertheless entail the need for moralistic jurisprudence.

Several legal philosophers, of whom Dworkin is the most prominent, attribute the need for moralistic interpretation to the moral character of law.[101] Indeed, Coleman says that this defence of the moral-evaluation thesis 'has nearly risen to the level of conventional wisdom.'[102] Yet its success is contingent on the beliefs of legal actors. Only if they regard law as morally valuable can these philosophers establish the necessity of moralistic jurisprudence.

According to Dworkin, the concept of law is concerned with the ideal of 'legality'. He regards this aspiration as evident in the convictions of legal actors.[103] But is Dworkin's portrayal of their beliefs accurate? The answer is not readily apparent. W.B. Gallie, for whom disputes about concepts of moral significance are inevitable, implicitly denies the morality of legal practice when he declares that law is not an 'essentially-contested' concept.[104] In any event, the moral nature of law is

[100] Richard Posner makes the latter assumption about moral philosophy when he derides 'academic moralists' for their alleged failure to reform conventional morality: see Posner 1999: Chap. 1. Insofar as he condemns these theorists for their practical impotence, his critique is rather Marxist, as Brian Leiter notes: see Leiter 2002: 1132.

[101] For discussion of this argument, see Bix 1995: 473.

[102] Coleman 2001: 174.

[103] See Dworkin 1984: 256.

[104] See Gallie 1968: 190. See also Green 1987: 18–19.

insufficient to prove the moral-evaluation thesis. To infer the need for moralistic interpretation from the morality of a practice, one must suppose that the beliefs of participants determine the methodological norms to which a philosopher refers.

Dworkin says that 'interpretation takes different forms in different contexts only because different enterprises engage different standards of value or success.'[105] He maintains that a theorist of a practice must share the perspective of its participants.[106] For him, an external observer can do no more than report participants' various convictions as articulated, whether explicitly or implicitly, in their speech. The outcome of this lexicographical exercise is an account of a practice that simply notes the different opinions of its participants. Yet Dworkin contends that a philosopher must evaluate these beliefs and so take sides in participants' disputes about their conduct. Such appraisal, he says, requires adoption of the internal point of view. He regards acceptance of the sort of norms by which participants are motivated as vital for philosophical understanding of a practice.

According to the version of philosophy on which Dworkin insists, a philosopher simultaneously describes and participates in a practice. Philosophy, on this account, is a way of taking part in (and is not itself) a particular practice. The opinions of a philosopher are simply less concrete than those of other participants. Regarding jurisprudence, therefore, Dworkin states: '[A] legal philosopher's theory of law is not different in character from, though it is of course much more abstract than, the ordinary legal claims that lawyers make from case to case.'[107]

But Dworkin is wrong to think that a philosopher must describe a practice from the inside. Even though he is right about the necessity of interpretation, his claim that it depends on internal observation is false. He ignores the possibility of interpretation from the external point of view.

Dworkin fails to grasp the potential for such evaluation because of his belief that external theorists are guilty of 'obscurantism'.[108] He contends that they are unable to contribute to non-philosophical discussions and that their work is relevant to them alone.[109] This allegation follows from his assumption that they cannot do more than record debates between participants. One might, however, interpret a practice in which one does not (currently[110]) take part. To evaluate the convictions of participants, one need not share their 'critical-reflective attitude'.[111] Rather, one can assess their opinions from the 'hermeneutic' perspective of another practice.[112] My account of pure interpretation indicates a discrete order of norms on which a philosopher might rely. A pure theorist evaluates the deliberate conduct of others by accepting

[105]Dworkin 1986: 53.

[106]See Dworkin 1986: 64, 2006: 141. See also Perry 2001: 346.

[107]Dworkin 2006: 141. See also Dworkin 1986: 90.

[108]Dworkin 2006: 170.

[109]See Dworkin 2006: 185–186.

[110]One might, of course, participate in a practice both prior to and following external analysis of it.

[111]See Hart 1994: 57.

[112]See MacCormick 2008: 52–54.

distinct criteria, such as clarity and consistency. Philosophy, therefore, can be more than a sophisticated mode of participation. It might be an autonomous practice from which other practices, including law, are analysed.

Yet Dworkin implies that this brand of philosophy is elitist. He says that external theorists 'look down' on the behaviour that they describe.[113] But this slur is no more warranted than his charge of obscurantism. These philosophers take up a perspective that everyone might adopt. Moreover, the practice in which they participate is not better than, but only *different* from, any other. Rather than observe from above, they look *across* at the conduct of people whose critical reflective attitude they do not (presently) share.

Given this alternative conception of philosophy, one can defend an understanding of a practice other than philosophy, which is necessarily self-justifying, from the outside. Interpretation is possible without acceptance of the sort of norms by which participants are motivated. Hence, a philosopher might justify an understanding of a practice whose participants imbue their behaviour with moral value in purely non-moral terms.[114]

None of the three objections to the possibility of pure interpretation is successful. Neither the belief that pure theorists always disagree, the perception that they have no impact on the conduct that they describe nor the allegation that they are unable to make sense of practices with moral content demonstrates the necessity of moralistic interpretation. My present denial of the need for a theorist to cite moral values in support of an understanding of legal practice is thus complete. Given my consideration of no more than three objections to the possibility of pure interpretation, however, my conclusion that a legal philosopher might rely exclusively on meta-theoretical norms is merely provisional. Nevertheless, I wish to end by asserting my preference for pure analysis and by appealing for greater reliance on it in the hope that its frequent application will demonstrate its relative worth. After all, as Neil MacCormick observes, 'the greatest test of any method of inquiry is [...] the quality of the results achieved.'[115]

References

Bayles, M. 1990. What is jurisprudence about? Theories, definitions, concepts or conceptions of law. *Philosophical Topics* 18: 23.
Bayles, M. 1991. Hart vs Dworkin. *Law and Philosophy* 10: 349.
Bix, B. 1995. Conceptual questions and jurisprudence. *Legal Theory* 1: 465.
Bix, B. 2003. Book review. *Australian Journal of Legal Philosophy* 28: 231.
Clark, D. 2001. To explain is not to excuse. *The Guardian*, 21 September.
Coleman, J. 2001. *The practice of principle: In defense of a pragmatist approach to legal theory.* Oxford: Oxford University Press.

[113]Dworkin 2006: 141.

[114]See Coleman 2001: 195; Hart 1994: 244.

[115]MacCormick 2007: 7.

Coleman, J. 2002. Methodology. In *The Oxford handbook of jurisprudence and philosophy of law*, ed. J. Coleman and S. Shapiro. Oxford: Oxford University Press.
Dickson, J. 2001. *Evaluation and legal theory*. Oxford: Hart Publishing.
Dickson, J. 2004. Methodology in jurisprudence: A critical survey. *Legal Theory* 10: 117.
Dworkin, R. 1984. A reply by Ronald Dworkin. In *Ronald Dworkin and contemporary jurisprudence*, ed. M. Cohen. London: Duckworth.
Dworkin, R. 1985. *A matter of principle*. Oxford: Clarendon.
Dworkin, R. 1986. *Law's empire*. London: Fontana.
Dworkin, R. 2006. *Justice in robes*. Cambridge: Harvard University Press.
Dyzenhaus, D. 1991. *Hard cases in wicked legal systems: South African law in the perspective of legal philosophy*. Oxford: Clarendon.
Dyzenhaus, D. 1997. *Legality and legitimacy: Carl Schmitt, Hans Kelsen and Hermann Heller in Weimar*. Oxford: Oxford University Press.
Endicott, T. 2001. Herbert Hart and the semantic sting. In *Hart's postscript: Essays on the postscript to the concept of law*, ed. J. Coleman. Oxford: Oxford University Press.
Farrell, I.P. 2006. Book review essay: H.L.A. Hart and the methodology of jurisprudence. *Texas Law Review* 84: 983.
Finnis, J. 1980. *Natural law and natural rights*. Oxford: Clarendon.
Friedman, T.L. 2005. Giving the hatemonger no place to hide. *The New York Times*, 22 July.
Fuller, L.L. 1958. Positivism and fidelity to law—A reply to Professor Hart. *Harvard Law Review* 71: 630.
Gallie, W.B. 1968. Essentially contested concepts. In *Philosophy and the historical understanding*, 2nd ed. New York: Schocken Books.
Gardner, J. 2001. Legal positivism: 5½ myths. *American Journal of Jurisprudence* 46: 199.
Green, L. 1987. The political content of legal theory. *Philosophy of the Social Sciences* 17: 1.
Green, L. 1996. The concept of law revisited. *Michigan Law Review* 94: 1687.
Guest, S. 1992. *Ronald Dworkin*. Edinburgh: Edinburgh University Press.
Guest, S. 1996. Two strands in Hart's theory of law: A comment on the "Postscript" to Hart's The concept of law. In *Positivism today*, ed. S. Guest. Aldershot: Dartmouth.
Guest, S. 1998. Justice, law and Ronald Dworkin: Jurisprudence at the end of the century. *Current Legal Problems* 51: 335.
Hart, H.L.A. 1983. Positivism and the separation of law and morals. In *Essays in jurisprudence and philosophy*. Oxford: Clarendon.
Hart, H.L.A. 1987. Comment. In *Issues in contemporary legal philosophy: The influence of H.L.A. Hart*, ed. R. Gavison. Oxford: Clarendon.
Hart, H.L.A. 1994. *The concept of law*, 2nd ed. Oxford: Clarendon.
Himma, K.E. 2001. Book review. *Law and Politics Book Review* 11: 567.
Jackson, F. 1998. *From metaphysics to ethics: A defence of conceptual analysis*. Oxford: Clarendon.
Kelsen, H. 1966. On the pure theory of law. *Israel Law Review* 1: 1.
Kramer, M.H. 1999. *In defense of legal positivism: Law without trimmings*. Oxford: Oxford University Press.
Kramer, M. 2001. Dogmas and distortions: Legal positivism defended. *Oxford Journal of Legal Studies* 21: 673.
Kramer, M.H. 2003. Book review. *Cambridge Law Journal* 62: 210.
Leiter, B. 2002. Book review: Marxism and the continuing irrelevance of normative theory. *Stanford Law Review* 54: 1129.
Leiter, B. 2007. *Naturalizing jurisprudence: Essays on American legal realism and naturalism in legal philosophy*. Oxford: Oxford University Press.
Lyons, D. 1984. Moral aspects of legal theory. In *Ronald Dworkin and contemporary jurisprudence*, ed. M. Cohen. London: Duckworth.
MacCormick, D.N. 1985. A moralistic case for a-moralistic law? *Valparaiso University Law Review* 20: 1.
MacCormick, D.N. 1994. *Legal reasoning and legal theory*, 2nd ed. Oxford: Clarendon.
MacCormick, D.N. 2007. *Institutions of law: An essay in legal theory*. Oxford: Oxford University Press.

MacCormick, D.N. 2008. *H.L.A. Hart*, 2nd ed. Stanford: Stanford University Press.
McBride, M. 2003. Book review. *Modern Law Review* 66: 661.
Morriss, P. 1987. *Power: A philosophical analysis*. Manchester: Manchester University Press.
Perry, S.R. 1995. Interpretation and methodology in legal theory. In *Law and interpretation: Essays in legal philosophy*, ed. A. Marmor. Oxford: Clarendon.
Perry, S.R. 2001. Hart's methodological positivism. In *Hart's postscript: Essays on the postscript to the concept of law*, ed. J. Coleman. Oxford: Oxford University Press.
Posner, R.A. 1999. *The problematics of moral and legal theory*. Cambridge: Harvard University Press.
Postema, G.J. 1998. Jurisprudence as practical philosophy. *Legal Theory* 4: 329.
Rawls, J. 1999. *A theory of justice*. Revised edition. Oxford: Oxford University Press.
Raz, J. 1995. *Ethics in the public domain: Essays in the morality of law and politics*. Revised edition. Oxford: Clarendon Press.
Raz, J. 2009a. *Between authority and interpretation: On the theory of law and practical reason*. Oxford: Oxford University Press.
Raz, J. 2009b. *The authority of law: Essays on law and morality*, 2nd ed. Oxford: Oxford University Press.
Schauer, F. 1998. Positivism through thick and thin. In *Analyzing law: New essays in legal theory*, ed. B. Bix. Oxford: Clarendon.
Schauer, F. 2005. The social construction of the concept of law: A reply to Julie Dickson. *Oxford Journal of Legal Studies* 25: 493.
Sereny, G. 1998. *Cries unheard: The story of Mary Bell*. London: Macmillan.
Soper, P. 1987. Choosing a legal theory on moral grounds. In *Philosophy and law*, ed. J. Coleman and E.F. Paul. Oxford: Basil Blackwell.
Stavropoulos, N. 2001. Hart's semantics. In *Hart's postscript: Essays on the postscript to the concept of law*, ed. J. Coleman. Oxford: Oxford University Press.
Tamanaha, B.Z. 2001. *A general jurisprudence of law and society*. Oxford: Oxford University Press.
Waldron, J. 2002. Is the rule of law an essentially contested concept (in Florida)? *Law and Philosophy* 20: 137.
Waluchow, W.J. 1994. *Inclusive legal positivism*. Oxford: Clarendon.

MIX
Papier aus verantwortungsvollen Quellen
Paper from responsible sources
FSC® C105338

If you have any concerns about our products,
you can contact us on
ProductSafety@springernature.com

In case Publisher is established outside the EU,
the EU authorized representative is:
Springer Nature Customer Service Center GmbH
Europaplatz 3, 69115 Heidelberg, Germany

Printed by Libri Plureos GmbH
in Hamburg, Germany